WORKSHOP MAINTENANCE MANUAL

FOR THE

Royal Enfield
'Made like a Gun'

"350 BULLET"   1949-1955

"500 BULLET"   1953-1955

A Floyd Clymer Publication
This edition published in 2024 by
www.VelocePress.com

All rights reserved. This work may not be reproduced or transmitted in any form without the express written consent of the publisher.

IMPORTANT NOTE ON PAGE NUMBERING

The 1948 to 1955 manual starts on page 1 and ends on page 110. The 1956 to 1962 manual starts on page 111 and ends on page 206. The original manuals did not have page numbers and the contents were only identified by 'sections'. Consequently, the addition of page numbers can be useful as an 'identifier' in order to locate a particular 'section'.

INTRODUCTION

Welcome to the world of digital publishing ~ the book you now hold in your hand was printed using the latest state of the art digital technology. The advent of print-on-demand has forever changed the publishing process, never has information been so accessible and it is our hope that this book serves your informational needs for years to come. If this is your first exposure to digital publishing, we hope that you are pleased with the results. Many more titles of interest to the classic automobile and motorcycle enthusiast, collector and restorer are available via our website at www.VelocePress.com. We hope that you find this title as interesting as we do.

NOTE FROM THE PUBLISHER

The information presented is true and complete to the best of our knowledge. All recommendations are made without any guarantees on the part of the author or the publisher, who also disclaim all liability incurred with the use of this information.

TRADEMARKS

We recognize that some words, model names and designations, for example, mentioned herein are the property of the trademark holder. We use them for identification purposes only. This is not an official publication.

INFORMATION ON THE USE OF THIS PUBLICATION

This manual is an invaluable resource for those interested in performing their own maintenance. However, in today's information age we are constantly subject to changes in common practice, new technology, availability of improved materials and increased awareness of chemical toxicity. As such, it is advised that the user consult with an experienced professional prior to undertaking any procedure described herein. While every care has been taken to ensure correctness of information, it is obviously not possible to guarantee complete freedom from errors or omissions or to accept liability arising from such errors or omissions. Therefore, any individual that uses the information contained within, or elects to perform or participate in do-it-yourself repairs or modifications acknowledges that there is a risk factor involved and that the publisher or its associates cannot be held responsible for personal injury or property damage resulting from the use of the information or the outcome of such procedures.

WARNING!

One final word of advice, this publication is intended to be used as a reference guide, and when in doubt the reader should consult with a qualified technician.

346 c.c. O.H.V. SPRING FRAME "350 BULLET"

499 c.c. O.H.V. SPRING FRAME "500 BULLET"
(*Frontispiece*)

Contents

SECTION A2a—TECHNICAL DATA ("350 Bullet" Engine)

SECTION A2b—TECHNICAL DATA ("500 Bullet" Engine)

SECTION B2—ENGINE SPECIFICATION

	Sub-section	Page
Engine	1	1
Cylinder Head	2	1
Cylinder	3	1
Piston	4	1
Connecting Rod	5	1
Crankcase	6	1
Crankshaft and Flywheel	7	1
Main Bearings	8	1
Cams	9	1
Valves	10	1
Valve Gear	11	1
Timing Drive	12	2
Ignition and Lighting System	13	2
Carburettor	14	2
Air Filter	15	2
Lubrication System	16	3
Breather	17	3
Gearbox	18	3
Clutch	19	3

SECTION C2—SERVICE OPERATIONS WITH ENGINE IN FRAME

	Sub-section	Page
Removal of the Timing Cover	1	1
Valve Timing	2	1
Tappet Adjustment	3	1
Ignition Timing	4	2
Removal of the Petrol Tank	5	2
Removal of the Cylinder Head	6	2
Removal of the Valves	7	3
Removal of the Rockers	8	3
Removal of the Valve Guides	9	3
Removal of the Cylinder Barrel	10	3
Removal of the Piston	11	3
Decarbonising	12	4
Grinding in the Valves	13	4
Re-assembly after Decarbonising	14	4
Cleaning the Oil Filter	15	4
Overhaul of Oil Pumps	16	5
Removal of Pump Worm and Timing Pinion	17	5
Removal of the Magdyno Pinion	18	5
Primary Chain Adjustment	19	5
Removal of the Engine Sprocket	20	6
Removal of the Tappets and Guides	21	6
Dismantling the Breather	22	6
Removal of the Clutch	23	6
Removal of the Final Drive Sprocket	24	6
Pressure Relief Valves	25	6
Removal of the Magdyno	26	7

Contents—contd.

SECTION D2—SERVICE OPERATIONS WITH ENGINE REMOVED

	Sub-section	Page
Removal of the Engine from the Frame	1	1
Removal of the Gearbox	2	1
Dismantling the Crankcase	3	1
Main Bearings	4	1
Replacement of the Cam and Idler Spindles	5	1
Flywheel Assembly	6	2
Reassembly of the Crankcase	7	3

SECTION E1—GEARBOX AND CLUTCH

	Sub-section	Page
Removal of Gearbox	1	1
To Dismantle the Gearbox	2	1
Removal of the Ball Races	3	3
Change-Gear Mechanism	4	3
Re-assembling the Gearbox	5	3
Dismantling and Re-assembly of the Clutch	6	3
Adjustment of the Clutch Control	7	3
Adjustment of the Neutral Finder	8	4
Gearbox Oil Level	9	4

SECTION F1—AMAL NEEDLE TYPE CARBURETTOR

	Sub-section	Page
General Description	1	1
Tuning the Carburettor	2	1
Dismantling Carburettor	3	3
Causes of High Petrol Consumption	4	4

SECTION F2—AMAL MONOBLOC CARBURETTOR

	Sub-section	Page
General Description	1	1
Tuning the Carburettor	2	1
Dismantling Carburettor	3	2
Causes of High Petrol Consumption	4	4

SECTION G1c—LUCAS MAGDYNO

	Sub-section	Page
General	1	1
Routine Maintenance	2	1
Lubrication	2(a)	1
Adjustments	2(b)	2
Cleaning	2(c)	2
Renewing High Tension Cable	2(d)	2
Renewing Timing Control Cable	2(e)	2
Contact Breaker Spring	2(f)	3
Testing Magdyno in Position on Engine	3	3

Contents—contd.

SECTION G2b—LUCAS DYNAMO MODEL E3LM

	Sub-section	Page
General	1	1
Lubrication	2(a)	1
Inspection of Commutator and Brush Gear	2(b)	1
Test Data	3	1
Testing in Position to Locate Fault in Charging Circuit	4(a)	1
To Dismantle	4(b)	2
Commutator	4(c)	3
Field Coil	4(d)	3
Armature	4(e)	4
Bearings	4(f)	4
Reassembly	4(g)	4
Dynamo Polarity	5	4

SECTION G3a—CONTROL BOX

	Sub-section	Page
General	1	1
Setting Data	2	1
Servicing	3	1

SECTION G4a—BATTERY MODEL PUZ7E

	Sub-section	Page
General	1	1
Preparation for Service	2	1
Routine Maintenance	3	1
Servicing	4	2

SECTION G5a—HEAD AND TAIL LAMPS

	Sub-section	Page
Headlamp	1	1
Lucas Light Unit	2	1
Replacing Light Unit and Bulb	3	2
Parking Light	4	2
Tail Light	5	2

SECTION H1—FRAME

	Sub-section	Page
Description of Frame	1	2
Steering Head Races	2	2
Removal of Rear Suspension Unit	3	2
Servicing Rear Suspension Units	4	2
Removal of Swinging Arm Chain Stays	5	4
Centre Stand	6	4
Wheel Alignment	7	5
Lubrication	8	5

Contents—contd.

SECTION J1—FRONT FORK WITH CASQUETTE, USED ON "500 BULLET" & "350 BULLET," 1954 ONWARDS

	Sub-section	Page
Description	1	1
Operation of the Fork	2	1
Dismantling the Fork to Replace Spring, Oil Seal or Bearing Bushes	3	2
Spring	4	3
Reassembly of Parts	5	3
Steering Head Races	6	3
Removal of Complete Fork	7	3
Lubrication	8	4
Air Vents	9	4

SECTION J3—FRONT FORK WITH FACIA PANEL. USED ON "500 BULLET," 1953

	Sub-section	Page
Description	1	1
Operation of Fork	2	1
Dismantling the Fork to Replace Spring, Oil Seal or Bearing Bushes	3	2
Spring	4	2
Steering Head Races	5	3
Removal of Facia Panel Fork Head, Spring, etc.	6	3
Removal of Main Tubes	7	4
Reassembly of Parts	8	4
Lubrication	9	4

SECTION J4—FRONT FORK WITH FACIA PANEL. USED ON "350 BULLET," 1950-53 INCLUSIVE

	Sub-section	Page
Description	1	1
Dismantling Fork to Replace Spring, Oil Seal or Bearing Bushes	2	1
Spring	3	1
Steering Head Races	4	1
Removal of Facia Panel Fork Head, Spring, etc.	5	3
Removal of Main Tubes	6	3
Reassembly of Parts	7	3
Lubrication	8	3

SECTION K1—FRONT WHEEL WITH DUAL BRAKE. FITTED TO "500 BULLET" & "350 BULLET" 1955 ONWARDS

	Sub-section	Page
Removal from Fork	1	1
Removal of Brake Cover Plate Assemblies	2	1
Removal of Brake Shoes and Springs	3	1
Replacing Brake Linings	4	2
Removal of Hub Spindle and Bearings	5	2
Hub Bearings	6	2
Fitting Limits for Bearings	7	2
Refitting Ball Bearings	8	2
Reassembly of Brake Shoes on to Cover Plates	9	3
Floating Cam Housings	10	3
Refitting Brake Cover Plates	11	3
Wheel Rim	12	3
Spokes	13	4
Wheel Building and Truing	14	4
Tyre	15	4
Tyre Pressure	16	4
Lubrication	17	4

Contents—contd.

SECTION K2—FRONT WHEEL WITH SINGLE BRAKE. FITTED TO "500 BULLET" & "350 BULLET" UP TO END OF 1954

	Sub-section	Page
Removal from Fork	1	1
Removal of Brake Cover Plate Assembly	2	1
Removal of Brake Shoes and Springs	3	1
Replacing Brake Linings	4	1
Removal of Hub Spindle and Bearings	5	1
Hub Bearings	6	2
Fitting Limits for Bearings	7	2
Refitting Ball Bearings	8	2
Reassembly of Brake Shoes to Cover Plate	9	3
Floating Cam Housing	10	3
Refitting Brake Cover Plate	11	3
Wheel Rims	12	3
Spokes	13	4
Wheel Building and Truing	14	4
Tyres	15	4
Tyre Pressures	16	5
Lubrication	17	5

SECTION L1—REAR WHEEL (DETACHABLE TYPE)

	Sub-section	Page
Description	1	1
Removal and Replacement of Main Portion of Wheel for Tyre Repairs, etc.	2	1
Removal and Replacement of complete Wheel for Access to Brake	3	2
Removal of Brake Shoes for Replacement, Fitting New Linings, etc.	4	3
Replacing Brake Linings	5	3
Removal of Brake Operating Cam and Brake Shoe Pivot Pin	6	3
Cush Drive	7	3
Removal of Ball Bearings	8	4
Hub Bearings	9	4
Fitting Limits for Bearings	10	4
Refitting Ball Bearings	11	4
Reassembly of Brake Shoes, Pivot Pin and Operating Cam into Cover Plate	12	5
Centering Cam Housing	13	5
Final Reassembly of Hub before Replacing Wheel	14	5
Wheel Rim	15	5
Spokes	16	5
Wheel Building and Truing	17	5
Tyre	18	5
Tyre Pressures	19	5
Lubrication	20	6

Contents—contd.

SECTION L2—REAR WHEEL (NON-DETACHABLE TYPE)

	Sub-section	Page
Description	1	1
Removal and Replacement of Wheel	2	1
Removal of Brake Shoes for Replacement, Fitting New Linings, etc.	3	2
Replacing Brake Linings	4	2
Removal of Hub Spindle and Bearings	5	2
Hub Bearings	6	2
Fitting Limits for Bearings	7	2
Refitting Ball Bearings	8	2
Removal of Brake Operating Cam and Brake Shoe Pivot Pin	9	3
Cush Drive	10	3
Reassembly of Brake Shoes, Pivot Pin and Operating Cam into Cover Plate	11	4
Centering Cam Housing	12	4
Final Reassembly of Hub before Replacing Wheel	13	4
Wheel Rims	14	4
Spokes	15	4
Wheel Building and Truing	16	4
Tyre	17	5
Tyre Pressures	18	5
Lubrication	19	5

SECTION M2—SPECIAL TOOLS

List of Illustrations

FRONTISPIECE

Offside views of "350 Bullet" and "500 Bullet"

SECTION B2—ENGINE SPECIFICATION

Page

Fig.	1	Exploded View of "Bullet" Engine	(Section A2a) 2
Fig.	2	Diagram of Lubrication System	2
Fig.	3A	Diagram of "350 Bullet" Oil Pump (Feed)	4
Fig.	3B	Diagram of "350 Bullet" Oil Pump (Return)	4
Fig.	4A	Diagram of "500 Bullet" Oil Pump (Feed)	5
Fig.	4B	Diagram of "500 Bullet" Oil Pump (Return)	5

SECTION C2—SERVICE OPERATIONS WITH ENGINE IN FRAME

Fig.	1	Valve Timing Marks	1
Fig.	2	Adjusting Tappets	2
Fig.	3	Valve Cap Removal	3
Fig.	4	Valve Spring Compressor	3
Fig.	5	Detail of Felt Oil Cleaner	4
Fig.	6	Primary Chain Adjustment	5

SECTION E1—GEARBOX AND CLUTCH

Fig.	1	Gearbox with Outer Cover Removed	1
Fig.	2	Exploded View of Clutch	1
Fig.	3	Exploded View of Gearbox	2
Fig.	4	Clutch Adjustment on Current Gearboxes	4
Fig.	5	Clutch Adjustment on Early Gearboxes	4

SECTION F1—AMAL STANDARD NEEDLE TYPE CARBURETTOR

Fig.	1	Sectional View showing Air Valve and Throttle Closed	1
Fig.	2	Sequence of Tuning	2
Fig.	3	Exploded View of Carburettor	2

SECTION F2—AMAL MONOBLOC CARBURETTOR

Fig.	1	Section through Mixing Chamber	1
Fig.	2	Sequence of Tuning	2
Fig.	3	Exploded View of Monobloc Carburettor	3

SECTION G1c—LUCAS MAGDYNO

Fig.	1	Exploded View of Shock Absorbing Drive	1
Fig.	2	Contact Breaker	1
Fig.	3	Detail of High Tension Connector	2
Fig.	4	Wiring Diagram	4

List of Illustrations—contd.

SECTION G2b—LUCAS DYNAMO MODEL E3LM

			Page
Fig.	1	Exploded View of Dynamo	1
Fig.	2	Testing Brush Spring Tension	2
Fig.	3	Undercutting Commutator Insulation	3
Fig.	4	Removing Pole Shoe Retaining Screw	3
Fig.	5	Use of Pole Shoe Expander	3
Fig.	6	Dynamo Brush Gear	4

SECTION G3a—CONTROL BOX.

Fig.	1	Terminal Connections to Control Box RB107	1
Fig.	2	Internal View of Control Box RB107	2

SECTION G4a—BATTERY MODEL PUZ7E

Fig.	1	Sectioned View of Battery	1
Fig.	2	Topping-Up with Distilled Water	2
Fig.	3	Measuring Specific Gravity	2

SECTION G5a—HEAD AND TAIL LAMPS

Fig.	1	Headlamp with Underslung Parking Light	1
Fig.	2	Headlamp with Parking Light in Reflector	1
Fig.	3	Light Unit MCF700	1
Fig.	4	Parking Light 550	2
Fig.	5	Rear Lamp	2
Fig.	6	Tail Lamp 480	2
Fig.	7	Stop-Tail Lamp L.529	3
Fig.	8	Stop-Tail Lamp 525	3
Fig.	9	Stop-Tail Lamp L.564	3

SECTION H1—FRAME

Fig.	1	Exploded View of Frame	1
Fig.	2	Rear Spring Compressor	2
Fig.	3	Rear Suspension Unit. Mark I	3
Fig.	4	Rear Suspension Unit. Mark II	4

SECTION J1—FRONT FORK WITH CASQUETTE

Fig.	1	Section of Fork Leg	1
Fig.	2	Main Tube Spanner	2
Fig.	3	Main Tube Seal Guide	2
Fig.	4	Clamp Bolts securing Steering Stem and Fork Tubes	3
Fig.	5	Outer Cover Centralising Bushes	3

SECTION J3—FRONT FORK WITH FACIA PANEL
("500 BULLET," 1953)

Fig.	1	Section of Fork Leg	1
Fig.	2	Clamp Bolts securing Steering Stem and Fork Tubes	2
Fig.	3	Outer Cover Centralising Bushes	3
Fig.	4	Drift for Parting Clamp Sleeves	3
Fig.	5	Main Tube Seal Guide	4

List of Illustrations—contd.

SECTION J4—FRONT FORK WITH FACIA PANEL ("350 BULLET," 1950-53)

			Page
Fig.	1	Sectioned View	2

SECTION K1—FRONT WHEEL WITH DUAL BRAKE

Fig.	1	Dual Front Brake	1
Fig.	2	Removal of Brake Shoe Assembly	2
Fig.	3	Drift for Refitting Bearings	2

SECTION K2—FRONT WHEEL WITH SINGLE BRAKE

Fig.	1	Front Hub in Exploded View	1
Fig.	2	Removal of Brake Shoe Assembly	2
Fig.	3	Drift for Refitting Bearings	2
Fig.	4A	Wheel Lacing—Dunlop Rim	4
Fig.	4B	Wheel Lacing—Palmer Rim	4

SECTION L1—REAR WHEEL (DETACHABLE TYPE)

Fig.	1	Exploded View of Wheel	1
Fig.	2	Removal of Main Portion of Wheel	2
Fig.	3	Reassembly of Cush Drive	3
Fig.	4	Drift for Refitting Bearing (Fixed Section)	4

SECTION L2—REAR WHEEL (NON-DETACHABLE TYPE)

Fig.	1	Rear Hub in Exploded View	1
Fig.	2	Drift for Refitting Bearings ("350 Bullet")	3
Fig.	3	Drift for Refitting Bearings ("500 Bullet")	3
Fig.	4	Reassembly of Cush Drive	3
Fig.	5A	Wheel Lacing—Dunlop Rim	5
Fig.	5B	Wheel Lacing—Palmer Rim	5

SECTION M2—SPECIAL TOOLS

SECTION A2a

Technical Data

"350 Bullet" Engine

Cubic Capacity	346 c.c.
Stroke	90 m.m.
Bore ... Nominal	70 m.m.
Actual	69·874 m.m./2·751 in.

(Rebore to ·020 in. when wear exceeds ·0065 in. and again to ·040 in. after a further ·0065 in. wear.)

Compression Ratio
- Up to and including 1954 ... 6¼ to 1
- Up to and including 1955 ... 7¼ to 1

Piston Diameter—
- Bottom of Skirt—Fore and Aft 69·811/69·786 m.m.
- Top Lands 69·32/69·27 m.m.

Piston Rings—
- Width—Plain Rings. (Two) ... ·0635/·0625 in.
- Scraper Ring. (One) ... ·156/·155 in.
- Radial Thickness ... 3·085/2·833 m.m.
- Clearance in Grooves—Plain Rings ·003/·001 in.
- Scraper Ring ·004/·002 in.

(Renew Piston Rings when gap exceeds 1/16 in.)
Oversize Pistons and Rings available ·020 in. and ·040 in.

Piston Boss Internal Diameter	·7501/·7499 in.
Gudgeon Pin Diameter	·7501/·7499 in.
Con. Rod Small End Diameter	·7507/·7505 in.
Con. Rod Big End Diameter	1·62625/1·62575 in.
Crank Pin Diameter	1·24900/1·24875 in.

Con. Rod Floating Bush—
- Outside Diameter ... 1·6235/1·6230 in.
- Inside Diameter ... 1·2502/1·2498 in.
- Width ... ·983/·980 in.

*Driving Side Main Ball Bearings Type (Two) SKF.CRL.8. and SKF.RLS.8.
- Outside Diameter ... 2·25 in.
- Inside Diameter ... 1 in.
- Width ... ·625 in.

Timing Side Main Roller Bearing—
- Outside Diameter ... 1·876/1·875 in.
- Inside Diameter ... 1·5002/1·4998 in.
- Width ... ·750 in.

Size of Rollers—
- Nominal Size ... ¼ in. dia. × 21/64 in. long
- Diameter ... ·2500/·2490 in.
- Length ... ·328/·327 in.

Graded rollers are available in steps of ·0001 from ·2490 to ·2500 in.

Rocker Bearing Inside Diameter	·626/·625 in.
Rocker Spindle Diameter	·6240/·6235 in.
Inlet Valve Stem Diameter	·3430/·3425 in.
Exhaust Valve Stem Diameter	·3410/·3405 in.
Valve Guide Internal Diameter	·3447/·3437 in.
Valve Guide External Diameter	·6275/·6270 in.
Guide Hole in Cylinder Head	·626/·625 in.
Tappet Stem Diameter	·375/·374 in.
Tappet Guide Internal Diameter	·3760/·3752 in.
Tappet Guide External Diameter	·7510/·7505 in.
Guide Hole in Crankcase	·750/·7505 in.

Tappet Clearance with cold engine—
- Inlet ... Nil
- Exhaust ... Nil

Valve Spring Free Length—
- Inner ... 2·02 in.
- Outer ... 2·095 in.

(Renew when reduced by 3/16 in.)

Valve Timing with ·012 in. clearance—
- Exhaust Opens ... 75° before B.D.C.
- Exhaust Closes ... 35° after T.D.C.
- Inlet Opens ... 30° before T.D.C.
- Inlet Closes ... 60° after B.D.C.

Cam Spindle External Diameter	·6240/·6235 in.
Cam Bush Internal Diameter	·6255/·6250 in.
Cam Lift	·3125 in.
Valve Lift (approximately)	·3125 in.

Magdyno—
- Speed ... ½ Engine Speed
- Points ... ·012/·015 in.
- Timing ... ½–7/16 in. before T.D.C.

Engine Sprocket	25 Teeth
Clutch Sprocket	56 Teeth
Final Drive Sprocket	15 Teeth

Primary Chain—
- Type ... Duplex No. 114038 Endless
- Length ... 90 Pitches
- Width ... ·628 in.
- Pitch ... ·375 in.

Feed Oil Pump—
- Speed ... 1/12 Engine Speed
- Piston Diameter ... ·24975/·24950 in.
- Stroke ... ·5 in.

Return Oil Pump—
- Speed ... 1/12 Engine Speed
- Piston Diameter ... ·37475/·37450 in.
- Stroke ... ·5 in.

Sparking Plug—
- Type ... Lodge H.14, KLG F.70, Champion L10S
- Diameter ... 14 m.m.

---

* Earlier engines have two RLS8 bearings instead of one RLS8 and one CRL8.

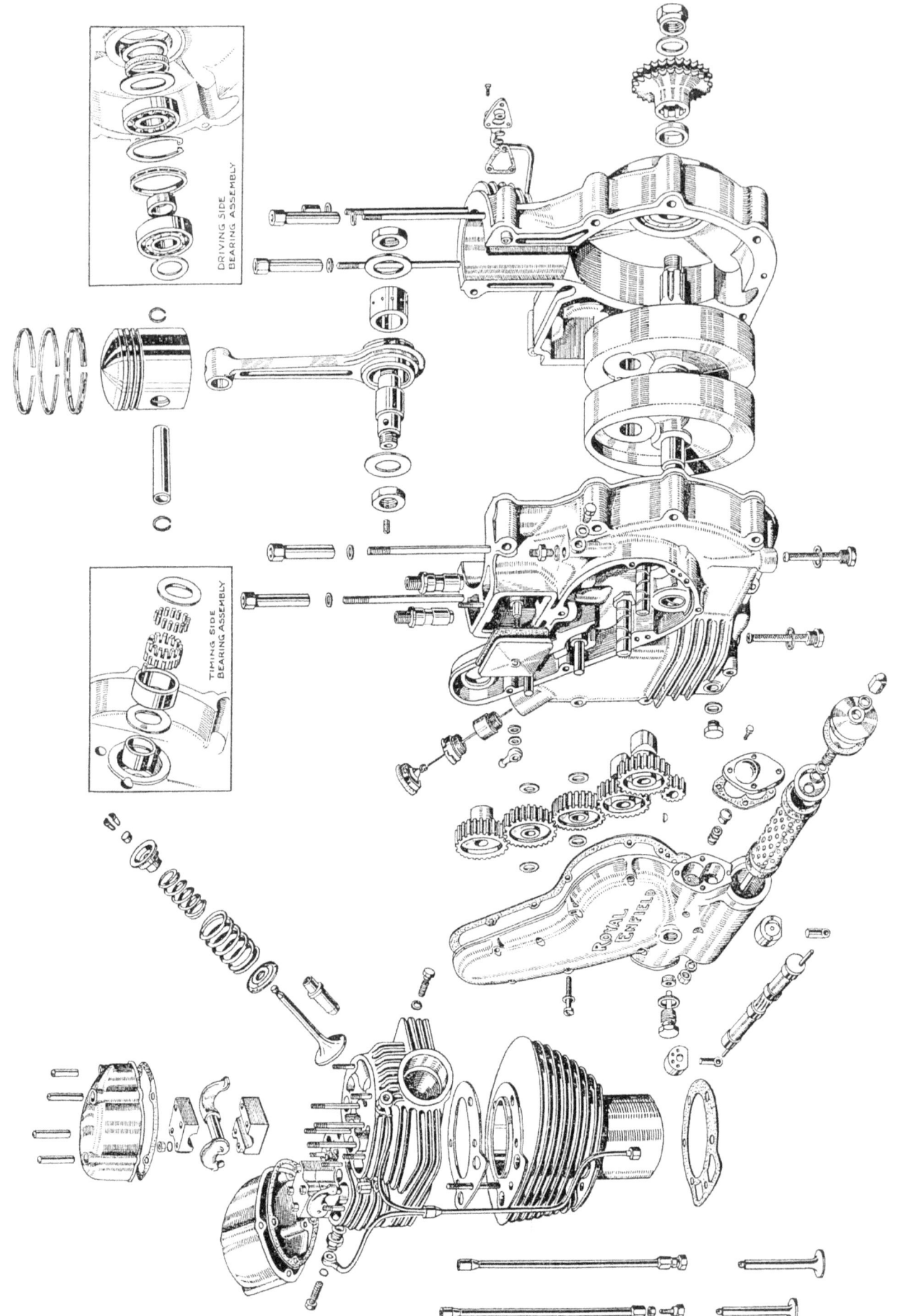

EXPLODED VIEW OF "BULLET" ENGINE Fig. 1

SECTION A2b

Technical Data

"500 Bullet" Engine

Cubic Capacity ... ... 499 c.c.
Stroke ... ... 90 m.m.
Bore ... ... Nominal 84 m.m.
                 Actual ... 3·30725/3·30675 in.
(Rebore to ·020 in. when wear exceeds ·008 in. and again to ·040 in. after a further ·008 in. wear.)
Compression Ratio ... ... 6·75 to 1
Piston Diameter—
    Bottom of Skirt—Fore and Aft ... 3·3047/3·3042 in.
                 Top Lands ... 3·284/3·281 in.

Piston Rings—
    Width—Plain Rings (Two) ... ·063/·062 in.
           Scraper Ring (One) ... ·156/·155 in.
    Radial Thickness ... ... ·115/·108 in.
    Clearance in Grooves—Plain Rings ·0035/·0015 in.
                    ScraperRing ·0035/·0015 in.
(Renew Piston Rings when gap exceeds $\frac{1}{16}$ in.)
Oversize Pistons and Rings available ... ·020 in. and ·040 in.

Piston Boss Internal Diameter ... ·7500/·7497 in.
Gudgeon Pin Diameter... ... ... ·7500/·7497 in.
Con. Rod Small End Diameter ... ·7507/·7505 in.
Con. Rod Big End Diameter ... 1·62625/1·62575 in.
Crank Pin Diameter ... ... 1·24900/1·24875 in.
Con. Rod Floating Bush—
    Outside Diameter ... ... 1·6235/1·6230 in.
    Inside Diameter ... ... 1·2502/1·2498 in.
    Width ... ... ·983/·980 in.

Driving Side Main Ball Bearings Type (Two)
SKF.CRL.8. and SKF.RLS.8.
    Outside Diameter ... ... 2·25 in.
    Inside Diameter ... ... 1 in.
    Width ... ... ·625 in.

Timing Side Main Roller Bearing—
    Outside Diameter ... ... 1·876/1·875 in.
    Inside Diameter ... ... 1·5002/1·4998 in.
    Width ... ... ·750 in.

Size of Rollers—
    Nominal Size ... ... $\frac{1}{4}$ in. dia. × $\frac{21}{64}$ in. long
    Diameter ... ... ·2500/·2490 in.
    Length ... ... ·328/·327 in.
Graded rollers are available in steps of ·001 from ·2490 to ·2500 in.
Rocker Bearing Inside Diameter ... ·626/·625 in.
Rocker Spindle Diameter ... ... ·6240/·6235 in.
Inlet Valve Stem Diameter ... ·3430/·3425 in.
Exhaust Valve Stem Diameter... ... ·3410/·3405 in.
Valve Guide Internal Diameter ... ·3447/·3437 in.
Valve Guide External Diameter ... ·6275/·6270 in.
Guide Hole in Cylinder Head ... ·626/·625 in.
Tappet Stem Diameter ... ... ·375/·374 in.
Tappet Guide Internal Diameter ... ·3760/·3752 in.

Tappet Guide External Diameter ... ·7510/·7505 in.
Guide Hole in Crankcase ... ... ·750/·749 in.

Tappet Clearance with cold engine—
    Inlet ... ... Nil
    Exhaust ... ... Nil

Valve Spring Free Length—
    Inner ... ... 2·032 in.
    Outer ... ... 2·095 in.
(Renew when reduced by $\frac{3}{16}$ in.)

Valve Timing with ·012 in. clearance—
    Exhaust Opens ... ... 75° before B.D.C.
    Exhaust Closes ... ... 35° after T.D.C.
    Inlet Opens ... ... 40° before T.D.C.
    Inlet Closes ... ... 70° after B.D.C.

Cam Spindle External Diameter ... ·6240/·6230 in.
Cam Bush Internal Diameter ... ... ·6255/·6250 in.
Cam Lift ... ... ·3125 in.
Valve Lift (approximately) ... ... ·3125 in.

Magdyno—
    Speed ... ... $\frac{1}{2}$ Engine Speed
    Points ... ... ·012/·015 in.
    Timing ... ... $\frac{5}{16}$ in. before T.D.C.

Engine Sprocket... ... ... 25 Teeth
Clutch Sprocket ... ... 56 Teeth
Final Drive Sprocket—
    Solo ... ... 21 Teeth
    Sidecar ... ... 18 Teeth

Primary Chain—
    Type... ... ... Duplex No. 114038
                            Endless
    Length ... ... 90 Pitches
    Width ... ... ·628 in.
    Pitch ... ... ·375 in.

Feed Oil Pump—
    Speed ... ... 1/12 Engine Speed
    Piston Diameter ... ... ·24975/·24950 in.
    Stroke ... ... ·5 in.

Return Oil Pump—
    Speed ... ... 1/12 Engine Speed
    Piston Diameter ... ... ·37475/·37450 in.
    Stroke ... ... ·5 in.

Sparking Plug—
    Type...   Lodge HLN, KLG FE80, Champion L10S
                                   Long Reach
    Diameter ... ... 14 m.m.

SECTION B2

Engine Specification

"350 and 500 Bullet" Models (Standard)

1. Engine

The engine is a 346 or 499 c.c. vertical single-cylinder four-stroke with separate cylinder head and fully enclosed pressure-fed overhead valve gear. It has dry sump lubrication with the oil tank integral with the crankcase and a built-up steel crankshaft.

2. Cylinder Head

The cylinder head is die-cast from aluminium alloy with ample finning to ensure adequate cooling. The valve inserts are of austenitic iron and are shrunk in so that they are replaceable (except on early models).

The large bore induction port is streamlined and blended to the valve seating.

3. Cylinder

The cylinder barrel is of cast iron, with internal tunnels enclosing the push rods.

The bore of the 350 engine is nominally 70 m.m. and the stroke 90 m.m., giving a cubic capacity of 346 c.c.

The bore of the 500 engine is nominally 84 m.m. and the stroke 90 m.m., giving a cubic capacity of 499 c.c.

4. Piston

The piston is of low expansion aluminium alloy, heat treated, and form-turned oval. There are three piston rings, the top two of which are compression rings. The top ring is chromium plated and the bottom one taper ground. The third ring is for oil control and is slotted.

Different compression ratios are available as follows:—

$\quad$ 350 c.c. Engine $\quad$ 6, $6\frac{1}{2}$, $7\frac{1}{4}$, $7\frac{1}{2}$, $8\frac{1}{2}$ and $10\frac{1}{2}$ to 1.

$\quad$ 500 c.c. Engine $\quad$ $6\frac{1}{4}$, 8 and $9\frac{1}{2}$ to 1.

5. Connecting Rod

The connecting rod is produced from a stamping of Hiduminium RR56 light alloy. The little end bearing is of alloy direct on to the gudgeon pin. In case of wear after long service the little end can be bored out and fitted with a bush, but this is rarely necessary.

The big end has a hardened chrome steel bush pressed in and a floating bush made from mild steel and white-metalled.

6. Crankcase

The combined crankcase and oil tank are die-cast from light alloy in two halves, being split vertically.

7. Crankshaft and Flywheel

The crankshaft is built up from two steel flywheels bolted to the crank pin and bolted and keyed to the engine shafts, the whole being carefully balanced.

8. Main Bearings

On the driving side there are two bearings, one ball and one roller,* both having inner and outer races, while on the timing side there are a roller bearing, with the rollers running on the shaft and a plain phosphor bronze bush for retaining oil in the timing chest.

9. Cams

The cams are integral with the cam pinions, being machined from carbon steel and case hardened. They have internal bronze bushes running on fixed spindles in the timing chest. The cam profiles are produced with silencing ramps to ensure quiet running.

10. Valves

The inlet valve is machined from a stamping of Silicon-chrome valve steel and the exhaust valve is of austenitic steel.

11. Valve Gear

The valves are operated from the cams by means of large flat-based guided tappets, high quality tubular steel push rods, with steel cups, and overhead rockers. Two compression springs are fitted to each valve.

---

* Earlier "350 Bullet" engines had two ball bearings on the driving side.

12. Timing Drive

The cams are located in the timing chest and are driven at half engine speed from the crankshaft by a positive geared drive.

The magdyno is driven from the inlet cam pinion through two idler pinions which also act as a gear pump to return the oil from the timing chest to the oil tank.

13. Ignition and Lighting System

The lighting and ignition are supplied from a Lucas Magdyno, which consists of a magneto running at $\frac{1}{2}$ engine speed and a dynamo running at $1\frac{1}{3}$ engine speed.

14. Carburetter (See Sections F1 and F2).

350 c.c. Engine { Amal Type 276CX/1A.
{ Amal Type 376/29 Monobloc.
500 c.c. Engine—Amal Type 289T/1A.

15. Air Filter

The air supply to the carburettor is cleaned by a Vokes Micro-Vee felt and gauze dry filter,

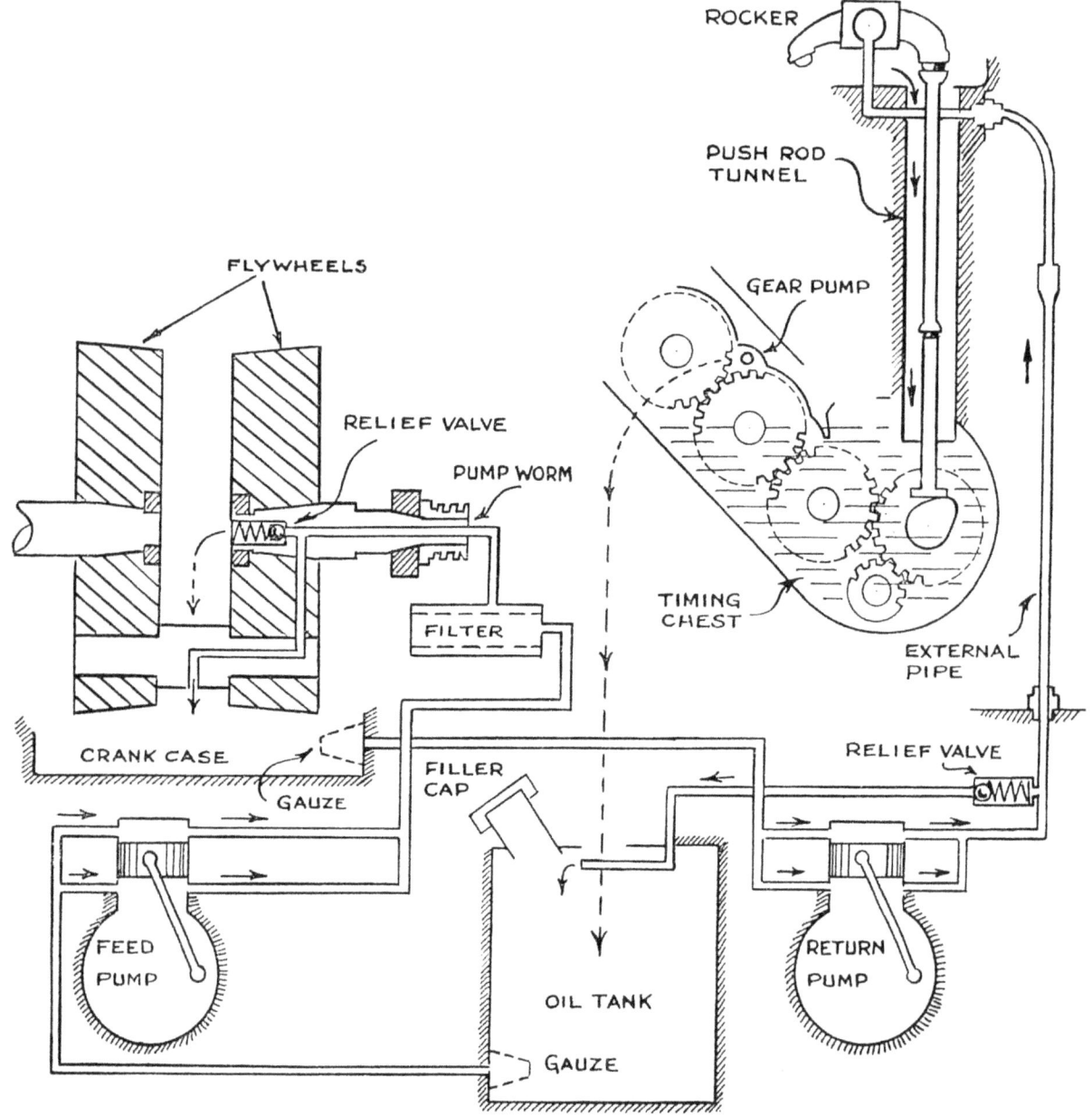

Fig. 2

housed in a box bolted to the frame behind the carburettor.

16. Lubrication System

Lubrication is by the Royal Enfield Dry-Sump which is entirely automatic and positive in action.

The oil tank is integral with the crankcase, ensuring the full rate of circulation immediately the engine is started and rapid heating of the oil in cold weather.

There are two piston type oil pumps running at $\frac{1}{12}$ engine speed, positively driven from the timing side engine shaft through a worm gear.

The feed pump at the rear of the timing cover is for pumping oil from the tank to the big end bearing. This oil drains to the bottom of the crankcase and is pumped by the return pump back to the tank.

Some of the return oil is by-passed to the cylinder head for lubricating the rocker gear, whence it flows down the push rod tunnels to the timing chest.

From here it is returned to the tank by the two idler pinions in the timing drive which act as a gear pump.

The return pump has a capacity of approximately double that of the feed pump, which ensures that oil does not accumulate in the crankcase.

Both pumps are double-acting, but the two sides of the feed pump are interconnected, thereby giving an augmented and more even supply to the big end. Both sides of the return pump are also interconnected for draining the crankcase.

Separate spring-loaded relief valves control the pressure to the big end and to the valve gear. The oil supply to the big end is through internally drilled passages and that to the valve gear is through an external pipe.

Gauze strainers are provided for the feed oil leaving the tank and for the return oil from the crankcase. In addition, the feed oil to the big end is pumped under pressure through a large capacity felt filter.

An important feature of the design of this filter is that the internal arrangement is such that, should it be neglected and become clogged, the oil pressure will lift the spring and cap off its seating thereby automatically by-passing the filter so that the big end will not be deprived of lubrication, even though the oil may be dirty.

17. Breather

The efficient operation of the breather is of paramount importance to the performance of the engine because it acts as a non-return valve between the crankcase and the outside atmosphere, causing a partial vacuum in the crankcase and rocker boxes which prevents the passage of oil into the cylinder and consequent smoking and oiling of the plug.

On the 500 c.c. engine the breather is located on the driving side of the crankcase and consists of a small housing containing two pen-steel discs covering two holes drilled in the crankcase.

Accurate seating of the discs is ensured by a pen-steel plate held between the breather body and the crankcase.

On the 350 c.c. engine the breather consists of a fibre disc in a small housing mounted on the crankcase immediately behind the magdyno.

18. Gearbox

The gearbox is bolted on to the back of the crankcase and has four speeds, which are foot controlled, and a patented neutral finder. All gears are in constant mesh, changes being effected by robust dog clutches.

The standard gear ratios are as follows:—
    350 c.c. Solo   5·67, 7·37, 10·20, 15·75 to 1.
    500 c.c. Solo   4·91, 6·40, 8·85, 13·65 to 1.
    500 c.c. Sidecar 5·72, 7·45, 10·30, 15·90 to 1.

19. Clutch

On the "500 Bullet" the clutch has six pressure plates and five friction plates, including the sprocket which is lined on both sides with friction material. The other friction plates have cork or "Klinger" inserts which give smooth operation and freedom from slipping in the presence of oil. The clutch centre is fitted with shock absorbers consisting of rubber blocks.

The clutch on the "350 Bullet" is similar to that described above except that it has five pressure plates and four friction plates, and the clutch centre is solid.

"350 BULLET" OIL PUMP DIAGRAMS

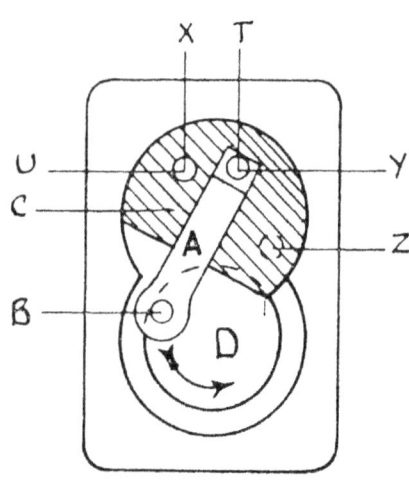

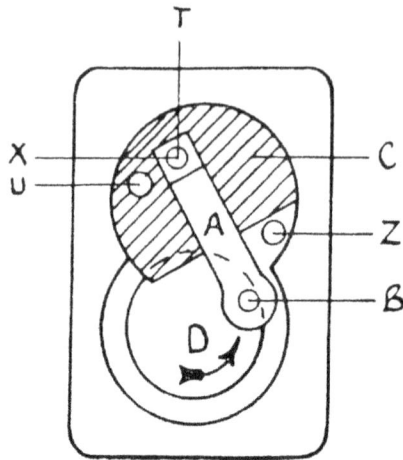

Fig. 3A

FEED PUMP POSITION 1

FEED PUMP POSITION 2

The ports in the housing are connected as follows:
- X — delivery to big end.
- Y — suction from oil tank
- Z — suction from oil tank

Position 1. The plunger A is being drawn out of the cylinder hole in the disc C by the action of the peg B on the shaft D. The port T in the disc C registers with the suction port Y in the housing, so that oil is drawn into the cylinder from the oil tank. At the same time the port U in the disc registers with the delivery port X in the housing, so that oil below the disc in the housing is forced through U and X to the big end.

Position 2. The plunger A is being pushed into the cylinder hole in the disc C. The port T in the disc now registers with the delivery port X in the housing, so that oil is forced out of the cylinder to the big end. At the same time the suction port Z in the housing is uncovered by the disc and oil is drawn into the housing below the disc from the oil tank.

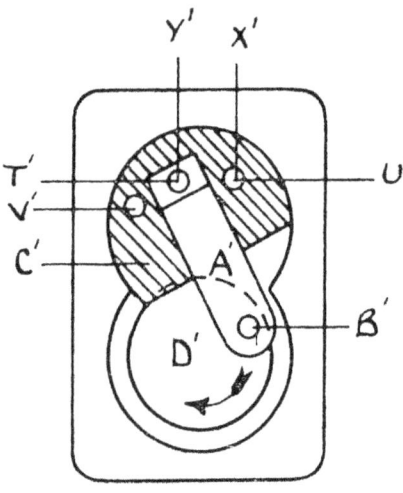

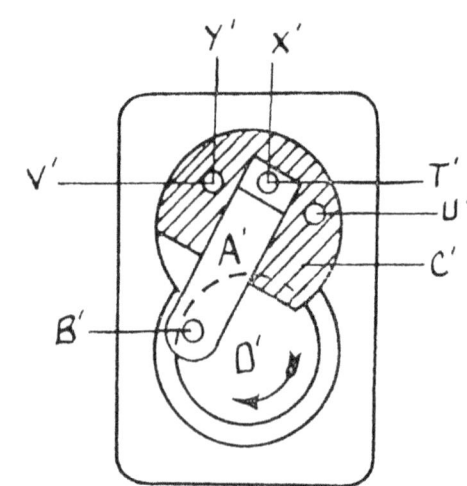

Fig. 3B

RETURN PUMP POSITION 1

RETURN PUMP POSITION 2

The ports in the housing are connected as follows:
- X' — delivery to rocker gear
- Y' — suction from crankcase.

Position 1. The plunger A' is being drawn out of the cylinder hole in the disc C'. The port T' in the disc registers with the suction port Y' in the housing, so that oil is drawn into the cylinder from the crankcase sump. At the same time the port U' in the disc registers with the delivery port X' in the housing, so that oil below the disc in the housing is forced through U' and X' to the rocker gear.

Position 2. The plunger A' is being pushed into the cylinder hole in the disc C'. The port T' now registers with the delivery port X' in the housing, so that oil is forced out of the cylinder to the rocker gear. At the same time, the port V' in the disc registers with the suction port Y' in the housing, so that oil is drawn into the housing below the disc from the crankcase sump through V' and Y'.

"500 BULLET" OIL PUMP DIAGRAMS

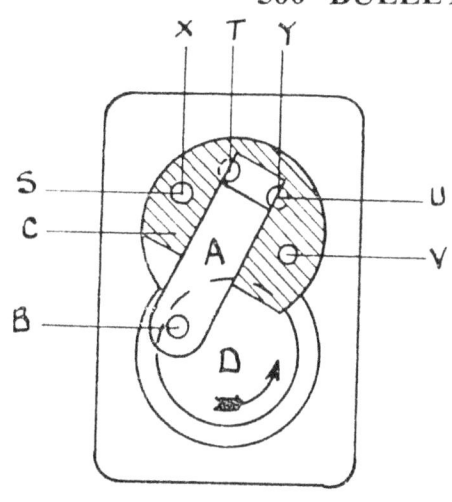

FEED PUMP POSITION 1

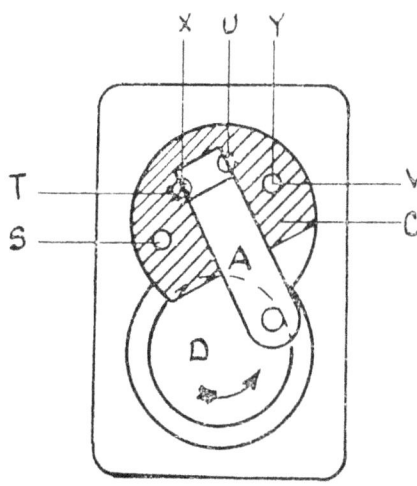

Fig. 4A

FEED PUMP POSITION 2

The ports are connected as follows:
X—in the housing is the delivery to the big end.
Y—in the housing is the suction from the oil tank.
S and V—are drilled through the disc.
T and U—are drilled from the underside of the disc into the cylinder hole.

Position 1. The plunger A is being drawn out of the cylinder hole in the disc C by the action of the peg B on the shaft D. The port U in the disc C registers with the suction port Y in the housing so that oil is drawn into the cylinder from the oil tank. At the same time the port S in the disc registers with the delivery port X in the housing so that oil below the disc in the housing is forced through S and X to the big end.

Position 2. The plunger A is being pushed into the cylinder hole in the disc C. The port T in the disc now registers with the delivery port X in the housing so that oil is forced out of the cylinder to the big end. At the same time the port V in the disc registers with the suction port Y in the housing and oil is drawn into the housing below the disc from the tank.

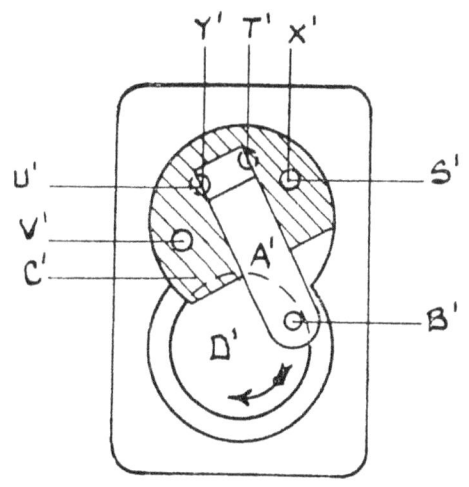

RETURN PUMP POSITION 1

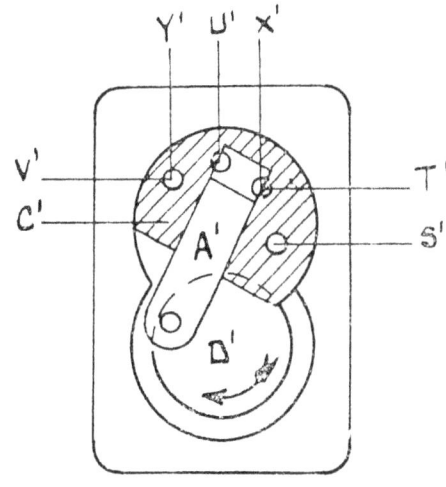

Fig. 4B

RETURN PUMP POSITION 2

The ports are connected as follows:
X'—in the housing is the delivery to the rocker gear.
Y'—in the housing is the suction from the crankcase.
S' and V'—are drilled through the disc.
T' and U'—are drilled from the underside of the disc into the cylinder hole.

Position 1. The plunger A' is being drawn out of the cylinder hole in the disc C by the action of the peg B' on the shaft D'. The port U' registers with the suction port Y' in the housing, so that oil is drawn into the cylinder from the crankcase sump. At the same time the port S' in the disc registers with the delivery port X' in the housing, so that oil below the disc in the housing is forced through S' and X' to the rocker gear.

Position 2. The plunger A' is being pushed into the cylinder hole in the disc C'. The port T' in the disc now registers with the delivery port X' in the housing, so that oil is forced out of the cylinder to the rocker gear. At the same time the port V' in the disc registers with the suction port Y' in the housing so that oil is drawn into the housing below the disc from the crankcase sump through V' and Y'.

SECTION C2

Service Operations with Engine in Frame

"350 and 500 Bullet" Engines

1. Removal of the Timing Cover

First place a tray under the engine to catch the oil which will escape when the cover is removed.

Remove the exhaust pipe and silencer.

Remove nine screws from the cover, taking care not to lose the sealing washers, one for each screw.

Draw off the timing cover, tapping it lightly if necessary.

In refitting the timing cover see that the joint washer is correctly located over the oil holes, using a little grease (not compound) to hold it in position.

See that the cork plug is in position in the hole in the pump worm. If the plug is damaged it should be renewed to ensure oil pressure to the big end bearing.

When refitting the timing cover it is important that the engine is turned gently forwards while the cover is being put in place. This will help the engagement of the pump worm with the pump spindle and prevent damage to the gears.

The filter chamber should be filled with clean oil before the timing cover is refitted.

To verify that the oil pumps are working after replacing the timing cover, start the engine up and remove the oil filler cap so that the oil return through the relief valve can be seen. It may take several minutes before there is sufficient oil in the engine for the return flow through the relief valve to commence.

2. Valve Timing

The cams are integral with the cam pinions and the position for correct timing is marked on the pinions by small dots.

Rotate the engine to top dead centre and put the exhaust (or right hand) cam pinion in position so that the pair of dots on it are opposite the pair of dots on the timing pinion on the crankshaft.

Put the inlet (or left hand) cam pinion in position so that the single dot on it is opposite the single dot on the exhaust cam pinion.

The correct timing at ·012 in. tappet clearance is as follows:—

"350 Bullet"
Exhaust opens 75° before bottom dead centre.
Exhaust closes 35° after top dead centre.
Inlet opens 30° before top dead centre.
Inlet closes 60° after bottom dead centre.

"500 Bullet"
Exhaust opens 75° before bottom dead centre.
Exhaust closes 35° after top dead centre.
Inlet opens 40° before top dead centre.
Inlet closes 70° after bottom dead centre.

3. Tappet Adjustment

The tappets are adjusted by the ball and socket joints which are located in a compartment at the side of the cylinder and access to which is obtained by removing the inspection cover.

Before checking the clearance or making any adjustment, rotate the engine until the piston is at the top of the firing stroke. This will ensure that both valves are closed and that the tappets are well clear of the silencing ramps on the cams. If the cylinder head has been dismantled, make sure that the end caps have been put back on the valve stems.

Because of the ball and socket joints at the bottom of the push rods, the tappet clearance cannot be measured there, but between the valve stems and rockers, with the rocker box covers removed. To remove the rocker box covers the petrol tank must be taken off. (See Subsection 5.)

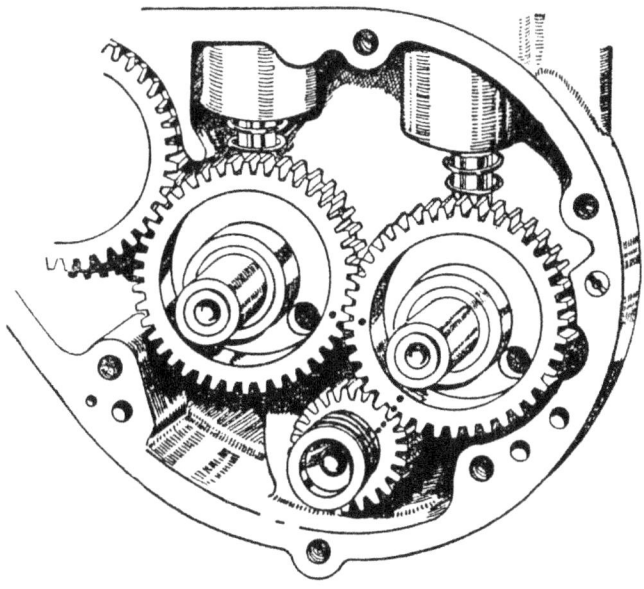

VALVE TIMING MARKS
Fig. 1

The correct clearance is nil or as little as possible with the engine **COLD.**

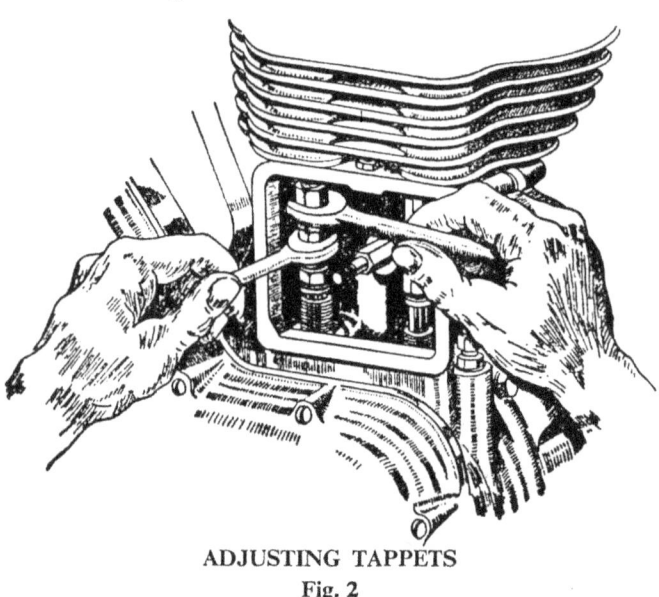

ADJUSTING TAPPETS
Fig. 2

To make the adjustment hold the push rod bottom end (top hexagon) and turn the locknut (middle hexagon) to the left. Screw the push rod cup (bottom hexagon) to the left to take up clearance or to the right to increase the clearance, at the same time holding the push rod bottom end (top hexagon). Lock the adjustment by tightening the locknut against the push rod end and then re-check the clearance.

Owing to the initial bedding down of the wearing surfaces, the tappets on new engines may require adjustment after the first few hundred miles.

4. Ignition Timing

The setting of the ignition timing depends upon the position of the magdyno pinion relative to the magdyno shaft.

To obtain access to the magdyno pinion it is necessary to remove the timing cover (see Subsection 1).

The pinion is mounted on a smooth taper on the magdyno shaft and held in position by a nut **(Right Hand Thread).** To remove the pinion undo the nut and use the special extractor tool supplied with the tool kit.

Before setting the timing adjust the contact breaker points to a clearance of ·012—·015 in. when fully opened and put the ignition lever in the full advance position. See that the stop screw in the magneto cam plate is in the end of the slot and that the plate is not sticking.

To set the timing, turn the engine until the piston is $\frac{7}{16}$ in.-$\frac{1}{2}$ in. for the 350 c.c. Engine, or $\frac{5}{16}$ in. for the 500 c.c. Engine, before top dead centre on the compression stroke, i.e., with both valves closed.

Insert a piece of thin tissue paper between the points of the contact breaker and turn the magneto forwards or clockwise, looking on the contact breaker, until the paper can just be pulled out. Give the pinion a sharp tap to secure it on the shaft and then lock it by tightening the nut.

5. Removal of the Petrol Tank

Turn off the petrol tap.
Disconnect the petrol pipe.
Remove the two bolts which secure the tank to the frame at front and rear and it can then be lifted clear.

6. Removal of the Cylinder Head

Remove the petrol tank (see Subsection 5).
Disconnect the engine steady.
Disconnect the plug lead and oil pipe.
Remove the exhaust pipe.
Push the carburettor back clear of the studs after removing the fixing nuts.
Remove the rocker box covers.
Remove the decompressor cable from the lever on the handlebar.
Turn the engine until both valves are closed.
Remove the rockers and bearings complete by undoing four $\frac{1}{4}$ in. nuts on each.
Lift out the push rods.
Remove six nuts, taking care not to lose the washers.
Remove the $\frac{1}{4}$ in. nut above the tappet chest to avoid possible damage to the crankcase.
Lift the cylinder head off the barrel, tapping it gently beneath the exhaust and inlet ports with a hide hammer to break the carbon seal. Do **not** tap the fins.

When fitting the head again, apply jointing compound to both sides of the gasket, replace the six nuts and tighten them progressively and diagonally from one side to the other to prevent distortion.

Replace the $\frac{1}{4}$ in. nut above the timing chest.
Replace the push rods with the adjustable parts downwards, remembering that the shorter rod is the inlet.
Replace the rockers and bearings, making sure that the oil feed holes are at the bottom and that the caps and bases are in line when tightened down. A sharp tap with a hammer on the end of the rocker will help to ensure this. See that the valve stem caps are in place.

After the engine has been run long enough to get thoroughly hot, the tightness of the nuts should be re-checked.

It will be found convenient for this purpose to use a small auxiliary petrol tank while the engine is being warmed up on the stand, because all the cylinder head nuts are not accessible with the proper tank in position.

See that the rocker box gaskets are intact and replace the rocker box covers.

After tightening the cylinder head nuts with the engine hot, recheck the tappet clearance at some convenient time when the engine is cold.

7. Removal of the Valves

Remove the cylinder head and rockers (see Subsection 6).

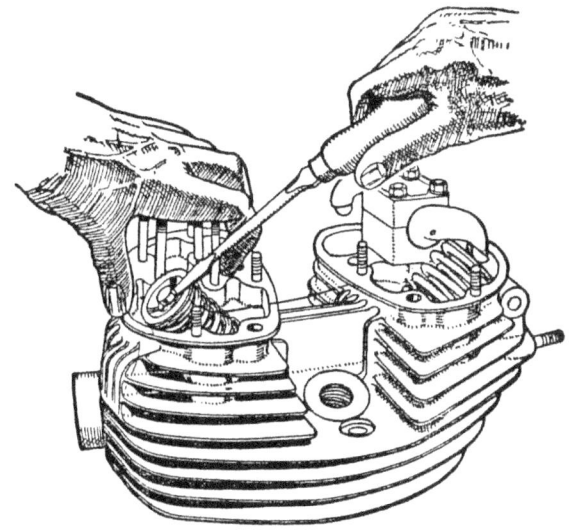

VALVE CAP REMOVAL
Fig. 3

Prise away the hardened steel thimble or end cap. If this has stuck it can be removed by means of a screwdriver.

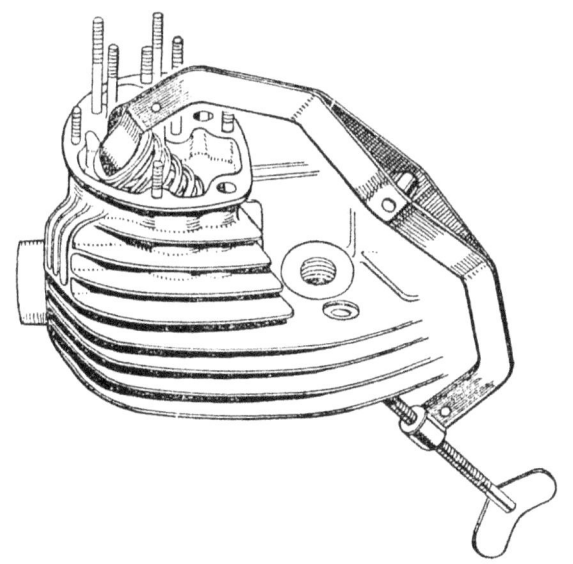

VALVE SPRING COMPRESSOR
Fig. 4

Using a suitable compressing tool, compress the valve springs and remove the split conical collets from the end of the valve stem.

Slacken back the compressing tool and release the springs.

Withdraw the valve and place its springs, top spring collar (and bottom collar if it is loose), the end cap and split conical collets together in order that they may be re-assembled with the valve from which they were removed.

Deal similarly with the other valve in the head.

If the valve will not slide easily through the valve guide, remove any slight burrs on the end of the valve stem with a carborundum stone. If the burrs are not removed and the valve is forced out, the guide may be damaged.

8. Removal of the Rockers

See Subsection 6.

9. Removal of the Valve Guides

To remove the valve guides from the head two special tools are required which can easily be made.

The first is a piece of tube with an internal bore of not less than $\frac{7}{8}$ in.

The second is a mandrel about 4 in. long made from $\frac{9}{16}$ in. diameter bar with the end turned down to $\frac{11}{32}$ in. diameter for $\frac{1}{2}$ in.

Support the cylinder head on the tube which fits over the collar of the valve guide. Using the mandrel, force the guide out of the head with a hand press or by using a hammer.

To fit a new guide, support the head at the correct angle and use a hand press and the same mandrel. If a hand press is not available and the guide is replaced by a hammer, use the mandrel to prevent damage to the guide which is of cast iron and must be treated with great care.

It is necessary to re-cut the valve seat to the correct profile and grind in the valve after a guide has been replaced.

10. Removal of the Cylinder Barrel

Remove the Cylinder Head (see Subsection 6).
Put the piston at bottom dead centre.
Remove the $\frac{1}{4}$ in. nut above the tappet chest and lift the barrel off.

When replacing the cylinder barrel, clean off the joint faces and fit a new paper washer.

11. Removal of the Piston

Remove the cylinder head and cylinder barrel (see Subsections 6 and 10).

With the tang of a file remove the wire circlip retaining the gudgeon pin on the timing side.

Extract the gudgeon pin using Special Tool No. E.5477 (with adaptor if necessary), having first marked the pin so that it, and the piston, may be replaced the same way round, i.e. split skirt to the front.

During this operation put a piece of clean rag in the top of the crankcase to prevent foreign matter getting in. In particular, take care not to drop the circlip in the crankcase.

12. Decarbonising

Having removed the cylinder head as described in Subsection 6, scrape away all carbon, bearing in mind that you are dealing with aluminium which is easily damaged. Scrape gently to avoid scoring the combustion chamber or the valve seats, which are of austenitic iron shrunk into the head. Be careful not to injure the joint face which beds down on to the head gasket.

Do not, in any circumstances, use caustic soda or potash for the removal of carbon from aluminium alloy.

Scrape away all carbon from the valve heads and beneath the heads, being careful not to cause any damage to the valve faces.

If the piston rings are removed, the grooves can be cleaned out and new ones fitted. For cleaning the grooves a suitable tool is a piece of broken ring thrust into a wooden handle and filed to a chisel point.

While the cylinder and piston are not in position, cover the crankcase with a clean cloth to prevent the ingress of dust and dirt of all kinds. Do not, of course, attempt to scrape the carbon from the piston when the mouth of the crankcase is open.

13. Grinding in the Valves

Wipe the valve faces clean and examine them carefully. If they are at all pitted, have the faces re-cut. Pay similar attention to the valve seats in the head; excessive grinding will form a pocket and the gas flow will be restricted. The angle of the valve face should be 45 degrees to the axis of the valve stem.

To grind a valve, smear the seating with a little grinding-in compound, place a light, short coil spring over the valve stem and beneath the head, insert the valve into its appropriate guide, press it on to the seat, using a tool with a suction cup and with a backwards and forwards rotary motion, grind it on to its seat. Alternatively, use a tool which grips the valve stem and pulls the valve on to its seat. Frequently lift the valve and move it round so that an even and true seating is obtained. Continue grinding until a bright ring is visible on both valve and seating.

14. Re-Assembly after Decarbonising

Before building up the engine, see that all parts are scrupulously clean and place them conveniently to hand on a clean sheet of brown paper.

When re-assembling the engine, it is advisable to fit a new paper washer between the cylinder barrel and the crankcase.

Smear clean oil over the piston and space the ring gaps, having replaced the rings if these have been removed. The taper ring is marked "TOP" on the upper face. Lower the piston over the connecting rod and insert the gudgeon pin. Fit the circlip securing the gudgeon pin.

If the piston ring gaps exceed $\frac{1}{16}$ in. when the rings are in position in the barrel, new rings should be fitted. The correct gap for new rings is ·011 in.—·015 in. The gap should be measured in the least worn part of the cylinder, which will be found to be the extreme top of bottom of the bore.

Oil the cylinder bore and lower the barrel over the piston and seat it gently on the paper washer. Tighten down the nut above the tappet chest and replace the cylinder head and rockers as described in Subsection 4.

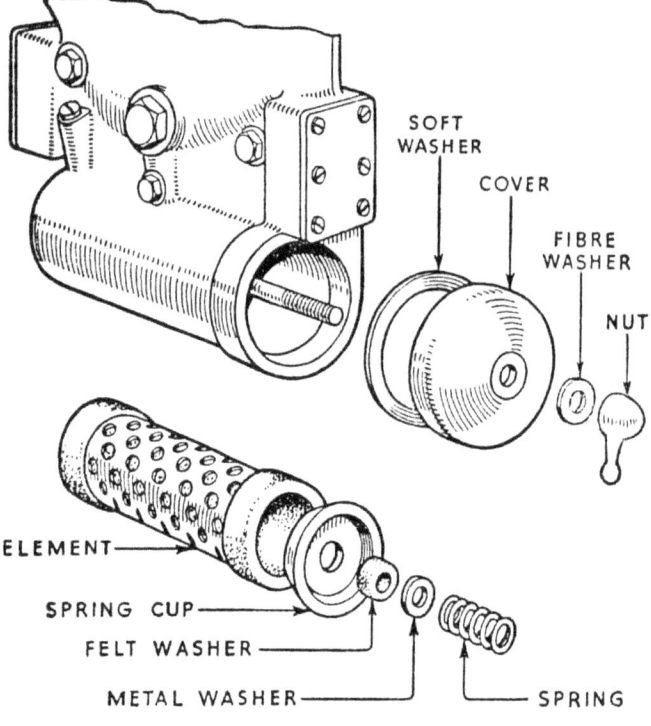

DETAIL OF FELT OIL CLEANER
Fig. 5

15. Cleaning the Oil Filter

The oil filter is located in the timing cover immediately below the oil pumps. The felt element should be taken out and washed in petrol after the first 500 miles and every subsequent 2,000 miles. Fit a new element every 5,000 miles.

The filter element is removed by unscrewing the nut holding the end cap in position. When re-assembling the filter after cleaning, take care that no grit or other foreign matter is sticking to it. After emptying the filter chamber it is essential to run the engine slowly for about five minutes to ensure that oil is reaching the big ends. If the timing cover has been removed, fill the filter chamber with clean oil before replacing the cover.

16. Overhaul of Oil Pumps

Remove the timing cover, as described in Subsection 1.

Remove the end plates from both pumps.

Remove the pump discs and plungers.

Remove the pump spindle which can be pulled out from the front or return pump end.

Check the fit of the plungers in the pump discs which should have a minimum of clearance but should be able to be moved in and out by hand.

If, when fitting a new disc or plunger, the plunger is found to be too tight a fit, carefully lap with metal polish until it is just free. If the pump disc is not seating properly or if a new pump disc is being fitted, it should be lapped to the seating with Special Tool No. E.5425, using carborundum 360 fine paste or liquid metal polish, until an even grey surface is obtained.

Replacement pump discs have a lip left on the flat, at the opposite side to the lapped face. The purpose of this is to hold the disc central in the housing during lapping-in. It should be filed off before the pump is finally assembled, care being taken not to damage the lapped face.

Wash all passages, etc., thoroughly with petrol after lapping to remove all traces of grinding paste.

Check the pump disc springs for fatigue by assembling in the timing cover and placing the pump covers in position. The latter should be held $\frac{1}{8}$ in. off the timing cover if the springs are correct.

In the case of the 500 c.c. engine see that the steel end pads are in position on the outer ends of the springs.

The pump spindle should be renewed if excessive wear has taken place on the teeth.

Re-assemble the oil pumps, replacing the paper cover gaskets if necessary. Before fitting each cover fill the pump chamber with clean oil.

Having assembled the pumps, lay the timing cover flat and fill the oil ports by means of an oilcan. Turn the pump spindle with a screwdriver in a clockwise direction looking on the front and it can then be seen whether the pumps are operating correctly.

Before replacing the timing cover on the engine, fill the filter chamber with clean oil.

The oil feed to the big end can be checked by partially unscrewing the feed plug in the timing cover between the oil pumps while the engine is running and the oil return to the tank can be checked by removing the oil filler cap.

17. Removal of Pump Worm and Timing Pinion

Remove the timing cover as described in Subsection 1.

Unscrew the worm shaft by a hexagon head behind the worm, using Special Tool No. E.5451. This is a **Left Hand Thread**.

Withdraw the timing pinion by means of a flat chisel placed behind the pinion and tapped gently.

When refitting the timing cover see that the cork or rubber plug is in position in the hole in the pump worm and is undamaged.

18. Removal of the Magdyno Pinion

Remove the timing cover and take off the hexagon nut holding the pinion.

Extract the pinion with the Special Tool supplied with tool kit.

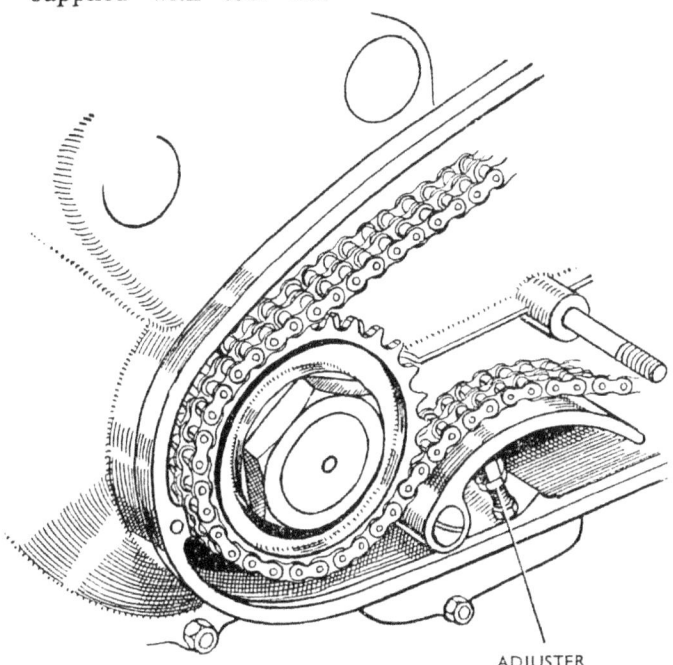

PRIMARY CHAIN ADJUSTMENT
Fig. 6

To take up slack in the primary chain, unscrew the locknut and turn the adjuster beneath the curved slipper until correct chain tension is obtained; re-tighten the locknut.

19. Primary Chain Adjustment

Access to the primary chain adjuster is gained by removing the primary chain cover, which is held in position by a single nut. Before removing the nut, place a tray under the engine to catch the oil from the chaincase.

Beneath the bottom run of the chain is a curved slipper on which the chain rests and which may be raised or lowered by turning the adjusting screw after having first slackened the locknut.

The chain should be adjusted so that there is ¼ in. up and down movement at the centre of the top run of the chain.

After replacing the chain cover, remember to replenish the chaincase with oil.

20. Removal of the Engine Sprocket

The primary chain is endless and it is therefore necessary to remove both the engine and clutch sprockets simultaneously.

Unscrew the engine sprocket nut so that the engine sprocket, which is mounted on splines, can then be removed with the clutch sprocket (on some early models the sprocket was mounted on a taper instead of splines).

To remove the clutch sprocket unscrew the three clutch spring pins and lift away the spring cap, springs and distance pieces, clutch front plate, centre or plate retaining ring and the assembly of the driving and driven clutch plates. The clutch sprocket can then be withdrawn from the clutch centre after removal of the large circlip which secures it.

21. Removal of the Tappets and Guides

It is only necessary to remove the tappets and guides if they have become worn.

To remove the guides use Special Tool No. E.5410.

The guide should have an interference fit of ·0015 in. to ·0025 in. in the crankcase and can be driven in with a bronze drift, care being taken when the guide is nearly home to avoid damaging the collar. Excessive hammering may close up the bore of the guide which would necessitate removing the tappet and reaming again. In no circumstances should the guide be reamed in position on the 350 c.c. engine as swarf might get into the recess in the guide.

22. Dismantling the Breather

If the breather is not operating efficiently, it may cause pressure in the crankcase, instead of a partial vacuum, giving rise to smoking or over-oiling.

500 c.c. Engine. See that the discs and backplate are clean and undamaged and that the discs are seating properly.

When re-assembling the breather, apply jointing compound very sparingly to the back of the steel plate taking great care to keep it away from the discs or their seatings.

350 c.c. Engine. Unscrew the body of the breather and examine the disc. If it is faulty, a new breather unit should be fitted as the disc cannot readily be taken out of the body.

23. Removal of the Clutch

Remove the engine sprocket and clutch sprocket together as described in Subsection 20.

To remove the clutch centre, hold the clutch with Special Tool No. E.4871, and remove the centre retaining nut and washer with a box spanner.

The clutch centre can then be withdrawn from the shaft with Special Tool No. E.5414.

If the circlip is not removed the sprocket and clutch centre can be removed together.

24. Removal of the Final Drive Sprocket

Remove the clutch as described in Subsection 23.

Remove the primary chain tensioner.

Remove the rear half of the primary chaincase by taking out three socket screws.

Remove the grub screw locking the final drive sprocket nut.

Hold the sprocket and remove the nut (**Right Hand Thread**). The sprocket can then be withdrawn.

25. Pressure Relief Valves

There are two Pressure Relief Valves in the oil feeds to the big end and to the rocker gear respectively. Their function is to prevent excessive pressure and their setting is not critical. The feed to the rocker gear comes from the return oil from the crankcase to the tank.

The pressure relief valves are set before leaving the Works and should not normally require to be disturbed. If, however, it is found necessary to dismantle either of them, they can be reset as follows:—

Rocker Feed Relief Valve. This is located on the outside of the crankcase immediately below the lower end of the external oil pipe. It has a hexagon head and can be removed complete by unscrewing it out of the case.

The valve itself cannot be dismantled and, if found to be faulty, should be replaced by a new one.

Big End Relief Valve. This is located in the timing-side crankshaft and can only be adjusted when the crankshaft has been dismantled. It consists of a $\frac{5}{16}$ in. diameter steel ball and spring held in position by a screwed plug.

The valve is set to open when the oil pressure exceeds about 35 lbs. per square inch and when set correctly there is a movement of about $\frac{3}{32}$ in. of the ball off the seat. This can be measured without dismantling the crankshaft by pushing a thin rod through the hole in the pump worm with the oil feed plug in the timing cover removed.

If the crankshaft is dismantled for any reason, it is always advisable to fit a new spring to the relief valve in case the original one has become weak.

If the valve is set to give too high a pressure, the pump disc will be forced off its seating.

26. Removal of the Magdyno

Remove the magdyno pinion. (See Sub-section 18.)

Unscrew the nut on the fixing strap bolt and swing the strap clear. The magdyno can then be withdrawn.

In replacing the magdyno, see that the felt washer, retainer and spring are in position.

SECTION D2

Service Operations with Engine Removed

"350 and 500 Bullet" Engines

1. Removal of the Engine from the Frame

Disconnect the battery leads and remove the battery.
Turn off the petrol and disconnect the petrol pipe.
Take the slides out of the carburettor.
Remove the air cleaner.
Remove the exhaust pipe.
Disconnect the electric horn leads.
Disconnect the control cable from the magdyno.
Disconnect the engine steady.
Remove the rear chain.
Remove the footrest bar.
Support the engine on a suitable box or wood block.
Remove the centre stand and the stand stop.
Remove the front engine plates.
Remove the bolt securing the rear engine plate to the frame.
Lift out the engine.

2. Removal of the Gear Box

Remove the primary chain case, engine sprocket and clutch (see Section C2, Subsection 24).
Remove four ⅜ in. nuts and the gearbox can then be withdrawn from the engine.

3. Dismantling the Crankcase

350 c.c. Engine. Drain the oil tank by removing the drain plug.

Having removed the engine from the frame as described in Subsection 1, dismantle the cylinder head, barrel, piston, timing gear, magdyno, etc., as described in Section C2.

Remove the nuts on the driving side of the engine from four fixed studs at the rear of the crankcase.

Remove six studs passing through the crankcase.

The two halves of the crankcase can then be separated.

The timing side outer roller race and the bronze bush will remain in the timing side half of the crankcase.

The driving side ball race and the driving side outer roller race will remain in the driving side half of the crankcase.

The driving side inner roller race and the inner distance piece will remain on the engine shaft.

The flywheel assembly may be difficult to remove from the driving side of the crankcase owing to the shaft being a tight fit in the inner race of the ball bearings. This is particularly likely in the earlier engines with two ball bearings. In this case push the shaft out of the bearings using crankshaft extractor E.5121.

500 c.c. Engine. The procedure is exactly the same as for the 350 c.c. except that there is a double roller race on the timing side of the 500 c.c.

4. Main Bearings

To remove the outer roller race(s) (or the inner ball race on earlier 350 Bullet engines) from the crankcase halves, heat to 100°C or more and drop the half case sharply on a flat block of wood or bench, when the race(s) will drop out, together with the distance piece in the case of the driving side and the thrust washer in the case of the timing side.

Remove the circlip from the driving side crankcase and re-heat to remove the second ball race.

To replace the bearings, heat the crankcase and press in the races in the following order:—

    Driving Side. Use Special Tool No. 4817.
        Small steel washer.
        Cork oil-retaining washer.
        Large steel washer.
        Ball bearing complete.
        Circlip.
        Outer distance piece ⎫ on
        Outer roller race ⎬ 500
          c.c. and later 350 c.c. engines;
        or distance piece and inner ball race on earlier 350 c.c. engines.

    Timing Side. Use Special Tool No. 4816.
        Steel thrust washer.
        Outer roller race(s).

Care must be taken to see that the lead on the outside of the outer roller race enters the case first to make sure that it is square with the housing.

5. Replacement of the Cam and Idler Spindles

To remove the cam spindles heat the crankcase and tap the spindles out from inside.

To remove the idler spindles heat the crankcase as before, hold the spindles in a vice and tap the crankcase lightly with a hide hammer

To replace the spindles use Special Tool No. E.6462 which is a locating plate for all the spindles.

Start the spindles in the holes in the crankcase by tapping them lightly.

Offer the locating plate to the spindles, making sure that they are all upright. Tap the plate over the spindles until it touches the timing chest face, having first made sure that the latter is quite clean.

Drive the spindles home with a small hammer (not heavier than ½ lb.) and a drift.

Remove the locating plate.

6. Flywheel Assembly

350 c.c. Engine. The flywheel assembly consists of the crankshaft and the connecting rod.

To dismantle the crankshaft remove the set screws securing the crankpin nuts.

Holding the crankshaft in a Special Jig, No. E.2775, remove the crankpin nuts.

Using E.2775, with a pair of steel bars (about 1 in. × ⅜ in. × 9 in. long) placed across, press out the crankpin with a hand press.

The connecting rod can then be removed.

Turn the crankshaft over in the jig and repeat with the other side if necessary.

To remove the main shafts, remove the set screws from the shaft nuts and unscrew the nut. Drive the shafts out with a hammer and drift.

To replace the main shafts, reverse the above process, making sure that the keys are a good fit.

To re-assemble the crankshaft, press the crankpin into the timing side flywheel, making sure that the oil hole is in the correct position and that the thrust washer is facing the right way, i.e., with the chamfer **away** from the flywheel.

Test the oil passages with an air line or oil gun to make sure that they are clear.

Smear oil over crankpin and floating bush.

Put the floating bush over the crankpin.

Put the connecting rod over the floating bush.

Place the other thrust washer over the crankpin, **also with the chamfer away from the flywheel.**

Press the driving side flywheel on.

Put the flywheel in the assembly jig E.2775, to ensure that the flywheels and shafts are in line and replace the nuts, tighten securely and refit the set screws.

Test the oil passages again to ensure that they are clear.

If the same crankpin has been put back, it will be necessary to drill out the grub screw, in order to clean the oil passages after which a new grub screw must be fitted.

Mount the crankshaft between centres and true up to ·0005 in. on either side of the shafts.

If the readings for the two shafts are high on opposite sides, the error can be corrected by gently tapping either or both of the flywheels.

If the readings are high on the same side of the two shafts, it is probably due to dirt or foreign matter in the joints and the crankshaft should be dismantled again, carefully examined and cleaned and re-assembled.

500 c.c. Engine. The flywheel assembly consists of the crankshaft and the connecting rod.

To dismantle the crankshaft remove the set screws securing the crankpin nuts.

Holding the crankshaft in a special jig, No. E.2774, remove the crankpin nuts.

Using E.2774 with a pair of steel bars (about 1 in. × ⅜ in. × 9 in. long) placed across, press out the crankpin with a hand press.

The connecting rod can then be removed.

Turn the crankshaft over in the jig and repeat with the other side if necessary.

To remove the timing side main shaft, take the set screw from the shaft nut and unscrew the nut. Drive the shaft out with a hammer and drift. To replace the timing side shaft, reverse the above process, making sure that the key is a good fit and that the nut is tightened securely by means of a box spanner with a 12 in. tommy bar.

The driving shaft has no nut but is secured by tightening the sprocket nut after the assembly of the engine. It should be pressed in and out with a hand press or a hammer and drift. If the latter is used care must be taken not to damage the centre.

To re-assemble the crankshaft, press the crankpin into the timing side flywheel, making sure that the oil hole is in the correct position and that the thrust washer is facing the right way, i.e. with chamfer **away** from the flywheel.

Test the oil passages with an air line or oil gun to make sure that they are clear.

Put the floating bush over the crankpin.

Put the connecting rod over the floating bush.

Place the other thrust washer over the crankpin, **also with the chamfer away from the flywheel.**

Press the driving side flywheel on.

Put the flywheel in the assembly jig, E.2774, to ensure that the flywheels and shafts are in line and replace the nuts, tighten securely and refit the set screws.

Test the oil passages again to ensure that they are clear.

If the same crank pin has been put back, it will be necessary to drill out the grub screw, in order to clean the oil passages after which a new grub screw must be fitted.

Mount the crankshaft between centres and true up to ·0005 in. on either side of the shafts.

If the readings for the two shafts are high on opposite sides, the error can be corrected by gently tapping either or both of the flywheels.

If the readings are high on the same side of the two shafts, it is probably due to dirt or foreign matter in the joints and the crankshaft should be dismantled again, carefully examined and cleaned and re-assembled.

7. Reassembly of the Crankcase

Replace the outer roller races, etc., in the crankcase halves as described in Subsection 4.

Fit the inner distance piece and the rollers and cage in the driving side crankcase.

Lay the thrust washer on the bearing.

Assemble the flywheel into the bearing, if necessary using the sprocket nut with suitable packing piece to draw the driving shaft through the inner race(s) of the ball bearing(s).

Make sure that the crankcase face is clean and apply jointing compound to it.

Put the thrust washer on the timing side shaft and the rollers and cage.

Put the magdyno straps over the studs in the timing side crankcase and place the latter in position over the flywheel.

Bolt the two halves of the crankcase together, making sure that the joint matches correctly so that the cylinder base is flat.

SECTION E1
Gearbox and Clutch

"Meteor 700"; "500 Twin"; "500 Bullet"; "350 Bullet."

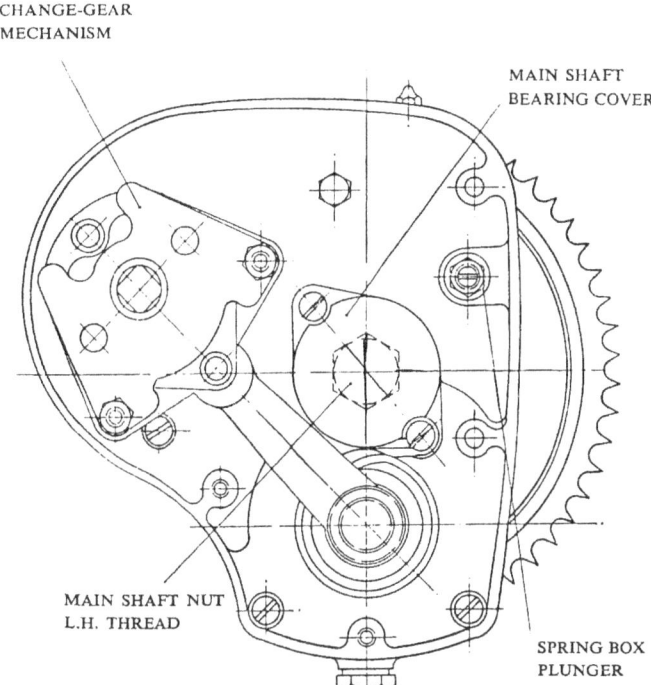

GEARBOX WITH OUTER COVER REMOVED
Fig. 1

1. Removal of Gearbox

This is described in Section D1 or D2.

The gearbox can, however, be completely dismantled with the engine in the frame except for the removal of the inside operator and the bearings in the gearbox shell.

2. To Dismantle the Gearbox

First remove the kickstart crank, the change-gear lever and the neutral finder and pointer.

Remove the top small inspection cover and disconnect the clutch cable.

Remove four screws and the gearbox outer cover can then be detached.

Remove the change-gear mechanism by taking off the two nuts securing it.

Remove the main shaft bearing cover which is attached by two screws.

Remove four cheese-headed screws and one hexagon bolt.

Remove the spring box locating plunger nut and washer.

Remove the main shaft nut (**Left Hand Thread**).

The gearbox inner cover can then be removed.

The mainshaft can be drawn straight out if the clutch has been removed, which, however, should be done before taking off the gearbox inner cover.

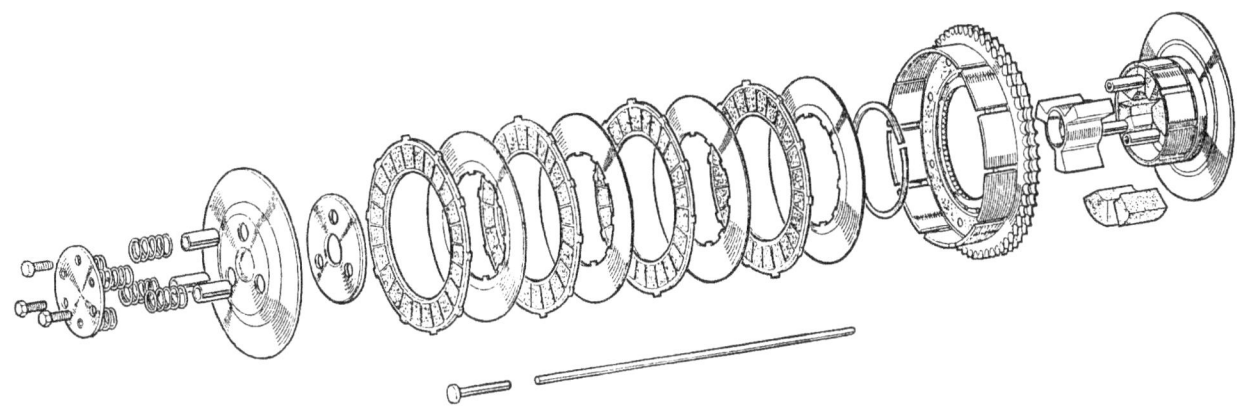

EXPLODED VIEW OF CLUTCH
Fig. 2

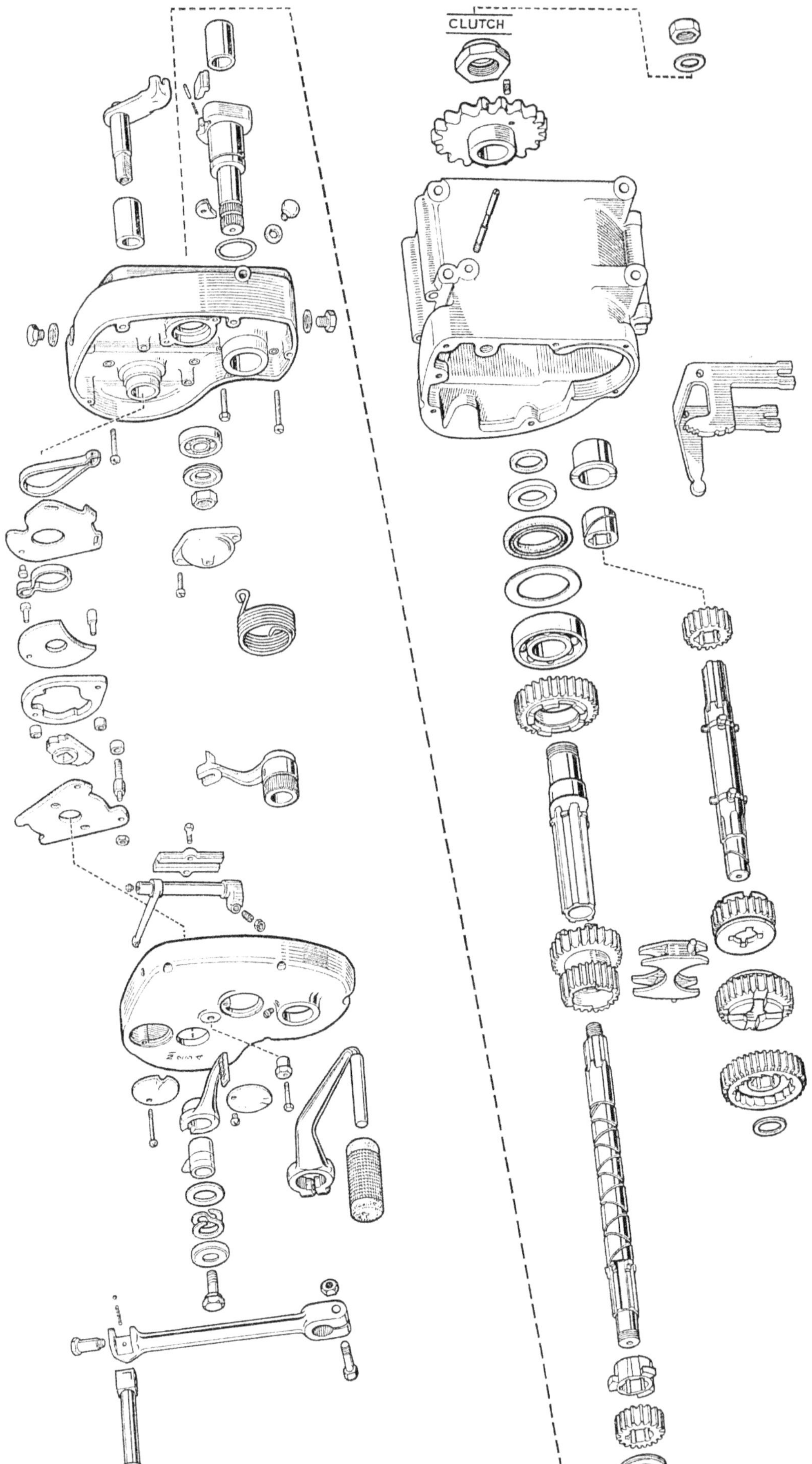

EXPLODED VIEW OF GEARBOX
Fig. 3

(See Section C1 or C2.) The top gear pinion and dog will come away with the mainshaft.

The layshaft can then be removed and the 2nd and 3rd gears drawn off the final drive sleeve together with the operator fork.

To take out the final drive sleeve, the final drive sprocket must be removed and this is preferably done before removing the inner cover. (See Section C1 or C2.)

3. Removal of the Ball Races

The mainshaft ball bearings can be removed by using a stepped drift $1\frac{7}{16}$ in.—$1\frac{11}{64}$ in. diameter for the bearing in the box and $\frac{13}{16}$ in.—$\frac{39}{64}$ in. diameter for the bearing in the cover.

When refitting the bearings stepped drifts of $2\frac{5}{16}$ in.—$1\frac{11}{64}$ in. diameter and $1\frac{11}{16}$ in.—$\frac{39}{64}$ in. diameter must be used for the bearings in the box and cover respectively.

Note the felt washer in the recess behind the larger main shaft bearing and the dished pen-steel washer between the bearing and the felt washer. The second dished pen-steel washer, if fitted, has a smaller central hole and is on the other side of the main shaft bearing and is nipped between the inner face of the bearing and the shoulder on the final drive sleeve. See that both of the dished pen-steel washers have their raised portions facing towards the clutch and final drive sprocket.

4. Change-Gear Mechanism

If the two nuts securing the change-gear ratchet mechanism are slackened, the adjuster plate can be set in the correct position. In this position the movement of the gear lever necessary to engage the ratchet teeth will be approximately the same in each direction.

If the plate is incorrectly adjusted, it may be found that, after moving from top to third or from bottom to second gear, the outer ratchets do not engage the teeth on the inner ratchets correctly.

If, when fitting new parts, it is found that the gears do not engage properly, ascertain whether a little more movement is required or whether there is too much movement so that the gear slips right through second or third gear into neutral. If more movement is required, this can be obtained by filing the adjuster plate very slightly at the points of contact with the pegs on the ratchet ring.

If too much movement is already present, a new adjuster plate giving less movement must be fitted.

5. Re-Assembling the Gearbox

The procedure is the reverse of that given in Subsection 2 but the following points should be noted:—

If the main shaft top gear pinion and dog have been removed, make sure that the dog is replaced the right way round or third and top gears can be engaged simultaneously.

Make sure that the trunnions on the operator fork engage with the slots in the inside operator.

See that the main shaft is pushed right home. (It may tighten in the felt washer inside the final drive shaft nut.)

The layshaft top gear and kickstarter pinion should be assembled on the layshaft and the kickstarter shaft and ratchet assembled on to it before fitting the end cover. Do not forget the washer on the layshaft between the kickstarter pinion and the kickstarter shaft.

The joint between the gearbox and the inner cover should be made with gold size, shellac or a similar jointing compound.

Make sure that all parts are clean before commencing assembly. In normal climates the recesses in the gearbox should be packed with soft grease and the box should be filled up to the correct level with engine oil. (See Subsection 9.) **On no account must heavy yellow grease be used.**

6. Dismantling and Re-assembly of the Clutch

The method of removing the clutch is described in Section C1 or C2.

When re-assembling, note that two of the steel plates are dished and that the other(s) are flat. The correct order of assembly is shown on the exploded drawing.

Do not forget to replace the cush rubber or plate retaining cover before fitting the pressure plate.

Make sure that the distance tubes inside three of the springs pass through the holes in the pressure plate. The other three springs are located by means of bosses on the clutch cap.

Tighten the spring pins as far as they will go.

If the clutch lifts unevenly it is probable that one of the springs has taken a set, in which case new springs should be fitted.

7. Adjustment of the Clutch Control

It is essential that there should be about $\frac{1}{16}$ in. free movement in the clutch cable, to ensure that all the spring pressure is exerted on the plates.

There are two points of adjustment for the clutch cable. The first is at the top of the gearbox just behind the oil filler plug and is provided for taking up any stretch in the cable. The adjustment is made by screwing the collar in or out of the gearbox shell. The connection between the end of the cable and the horizontal lever can be seen if the top small inspection cover on the front of the gearbox is removed. Tighten the locknut on the screwed collar after adjustment has been made.

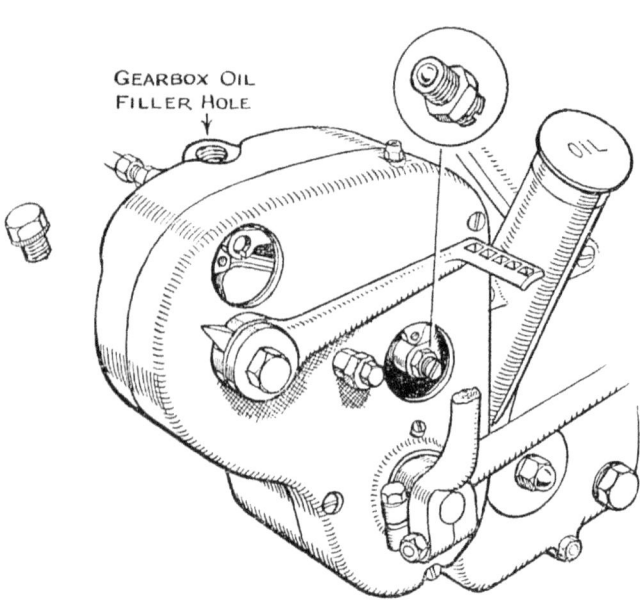

CLUTCH ADJUSTMENT ON CURRENT GEARBOXES
Fig. 4

The other point of adjustment is behind the lower inspection cover on the front of the gearbox and is for compensating for wear on the clutch plate inserts. To make the adjustment, remove the inspection cover, slacken the locknut and turn the central screw. Tighten the locknut after adjustment has been made.

The reason for the two points of adjustment is to enable the lever behind the cover to be kept in its proper position whether the need for adjustment is caused by plate wear or cable stretch.

Owing to initial bedding down of the clutch plate inserts, the clutch control may require adjustment after the first few hundred miles with a new machine. This point should therefore be examined soon after delivery and adjustment made if necessary.

On earlier models the clutch operating mechanism is exposed on the front of the gearbox, but the adjustments are, however, the same in principle as those described above.

The cable adjustment is at the bottom of the front of the gearbox just in front of the kickstart lever. The collar is screwed in or out of a lug on the gearbox cover and is secured by a locknut as before.

The other adjustment is made by slackening the clamping bolt in the horizontal lever and turning the lever on its spindle, which is the end of the operating worm in the gearbox cover.

When correctly adjusted, the lever should be approximately square with the cable when the clutch is fully lifted.

The position of the lever endwise on the worm spindle is important and it should be positioned so that it does not foul the kickstart lever.

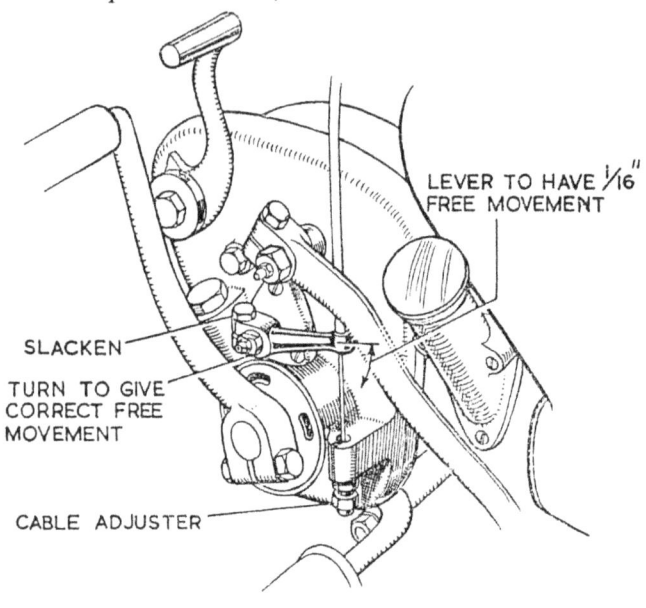

CLUTCH LEVER AND CABLE ADJUSTMENTS ON EARLY GEARBOXES
Fig. 5

8. Adjustment of the Neutral Finder

The neutral finder is adjusted by means of an eccentric stop secured to the front of the gearbox cover by a bolt which limits the travel of the operating pedal. Slacken the bolt and turn the eccentric until the correct movement of the pedal is obtained.

9. Gearbox Oil Level

The gearbox is replenished with oil by removing a plug in the top and the correct level can be checked by removing a second plug lower down on the right hand side looking at the cover.

On earlier models a dip-stick is attached to the filler plug for measuring the level of the oil or was provided loose in the tool kit.

On some models the filler plug is on the side of the gearbox and in such cases the oil should be level with the plug hole and no dip-stick is required. The oil will be found to run into the box more easily on these models if the engine is started up and allowed to tick over so that the gears and shafts rotate.

SECTION F1

Amal Needle Type Carburetter

1. General Description

The Amal Standard Needle Type Carburetter has been in production for many years and has proved itself to be especially suitable for single and twin cylinder motor cycles in which there is a pulsating air flow through the carburetter.

The float chamber is a separate unit bolted on to the base of the mixing chamber and may have either a top or bottom petrol feed.

The supply of air to the engine is controlled by a throttle slide which carries a taper needle operating in the needle jet. The needle is secured to the throttle slide by a spring clip fitting in one of five grooves and the mixture strength throughout a large proportion of the throttle range is controlled by the position of this needle in the slide and by the size of the jet in which it works. There is, however, a restricting or main jet at the bottom of the needle jet and the size of this controls the mixture strength at the largest throttle openings. At very small throttle openings petrol and air are fed to the engine through a separate pilot system which has an outlet at the engine side of the throttle. The air supply to this pilot system is controlled by the pilot air screw and the slow running of the engine can be adjusted by means of this screw and a stop which holds the throttle open a very small amount. The throttle slide is cut away at the back and the shape of this cut-away controls the mixture at throttle openings slightly wider than that required for slow running. There is a compensating system to prevent undue enriching of the mixture with increasing engine speed, this system consisting of a primary choke surrounding the upper end of the needle jet through which air is drawn in increasing quantities as the depression in the main choke increases. This air supply and the supply to the pilot system are taken from a duct in the main air intake to the carburetter so that all the air passing to the engine can be filtered by fitting an air cleaner to the main carburetter air intake. A handlebar controlled air slide is provided to enrich the mixture temporarily when required.

2. Tuning the Carburetter

The throttle opening at which each tuning point is most effective is shown in Fig. 2. It should be remembered, however, that a change of setting at any point will have some effect on the setting required at other points; for instance, a change of main jet will have some effect on the mixture strength at half throttle which, however, is mainly controlled by the needle position. Similarly an alteration to the throttle cut-away may affect both the needle position required and the adjustment of the pilot air screw. For this reason it is necessary to tune the carburetter in a definite sequence, which is as follows:

First—Main Jet. The size should be chosen which gives maximum speed at full throttle with the air control wide open. If two

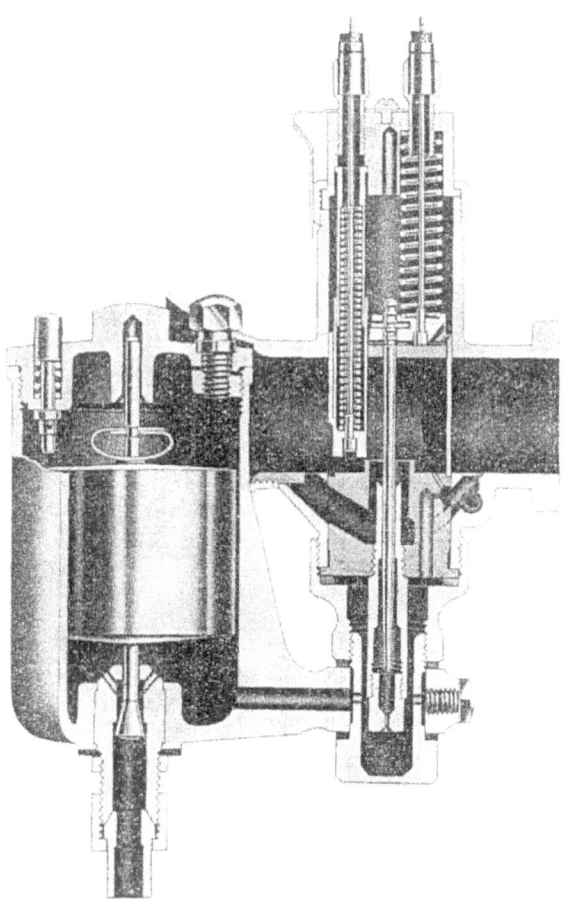

SECTIONAL VIEW SHOWING AIR VALVE AND THROTTLE CLOSED

Fig. 1

different sizes of jet give the same speed the larger should be chosen for safety as it is dangerous to run with too weak a mixture at full throttle.

Second—The pilot air screw should be set to give good idling.

Third—The throttle valve should be selected with the largest amount of cut-away which will prevent spitting or mis-firing when opening the throttle slowly from the idling position.

Fourth—The lowest position of the taper needle should be found consistent with good acceleration with the air slide wide open.

Fifth—The pilot air screw should be checked to improve the idling if possible. When setting the adjustment of the pilot air screw this should be done in conjunction with the throttle stop. Note that the correct setting of the air screw is the one which gives the fastest idling speed for a given position of the throttle stop. If the idling speed is then undesirably fast it can be slowed down by unscrewing the throttle stop a fraction of a turn.

PHASES OF AMAL NEEDLE JET CARBURETTER THROTTLE OPENINGS

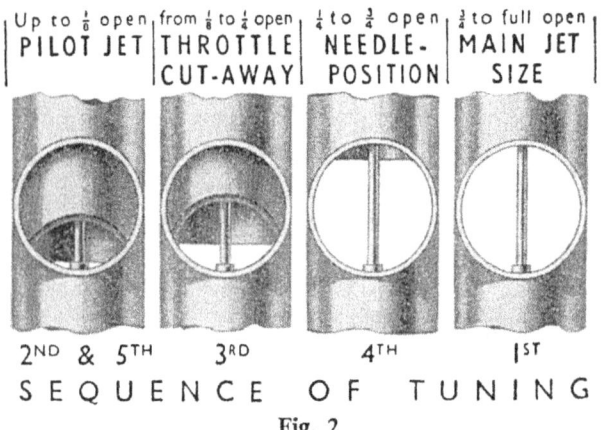

Fig. 2

It will be noted that of the four points at which adjustments are normally made, i.e. pilot air screw, throttle cut-away, needle position and main jet size, the first and third do not require changing of any parts of the carburetter. Assuming that the carburetter has the standard setting to suit the particular model of the motor cycle any small adjustments occasioned by atmospheric conditions, changes in quality of fuel, etc., can usually be covered by adjustment of the pilot air screw and raising or lowering the taper needle one notch. If, however, the machine is used at very high altitudes or with a very restricted air cleaner a smaller main jet will be necessary. The following table gives the reduction in main jet size required at different altitudes:

Altitude Ft.	Reduction %
3,000	5
6,000	9
9,000	13
12,000	17

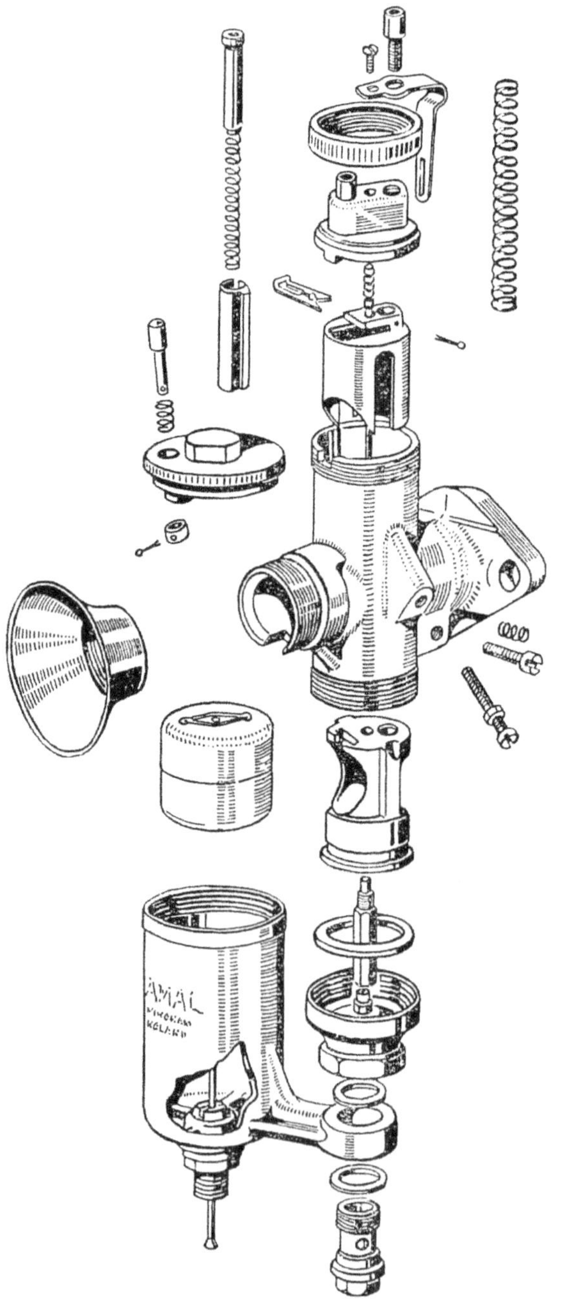

AMAL STANDARD NEEDLE TYPE CARBURETTER
Fig. 3

SETTINGS FOR AMAL STANDARD CARBURETTERS.

MODEL	Carburetter Code No.	Choke Dia. In.	Main Jet	Needle Jet	Needle Position	Throttle Valve	Pilot Outlet In.	REMARKS
"S 250" ohv	274BH/3A	26/32	75	Std.	2	4/4	.031	Stub Fitting
"S 250" ohv / "250 Clipper"	274 BS/3A	26/32	75	Std.	2	4/4	.031	Flange Fitting
"WD/C 350" sv	274 B/1A	26/32	85	Std.	3	4/5	.031	3-gauze Air Intake
"WD/CO 350" ohv	276AC/1A	15/16	130	Std.	3	6/4	.037	3-gauze Air Intake / Shallow Mixing Chamber Nut
"G 350" ohv	276BL/1A	15/16	130	Std.	3	6/4	.037	Shallow Mixing Chamber Nut
"350 Bullet" Std.	276CX/1A	1	140	Std.	3	6/4	.037	Shallow Mixing Chamber Nut
"350 Bullet" Trials	276EX/1A	15/16	140	Std.	3	6/3	.037	Shallow Mixing Chamber Nut
"J 500" ohv 1-Port	276CB/1A / 276CT/1A	1	150	Std.	3	6/4	.031	Stub Fitting / Flange Fitting
"J2 500" ohv 2-Port	276CZ/1A / 276DB/1A	1 1/16	170	Std.	2	6/4	.031	Reduced O/D Air Intake / Standard Air Intake
"500 Bullet"	289T/1A	1 1/8	180	Std.	2	29/3	.037	
"500 Twin"	276DU/1AT / 276GQ/1AT	15/16	150	109	2	6/4	.025	L.H. Pilot Screw & Throttle Stop / R.H. Pilot Screw & Throttle Stop
"Meteor 700"	276FJ/1AT / 276GR/1AT	1 1/16	170	Std.	3	6/4	.025	L.H. Pilot Screw & Throttle Stop / R.H. Pilot Screw & Throttle Stop

In the case of carburetters for engines running on alcohol fuel considerably larger jets are needed. In most cases a No. 113 needle jet will be required and the main jet size will require to be increased by an amount varying from 50% to 150% according to the grade of fuel used.

If the engine is run on fuel containing a small proportion of alcohol added to the petrol, a rough and ready guide is that the main jet should be increased by 1% for every 1% of alcohol in the fuel. In most cases alcohol blends **available from petrol pumps** do not contain sufficient alcohol to require any alteration to the carburetter setting.

The range of adjustment of the taper needle and the pilot air screw are determined by the size of the needle jet and of the pilot outlet respectively. Standard needle jets have a bore at the smallest point of .1065 in. and are not marked for size. Larger needle jets .1075 in., .109 in. and .113 in. bore are available and are marked 107, 109 and 113 respectively.

The standard pilot outlet bore is .031 in. but in some cases larger or smaller size pilot outlets are used. Since the pilot outlet is actually drilled in the body of the carburetter it is necessary to have a carburetter with the correct size pilot outlet if the best results are to be obtained.

The accompanying table shows the standard settings for all Amal standard needle type carburetters used on Royal Enfield machines from 1946 onwards.

3. Dismantling Carburetter

The construction of the carburetter is clearly shown in Fig. 3.

If the float chamber floods first make sure that the float is not punctured and partly filled with petrol, also that the clip on top of the float is engaged correctly with the groove in the fuel needle. If necessary lap the needle into its **seating** using only liquid metal polish for this purpose.

If it is necessary to remove the jet block do this with great care using a wooden drift and a light hammer to knock it out of the mixing chamber body. A single strand of an inner control cable is useful for clearing the small passages in the jet block and care must be taken not to enlarge these by forcing the wire through them. Compressed air from a pipe line or a tyre pump is preferable. A choked main jet should be cleared only by blowing through it.

4. Causes of High Petrol Consumption

If the petrol consumption is excessive first look for leaks either from the carburetter, petrol pipe, petrol tap(s) or tank. If coloured petrol is in use this will readily indicate the presence of any small leaks which otherwise might pass unnoticed. If the petrol system is free from leaks, carefully set the pilot adjusting screw as described in paragraph 2 to give the correct mixture when idling. Running with the pilot adjusting screw too far in is a common cause of excessive petrol consumption. If the consumption is still heavy, try the effect of lowering the taper needle in the throttle slide by one notch. Do not fit a smaller main jet as this will not affect consumption except when driving on nearly full throttle and may make the mixture too weak at large throttle openings, thus causing overheating.

SECTION F2

Amal Monobloc Carburetter

1. General Description

The Amal Monobloc Carburetter has been introduced as an improvement on the earlier standard needle type. In general it gives better petrol consumption, combined with improved starting and acceleration from low speeds and a small increase in maximum speed.

The float chamber is integral with the mixing chamber and contains a pivoted barrel-shaped float operating on a nylon fuel needle. There is a considerable leverage ratio between the float and the needle and, in consequence, flooding is rare unless there is dirt on the needle seating.

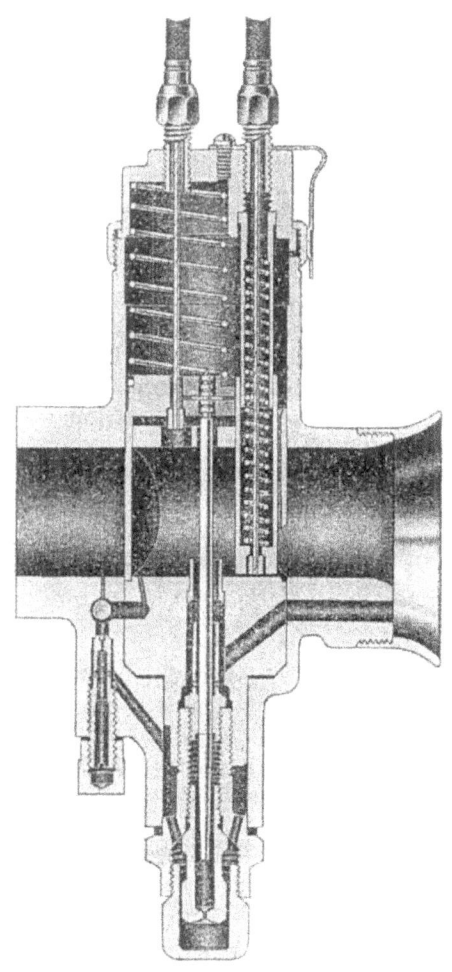

SECTION THROUGH MIXING CHAMBER, SHOWING AIR VALVE AND THROTTLE CLOSED

Fig. 1

The supply of air to the engine is controlled by a throttle slide which carries a taper needle operating in the needle jet. The needle is secured to the throttle slide by a spring clip fitting in one of five grooves and the mixture strength throughout a large proportion of the throttle range is controlled by the position of this needle in the slide and by the size of the jet in which it works. There is, however, a restricting or main jet at the bottom of the needle jet and the size of this controls the mixture strength at the largest throttle openings. At very small throttle openings petrol and air are fed to the engine through a separate pilot system, which has an outlet at the engine side of the throttle. The air supply to this pilot system is controlled by the pilot air screw and the slow running of the engine can be adjusted by means of this screw and a stop which holds the throttle open a very small amount. The throttle slide is cut away at the back and the shape of this cut-away controls the mixture at throttle openings slightly wider than that required for slow running. There is a compensating system to prevent undue enriching of the mixture with increasing engine speed, this system consisting of a primary choke surrounding the upper end of the needle jet through which air is drawn in increasing quantities as the depression in the main choke increases. This air supply and the supply to the pilot system are taken from two separate ducts in the main air intake to the carburetter so that all the air passing to the engine can be filtered by fitting an air cleaner to the main carburetter air intake.

Two small cross holes in the needle jet, at a level just below the static level in the float chamber, permit petrol to flow into the primary choke when the engine is not running or when it is running at very low speeds, thus forming a well of petrol which will be drawn into the engine on starting or accelerating from low speeds. At moderately high engine speeds the level of petrol in the float chamber falls slightly and in consequence no more fuel flows through the cross holes in the needle jet so that the petrol well remains empty until the engine slows down or stops.

A handlebar controlled air slide is provided to enrich the mixture temporarily when required.

2. Tuning the Carburetter

The throttle opening at which each tuning point is most effective is shown in Fig. 2. It should be remembered, however, that a change of setting at any point will have some effect on the setting required at other points; for instance, a change of main jet will have some effect on the mixture strength at half throttle which, however, is mainly controlled by the needle position. Similarly an alteration to the throttle cut-away may affect both the needle position required and the adjustment of the pilot air screw. For this reason it is necessary to tune the carburetter in a definite sequence, which is as follows:—

First—Main Jet. The size should be chosen which gives maximum speed at full throttle with the air control wide open. If two different sizes of jet give the same speed the larger should be chosen for safety as it is dangerous to run with too weak a mixture at full throttle.

Second—The pilot air screw should be set to give good idling. Note that the pilot jet is detachable and two sizes are available, 25 c.c. and 30 c.c. If the pilot air adjusting screw requires to be screwed out less than half a turn the larger size pilot jet should be used; if the air screw requires to be screwed out more than 2-3 turns fit the smaller size of pilot jet.

PHASES OF AMAL MONOBLOC CARBURETTER THROTTLE OPENINGS

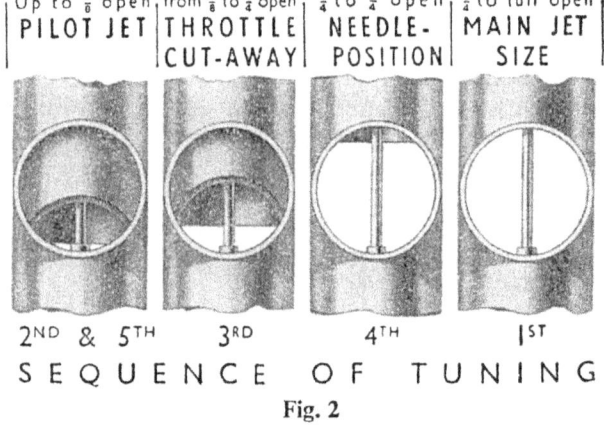

Fig. 2

Third—The throttle valve should be selected with the largest amount of cut-away which will prevent spitting or misfiring when opening the throttle slowly from the idling position.

Fourth—The lowest position of the taper needle should be found consistent with good acceleration with the air slide wide open.

Fifth—The pilot air screw should be checked to improve the idling if possible. When setting the adjustment of the pilot air screw this should be done in conjunction with the throttle stop. Note that the correct setting of the air screw is the one which gives the fastest idling speed for a given position of the throttle stop. If the idling speed is then undesirably fast it can be slowed down by unscrewing the throttle stop a fraction of a turn.

It will be noted that of the four points at which adjustments are normally made, i.e., pilot air screw, throttle cut-away, needle position and main jet size, the first and third do not require changing of any parts of the carburetter. Assuming that the carburetter has the standard setting to suit the particular type of engine any small adjustments occasioned by atmospheric conditions, changes in quality of fuel, etc., can usually be covered by adjustment of the pilot air screw and raising or lowering the taper needle one notch. If, however, the machine is used at very high altitudes or with a very restricted air cleaner a smaller main jet will be necessary. The following table gives the reduction in main jet size required at different altitudes:

Altitude, ft.	Reduction, %
3,000	5
6,000	9
9,000	13
12,000	17

In the case of carburetters for engine running on alcohol fuel considerably larger jets are needed. In most cases a No. 113 needle jet will be required and the main jet size will require to be increased by an amount varying from 50% to 150% according to the grade of fuel used.

If the engine is run on fuel containing a small proportion of alcohol added to the petrol, a rough and ready guide is that the main jet should be increased by 1% for every 1% of alcohol in the fuel. In most cases alcohol blends available from petrol pumps do not contain sufficient alcohol to require any alteration to the carburetter setting.

The range of adjustment of the taper needle and the pilot air screw are determined by the size of the needle jet and of the pilot outlet respectively. Standard needle jets have a bore at the smallest point of ·1065 in. and are marked 106. Alternative needle jets ·1055 in., ·1075 in., ·109 in. and ·113 in. bore are available and are marked 105, 107, 109 and 113 respectively.

The standard pilot outlet bore is ·025 in. but in some cases larger size pilot outlets are used. Since the pilot outlet is actually drilled in the body of the carburetter it is necessary to have a carburetter with the correct size pilot outlet if the best results are to be obtained.

The accompanying table shows the standard settings for Amal Monobloc Carburetters used on Royal Enfield motor cycles.

3. Dismantling Carburetter

The construction of the carburetter is clearly shown in Fig. 3.

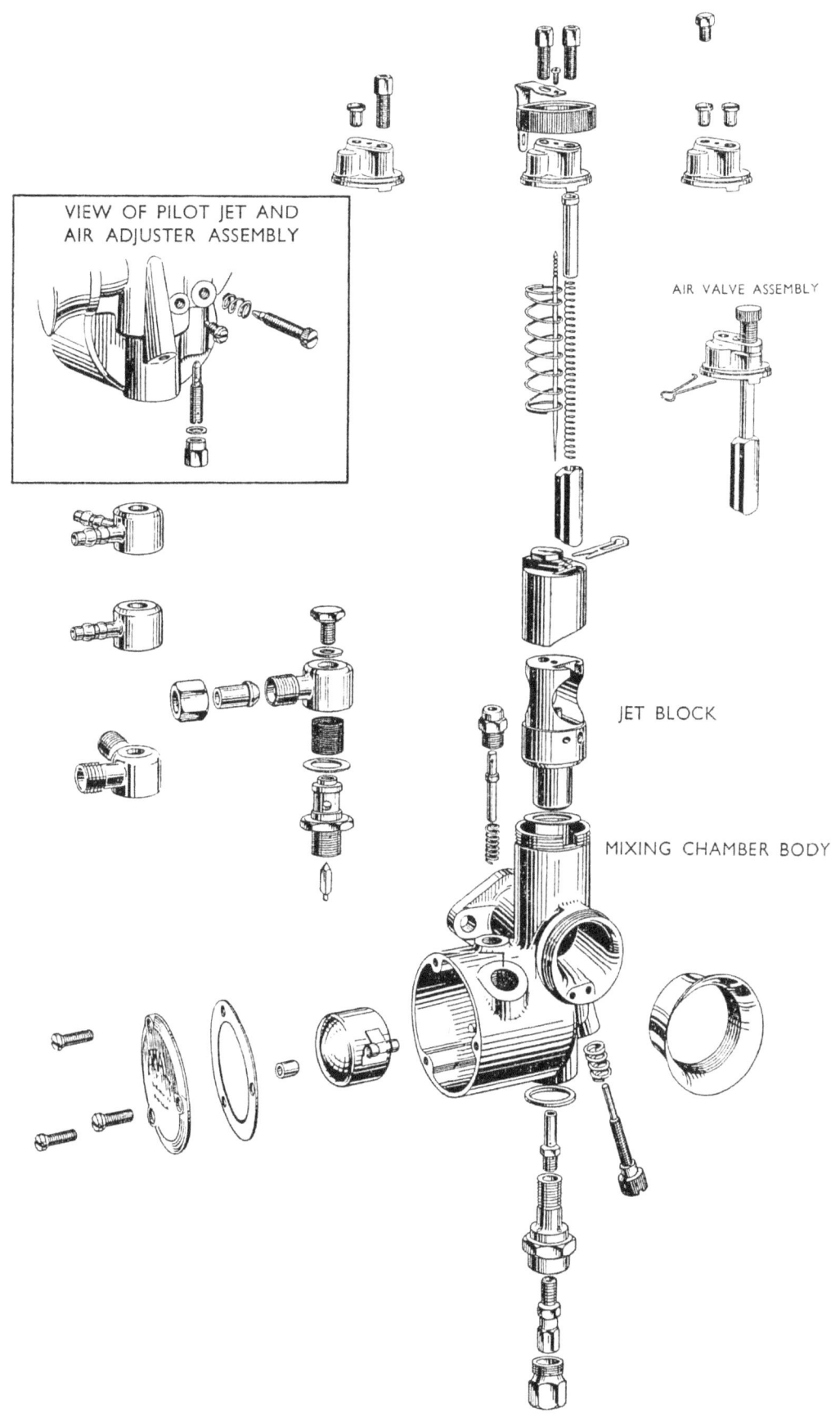

Fig. 3

If the float chamber floods, first make sure that there is no dirt on the fuel needle seating. Owing to the use of a nylon needle and the leverage ratio between float and needle, flooding is very unlikely with this type of carburetter unless dirt is present or, of course, the float is punctured.

If it is necessary to remove the jet block note that this is withdrawn from the upper end of the mixing chamber after unscrewing the jet holder. Be careful not to damage the jet block when removing or refitting it. Note that the large diameter of the jet block pulls down on to a thin washer.

A single strand of an inner control cable is useful for clearing the small passages in the jet block and care must be taken not to enlarge these by forcing the wire through them. Compressed air from a pipe line or a tyre pump is preferable. A choked main jet should be cleared only by blowing through it.

4. Causes of High Petrol Consumption

If the petrol consumption is excessive first look for leaks either from the carburetter, petrol pipe, petrol tap(s) or tank. If coloured petrol is in use this will readily indicate the presence of any small leaks which otherwise might pass unnoticed. If the petrol system is free from leaks, carefully set the pilot adjusting screw as described in Subsection 2 to give the correct mixture when idling. Running with the pilot adjusting screw too far in is a common cause of excessive petrol consumption. If the consumption is still heavy try the effect of lowering the taper needle in the throttle slide by one notch. Do not fit a smaller main jet as this will not affect consumption except when driving on nearly full throttle and may make the mixture too weak at large throttle openings, thus causing overheating.

Settings for AMAL MONOBLOC carburetters on ROYAL ENFIELD motor cycles

Machine	Carburetter Type No.	Choke Bore in.	Main Jet c.c.	Needle Jet	Needle Position	Throttle Valve	Pilot Jet c.c.	Pilot outlet in.	Remarks
"250 Clipper" 1955 (late), 1956 and 1957	375/10	25/32	120	105	3	375/4	25	·025	Setting is for use with felt Air Filter.
"350 Bullet" 1955 (late), 1956 and 1957	376/29	1	180	106	3	376/4	30	·025	Setting is for use with felt Air Filter.
"500 Bullet" 1956 and 1957	389/9	$1\frac{1}{8}$	200	106	2	389/3½	30	·025	Setting is for use with felt Air Filter.
"Super Meteor" 1956 and 1957	376/41	$1\frac{1}{16}$	249	106	3	376/3½	30	·025	Setting is for use with felt Air Filter
"Crusader 250" 1957	375/16	$\frac{7}{8}$	120	105	3	375/3½	25	·025	Setting is for use with felt Air Filter.

SECTION G1c
Lucas Magdyno
Model MO1L for Single Cylinder Engines

1. General.

The Magdyno is a base-fixed magneto and dynamo unit, the body of the magneto portion being arranged to carry a standard strap-fixed dynamo. A shock absorbing drive is arranged between the magneto and dynamo portions. The magneto portion has a wound rotating armature and a high energy magnet case integral with the body.

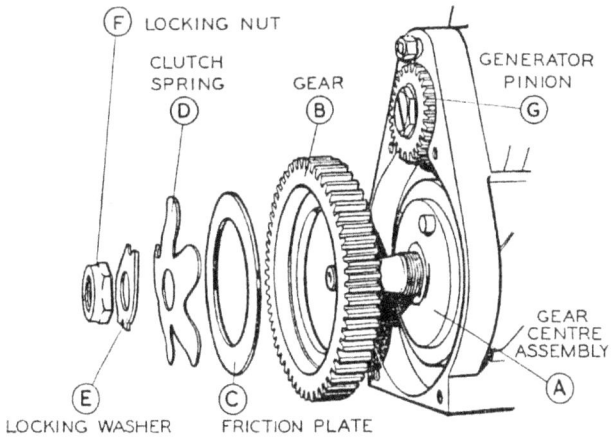

Fig. 1

The shock absorbing drive is incorporated in the larger of the two gears which transmit the drive from the magneto shaft to the dynamo and is shown exploded in Fig. 1. This drive, whilst permitting maximum dynamo output to be obtained, reduces peak shock loadings on the teeth of a bakelised fabric gear to a minimum value. The drive is taken from metal gear centre A, keyed to the magneto shaft, to fabric gear B by means of friction plate C and clutch spring D. A peg projecting from gear centre A prevents relative movement of the gear centre and tension spring D. In the event of a back-fire or an electrical short-circuit, slip will occur between the contacting surfaces of fabric gear B and gear centre A.

2. Routine Maintenance
2 (a). Lubrication

To be carried out every 3,000 miles.

The cam is lubricated by a wick located in the contact breaker casting (see Fig. 2). To reach the wick, remove the backing spring and spring arm by withdrawing the single securing screw. The wick is carried in a hollow hexagon headed screw which can now be withdrawn. Take care not to lose the insulating washer or tube. Moisten the wick with a few drops of thin machine oil and refit the hollow screw.

At this stage, bend back the brass locking tag from the hexagon head of the contact breaker securing screw and withdraw the screw. The contact breaker can now be removed. Take out the tappet which actuates the spring arm and lightly smear it with thin machine oil. Extract the wire ring and remove the face cam. Lightly smear both sides of the cam with Mobilgrease No. 2.

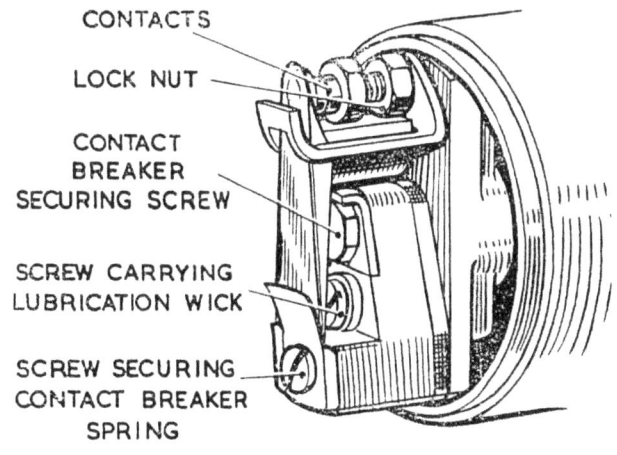

Fig. 2

Refit the cam, taking care that the stop peg in the housing and the plunger of the timing control engage with their respective slots. Note that a recess is provided for the "eye" of the wire ring.

Check that the tappet moves freely in the contact breaker casting.

Thread the special tag washer on the contact breaker securing screw and place the flat edge of the washer against the location provided for it in the contact breaker casting. Tighten the screw and lock it by bending the tag washer against one of the hexagon flats.

Wipe away any dirt or grease from the contacts with a petrol-moistened cloth. If necessary, use a very fine carborundum stone to polish the contacts, re-cleaning afterwards with a petrol-moistened cloth.

Refit the spring arm and backing spring. The bent portion of the spring arm must curve outwards. Place a lock washer over the fixing screw and tighten.

The main bearings of the Magdynos are packed with grease during manufacture and need no attention until a general overhaul is undertaken.

2 (b). Adjustments

Check every 3,000 miles.

(i) *Setting contact breaker gap.* The contact breaker gap must be set to 0·012 in.—0·015 in. when the contacts are fully separated. To adjust the gap, turn the engine until the contacts are fully opened. Slacken the locking nut of the adjustable contact and turn the contact by its hexagon head until a feeler gauge of appropriate thickness is a sliding fit in the gap. Tighten the lock nut and recheck the gap.

(ii) *Adjusting the timing control cable.* Any slackness in the cable can be taken up by sliding the waterproofing rubber shroud up the cable and turning the hexagon headed cable adjuster. After adjusting, return shroud to its original position over the adjuster and central barrel.

2 (c). Cleaning

To be carried out every 6,000 miles.

Check the contact breaker contacts and, if necessary, clean them as described in Subsection 2 (a). Wipe the outside of the magneto to remove dirt or grease. Check the cable adjuster and control barrel for signs of water ingress.

Remove the high tension pick-up and polish with a soft dry cloth. The carbon brush must move freely in its holder. If necessary, clean it with a petrol-moistened cloth. Should the brush be worn to within $\frac{1}{8}$ in. of the shoulder it must be renewed.

Whilst the pick-up moulding is removed, clean the slip ring track and flanges by holding a soft dry cloth against them with a suitably shaped piece of wood while the engine is slowly turned.

The high tension cable must be kept clean and dry.

2 (d). Renewing High Tension Cable

If, on inspection, the high tension cable shows signs of deterioration, it must be replaced, using neoprene covered rubber cable. To fit a new high tension cable, bare the end for about $\frac{3}{8}$ in., thread the knurled moulded nut over the cable and thread the bared cable through the washer removed from the old cable (see Fig. 3).

Bend back the strands radially and screw the nut into the pick-up moulding.

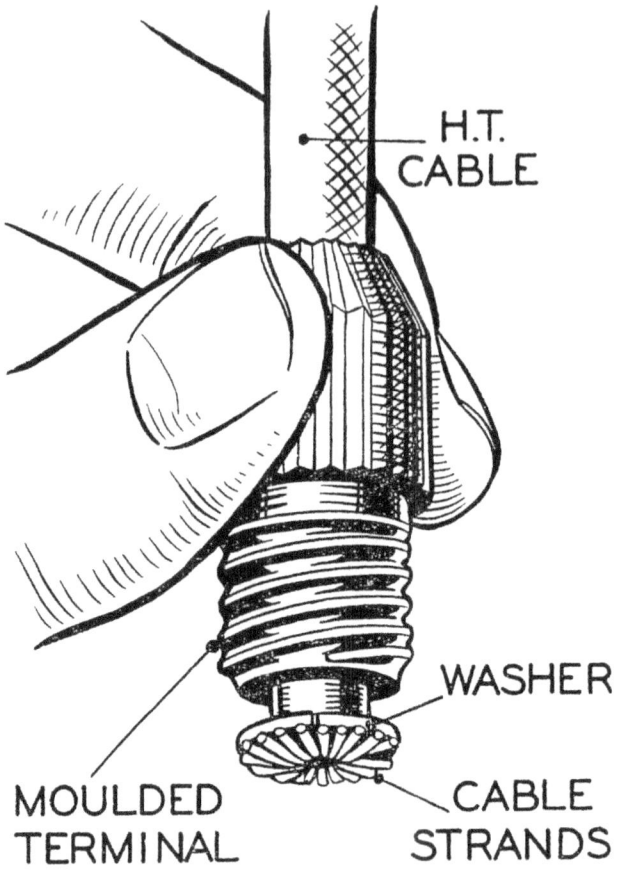

Fig. 3

2 (e). Renewing Timing Control Cable

The Bowden timing control cable should be renewed if it becomes frayed, otherwise moisture may enter the contact breaker housing.

To do this, slip back the rubber shroud and, by means of the hexagon at the base, unscrew the control barrel. If the cable and the plunger to which it is attached are now pulled upwards, the cable nipple can be disengaged from the plunger slot.

Soften the solder and remove the nipple.

Thread the new length of cable through the rubber shroud, cable adjuster, control barrel, sealing washer and restoring spring. Solder the nipple to the end of the cable. Engage the nipple with the slot in the plunger and screw the control barrel into the body, ensuring that the sealing washer is correctly fitted between the barrel and the body.

Take up any slackness in the cable by means of the adjuster before refitting the rubber shroud in position.

2 (f). Contact Breaker Spring

The correct contact breaker spring pressure, measured at the contacts, is 28—36 oz.

3. Testing Magdyno in Position on Engine

To locate cause of misfiring or failure of ignition, check as follows :—

(i) Remove the sparking plug from the engine. Hold the end of the H.T. cable about $\frac{1}{8}$ in. from the cylinder block and crank the engine. If strong and regular sparking is produced the fault lies with the sparking plug, which must be cleaned and adjusted or renewed.

(ii) If no sparking is produced, examine the H.T. cable and, if necessary, renew it as described above in Subsection 2 (d).

(iii) Very occasionally the fault may be due to a cracked or punctured pick-up moulding. This type of fault is not easily detected by inspection and a check should be made by substitution.

(iv) If the Magdyno has recently been replaced or removed it may be incorrectly timed (see Section C2, Subsection 4.)

(v) Check the contact breaker for cleanliness and correct contact setting as described in Subsection 2 (a).

If the cause of faulty operation cannot be traced from the foregoing checks, the cause may be an internal defect in the Magdyno. The Magdyno should therefore be removed from the engine for attention by a Lucas Agent.

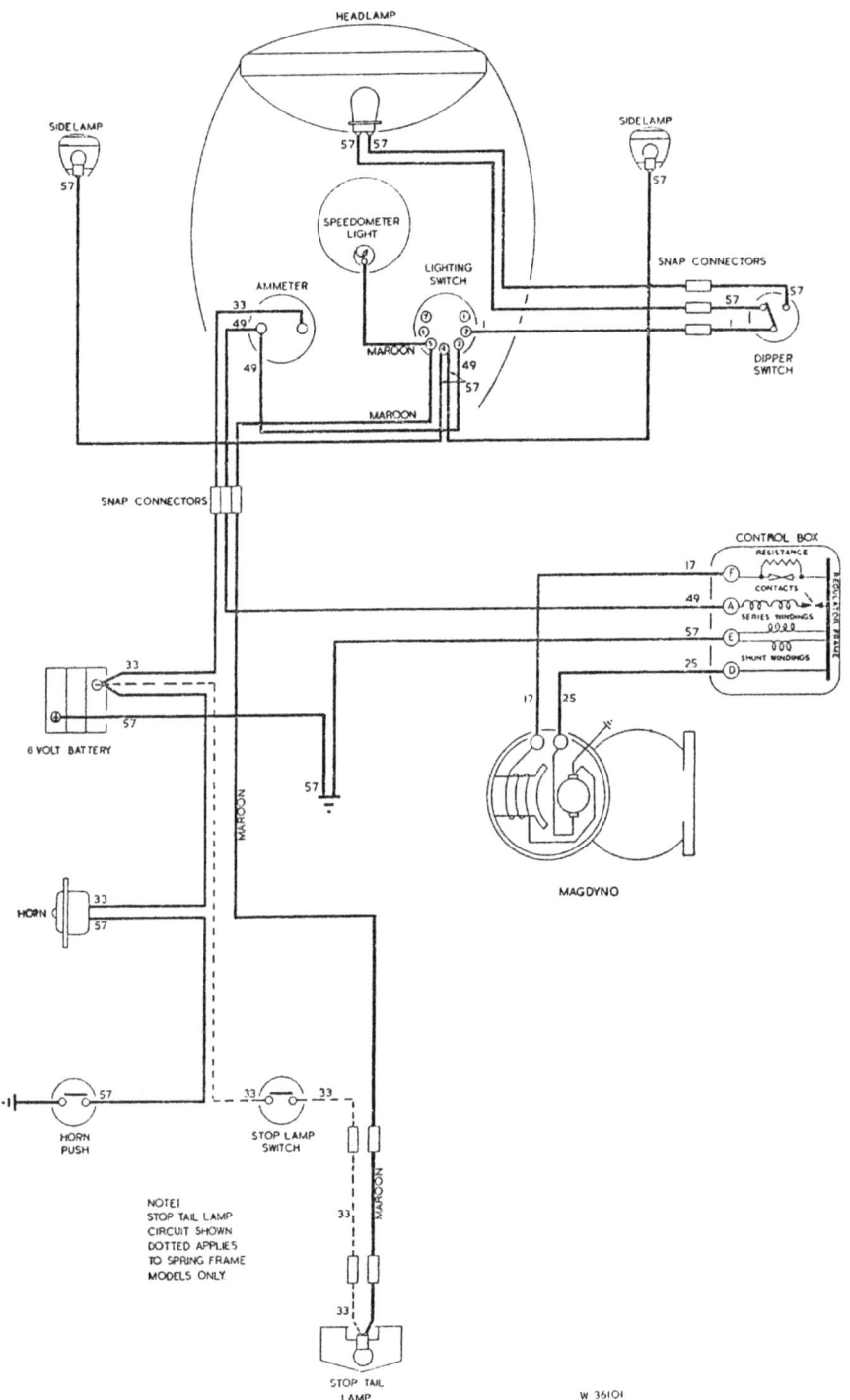

WIRING DIAGRAM
Fig. 4

SECTION G2b

Lucas Dynamo Model E3LM

Used on all Models fitted with Magdyno

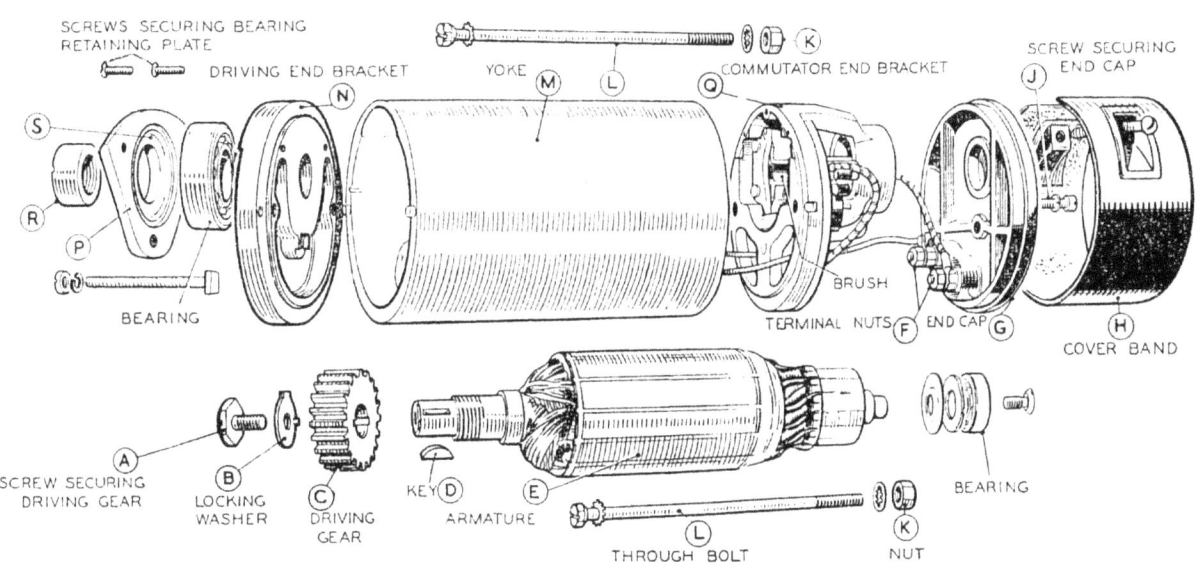

Fig. 1

1. General

The dynamo is a shunt-wound two-pole machine, arranged to work in conjunction with a regulator unit to give an output which is dependent on the state of charge of the battery and the loading of the electrical equipment in use. When the battery is in a low state of charge, the dynamo gives a high output, whereas, if the battery is fully charged, the dynamo gives only a trickle charge to keep the battery in a good condition without overcharging. In addition, an increase of output is given to balance the current taken by the lamps when in use. Model E3LM (see Fig. 1) is designed to be the upper portion of the "Magdyno" and has an output of 60 watts.

2 (a). Lubrication

No lubrication is necessary, as the ball bearings are packed with H.M.P. grease, which will last until the machine is taken down for a general overhaul, when the bearings should be repacked.

2 (b). Inspection of Commutator and Brush Gear

About once every six months remove the cover band for inspection of commutator and brushes, see Subsection 4 (a) (vi).

3. Test Data

Cutting-in Speed (Dynamo Cold)	Output Test	Field Resistance	Brush Spring Tension
1,050—1,200 r.p.m. at 7 volts	8·5 amps. at 1,850—2,000 r.p.m. at 7 volts*	2·8 ohms	16—20 oz.

*On resistance load of 0·82 ohm.

4 (a). Testing in Position to Locate Fault in Charging Circuit

In the event of a fault in the charging circuit, adopt the following procedure to locate the cause of trouble.

(i) Check that the dynamo and regulator units are connected correctly. The dynamo terminal "D" should be connected to the regulator unit terminal "D" and dynamo terminal "F" to regulator terminal "F."

(ii) Remove the cables from the dynamo terminals "D" and "F" and connect the two terminals with a short length of wire.

(iii) Start the engine and set to run at normal idling speed.

(iv) Connect the negative lead of a moving coil voltmeter, calibrated 0—10 volts, to one of the dynamo terminals and connect the positive lead to a good earthing point on the dynamo yoke or engine. Reverse voltmeter connections on negative earth machines.

(v) Gradually increase the engine speed, when the voltmeter reading should rise rapidly and without fluctuation. Do not allow the voltmeter reading to rise above 10 volts and do not race the engine in an attempt to increase the voltage. It is sufficient to run the dynamo up to a speed of 1,000 r.p.m. If there is no reading, check the brush gear, as described in (vi) below. If there is a low reading of approximately $\frac{1}{2}$ volt, the field winding may be at fault, see Subsection 4 (d). If there is a reading of approximately $1\frac{1}{2}$ to 2 volts, the armature winding may be at fault, see Subsection 4 (e).

(vi) Remove the cover band and examine the brushes and commutator. Hold back each of the brush springs and move the brush by pulling gently on its flexible connector. If the movement is sluggish, remove the brush from its holder and ease the sides by lightly polishing on a smooth file. Always replace brushes in their original positions. If the brushes are worn so that they do not bear on the commutator or if the brush flexible is exposed on the running face, new brushes must be fitted.

Test the brush spring tension with a spring scale (see Fig. 2). The correct tension is 16—20 oz. and new springs must be fitted if the tension is low.

If the commutator is blackened or dirty, clean it by holding a petrol-moistened cloth against it while the engine is turned slowly by means of the kick start, with sparking plug(s) removed.

Re-test the dynamo as in (v) above. If there is still no reading on the voltmeter there is an internal fault and the complete unit should be replaced if a spare is available. Otherwise the unit must be dismantled, see Subsection 4 (b) for internal examination.

(vii) If the dynamo is in good order, restore the original connections. Connect regulator unit terminal " D " to dynamo terminal " D " and regulator terminal " F " to dynamo terminal " F " and check the regulator.

4 (b). To Dismantle

Remove the dynamo from the motor cycle. To detach the dynamo from the Magdyno, unscrew the hexagon headed nut from the driving end cover and slacken the screws securing the band clip.

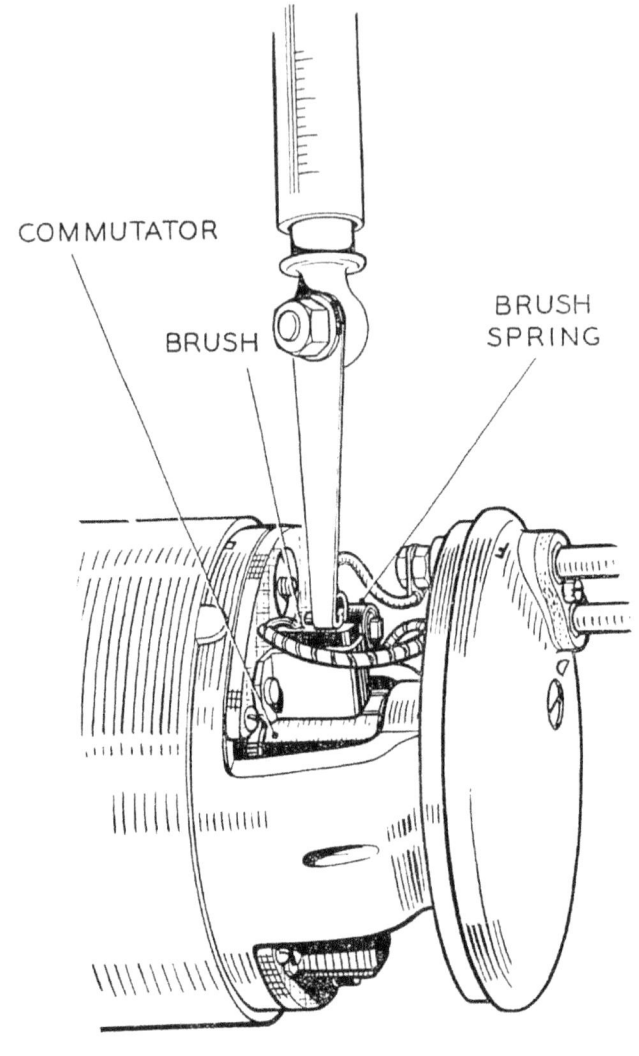

Fig. 2

To dismantle the dynamo proceed as follows :—

(i) Bend back the tag on the washer " B " locking the screw "A" (see Fig. 1). Remove this screw, withdraw the gear " C " from the shaft with the aid of an extractor and remove the key(s) " D " from the shaft.

(ii) Remove the cover band " H," hold back the brush springs and lift the brushes from their holders.

(iii) Take out the screw " J " with spring washer from the centre of the black moulded end cap " G." Draw the cap away from the end bracket, take off terminal nut " F " and spring washer, and lift the connections off the terminals.

(iv) Unscrew and remove from the drive end bracket the two through bolts " L " securing the drive end bracket " N " and commutator end bracket " Q " to the yoke " M." Hold the nuts

"K" at the commutator end while unscrewing the bolts and take care not to lose the nuts.

(v) Draw the drive end bracket complete with armature "E" out of the yoke.

(vi) Remove the nut "R" and press the armature out of the drive end bracket by means of a hand press.

(vii) Remove the bearing retaining plate "P" from the end bracket. This is secured by two screws and a long threaded bolt.

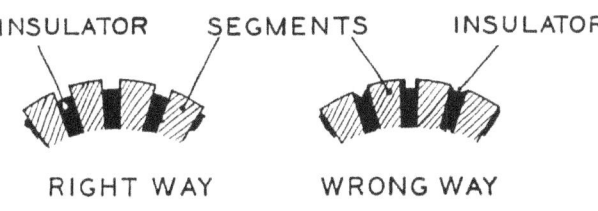

Fig. 3

(viii) Take out the screw securing the green field coil lead with the yellow sleeve to commutator end bracket and remove the end bracket "Q" withdrawing the connectors through the slot in the insulating plate.

(ix) Unscrew the three screws securing the insulating plate to the commutator end bracket and remove the plate with brush gear.

4 (c). Commutator

Examine the commutator. If it is in good condition it will be smooth and free from pits or burnt spots. Clean with a petrol-moistened cloth. If this is ineffective, carefully polish with a strip of very fine glass paper while rotating the armature.

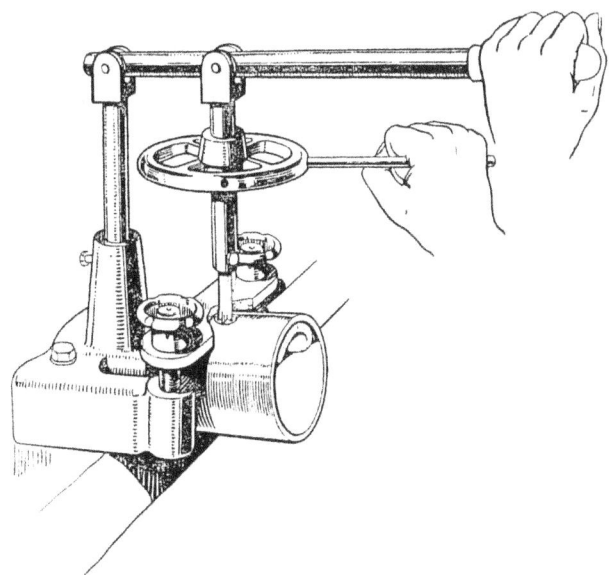

Fig. 4

To remedy a badly worn commutator, mount the armature with or without the drive end bracket in a lathe, rotate at high speed and take a light cut with a very sharp tool. Do not remove more metal than is necessary. Polish the commutator with very fine glass paper.

Undercut the insulation between the segments to a depth of $\frac{1}{32}$ in. with a hacksaw blade ground down until it is only slightly thicker than the insulation (see Fig. 3).

4 (d) Field Coil

Measure the resistance of the field winding by means of an ohm-meter. If this is not available, connect a 6-volt D.C. supply with an ammeter in series with the coil. The ammeter reading should be approximately 2 amps. No reading on the ammeter indicates an open circuit in the field winding.

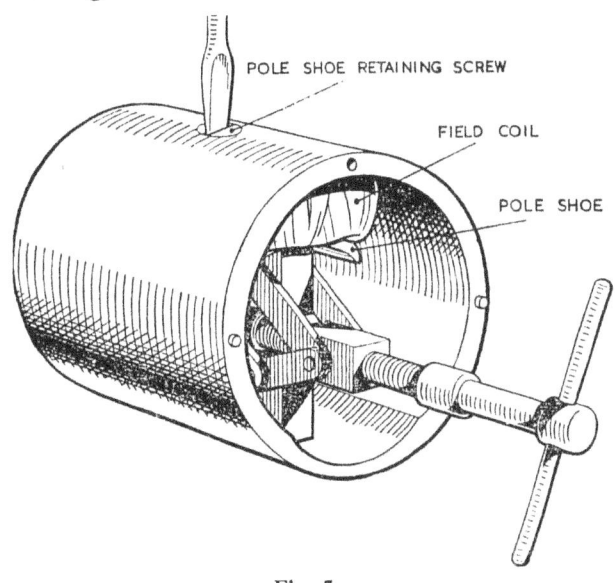

Fig. 5

To check for an earthed coil, connect a mains test lamp between one end of the coil and the yoke. If the bulb lights, there is an earth between coil and yoke.

In either case, unless a replacement dynamo is available, the field coil must be replaced but this should only be attempted if a wheel-operated screwdriver and pole shoe expander are at hand, the latter being especially necessary to ensure that there will be no air gap between the pole shoe and the inner face of the yoke.

To replace the field coil, proceed as follows :—

(i) Unscrew the pole shoe retaining screw by means of the wheel-operated screwdriver (see Fig. 4).

(ii) Draw the pole shoe and field coil out of the yoke and lift off the coil.

(iii) Fit the new field coil over the pole shoe and place it in position inside the yoke. Take care to ensure that the taping of the field coil is not trapped between the pole shoe and the yoke.

(iv) Locate the pole shoe and field coil by lightly tightening the fixing screw, insert the pole shoe expander (see Fig. 5), open to its fullest extent and tighten the screw. Remove the expander and give the screw a final tightening with the wheel-operated screwdriver. Lock the screw in position by caulking, that is, by tapping some of the metal of the yoke into the slot in the head of the screw.

4 (e). Armature

The testing of the armature winding requires the use of a voltdrop test or a growler. If these are not available, the armature should be checked by substitution. No attempt should be made to machine the armature core or to true a distorted armature shaft.

4 (f). Bearings

Ball bearings are fitted to both the commutator and drive end brackets. When the bearings become worn to such an extent that they allow side movement of the armature shaft, they must be replaced. To replace the ball bearing at the commutator end proceed as follows :—

(i) Remove the screw from the end of the armature shaft and, using a caliper type extractor, draw the bearing off the shaft.

(ii) Wipe out the bearing housing and pack the new bearing with H.M.P. grease.

(iii) Position the bearing on the end of the shaft and press it squarely home, applying pressure on the inner journal of the bearing.

To replace the ball bearing at the drive end proceed as follows :—

(i) Remove the bearing retaining plate from the drive end bracket as previously described.

(ii) Press the bearing out of the end bracket, using a metal drift locating on the inner journal of the bearing. Wipe out the bearing housing and pack the new bearing with H.M.P. grease.

(iii) Position the bearing in its housing and press it squarely home, applying pressure on the outer journal of the bearing.

4 (g). Reassembly

In the main, the reassembly of the dynamo is a reversal of the operation described in Subsection 4 (b), bearing in mind the following points :—

(i) The field coil lead fitted with the short length of yellow tubing must be connected, together with the eyelet of the earthed brush, to the commutator end bracket by means of the screw provided.

(ii) The second field lead coil must be con-

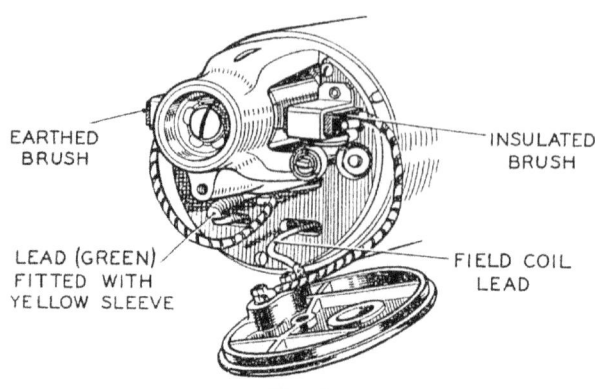

Fig. 6

nected to terminal " F " on the moulded cap (see Fig. 6).

(iii) The unearthed brush flexible lead must be connected direct to terminal " D " on the moulded end cap.

(iv) Take care to refit the cover band in its original position and make sure that the securing screw, when of flush-fitting pattern, does not "short" on the brush gear.

5. Dynamo Polarity

All replacement motor cycle dynamos are despatched from the Works suitable for immediate use on positive earth systems. If the negative terminal of the battery is earthed on the machine for which the replacement dynamo is intended, it will be necessary to re-polarize the dynamo before use to make it suitable for negative earth.

Similarly, if a dynamo has been incorrectly connected on the motor cycle and its polarity has become reversed, then it must be re-polarized.

To do this, fit the dynamo to the motor cycle but do not at this stage connect the cable to the " D " and " F " terminals. Temporarily connect a length of wire to the unearthed terminal of the battery and hold the other end of this wire in contact with dynamo terminal " F " for a few seconds only. This serves to re-polarize the dynamo. The temporary connection can now be removed and the original cables connected to " D " and " F " terminals.

The practice of closing the cut-out points to reverse the dynamo polarity is not recommended, as this method allows a high initial surge of current from the battery to pass through the armature, which can damage the windings, insulation, etc. and result in a decreased service life of the machine.

Generally speaking, motor cycles manufactured up to and including 1951 had the negative terminal of the battery connected to the frame. With a few exceptions, i.e. Miller coil ignition sets and rectifier sets on two-stroke machines, all Royal Enfield machines in current production have the positive terminal earthed.

SECTION G3a

Control Box

Used on Models G, J2, "350 Bullet," "500 Bullet," "500 Twin," "Meteor 700," 1950 onwards

MODEL RB107

1. General

In Model RB107 control box, the regulator and cut-out contacts are positioned, for ease of access, above their respective armatures. It will be noticed that some of the internal electrical joints are resistance brazed.

2. Setting Data

(a) **Cut-out**

Cut-in voltage	6·3—6·7 volts
Drop-off voltage	4·8—5·3 volts

(b) **Regulator**

Setting on open circuit relative to ambient temperature:—

10° C. (50° F.)	7·7—8·1 volts
20° C. (68° F.)	7·6—8·0 volts
30° C. (86° F.)	7·5—7·9 volts
40° C (104° F.)	7·4—7·8 volts

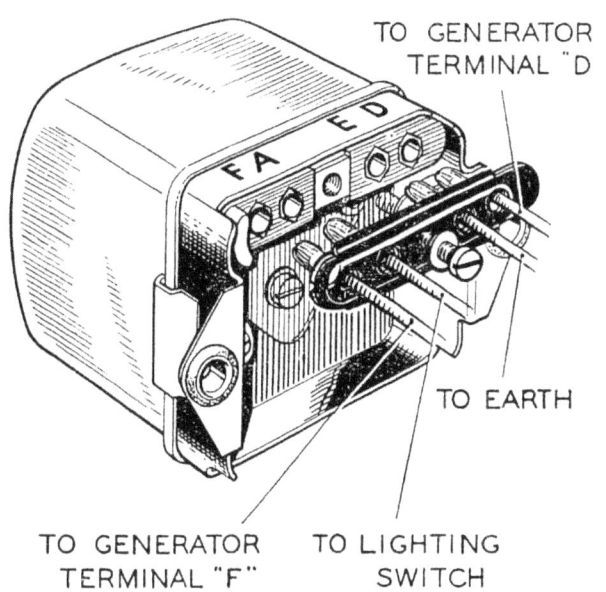

Fig. 1

3. Servicing

Before making any adjustment to the regulator, ensure that the dynamo and battery are in order. When a sound battery does not keep in a charged condition, or if the dynamo output does not fall when the battery is fully charged, the following procedure should be adopted:—

(a) **Checking the wiring between battery and regulator**

Remove the control box from its mountings and withdraw the cable from terminal "A" (see Fig. 1) and connect it to the negative terminal of a voltmeter.

Connect the positive terminal of the voltmeter to an earthing point on the machine. If a voltmeter reading is given, the circuit from the battery to terminal "A" is in order.

If there is no voltmeter reading, examine the wiring between the battery and the control box for defective cables or loose connections. Re-connect the cable to terminal "A."

Check that the dynamo terminal "D" is connected to control box terminal "D" and that the cable is in good condition. Similarly, check the cable between terminals "F" at the dynamo and control box.

(b) **Checking the electrical setting of the regulator**

The regulator is carefully set during manufacture and, in general, it should not be necessary to make further adjustment. If, however, the charging system is suspected it is important that only a good-quality **moving coil voltmeter** (0—20 volts) is used to check the system. The electrical setting of the regulator can be checked without removing the cover from the control box.

Withdraw the plug-in connectors a small distance, so that a voltmeter connection can be made to terminals "D" and "E."

Connect the negative lead of the voltmeter to control box terminal "D" and the positive lead to terminal "E."

Remove the negative terminal from the battery. If coil ignition is fitted, run a temporary connection from the negative terminal of the battery to the "SW" terminal of the coil.

With the ignition switch in the "OFF" position, start the engine.

Slowly increase the speed of the engine until the voltmeter needle "flicks" and then steadies. Note this value and stop the engine.

If this value lies outside the limits given in para. 2 (b), the regulator setting must be adjusted.

If the value is within the limits, examine the cut-out as described in para 3 (c).

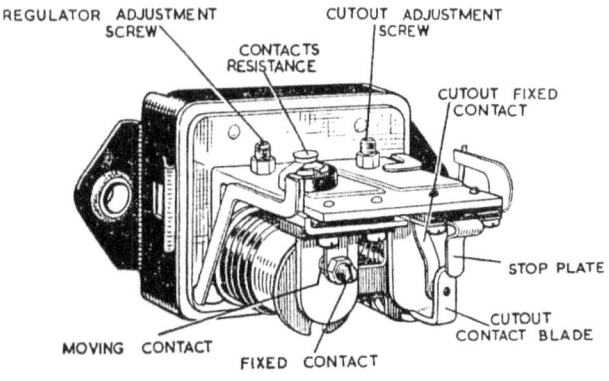

Fig. 2

(c) Adjusting the electrical setting of the regulator

Adjustment of the regulator requires removal of the control box cover. This is facilitated by removing the control box from the machine and providing temporary connections. Loosen the control box cover securing clips by slackening the securing screws set in the base of the control box, and lift off the cover.

It is important that regulator adjustments are carried out with the control box supported in a similar position to that on the machine.

Restart the engine.

Slacken the locknut of the regulator adjusting screw (see Fig. 2) and turn the screw in a clockwise direction to raise the setting or an anti-clockwise direction to lower the setting. Turn the screw only a fraction of a turn at a time and then tighten the locknut. Repeat as above until the correct setting is obtained.

Adjustment of regulator open-circuit voltage should be completed within 30 seconds, otherwise heating of the shunt winding will cause false settings to be made.

Stop the engine.

Remake the original connections and replace the cover. Ensure that the cover seats correctly on the sealing washer.

N.B.—A dynamo run at high speed on open circuit will build up a high voltage. Therefore, when adjusting the regulator, do not run the engine up to more than half throttle or a false setting will be made.

(d) Checking the electrical setting of the cut-out

If the regulator is correctly set but the battery is still not being charged, the cut-out may be out of adjustment.

Replace the control box in the testing position, remake the temporary connections and remove the control box cover. Connect a voltmeter between terminals "D" and "E."

Start the engine and slowly increase the speed until the cut-out contacts close. Note the voltage at which this occurs and stop the engine. This should be 6·3—6·7 volts. If operation of the cut-out takes place outside these limits, it will be necessary to adjust.

(e) Adjusting the electrical setting of the cut-out

Restart the engine.

Slacken the locknut securing the cut-out adjusting screw and turn the adjusting screw in a clockwise direction to raise the voltage setting or in an anti-clockwise direction to reduce the setting.

Turn the screw only a fraction of a turn at a time and then tighten the locknut. Test after each adjustment by increasing the engine speed and noting the voltmeter reading at the instant of contact closure.

Stop the engine.

Electrical setting of the cut-out, like the regulator, must be made as quickly as possible because of temperature-rise effects. Tighten the locknut after making the adjustment.

N.B.—If the cut-out does not operate, there may be an open-circuit in the wiring of the cut-out and regulator unit, in which case the unit should be removed for examination or replacement.

SECTION G4a
Battery Model PUZ7E

1. General

The model PUZ7E (see Fig. 1) is a "dry-charged" battery and is supplied without electrolyte but with its plates in a charged condition. When the battery is required for service it is only necessary to fill each cell with sulphuric acid of the correct specific gravity. No initial charging is required, but the battery must be left to stand at least one hour after filling before putting the machine into service.

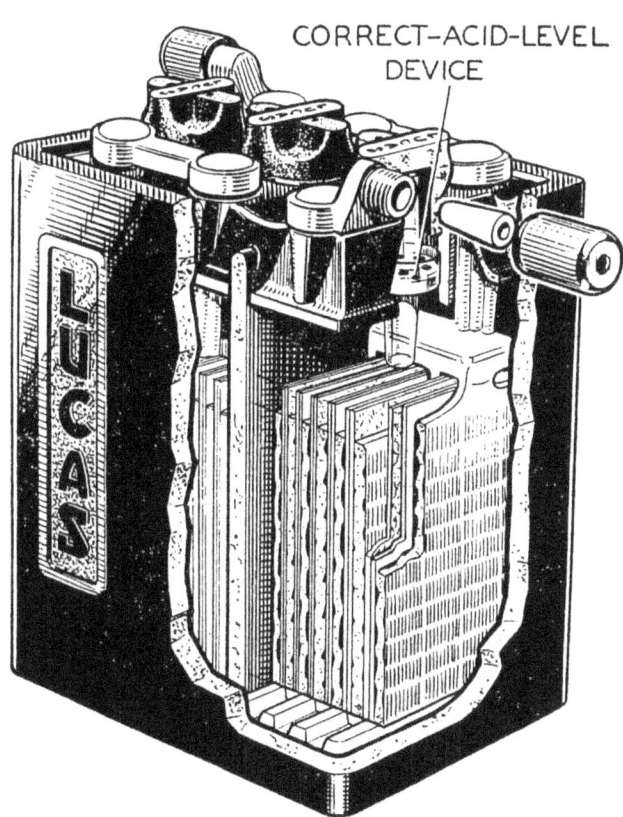

Fig. 1

2. Preparation for Service

The electrolyte is prepared by mixing together distilled water and concentrated sulphuric acid, using lead-lined tanks or suitable glass or earthenware vessels. Slowly add the acid to the water, stirring with a glass rod. Never add water to the acid, as this causes dangerous spurting of the concentrated acid. The specific gravity of the filling electrolyte depends on the climate in which the battery is to be used.

Specific gravity of electrolyte for filling "dry-charged" batteries:

Climates below 90°F. (32°C.)	Climates above 90°F. (32°C.)
Filling, 1.270	Filling, 1·210

The approximate proportions of acid and water to obtain these specific gravities:

To obtain specific gravity (corrected to 60°F.) of :	Add 1 vol. of 1·835 S.G. acid (corrected to 60°F.) to :
1·270	2·9 vols. of water.
1·210	4·0 vols. of water.

Heat is produced by the mixture of acid and water, the electrolyte should be allowed to cool before pouring it into the battery.

The specific gravity of the electrolyte varies with the temperature. For convenience in comparing specific gravities, they are always corrected to 60° F., which is adopted as a reference temperature.

The method of correction is as follows :—

For every 5°F. below 60°F., deduct ·002 from the observed reading to obtain the true specific gravity at 60°F. For every 5°F. above 60°F. add ·002 to the observed reading to obtain the true specific gravity at 60°F.

The temperature must be that indicated by a thermometer having its bulb actually immersed in the electrolyte and not the ambient temperature.

Fill the cells to the tops of the separators, *in one operation*. The battery filled in this way is 90% charged. Whentime permits, a short freshening charge for no more than four hours at the normal recharge rate of 1·5 amp. should be made.

3. Routine Maintenance

Fortnightly (or more frequently in hot climates) examine the level of electrolyte in the cells and if necessary add distilled water to bring the level up to the tops of the separators. The use of a Lucas Battery Filler will be found helpful, as it ensures that the correct electrolyte level is automatically maintained and also prevents distilled water from being spilled on the top of the battery (see Fig. 2).

Occasionally examine the terminals, clean and coat them with petroleum jelly. Wipe away all

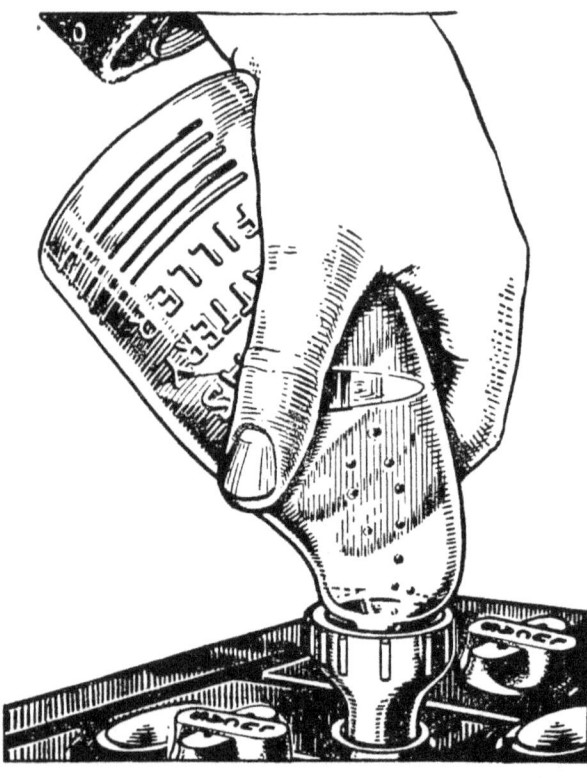

Fig. 2

dirt and moisture from the top of the battery and ensure that the connections are clean and tight.

4. Servicing

If the battery is subjected to long periods of night parking with the lights on, without suitable opportunities for recharging, a low state of charge is to be expected.

Measure the specific gravity of the acid of each cell in turn with a hydrometer (see Fig. 3).

The following table shows the state of charge at different values of specific gravities:

State of Charge	Temperature under 90°F.	Temperature over 90°F.
Battery fully charged	1·270—1·290	1·210—1·230
Battery about half charged	1·190—1·210	1·130—1·150
Battery fully discharged	1·110—1·130	1·050—1·070

If the battery is discharged, it must be recharged, either on the motor cycle by a period of daytime running or from an external D.C. supply at the normal recharge rate of 1·5 amp.

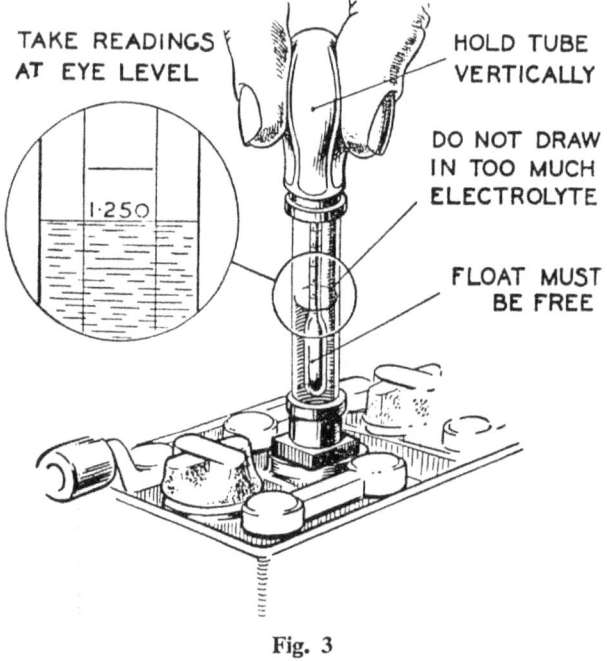

Fig. 3

SECTION G5a

Head and Tail Lamps

Used on Models G, J2, "350 Bullet," "500 Bullet," "500 Twin," "Meteor 700," 1950 onwards

1. Headlamp

In all the above Models the headlamp incorporates the Lucas Light Unit MCF700. This is either fitted into a lamp shell (see Figs. 1 and 2) carried on brackets in front of the facia panel type of fork head and housing a switch, ammeter and parking lamp, or, on later models, is built into the Casquette fork head which contains twin parking lamps as well as the ammeter and switch. On machines fitted with coil ignition the ammeter has a red central window with the ignition warning light beneath.

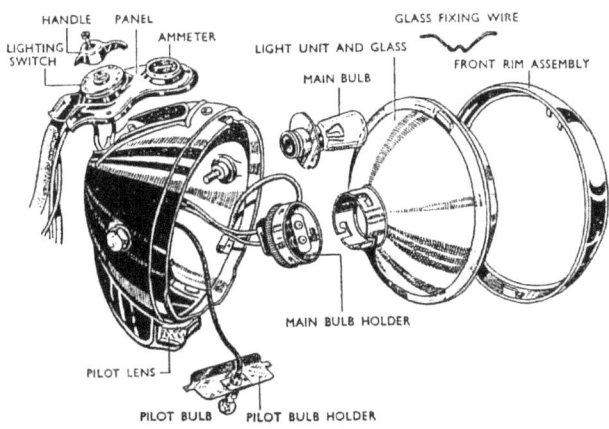

Fig. 1

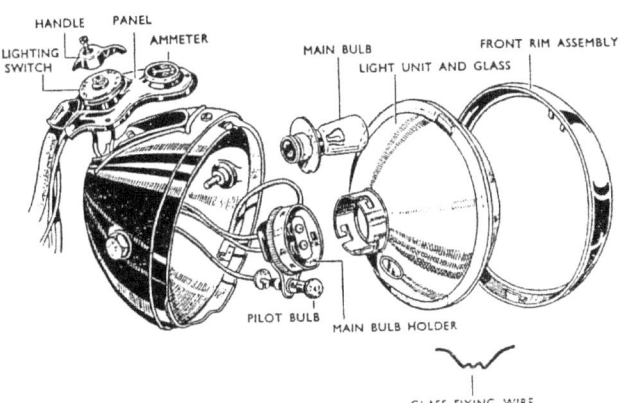

Fig. 2

2. Lucas Light Unit

The unit incorporates a combined reflector and front lens assembly (see Fig. 3). This construction ensures that the reflector and lenses are permanently protected, thus the unit keeps its high efficiency over a long period. A "prefocus" bulb is used, the filaments of which are accurately positioned with respect to the reflector, thus no focusing device is necessary.

The bulb has a large cap and a flange, which has been accurately positioned with relation to the bulb filaments during manufacture. A slot in the flange engages with a projection on the inside of the bulb holder positioned at the back of the reflector.

A bayonet-fitting adaptor with spring-loaded contacts secures the bulb firmly in position and carries the supply to the bulb contacts.

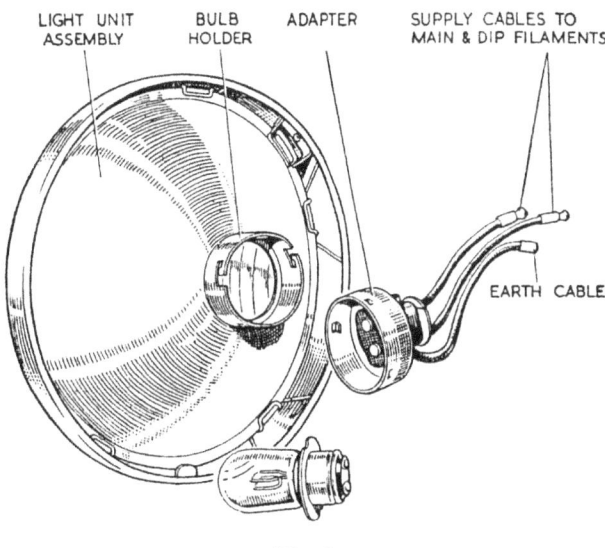

Fig. 3

The outer surface of the lens is smooth to facilitate cleaning. The inner surface is formed of a series of lenses which determine the spread and pattern of the light beams.

In the event of damage to either the lens or reflector a replacement light unit must be fitted.

3. Replacing the Light Unit and Bulb

Slacken the securing screw at the top of the headlamp rim. Remove the front rim and Light Unit assembly.

Withdraw the adaptor from the Light Unit by twisting it in an anti-clockwise direction and pulling it off. Remove the bulb from its locating sleeve at the rear of the reflector.

Disengage the Light Unit securing springs from the rim and lift out the Light Unit.

Position the new unit in the rim so that the word "TOP" on the lens is correctly located when the assembly is mounted on the headlamp. Refit the securing springs ensuring that they are equally spaced around the rim.

Replace the bulb and adaptor. The bulb must be the Lucas "prefocus" type—6 v. 30/24 watt Lucas No. 312.

Locate the bottom of the Light Unit and front rim assembly in the headlamp shell or in the fixing rim attached to the Casquette fork head. Press the front on and tighten the securing screw at the top of the headlamp.

4. Parking Lights

In the case of lamps having separate shells the parking bulb may be mounted either to show through a hole in the back of the main reflector (Fig. 1) or may be mounted in a separate housing beneath the lamp shell (Fig. 2). In the case of lamps fitted into a Casquette fork head twin parking lights are provided. In all cases the bulb is the same, i.e. 6 v. 3 watt M.B.C. Lucas Part No. 988.

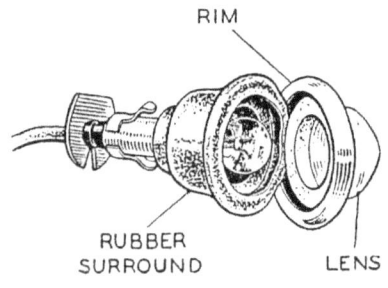

Fig. 4

Access to the parking bulb in the case of lamps with separate shells is obtained by removing the light unit as described in Subsection 2. In the case of lamps in which the parking bulb shows through a hole in the main reflector the bulb holder assembly should be removed. This will come away bringing with it the parking bulb which will then be readily accessible.

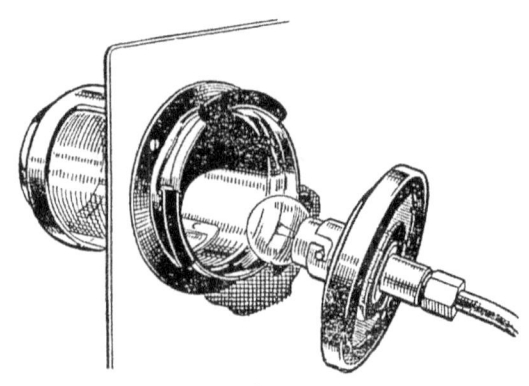

Fig. 5

In the case of lamps having the underslung parking light the parking bulb holder can be lifted out of the lamp shell after removal of the Light Unit.

In the case of lamps fitted into Casquette fork heads access to the parking bulbs is obtained by removing the parking lamp rim (see Fig. 4). This may merely be forced over the edge of the rubber lamp body or in the case of later machines is additionally secured by means of a small fixing screw. After removal of the lamp rim the parking lamp lens can be pulled out of the rubber body, after which the bulb will be accessible.

5. Tail Light

Earlier machines used a circular metal-bodied tail light, either Lucas No. MT110 (Fig. 5) or No. 480 (Fig. 6). In the former case, access to the bulb is obtained by removing the back of the lamp, which will come away bringing the bulb with it. In the latter case, the front of the lamp is removed, leaving the bulb carrier in position. In either case the bulb is the same, that originally fitted being 6 volt 3 watt S.B.C., Lucas Part No. 200, which, however, on machines of over 250 c.c. should now be replaced by 6 volt 6 watt S.B.C. Lucas No. 205.

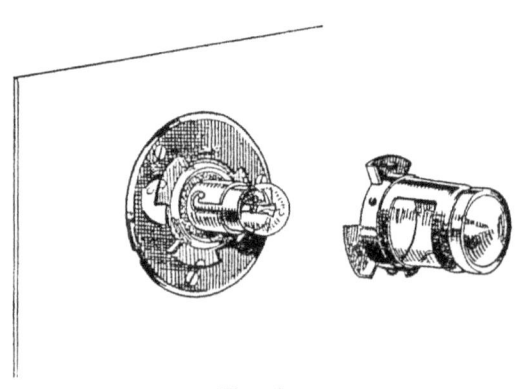

Fig. 6

Recent machines use lamps with red plastic covers, either Type 529 (Fig. 7), which is a tail lamp only; 525 (Fig. 8), which is a combined stop and tail lamp; or 564 (Fig. 9), which is a combined stop and tail lamp and reflector.

Access to the bulb is obtained by removing the two screws which secure the plastic cover.

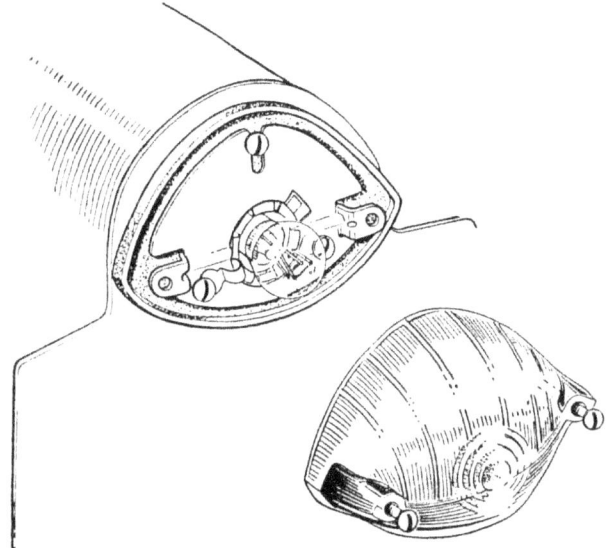

Fig. 7

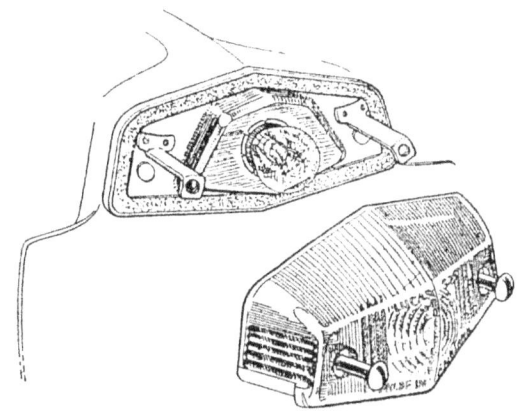

Fig. 8

Care must be taken that the leads to the stop tail lamp are correctly connected, as the use of the 18 watt filament on the normal tail light will not only discharge the battery but could cause trouble from excessive heat affecting the plastic cover. At the same time, the 3 or 6 watt filament, if used as a stop-tail light will be ineffective in bright sunlight.

The correct bulb for the 529 lamp is either Lucas No. 988 6 volt 3 watt M.B.C. or No. 951 6 volt 6 watt M.B.C.

The correct bulb for the stop tail lights 525 and 564 is either Lucas No. 352 6 volt 3/18 watt or Lucas No. 384 6 volt 6/18 watt. The 3 watt or 6 watt filament provides the normal tail light, while the 18 watt filament is illuminated on movement of the brake pedal.

6 watt bulbs are now required by law in Great Britain on machines of more than 250 c.c. capacity.

Fig. 9

SECTION H1

Frame

"Meteor 700"; "500 Twin"; "500 Bullet"; "350 Bullet"; "250 Clipper"

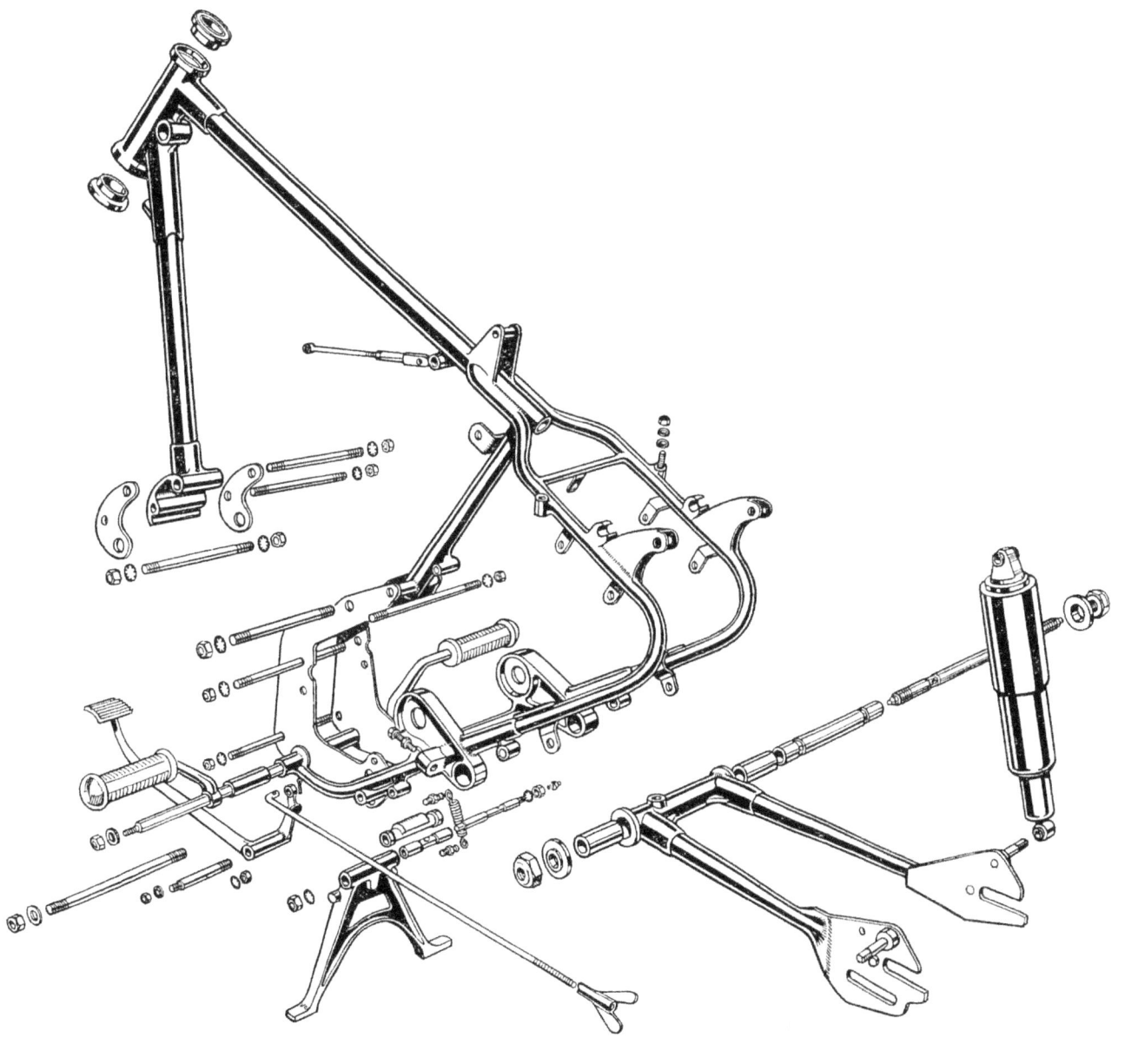

EXPLODED VIEW OF "250 CLIPPER" FRAME
Fig. 1

1. Description of Frame

The frames used on the above models are basically identical, with swinging arm rear suspension, but there are some small differences in the lugs for engine attachment, the method of attachment of the pivot point for the swinging arm and in the width between the brackets supporting the upper ends of the rear suspension units. For part numbers of frames see appropriate spares lists.

The frame is built throughout of cold drawn weldless steel tubing with brazed or welded joints, liners being fitted where necessary for extra strength. All the main frame members are made of chrome-molybdenum alloy steel tubing which retains its strength and resistance to fatigue after brazing or welding.

The swinging arm unit which forms the chain stays is provided with large diameter phosphor bronze bushes and pivots on a stout steel tube which is secured to the main frame by a long bolt passing through the pivot lugs. Hardened steel thrust washers are provided to deal with side thrust. The torsional rigidity of the swinging arm unit helps to maintain the rear wheel upright in the frame and thus relieves the wheel spindle of bending stresses to which it is subject with other types of rear suspension.

2. Steering Head Races

The steering head races, 34085, are the same at the top and bottom of the head lug and are the same for all models. They are easily removed by knocking them out with a hammer and drift and new races can be fitted either under a press or by means of a hammer and a wooden drift.

3. Removal of Rear Suspension Unit

The rear suspension units are readily removed by undoing the top pivot pin nut, driving out the pivot pin, then hinging the suspension unit back on the lower pivot pin, removing the lower nut and pushing the suspension unit off the pivot pin welded to the fork end.

4. Servicing Rear Suspension Units

(a) Proprietary Units. The proprietary units fitted to most 1954 and all 1955 models are sealed and servicing of the internal mechanism can be carried out only by the manufacturers.

The rubber bushes in the top and bottom eyes can easily be renewed and the spring can be removed by pushing down on the top spring cover so as to release the split collar above it. After removal of the split collar the top cover and spring can be lifted off. When reassembling, the spring should be greased to prevent rust and

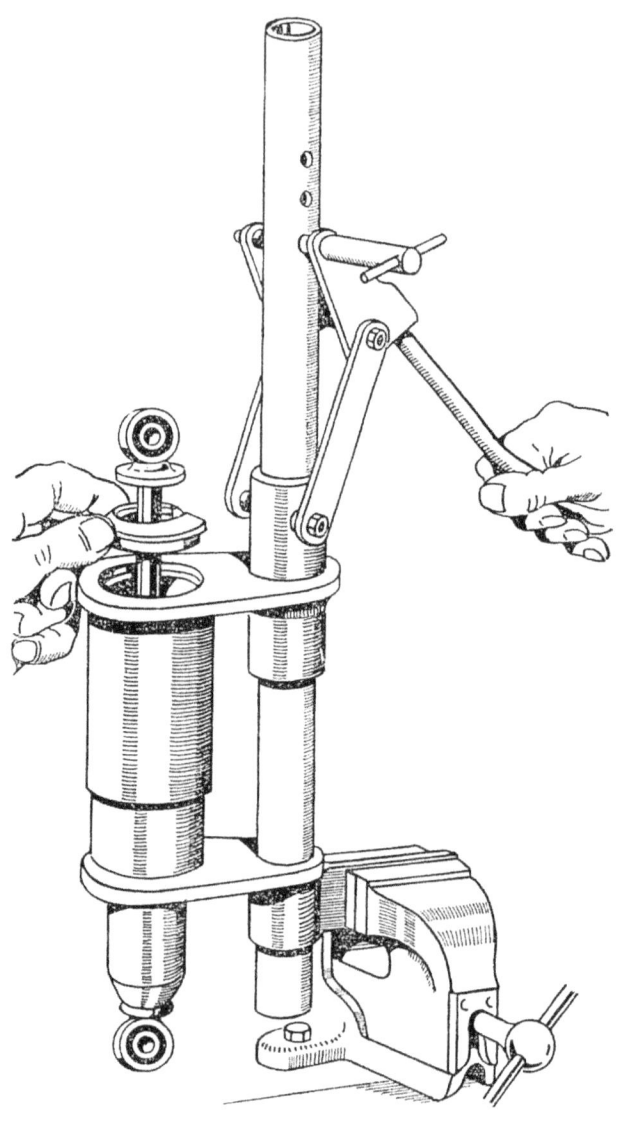

REAR SPRING COMPRESSOR
Fig. 2

squeaking if it should come into contact with either of the covers.

The standard solo springs have a rate of 100–105 lb. per inch and it is not difficult to compress these by hand. Heavier springs having a rate of 130 lb. per inch are available which may require the use of a spring compressor, as shown in Fig. 2.

(b) Royal Enfield Units. Mark I. Enfield rear suspension units, Part Number 34276 or 36451, are shown in Fig. 3. Units having Part No. 34276 are fitted with springs of ·252 in. diameter wire (Part No. 34284) having a rating of approximately 200 lb. per inch (when fitted on the scrolls). Units having Part No. 36451 have a spring of ·264 in. diameter wire (Part No. 35494) having a rating of approximately 250 lb. per inch. The free overall length of both types of spring is 7¾ in. New springs should be fitted if they have set more than ⅛ in.

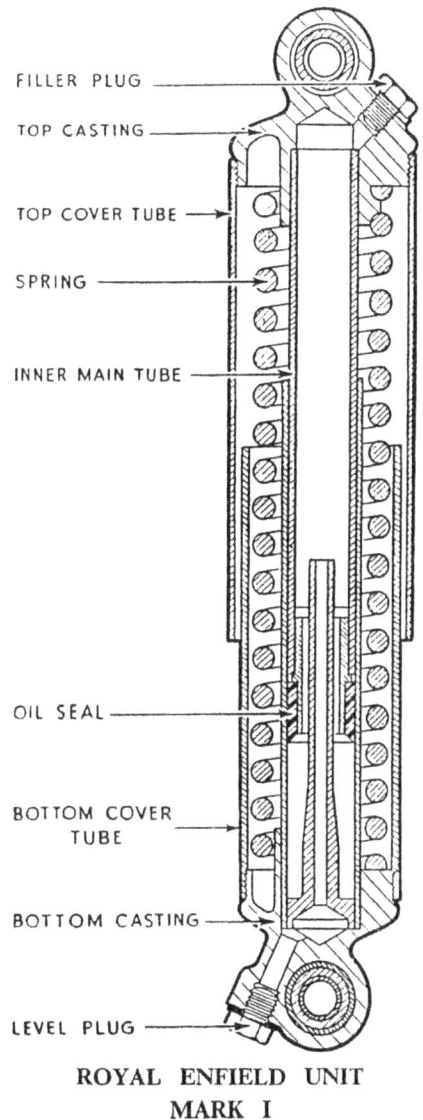

ROYAL ENFIELD UNIT MARK I

Fig. 3

This type of suspension unit was fitted on "350 Bullet" and "500 Twin" Models up to the early part of the 1954 season, and on the "250 Clipper" Model up to the later part of the 1954 season.

To dismantle the unit, remove it from the machine, grip the lower end of the bottom casting in a vice, unscrew the top cover tube, place a suitable bar through the Silentbloc bush in the top casting and turn so as to unscrew the spring from the scroll on either the top or bottom casting.

The top casting with the inner main tube (which is brazed into it) and the oil seal can now be withdrawn from the outer main tube and bottom casting. If the spring has remained attached to the bottom casting unscrew the bottom cover tube and unscrew the spring from the scroll on the bottom casting, if necessary tapping it with a hammer and a blunt chisel. The outer main tube is brazed into the bottom casting and the hollow damper post is brazed into the main tube.

Oil tightness of these units depends on the condition of the edge of the oil seal which must be handled with great care. The synthetic rubber seal is bonded to a hollow metal plug which forms the valve port in the hydraulic damping system. If the oil seal needs renewing the easiest way to remove it from the inner main tube is to pass a $\frac{13}{32}$ in. diameter bar through the hollow plug to prevent it closing in, then grip the oil seal in a vice, pass a bar through the eye in the top casting and pull and twist to withdraw the hollow metal plug from the end of the main tube. Take care not to damage the new seal when fitting it.

After reassembling, remove the oil filler and level plugs and fill with one of the following oils until it runs out through the level plug orifice:—

Castrolite; Mobiloil Arctic;
Shell X-100. 20/20w; Essolube 20;
B.P. Energol S.A.E. 20.

Wait till the oil has ceased running, then replace the oil filler and level plugs.

(c) **Royal Enfield Units. Mark II.** Enfield rear suspension units, Part No. 38109, are shown in Fig. 4. This type provides positive damping on the rebound stroke and in consequence does not need the spring to be anchored on scrolls. The range of movement is greater than the Mark I dampers and on account of this and the improved damping the ride is better, particularly on extended rough sections. The spring rate is 150 lb. per inch.

This type of unit was fitted on the "Meteor 700" model up to the early part of the 1954 season and on the "500 Bullet" model up to the later part of the 1954 season.

The Plunger Head contains a disc valve which on the bump stroke provides only a slight restriction to passage of oil between the inside of the Bottom Bearing Tube and the Damper Chamber which is bounded by the inside wall of the upper end of the bottom bearing tube, the outer wall of the lower end of the top bearing tube, the upper surface of the plunger head and the lower end of the bearing bush. Since there is not room in the damper chamber for all the oil displaced on the bump stroke, provision is made for the surplus to pass up the inside of the top bearing tube and into the hollow top end casting.

On the rebound stroke the disc valve in the plunger head closes under pressure in the damper chamber, so that the oil is forced past the clearance between the plunger head and the inside wall of the bottom bearing tube, thus providing positive damping on the rebound stroke.

At the end of the bump stroke the Oil Damping Post enters the open end of the top bearing tube thus providing a hydraulic cushion to prevent bottoming.

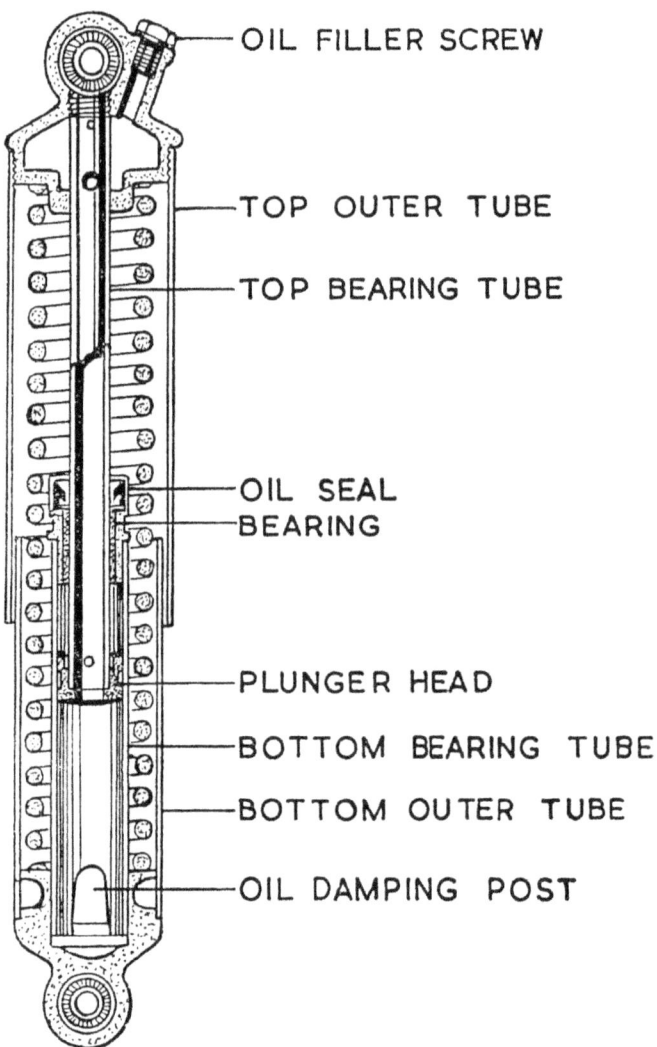

**ROYAL ENFIELD UNIT
MARK II
Fig. 4.**

To dismantle the unit, remove it from the machine, grip the lower end of the bottom casting in a vice and unscrew the top outer tube. Now insert a thin spanner ·820 in. across flats between the coils of the spring to engage the flats on the top bearing and oil seal assembly, unscrew this and withdraw the top casting, top bearing tube and plunger head from the bottom bearing tube, bottom casting and outer tube assembly.

The spring can now be lifted away. Its original free length is $8\frac{3}{4}$ in. If it has closed more than $\frac{1}{8}$—$\frac{3}{16}$ in. a new spring should be fitted.

If it is required to renew the bearing bush or oil seal, the plunger head must be dismantled by unscrewing it from the top bearing tube and then lifting away the Oil Control Valve and circlip. The top bearing assembly comprising the oil seal and bearing bush in a housing can now be withdrawn from the lower end of the top bearing tube. The oil seal and bearing bush are secured in the housing by spinning over the end of the latter. A new assembly must therefore be fitted if either oil seal or bearing require renewing.

After reassembly of the plunger head, fill the bottom bearing tube with oil of one of the grades given below. Remove the oil filler screw from the top casting, replace the spring, and carefully insert the plunger head into the bottom bearing tube, pushing it down slowly so as to spill as little oil as possible and allow time for oil to enter the damper chamber and pass up the inside of the top bearing tube. Tighten down the top bearing and oil seal assembly with a thin spanner inserted between the coils of the spring.

Now use a mandrel press or a vertical drilling machine to compress the damper unit fully and carefully insert oil through the filling orifice until the unit is completely full. Slightly release the pressure and then compress again fully several times to remove air bubbles. Release the pressure to allow the spring to expand about 1 in. before replacing the oil filler plug.

Use one of the following grades of oil:—
Castrolite;   Mobiloil Arctic;
Shell X-100 20/20w;   Essolube 20;
B.P. Energol S.A.E. 20.

5. Removal of Swinging Arm Chain Stays

First remove one of the pivot pin nuts and pull the pivot pin out from the other end. To release the pivot bearing it is necessary to spread the rear portion of the frame, using the frame expander E.5431, which will spread the frame sufficiently to enable the spigots on the thrust washers to clear the recesses in the pivot lugs forming part of the frame.

If it is necessary to remove the bronze bushes these can be driven out by means of a hammer and a suitable drift and new bushes can be fitted under a press without difficulty. After fitting the bushes they must be reamed to ·844/·843 in.

6. Centre Stand

To remove the centre stand unscrew the nut from one end of the stand spindle, knock out the latter and withdraw the stand complete with its bearing sleeve after disconnecting one end of the stand spring. Note that the position of the stand when raised is controlled by the stop on the rear engine plate spacer, Part No. 35060. This should be adjusted so that the stand is as high as possible without actually hitting the exhaust pipe.

7. Wheel Alignment

Note that it is not possible to guarantee that the wheels are correctly aligned when the same notch position is used on both adjuster cams. It is therefore not sufficient to count the notches and use the same position on both sides of the machine. The only way to guarantee that the wheels are in line is to check the alignment from front wheel to back using either a straight edge or a piece of taut string. The alignment should be checked on both sides of the machine and if the front and rear tyres are of different section allowance must be made for this.

It is usual to check the alignment of the wheels at a point about six inches above the ground but, if the alignment is checked also towards the top of the wheels, it will be possible to ascertain whether or not the frame is twisted so as to cause one wheel to be leaning while the other is vertical. To do this it is always necessary to remove the mudguards and, unless a straight edge cut away in its centre portion is available, it will be necessary also to remove the cylinder, toolboxes, battery, etc., in order to allow an unbroken straight edge or a piece of taut string to contact the front and rear tyres.

8. Lubrication

The steering head races, swinging arm pivot bearing and stand pivot bearing should be well greased on assembly. The swinging arm pivot and stand pivot are provided with grease nipples but no nipples are provided for the steering head as experience has shown that the provision of nipples at this point causes trouble through chafing and cutting of control and lighting cables. If the steering head bearings are well packed they will last for several years or many thousands of miles.

Recommended greases are Castrolease (Heavy), Mobilgrease (No. 4), Esso Grease, Energrease C.3 or Shell Retinax A.

SECTION J1

Front Fork

With Casquette and Aluminium Alloy Bottom Tubes

Used on "Meteor 700," "500 Twin," "500 Bullet," "350 Bullet," 1954 onwards

1. Description

The telescopic fork consists of two legs each of which comprises a main tube of chrome molybdenum alloy steel tubing which is screwed into the Casquette fork head at the upper end and securely clamped to the fork crown. Fitted over the lower end of the main tube is the bottom tube made of high strength aluminium alloy with an integral lug which carries the wheel spindle. Fitted on the lower end of the main tube is a steel bush which is a close fit in the bore of the bottom tube. The upper end of the bottom tube carries a bronze bush which is a close fit over the outside diameter of the main tube. The bush is secured to the bottom tube by means of a threaded housing which contains an oil seal. A stud known as the "spring stud" is fitted in the lower end of the bottom tube and a valve port is secured to the lower end of the main tube. As the fork operates oil is forced between the spring stud and the bore of the valve port forming a hydraulic damping system. A compression spring is fitted inside the main tube between the upper end of the spring stud and the upper end of the main tube. The lower end of the main tube and upper end of the bottom tube are protected by a cover secured to the fork crown.

A special fork is available for sidecar machines. This has bottom tubes with extended wheel lugs giving less trail and is fitted with stronger springs and a steering damper.

2. Operation of the Fork

The fork provides a range of movement of 6 in. from the fully extended to the fully compressed position. The movement is controlled by the compression spring and by the hydraulic damping system. The hydraulic damping is light on the bump stroke and heavier on the rebound stroke, thus damping out any tendency to pitching or oscillation without interfering unduly with the free movement of the fork when the wheel encounters an obstacle.

The fork is filled with a light oil (S.A.E. 20) to a point above the lower end of the spring so that the damper chamber "B" is always kept

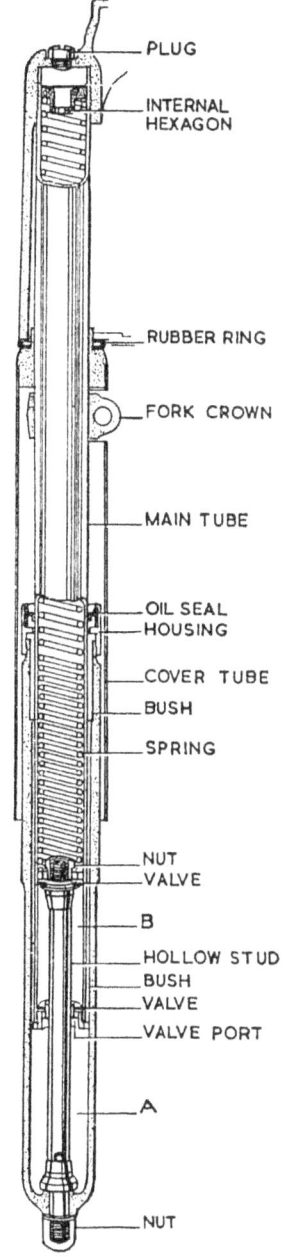

SECTION OF FORK LEG

Fig. 1

full of oil. Upward movement of the wheel spindle forces oil from the lower chamber "A" through the annular space between the spring stud (38067) and the bore of the main tube valve port (38138) into the damper chamber "B." During this stroke the pressure on the underside of the valve plate (38073) causes this to lift so that oil can also pass from "A" to "B" through the eight holes in the valve body. Since, however, the diameter of chamber "B" is less than that of chamber "A" there is not room in "B" to receive all the oil which must be displaced from "A" as the fork operates. The surplus oil passes through the cross hole in the spring stud and up the centre hole in the stud, spilling out through the nut (38076) which secures the upper end of the spring stud to the bronze guide at the lower end of the fork spring.

On the rebound stroke the oil in the damper chamber "B" is forced through the annular space between the spring stud and the bore of the main tube valve port. During this stroke pressure in chamber "B" closes the two disc valves at the upper and lower ends of the chamber so that the only path through which the oil can escape is the annular space between the spring stud and the port. Damping on the rebound stroke is therefore heavier than on the bump stroke. At the extreme end of either bump or rebound stroke a small taper portion on the spring stud enters the bore

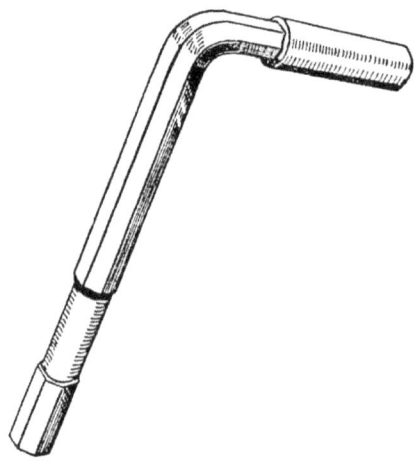

MAIN TUBE SPANNER

Fig. 2

of the valve port, thus restricting the annular space and increasing the amount of damping. At the extreme end of the bump stroke the larger diameter taper on the oil control collar (38075) enters the main counterbore of the valve port thus forming a hydraulic cushion to prevent metal to metal contact.

3. Dismantling the Fork to Replace Spring, Oil Seal or Bearing Bushes

Place the machine on the centre stand, disconnect the front brake control and remove the front wheel and mudguard complete with stays. Unscrew the bottom spring stud nut (38080) which will allow oil to run out of the fork down to

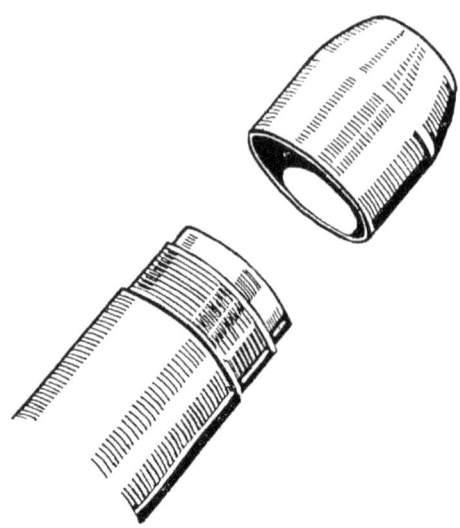

MAIN TUBE SEAL GUIDE

Fig. 3

the level of the cross hole in the spring stud. Now knock the spring stud upwards into the fork with a soft mallet, thus allowing the remainder of the oil to escape. Pull the fork bottom tube down as far as possible, thus exposing the oil seal housing (38157). Unscrew this housing either by means of a spanner on the flats with which it is provided or by using the gland nut hand grips (E.5417). The bottom tube can now be withdrawn completely from the main tube, leaving the bottom tube bush, oil seal housing and oil seal in position on the main tube.

Now unscrew the main tube valve port using "C" spanner (E5418). The spring stud and spring can now be withdrawn from the lower end of the main tube.

The steel main tube bush (38156) can now be tapped off the lower end of the tube, if necessary using the bottom tube bush for this purpose. Before doing this, however, it is advisable to mark the position of the bush with a pencil line so as to ensure reassembling it in the same position on the main tube. The reason for this is that these bushes are finish ground to size after fitting on to the tubes so as to ensure concentricity. After removal of the main tube bush the bottom tube bush, oil seal housing and oil seal can be removed.

In case of difficulty in removing the main tube bush it is possible to withdraw the oil seal housing after loosening the crown clip bolt 39038, removing the plug screw 38968 and unscrewing the main tube from the fork head by means of a hexagon bar ·500 in. across flats (Unbrako wrench W.11) or the special tool shown in Fig. 2.

4. Spring

Solo and Sidecar springs are available. The free length of each is 20½ ins. The spring should be replaced if it has closed by more than 1 inch.

5. Reassembly of Parts

When refitting the oil seal, or fitting a new one, great care must be exercised not to damage the synthetic rubber lip which forms the actual seal. If the seal has been removed from the upper end of the main tube and is refitted from this end a special nose piece (Fig. 3) must be fitted over the end of the tube to prevent the thread from damaging the oil seal.

The spring stud is a tight fit in the hole at the lower end of the bottom tube. Once the stud has been entered in the hole push the bottom tube up sharply against the spring until two or three threads on the stud project beneath the end of the bottom tube. Now fit the nut and washer and pull the stud into position by tightening the nut. If necessary fit the nut first without the washer until sufficient thread is projecting to enable the washer to be fitted.

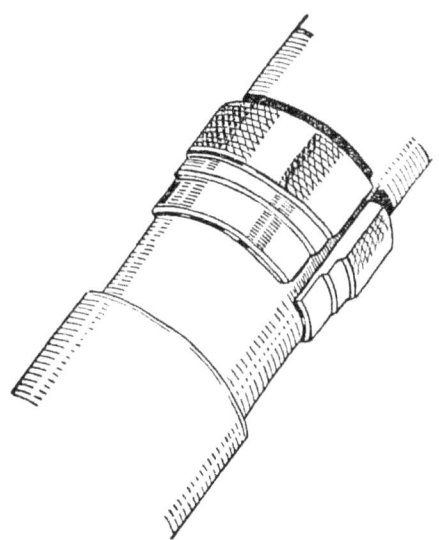

OUTER COVER CENTRALISING BUSHES

Fig. 5

6. Steering Head Races.

The steering head bearing consists of two deep groove thrust races each containing nineteen ¼ in. diameter balls. The bearing is adjusted by tightening the steering stem locknut after loosening the ball head clip screw and both the fork crown clamp bolts. The head should be adjusted so that, when the front wheel is lifted clear of the ground, a light tap on the handlebars will cause the steering to swing to full lock in either direction, while at the same time there should be only the slightest trace of play in the bearings. When testing for freedom of movement the steering damper, if fitted, should be disconnected by unscrewing the anchor plate pin. Do not forget to tighten the ball head clip screw and fork crown clamp bolts. Before tightening the latter make sure that the cover tubes are located centrally round the main tubes so that the bottom tube does not rub inside the cover tube. A pair of split bushes (Fig. 5) is useful to ensure centralisation of the cover tubes.

7. Removal of Complete Fork

The fork complete with front wheel and mudguard can be removed from the machine if necessary by adopting the following procedure.

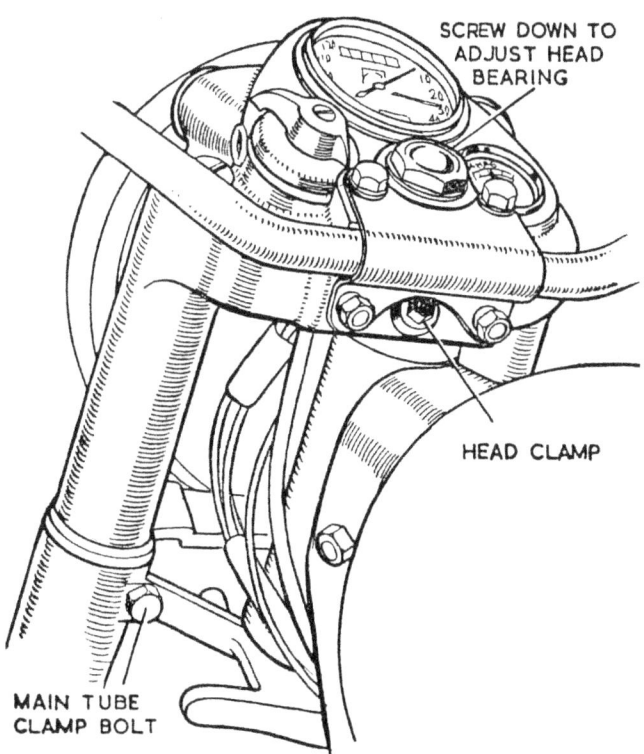

SHOWING THE POSITIONS OF THE CLAMP BOLTS SECURING THE STEERING STEM AND FORK TUBES

Fig. 4

The leads to the lighting switch and ammeter should be disconnected from the battery, regulator, tail lamp, etc. at their lower ends or by means of the plug and socket connectors when these are provided. The switch and ammeter are push fits into the rubber bushes in the fork head.

Disconnect the speedometer drive from the speedometer head and unscrew the steering damper knob and rod (on sidecar forks) after removal of the split pin through the lower end of the rod. Undo the steering damper anchor plate pin so as to disconnect the damper from the frame of the machine.

Remove the two plug screws (38968) and loosen the steering head clip bolt and the two fork crown clamp bolts.

Now unscrew the fork main tubes from the fork head and the steering stem locknut from the top of the steering stem, turning each tube and the nut a turn or two at a time. When the nut has been removed from the steering stem and the main tubes have been completely unscrewed from the fork head the complete fork and wheel with steering stem can be lifted out of the head lug of the frame.

8. Lubrication

The lubrication of the fork bearings is effected by the oil which forms the hydraulic damping medium. All that is necessary is to keep sufficient oil in the fork to ensure that the top end of the bottom spring stud is never uncovered even in the full rebound position. The level of oil in the fork can be gauged by removing the top plug screw and inserting a long rod about $\frac{3}{8}$ in. diameter. If slightly tilted this will ledge against the nut at the upper end of the bottom spring stud and indicate the level of oil above the stud. If the fork is empty to start with the quantity required is approximately $7\frac{1}{2}$ fluid ounces in each leg. Recommended grades of oil are Castrolite, Mobiloil Arctic, Essolube 20, B.P. Energol S.A.E. 20 and Shell X-100 20/20W.

9. Air Vents

The earlier forks of this type were provided with holes at the upper end of each main tube communicating with small vent holes in the Casquette head. Experience has shown that on rough roads oil may escape through these air vents which in consequence are now omitted. Escape of oil from the earlier forks can be largely eliminated by fitting specially long plug screws which are available. The Part Number is 40118. If these are fitted and the final vent hole is stopped up with a wooden plug leakage at this point is impossible. Fitting the special plug screws alone is sufficient in most instances.

SECTION J3

Front Fork

With Facia Panel and Aluminium Alloy Bottom Tubes
Used on "500 Bullet," 1953; "Meteor 700," 1953

1. Description

The telescopic fork consists of two legs each of which comprises a main tube of chrome molybdenum alloy steel tubing which is securely clamped to the Facia Panel Fork Head and to the fork crown. Fitted over the lower end of the main tube is the bottom tube made of high strength aluminium alloy with an integral lug which carries the wheel spindle. Fitted on the lower end of the main tube is a steel bush which is a close fit in the bore of the bottom tube. The upper end of the bottom tube carries a bronze bush which is a close fit over the outside diameter of the main tube. The bush is secured to the bottom tube by means of a threaded housing which contains an oil seal. A stud, known as the "spring stud," is fitted in the lower end of the bottom tube and a valve port is secured to the lower end of the main tube. As the fork operates oil is forced between the spring stud and the bore of the valve port forming a hydraulic damping system. A compression spring is fitted inside the main tube between the upper end of the spring stud and the upper end of the main tube. The main tube and upper end of the bottom tube are protected by a one-piece cover secured to the fork crown and carrying a pressed steel lamp bracket welded to it.

A special version of the fork is available for sidecar use. This has a modified fork head and fork crown setting the main tubes $1\frac{1}{2}$ in. further forward thus giving less trail and providing lighter steering when used with a sidecar. These sidecar forks also are fitted with a steering damper and have stronger springs.

2. Operation of Fork

The fork provides a range of movement of 6 in. from the fully extended to the fully compressed position. The movement is controlled by the compression spring and by the hydraulic damping system. The hydraulic damping is light on the bump stroke and heavier on the rebound stroke, thus damping out any tendency to pitching or oscillation without interfering unduly with the free movement of the fork when the wheel encounters an obstacle.

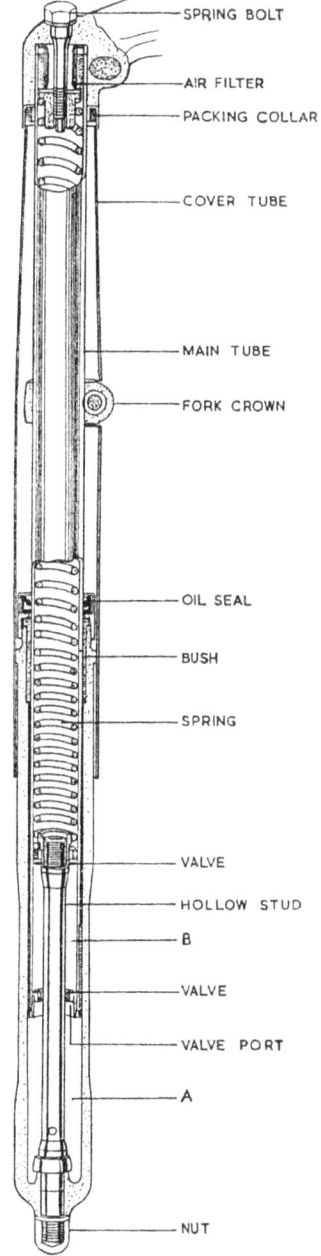

SECTION OF LEG

Fig. 1

The fork is filled with a light oil (S.A.E. 20) to a point above the lower end of the spring so that the damper chamber "B" is always kept full of oil. Upward movement of the wheel spindle forces oil from the lower chamber "A" through the annular space between the spring stud (38067) and the bore of the main tube valve port (38138) into the damper chamber "B." During this stroke the pressure on the underside of the valve plate (38073) causes this to lift so that oil can also pass from "A" to "B" through the eight holes in the valve body. Since, however, the diameter of chamber "B" is less than that of chamber "A" there is not room in "B" to receive all the oil which must be displaced from "A" as the fork operates. The surplus oil passes through the cross hole in the spring stud and up the centre hole in the stud, spilling out through the nut (38076) which secures the upper end of the spring stud to the bronze guide at the lower end of the fork spring.

On the rebound stroke the oil in the damper chamber "B" is forced through the annular space between the spring stud and the bore of the main tube valve port. During this stroke pressure in chamber "B" closes the two disc valves at the upper and lower ends of the chamber so that the only path through which the oil can escape is the annular space between the spring stud and the port. Damping on the rebound stroke is therefore heavier than on the bump stroke. At the extreme end of either bump or rebound stroke a small taper portion on the spring stud enters the bore of the valve port thus restricting the annular space and increasing the amount of damping. At the extreme end of the bump stroke the larger diameter taper on the oil control collar (38075) enters the main counterbore of the valve port thus forming a hydraulic cushion to prevent metal to metal contact.

3. Dismantling the Fork to Replace Spring, Oil Seal or Bearing Bushes

Place the machine on the centre stand, disconnect the front brake control and remove the front wheel and mudguard complete with stays. Unscrew the bottom spring stud nut (38080) which will allow oil to run out of the fork down to the level of the cross hole in the spring stud. Now knock the spring stud upwards into the fork with a soft mallet, thus allowing the remainder of the oil to escape. Pull the fork bottom tube down as far as possible, thus exposing the oil seal housing (38157). Unscrew this housing either by means of a spanner on the flats with which it is provided or by using the gland nut hand grips (E5417). The bottom tube can now be withdrawn completely from the main tube, leaving the bottom tube bush, oil seal housing and oil seal in position on the main tube.

Now unscrew the main tube valve port using "C" spanner (E5418). The spring stud and spring can now be withdrawn from the lower end of the main tube.

The steel main tube bush (38156) can now be tapped off the lower end of the tube, if necessary using the bottom tube bush for this purpose. Before doing this, however, it is advisable to mark the position of the bush with a pencil line so as to ensure reassembling it in the same position on the main tube. The reason for this is that these bushes are finish ground to size after fitting on to the tubes so as to ensure concentricity. After removal of the main tube bush the bottom tube bush, oil seal housing and oil seal can be removed.

In case of difficulty in removing the main tube bush it is possible to withdraw the oil seal housing from the upper end after removal of the main tube from the fork head and fork crown as described in paragraphs 6 and 7.

4. Spring

Solo and sidecar springs are available. The free length of each is 20½ in. The spring should be replaced if it has closed by more than 1 inch.

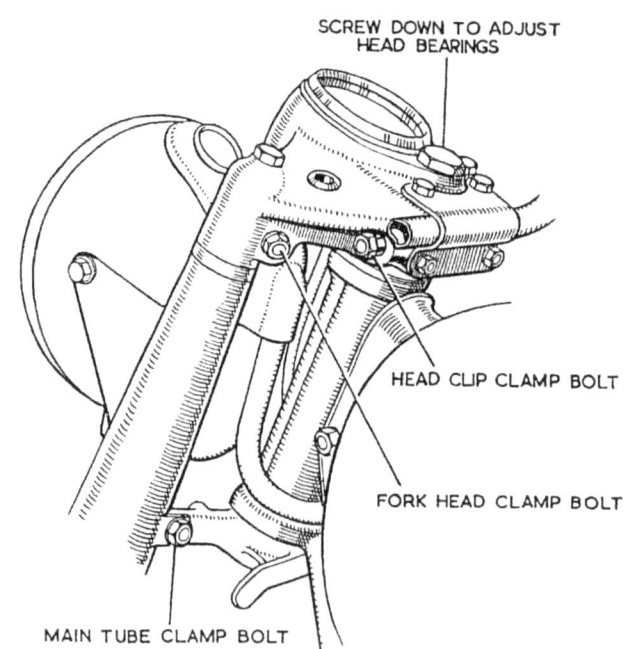

SHOWING THE POSITIONS OF THE CLAMP BOLTS SECURING THE STEERING STEM AND FORK TUBES

Fig. 2

5. Steering Head Races

The steering head bearing consists of two deep groove thrust races each containing nineteen $\frac{1}{4}$ in. diameter balls. The bearing is adjusted by tightening the steering stem locknut after loosening the nuts on the three pinch bolts which secure the fork head to the steering stem and to the two main tubes. The head should be adjusted so that when the front wheel is lifted clear of the ground a

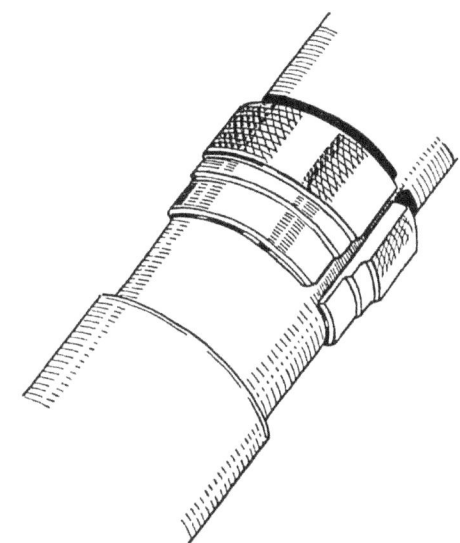

OUTER COVER CENTRALISING BUSHES

Fig. 3

light tap on the handlebars will cause the steering to swing to full lock in either direction, while at the same time there should be only the slightest trace of play in the bearings. When testing for freedom of movement the steering damper, if fitted, should be disconnected by unscrewing the anchor plate pin.

Adjustment of the steering head depends on the ability of the fork head to slide on the steering stem and on the fork main tubes. A rubber washer is interposed between the fork head and the top of the lamp bracket tube to permit the necessary movement. If this rubber washer is fully compressed while there is still some play in the steering head it will be necessary to remove the fork head (see paragraph 6) and shorten the lamp bracket tube by, say, $\frac{1}{32}$ in. Alternatively, if the lamp bracket tube is loose when the steering head is correctly adjusted, it can be tightened by fitting an additional steel washer (Part No. 35974) beneath the rubber washer.

It is also possible that the steering head cannot be adjusted because the main tube is bottoming in the recess in the fork head in which it fits. In this case the nuts on the fork crown clamp studs must be loosened and the sleeves separated (see paragraph 7) thus permitting the main tubes to slide through the fork crown. Do not forget to tighten the fork head pinch bolts and the nuts on the fork crown clamp studs after adjusting the steering head. Before tightening the latter make sure that the cover tubes are located centrally round the main tubes so that the bottom tube does not rub inside the lower end of the cover tube. A pair of split bushes (Fig. 3) is useful to ensure centralisation of the cover tubes.

6. Removal of Facia Panel Fork Head, Spring, etc.

To remove the Facia Panel Fork Head for access to the lamp bracket tubes (or to change the fork spring without disturbing the bearings) proceed as follows—disconnect all control cables at the handlebar end and remove the headlamp from the lamp brackets. The switch panel can conveniently be removed from the back of the lamp so that the body of the lamp can be removed completely.

Now remove the two Fork Spring Guide Bolts from the fork head, unscrew the nuts on the fork head clip bolt and the two main tube clip bolts, remove the three clip bolt sleeves and knock out the three clip bolts. The facia panel fork head can now be tapped gently upwards with a hide mallet or a hammer and a wooden drift but care must be taken to hit only the more solid parts of the fork head, i.e. beneath the handlebar clip and at the back of the main tubes, avoiding the underside of the comparatively thin portion in front of the speedometer.

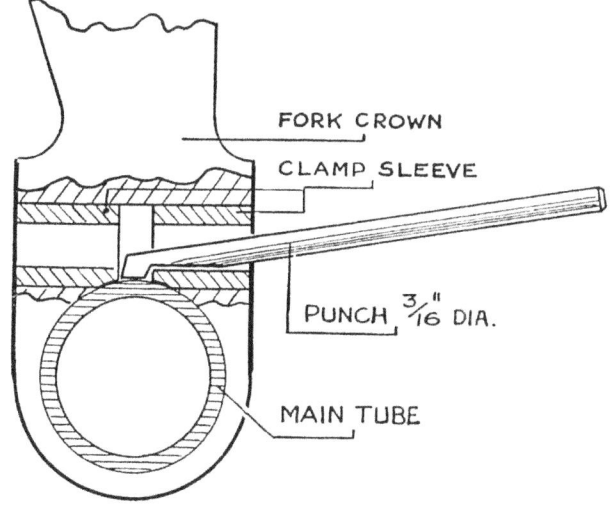

DRIFT FOR PARTING CLAMP SLEEVES

Fig. 4

After removal of the fork head the lamp bracket tubes can be lifted straight off and the springs can be withdrawn from the upper end of the main tubes.

7. Removal of Main Tubes

To remove the main tubes first dismantle the fork as described in paragraph 3 then remove the facia panel fork head and lamp bracket tubes as described in paragraph 6. Now remove one nut from each of the fork crown clamp studs, remove the studs and separate the clamp sleeves with a drift of the form shown in Fig. 4. Now knock the main tubes out of the fork crown either upwards or downwards as may be most convenient. If the machine has been in an accident and the tube is badly bent both above and below the fork crown, it may be necessary to cut through the tube with a hacksaw before it can be withdrawn.

8. Reassembly of Parts

No difficulty should be experienced with this. When refitting the main tube use the lamp bracket tube as a guide to its correct position in the fork crown. The small shoulder some $1\frac{1}{2}$ in. from the upper end of the tube should be $\frac{1}{8}$ in. above the top of the lamp bracket tube when the latter is in position on the fork crown. With the main tube in this position tighten the fork crown clamp screws before fitting the facia panel fork head.

The cover tube must be fitted in position on the fork crown and the clamp sleeves placed in position before the main tube is fitted. To keep the clamp sleeves in position it is convenient to insert a short piece of tube or bar in the eye of the fork crown before putting the cover tube in position. The short piece of tube will be pushed out when inserting the main tube. Before tightening the nuts on the three fork head clip bolts make sure that the bolt heads and the sleeves are correctly positioned with the cut-away portion engaging the main tube or steering stem. Failure to do this may result in a cracked fork head.

When refitting the oil seal or fitting a new one great care must be exercised not to damage the synthetic rubber lip which forms the actual seal. If the seal has been removed from the upper end of the main tube and is refitted from this end a special nose piece (Fig. 5) must be fitted over the end of the tube to prevent the thread from damaging the oil seal.

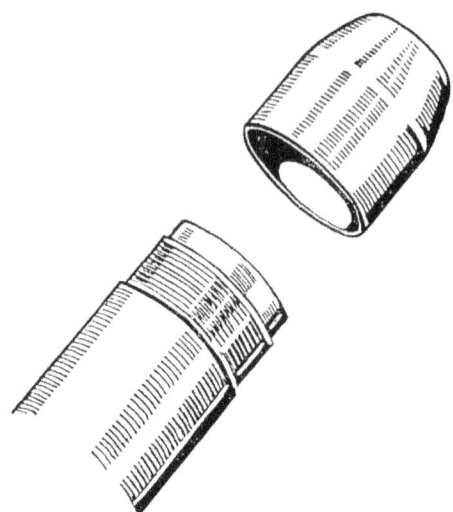

MAIN TUBE SEAL GUIDE

Fig. 5

The spring stud is a tight fit in the hole at the lower end of the bottom tube. Once the stud has been entered in the hole push the bottom tube up sharply against the spring until two or three threads on the stud project beneath the end of the bottom tube. Now fit the nut and washer and pull the stud into position by tightening the nut. If necessary fit the nut first without the washer until sufficient thread is projecting to enable the washer to be fitted.

9. Lubrication

The lubrication of the fork bearings is effected by the oil which forms the hydraulic damping medium. All that is necessary is to keep sufficient oil in the fork to ensure that the top end of the bottom spring stud is never uncovered even in the full rebound position. The level of oil in the fork can be gauged by removing the top plug screw and inserting a long rod about $\frac{3}{8}$ in. diameter. If slightly tilted this will ledge against the nut at the upper end of the bottom spring stud and indicate the level of oil above the stud. If the fork is empty to start with the quantity required is approximately $7\frac{1}{2}$ fluid ounces in each leg. Recommended grades of oil are Castrolite, Mobiloil Arctic, Essolube 20, B.P. Energol S.A.E. 20 and Shell X-100 20/20 w.

SECTION J4

Front Fork

With Facia Panel and Steel Bottom Tubes

Used on "350 Model G," "500 Model J2," 1951 onward;
"350 Bullet," "500 Twin," 1950-53 inclusive

1. Description

The telescopic fork consists of two legs each of which comprises a main tube of chrome molybdenum alloy steel tubing which is securely clamped to the facia panel fork head at the upper end and to the fork crown. Fitted over the lower end of the main tube is the bottom tube made of steel tubing with a forged steel fork end flash-welded to it.* Fitted on the lower end of the main tube is a bronze bush which is a close fit in the bore of the bottom tube. The upper end of the bottom tube carries a bronze bush which is a close fit over the outside diameter of the main tube. The bush is secured to the bottom tube by means of a gland nut with an oil seal fitted inside it. A stud, known as the "spring stud," is fitted in the lower end of the bottom tube and a valve port is secured to the lower end of the main tube. As the fork operates oil is forced through the annular space between the bore of the valve port and the outside diameter of the "spring stud," which is formed with a double taper. Thus hydraulic damping is provided which is light at the normal position of the fork and becomes increasingly effective towards each end of the fork's travel. A compression spring is fitted inside the main tube and is secured by scrolls so that it is in tension on the rebound. The lower end of the main tube and upper end of the bottom tube are protected by a cover tube screwed to the fork crown. The upper end of the main tube is covered by a tube with a pressed steel lamp bracket welded to it.

The fork is filled with a light oil (S.A.E. 20) up to a level above the valve port, this oil providing both the damping medium and the lubricant for the bearings.

A special version of the fork is available for sidecar use. This has a modified fork head and fork crown setting the main tubes 1½ in. further forward, thus giving less trail and providing lighter steering when used with a sidecar. These sidecar forks also are fitted with a steering damper and have stronger springs.

2. Dismantling Fork to Replace Spring, Oil Seal or Bearing Bushes

Place the machine on the stand and in the case of Model "G" or "J2" place a box beneath the crankcase to raise the front wheel from the ground. Disconnect the front brake control and remove the front wheel and mudguard complete with stays. Unscrew the oil level plug after placing a tray to catch any oil which may run out. Undo the nut which secures the spring stud to the fork end and knock the spring stud upwards into the fork with a soft mallet, thus allowing the remainder of the oil to escape.

Unscrew the outer cover tube using the hand grips E4912† thus exposing the gland nut which can be unscrewed with the hand grips E5417,† using a bar through the bracket for the wheel spindle to prevent the bottom tube from turning. The bottom tube can now be withdrawn completely from the main tube leaving the bottom tube bush, oil seal and gland nut on the main tube.

Now unscrew the main tube valve port using "C" spanner E5418.† The spring stud and spring can now be withdrawn from the lower end of the main tube.

The bronze main tube bush can be now tapped off the lower end of the tube using the bottom tube bush for this purpose. The bottom tube bush, oil seal and gland nut can then be withdrawn.

3. Spring

The original length of the spring is 19 in. overall. A new spring should be fitted if the old one has set by more than 1 inch.

4. Steering Head Races

The steering head bearing consists of two deep groove thrust races each containing nineteen

---

*On early models the fork end was made of aluminium alloy screwed on to the bottom tube.

† See Manual of Service Tools.

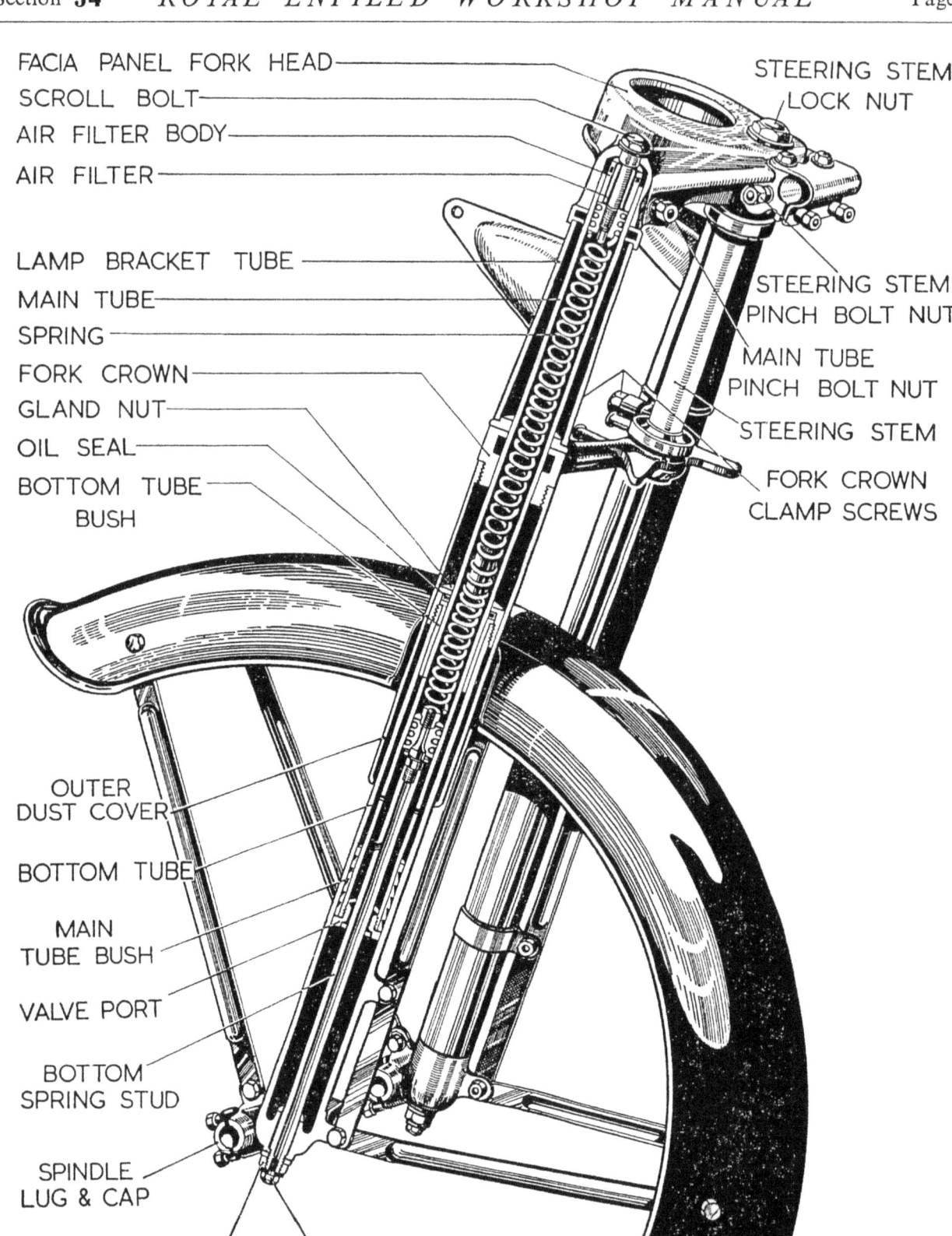

SECTIONED VIEW OF TELESCOPIC FORK
Fig. 1

$\frac{1}{4}$ in. diameter balls. The bearing is adjusted by tightening the steering stem locknut after loosening the nuts on the three pinch bolts which secure the fork head to the steering stem and to the two main tubes. The head should be adjusted so that when the front wheel is lifted clear of the ground a light tap on the handlebars will cause the steering to swing to full lock in either direction, while at the same time there should be only the slightest trace of play in the bearings. When testing for freedom of movement the steering damper, if fitted, should be disconnected by unscrewing the anchor plate pin.

Adjustment of the steering head depends on the ability of the fork head to slide on the steering stem and on the fork main tubes. A rubber washer is interposed between the fork head and the top of the lamp bracket tube to permit the necessary movement. If this rubber washer is fully compressed while there is still some play in the steering head it will be necessary to remove the fork head (see paragraph 5) and shorten the lamp bracket tube by, say, $\frac{1}{32}$ in. Alternatively, if the lamp bracket tube is loose when the steering head is correctly adjusted, it can be tightened by fitting an additional steel washer (Part No. 35974) beneath the rubber washer.

It is also possible that the steering head cannot be adjusted because the main tube is bottoming in the recess in the fork head in which it fits. In this case the fork crown clamp screws must be loosened, thus permitting the main tubes to slide through the fork crown. Do no forget to tighten the fork head pinch bolts and the fork crown clamp screws after adjusting the steering head.

5. Removal of Facia Panel Fork Head, Spring, etc.

To remove the Facia Panel Fork Head for access to the lamp bracket tubes (or to change the fork spring without disturbing the bearings) proceed as follows—disconnect all control cables at the handlebar end and remove the headlamp from the lamp brackets. The switch panel can conveniently be removed from the back of the lamp so that the body of the lamp can be removed completely.

Now unscrew the two Fork Spring Scroll Bolts from the fork head, unscrew the nuts on the fork head clip bolt and the two main tube clip bolts, remove the three clip bolt sleeves and knock out the three clip bolts. The facia panel fork head can now be tapped gently upwards with a hide mallet or a hammer and a wooden drift but care must be taken to hit only the more solid parts of the fork head, i.e. beneath the handlebar clip and at the back of the main tubes, avoiding the underside of the comparatively thin portion in front of the speedometer.

After removal of the fork head the lamp bracket tubes can be lifted straight off and the springs can be withdrawn from the upper end of the main tubes after unscrewing the oil level plug and the nut which secures the spring stud to the fork end and knocking the spring stud upwards.

6. Removal of Main Tubes

To remove the main tubes first dismantle the fork as described in paragraph 2 then remove the facia panel fork head and lamp bracket tubes as described in paragraph 5. Now loosen the fork crown clamp screws and knock the main tubes out of the fork crown either upwards or downwards as may be most convenient. If the machine has been in an accident and the tube is badly bent both above and below the fork crown, it may be necessary to cut through the tube with a hacksaw before it can be withdrawn.

7. Reassembly of Parts

No difficulty should be experienced with this. When refitting the main tube use the lamp bracket tube as a guide to its correct position in the fork crown. The small shoulder some $1\frac{1}{2}$ in. from the upper end of the tube should be flush with the top of the lamp bracket tube when the latter is in position on the fork crown. With the main tube in this position tighten the fork crown clamp screws before fitting the facia panel fork head.

If new oil seals have been fitted it may be found that the action of the fork is very stiff when the gland nuts are tightened down fully. In this case the nuts may be left half a turn or so slack until the seals have freed off, after which they should be tightened down. Note that the seals must be fitted with the larger bore uppermost, i.e. with the scraping edges facing downwards.

When refitting the three clip bolts, which secure the fork head to the main tubes and steering stem, make sure that the clip bolts and their sleeves are correctly fitted so that the cut-away portions of them bear against the tubes. Any attempt to tighten the nuts with the bolts or sleeves incorrectly fitted may result in cracking the facia panel fork head.

8. Lubrication

The lubrication of the fork bearings is effected by the oil which forms the hydraulic damping medium. The oil level is fixed by a cross hole in the spring stud leading to a drilled passage terminating in the oil level plug. To fill each fork leg to the correct level remove the plug screws from the fork head and the oil level plugs from the fork ends. Pour oil in at the top until it runs out at the bottom of the fork. Wait till oil has stopped running and replace level plugs and plug screws.

Recommended grades of oil are Castrolite, Mobiloil Arctic, Essolube 20, B.P. Energol S.A.E. 20, Shell X-100 20/20 w.

SECTION K1

Front Wheel

With Dual 6 in. Brake

Fitted to "Meteor 700," 1953 onwards;
"500 Twin," "500 Bullet," "350 Bullet," 1955 onwards

1. Removal from Fork

To remove the front wheel from the fork place the machine on the centre stand and front stand, if fitted, or alternatively with sufficient packing (about 2 in.) beneath each side of the stand to lift the wheel clear of the ground when tilted back on to the rear wheel. Slacken brake cable adjustments and disconnect cables from handlebar lever and from operating cam levers on hub. Unscrew the four nuts securing the fork bottom tube lug caps (Part No. 38593) and allow the wheel to drop forwards out of the front fork. Make sure that the machine stands securely on the rear wheel and centre stand—if necessary place a weight on the saddle or a strut beneath the fork to ensure this.

2. Removal of Brake Cover Plate Assemblies

Lock the brake "on" by pressure on the operating lever, 38905 (R.H.) or 38906 (L.H.), and unscrew the cover plate nuts 31347. The right and left hand cover plate assemblies can then be withdrawn from the respective brake drums.

3. Removal of Brake Shoes and Springs

This is best done by unscrewing the pivot pin locknuts, 28715, and the operating lever nuts, 10314, after which the assembly of brake shoes, return springs, pivot pin and operating cam can be removed from the cover plate by light blows with a hammer and drift on the ends of the pivot pin and the operating cam. The return springs, 29236, can then be unhooked from the spring posts

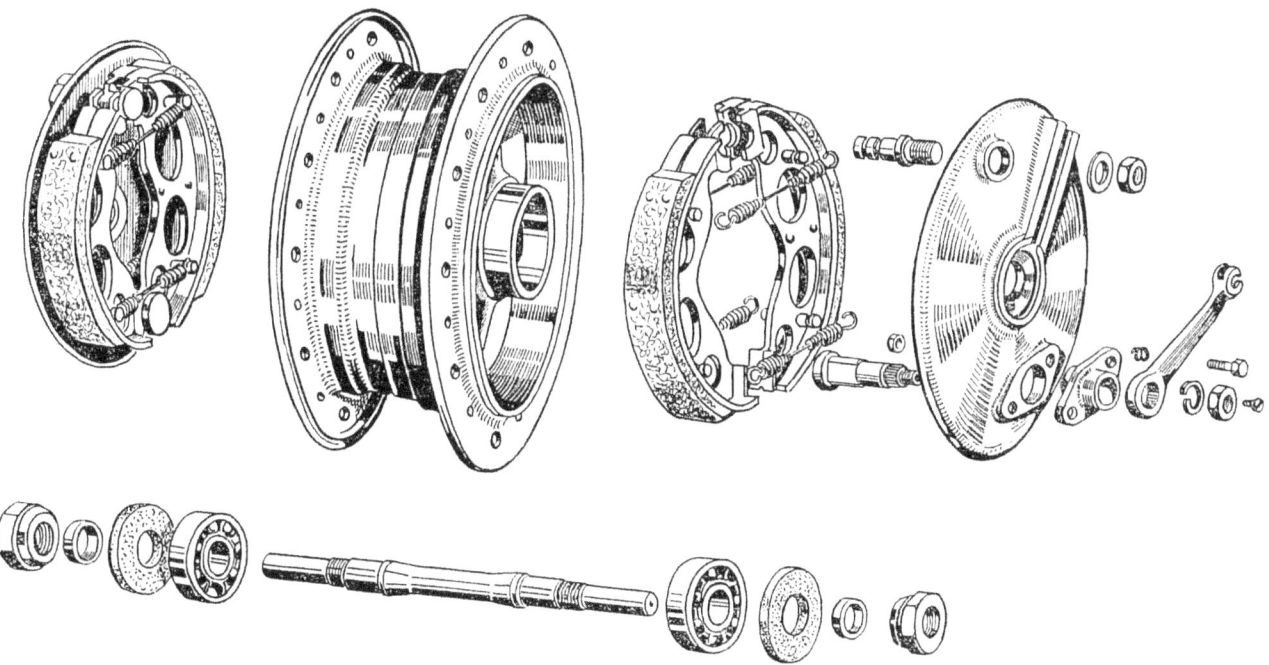

DUAL FRONT BRAKE
Fig. 1

in the brake shoes thus allowing the whole assembly to fall apart.

4. Replacing Brake Linings

Brake linings are supplied either in pairs ready drilled complete with rivets (Part No. 37786BX) or ready fitted to service replacement brake shoes (Part No. 38042). When riveting linings to shoes secure the two centre rivets first so as to ensure that the lining lies flat against the shoe. Standard linings are Ferodo MR41, which are drilled to receive cheese headed rivets.

5. Removal of Hub Spindle and Bearings

To remove the hub spindle and bearings having already removed the brake cover plate assemblies, lift out the felt washers, Part No. 21466, and distance washers, Part No. 30538. Now hit one end of the wheel spindle with a copper hammer or mallet, thus driving it out of the hub bringing one bearing with it and leaving the other in position in the hub. Drive the bearing off the spindle and insert the latter once more in the hub at the end from which it was removed. Now drive the spindle through the hub the other way, when it will bring out the remaining bearing.

6. Hub Bearings

These are deep groove single row journal ball bearings $\frac{5}{8}$ in. i/d by $1\frac{9}{16}$ in. o/d by $\frac{7}{16}$ in. wide. The Skefko Part No. is RLS5. Equivalent bearings of other makes are Hoffmann LS7, Ransome and Marles LJ$\frac{5}{8}$ in., Fischer LS7.

7. Fitting Limits for Bearings

The fit of the bearings in the hub barrel is important. The bearings are locked on the spindle between shoulders and the distance pieces, 30538, which in turn are held up by the cover plate nuts 31347. In order to prevent endways pre-loading of the bearings it is essential that there is a small clearance between the inner edge of the outer race of the bearing and the back of the recess in either end of the hub barrel. To prevent any possibility of sideways movement of the hub barrel on the bearings it is, therefore, necessary for the bearings to be a tight fit in the barrel but this fit must not be so tight as to close down the outer race of the bearing and thus overload the balls. The following are the manufacturing tolerances which control the fit of the bearings. The figures for the bearings themselves are for SKF bearings but other manufacturers' tolerances are similar.

Bearing o/d	1·5622/1·5617 in.
Housing bore	1·5620/1·5616 in.
Bearing bore	·6252/·6247 in.
Shaft diameter	·6252/·6248 in.

8. Refitting Ball Bearings

To refit the bearings in the hub two hollow drifts are required, as shown in Fig. 2. One

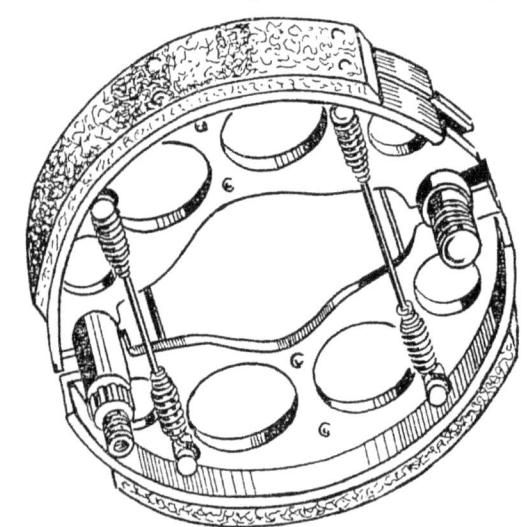

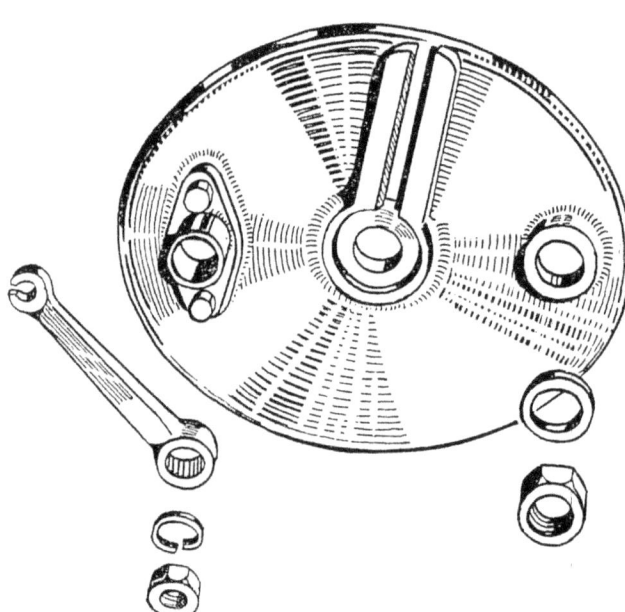

REMOVAL OF BRAKE SHOE ASSEMBLY
Fig. 2

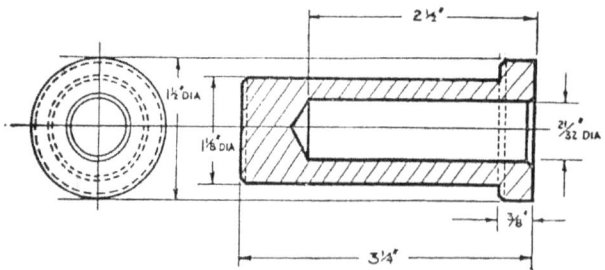

DRIFT FOR REFITTING BEARINGS
Fig. 2

bearing is first fitted to one end of the spindle by means of the hollow drift; the spindle and bearing are then entered into one end of the hub barrel which is then supported on one of the hollow drifts. The other bearing is then threaded over the upper end of the spindle and driven home by means of the second hollow drift either under a press or by means of a hammer which will thus drive both bearings into position simultaneously. In order to make quite sure that there is clearance between the inner faces of the outer bearing races and the bottom of the recesses, fit the distance washers, 30538, and the cover plate nuts, 31347, with either the cover plates themselves or additional packing washers behind the nuts. Tightening the nuts should not have any effect on the ease with which the spindle can be turned. If tightening the nuts makes the spindle hard to turn this may be taken as proof that the bearings are bottoming in the recesses in the hub barrel before they are solid against the shoulders on the spindle. In this case the bearing should be removed and a thin packing shim fitted between the inner race and the shoulder on the spindle.

9. Reassembly of Brake Shoes on to Cover Plates

Assemble each pair of shoes with their return springs on to the pivot pin and operating cam, putting a smear of grease in the grooves of the pivot pin and on the operating faces of the cam. Now fit the assembly into the cover plate, putting a smear of grease on to the cylindrical bearing surface of the operating cam and secure with the pivot pin locknut, 28715, and washer, 17551. Fit the operating lever, 38905 or 38906, on its splines in a position to suit the extent of wear on the linings and secure with the nut, 10314, and washer, 14613. Note that the position of the operating levers may have to be corrected when adjusting the brake after refitting the wheel. The range of adjustment can be extended by moving these levers on to different splines. Limit of wear is reached when the cam is turned through nearly 90° with the brake hard on so that there is a danger that the operating springs cannot return the brake to the off position.

10. Floating Cam Housings

Note that the cam housings, Part No. 26836, are intended to be left free to float. The bolt holes in the cam housings are slotted and the securing pins, Part No. 252, are provided with double coil spring washers beneath their heads to enable them to be tightened sufficiently to prevent the cam housings moving under the influence of road shocks, while at the same time they can be, and should be, left free enough to be capable of being moved by hand in the direction of the slots.

The pins, 252, are secured by locknuts, 7916, which are centre punched as an additional precaution.

The leading shoes (i.e. those towards the rear of the machine) have a servo action which render them more effective than the trailing shoes. This servo action causes the linings on the leading shoes to wear more quickly than those on the trailing shoes and at the same time tends to lift the leading shoes off the cams and press the trailing shoes harder on to the cams. With a fixed cam housing the result is that the majority of the cam pressure is applied to the less efficient trailing shoe. By leaving the housing free to float the cam can follow up the leading shoe thus maintaining equal pressure between the cam and the two shoes and so making full use of the more efficient leading shoe. Owing to the servo action the wear on the leading shoe with a floating cam housing is greater than that of the trailing shoe and in time the limit of float of the cam housing will be reached, after which the brake will continue to function as a fixed cam brake with some loss of efficiency. This can be restored by removing the shoes and fitting them in the opposite positions. Floating cam brakes are self-centering and there is no need to take any special precautions to see that the two linings are of equal thickness or that the brake shoe assembly is centered in the drum.

11. Refitting Brake Cover Plates

After assembling the brake shoe pivot pins and operating cams into the cover plates repack the hub bearings with grease. The recommended greases are Castrolease (Heavy), Mobilgrease (No. 4), Esso Grease, Energrease C3 or Shell Retinax A. These are all medium heavy lime soap or aluminium soap greases. The use of H.M.P. greases which have a soda soap base is not recommended as these tend to be slightly corrosive if any damp finds its way into the hubs.

Before fitting the distance washers and felt washers make sure that the inside of the brake drums are quite clean and free from oil or grease, damp, etc., and replace the brake cover plate assemblies. Securely tighten the cover plate nuts, 31347.

12. Wheel Rim

The rim is Type WM2—19 in. plunged and pierced with forty holes for spoke nipples. The spoke holes are symmetrical, i.e. the rim can be assembled to the hub either way round. Rim diameter after building is 19·062 in., tolerances on the circumference of the rim shoulders where the tyre fits being 59·930/59·870 in. The standard steel measuring tape for checking rims is $\frac{5}{16}$ in. wide, ·011 in. thick and its length is 59·964/59·904 in.

13. Spokes

The spokes are of the single butted type 8—10 gauge with 90° countersunk heads, angle of bend 95°—100°, length 6⅜ in., thread diameter ·144 in., 40 threads per inch, thread form British Standard Cycle.

14. Wheel Building and Truing

The spokes are laced one over two and the wheel rim must be built central in relation to the nuts which secure the brake cover plates. The rim should be trued as accurately as possible, the maximum permissible run-out both sideways and radially being plus or minus $\frac{1}{32}$ in.

15. Tyre

The standard tyre is Dunlop 3·25—19 in. Ribbed tread.

When removing the tyre always start close to the valve and see that the edge of the cover at the other side of the wheel is pushed down into the well in the rim.

When replacing the tyre fit the part by the valve last, also with the edge of the cover at the other side of the wheel pushed down into the well.

If the correct method of fitting and removal of the tyre is adopted it will be found that the covers can be manipulated quite easily with the small levers supplied in the toolkit. The use of long levers and/or excessive force is liable to damage the walls of the tyre. After inflation make sure that the tyre is fitting evenly all the way round the rim. A line moulded on the wall of the tyre indicates whether or not the tyre is correctly fitted. If the tyre has a white mark, indicating a balance point, this should be fitted near the valve.

16. Tyre Pressure

The recommended pressure for the front tyre is 18 lb. per square inch for wheel loads up to 240 lb.

17. Lubrication

Two greasing points are provided both of which lead grease to the centre of the hub barrel. Unless the barrel is packed full with grease on assembly (which is apt to lead to trouble through grease finding its way past the felt seals on to the brake linings) these greasing points are of little value and the best way to grease the bearings is by packing them with grease after dismantling the hub as described above.

Note that the brake cams are drilled for grease passages but the ends of these are stopped up with countersunk screws instead of being fitted with grease nipples. This is done to prevent excessive greasing by over-enthusiastic owners. If the cams are smeared with grease on assembly they should require no further attention but in case of necessity it is possible to remove the screws, fit grease nipples in their place and grease the cams by this means.

SECTION K2

Front Wheel
With Single 6 in. Brake

Fitted to "250 Clipper," Model "S," Model "G" and Model "J2."
Also "350 Bullet," "500 Bullet," and "500 Twin" up to the end of 1954.

1. Removal from Fork

To remove the front wheel from the fork place the machine on the centre stand (in the case of the spring frame models) with sufficient packing (about 2 in.) beneath each side of the stand to lift the wheel clear of the ground when tilted back on to the rear wheel. In the case of Models G and J2 place the machine on the rear stand and place a suitable box or block beneath the crankcase to lift the front wheel clear of the ground. Slacken the brake cable adjustment and disconnect the cable from the handlebar lever and from the operating cam lever on the hub. Unscrew the four nuts securing the fork bottom tube lug caps (Part No. 38593) and allow the wheel to drop forwards out of the front fork. Make sure that the machine stands securely on the rear wheel and centre stand—if necessary place a weight on the saddle or a strut beneath the fork to ensure this.

2. Removal of Brake Cover Plate Assembly

Lock the brake "on" by pressure on the operating lever and unscrew the cover plate nut. The cover plate assembly can then be withdrawn from the brake drum.

3. Removal of Brake Shoes and Springs

This is best done by unscrewing the pivot pin locknuts and the operating lever nuts, after which the assembly of brake shoes, return springs, pivot pin and operating cam can be removed from the cover plate by light blows with a hammer and drift on the ends of the pivot pin and the operating cam. The return springs can then be unhooked from the spring posts in the brake shoes thus allowing the whole assembly to fall apart.

4. Replacing Brake Linings

Brake linings are supplied either in pairs ready drilled complete with rivets (Part No. 37786BX) or ready fitted to service replacement brake shoes (Part No. 38042). When riveting linings to shoes secure the two centre rivets first so as to ensure that the lining lies flat against the shoe. Standard linings are Ferodo MR41, which are drilled to receive cheese headed rivets.

5. Removal of Hub Spindle and Bearings

To remove the hub spindle and bearings having first removed the brake cover plate, unscrew the retaining nut and remove the dust excluder from the non-brake side of the hub. Now remove the felt washers and the distance washer from the brake side and hit one end of the spindle with a copper hammer or mallet, thus driving it out of the hub bringing one bearing with it and leaving the other in position in the hub. Drive the

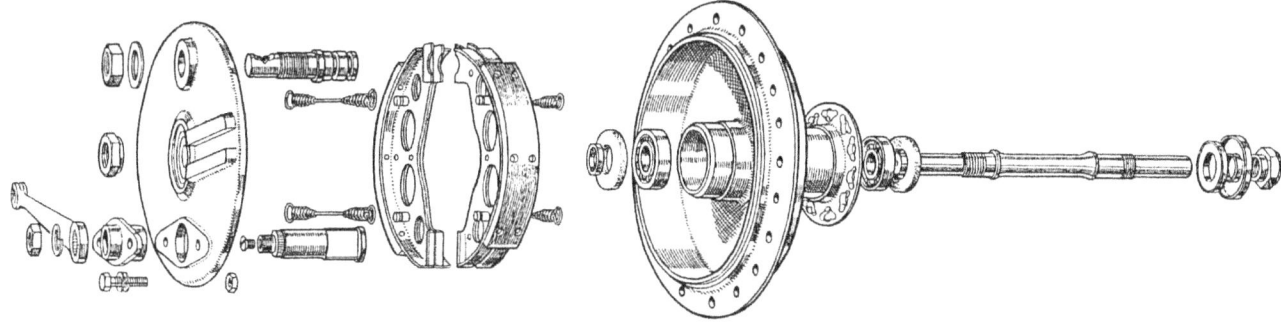

FRONT HUB
Fig. 1

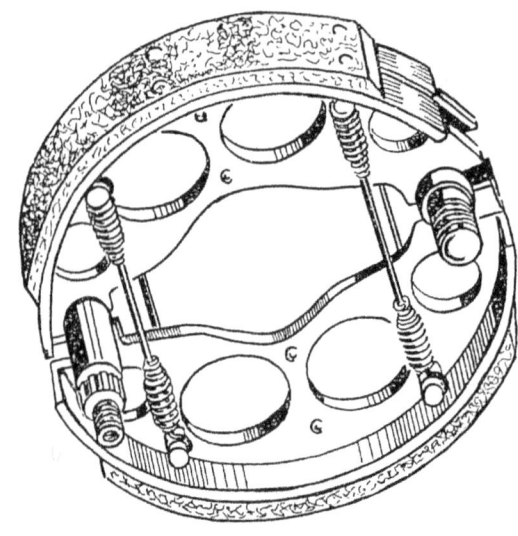

7. Fitting Limits for Bearings

The fit of the bearings in the hub barrel is important. The bearings are locked on the spindle between shoulders and the distance pieces, 30528, which in turn are held up by the nuts on the spindle. In order to prevent endways pre-loading of the bearings it is essential that there is a small clearance between the inner edge of the outer race of the bearing and the back of the recess in either end of the hub barrel. To prevent any possibility of sideways movement of the hub barrel on the bearings it is, therefore, necessary for the bearings to be a tight fit in the barrel but this fit must not be so tight as to close down the outer race of the bearing and thus overload the balls. The following are the manufacturing tolerances which control the fit of the bearings. The figures for the bearings themselves are for SKF bearings but other manufacturers' tolerances are similar.

Bearing o/d	1·5622/1·5617 in.
Housing bore	1·5620/1·5616 in.
Bearing bore	·6252/·6247 in.
Shaft diameter	·6252/·6248 in.

8. Refitting Ball Bearings

Note that the two ends of the spindle are not identical. The end with the longer plain portion between the thread and the shoulder is fitted to the brake side of the wheel. To refit the bearings in the hub two hollow drifts are required, as shown in Fig. 3. One bearing is first fitted to one end of the spindle by means of the hollow drift; the spindle and bearing are then entered into one end of the hub barrel which is then supported on one of the hollow drifts. The other bearing is then threaded over the upper end of the spindle and driven home by means of the second hollow drift either under a press, or by means of a hammer, which will thus drive both bearings into position simultaneously. In order to make quite sure that there is clearance between the inner faces of the outer bearing races and the bottom of the recesses, fit the distance washer, cover plate, dust excluder and the nuts on the spindle. Tightening

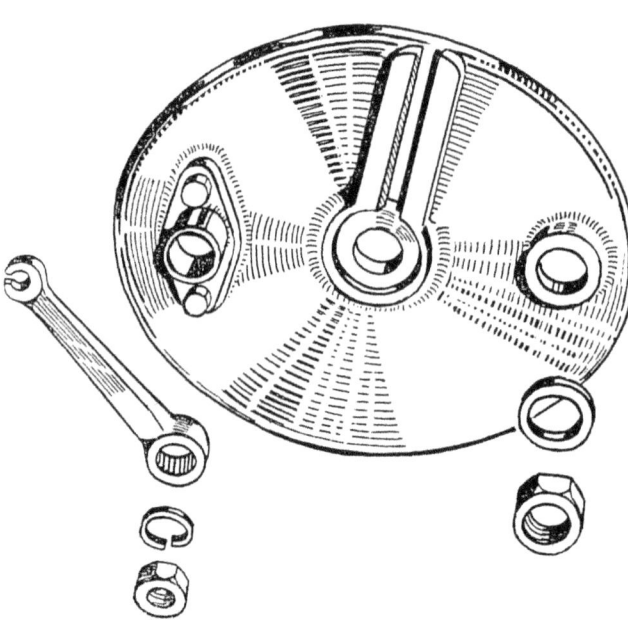

REMOVAL OF BRAKE SHOE ASSEMBLY
Fig. 2

bearing off the spindle and insert the latter once more in the hub at the end from which it was removed. Now drive the spindle through the hub the other way, when it will bring out the remaining bearing.

6. Hub Bearings

These are deep groove single row journal ball bearings, $\frac{5}{8}$ in. i/d by $1\frac{9}{16}$ in. o/d by $\frac{7}{16}$ in. wide. The Skefko Part No. is RLS5. Equivalent bearings of other makes are Hoffmann LS7, Ransome and Marles LJ$\frac{5}{8}$ in., Fischer LS7.

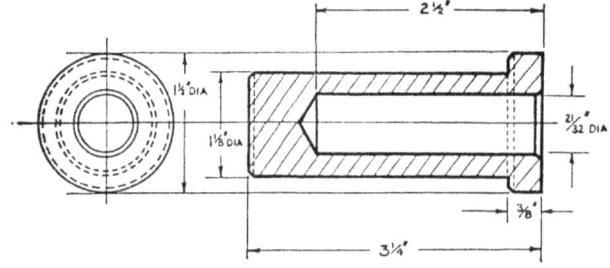

DRIFT FOR REFITTING BEARINGS
Fig. 3

the nuts should not have any effect on the ease with which the spindle can be turned. If tightening the nuts makes the spindle hard to turn this may be taken as proof that the bearings are bottoming in the recesses in the hub barrel before they are solid against the shoulders on the spindle. In this case the bearing should be removed and a thin packing shim fitted between the inner race and the shoulder on the spindle.

9. Reassembly of Brake Shoes to Cover Plate

Assemble the shoes with their return springs on to the pivot pin and operating cam, putting a smear of grease in the grooves of the pivot pin and on the operating faces of the cam. Now fit the assembly into the cover plate, putting a smear of grease on to the cylindrical bearing surface of the operating cam and secure with the pivot pin locknut and washer. Fit the operating lever on its spline in a position to suit the extent of wear on the linings and secure with the nut and washer. Note that the position of the operating lever may have to be corrected when adjusting the brake after refitting the wheel. The range of adjustment can be extended by moving this lever on to a different spline. Limit of wear is reached when the cam is turned through nearly 90° with the brake hard on so that there is a danger that the operating springs cannot return the brake to the off position.

10. Floating Cam Housing

Note that the cam housing is intended to be left free to float. The bolt holes in the cam housing are slotted and the securing pins are provided with double coil spring washers beneath their heads to enable them to be tightened sufficiently to prevent the cam housing moving under the influence of road shocks, while at the same time it can be, and should be, left free enough to be capable of being moved by hand in the direction of the slots. The pins are secured by locknuts which are centre punched as an additional precaution.

The leading shoe (i.e. the one towards the rear of the machine) has a servo action which renders it more effective than the trailing shoe. This servo action causes the lining on the leading shoe to wear more quickly than that on the trailing shoe and at the same time tends to lift the leading shoe off the cam and press the trailing shoe harder on to the cam. With a fixed cam housing the result is that the majority of the cam pressure is applied to the less efficient trailing shoe. By leaving the housing free to float the cam can follow up the leading shoe thus maintaining equal pressure between the cam and the two shoes and so making full use of the more efficient leading shoe. Owing to the servo action the wear on the leading shoe with a floating cam housing is greater than that of the trailing shoe and in time the limit of float of the cam housing will be reached, after which the brake will continue to function as a fixed cam brake with some loss of efficiency. This can be restored by removing the shoes and fitting them in the opposite positions. Floating cam brakes are self-centering and there is no need to take any special precautions to see that the two linings are of equal thickness, or that the brake shoe assembly is centered in the drum.

11. Refitting Brake Cover Plate

After assembling the brake shoe pivot pin and operating cam into the cover plate repack the hub bearings with grease. The recommended greases are Castrolease (Heavy), Mobilgrease (No. 4), Esso Grease, Energrease C3 or Shell Retinax A. These are all medium heavy lime soap or aluminium soap greases. The use of H.M.P. greases which have a soda soap base is not recommended as these tend to be slightly corrosive if any damp finds its way in to the hubs.

Before fitting the distance washer and felt washer make sure that the inside of the brake drum is quite clean and free from oil or grease, damp, etc. and replace the brake cover plate assembly. Securely tighten the cover plate nut.

12. Wheel Rims

The rim used on the "250 Clipper" and Model "S" is type WM1—19 in., internal width 1.60 in. The rim used on the other models is type WM2-19 in., internal width 1·850 in.

The rim diameter after building is the same in each case, i.e. 19·062 in., the tolerances on the circumference of the rim shoulders where the tyre fits being 59·930/59·870 in. The standard steel measuring tape for checking rims is $\frac{5}{16}$ in. wide, ·011 in. thick and its length is 59·964/59·904 in. All rims are pierced with forty holes for spoke nipples.

Note that two makes of rim are used— "Dunlop" and "Palmer Jointless." These differ in the positions of the pierced spoke holes. The Dunlop rims have a group of three holes on one side of the centre line, then a single hole on the other side, a further group of three and a single hole and so on. Palmer rims have the holes alternately spaced either side of the centre line. Both rims are interchangeable and both use the same length spokes but the method of lacing the wheel is different (see Subsection 14). Neither type of rim is symmetrical and care must be taken

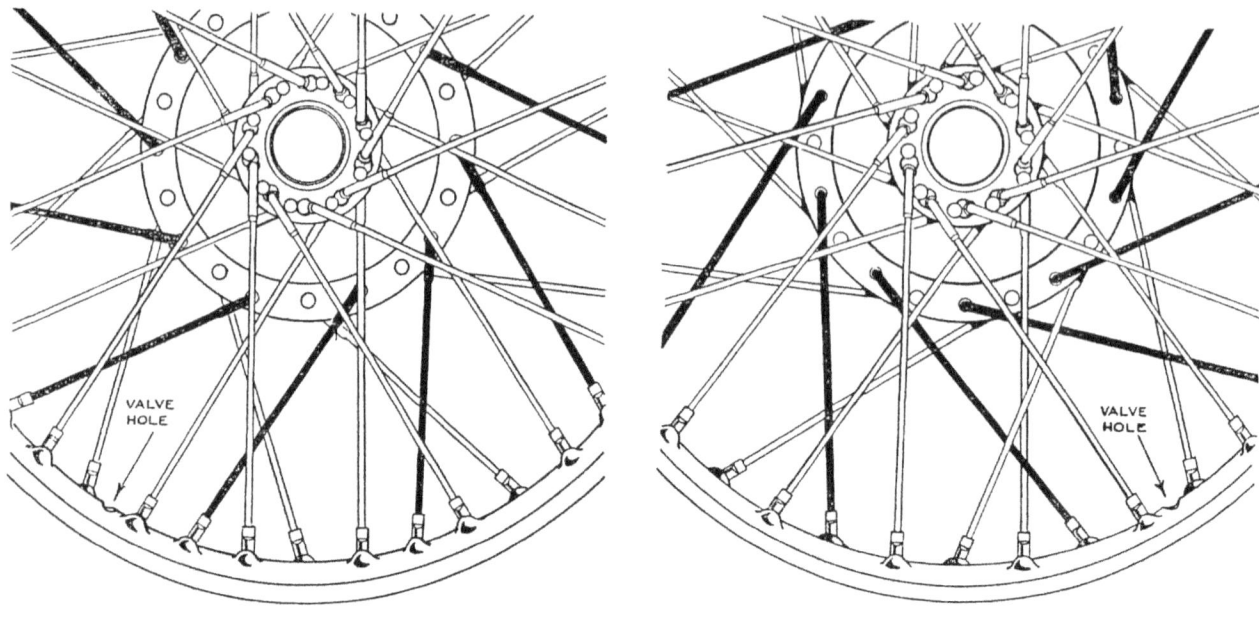

WHEEL LACING

Fig. 4A Dunlop Rim   Fig. 4B Palmer Rim

that they are built the right way round into the wheel.

13. Spokes

The spokes are of the single butted type 8—10 gauge with 90° countersunk heads, angle of bend 95°—100°, length $6\frac{5}{8}$ in. brake drum side, $8\frac{1}{2}$ in. spoke flange side, thread diameter ·144 in., 40 threads per inch, thread form British Standard Cycle.

14. Wheel Building and Truing

The spokes are laced one over two on the brake side and one over three on the spoke flange side of the wheel. The wheel must be built central in relation to the faces of the nuts on the spindle. The rim should be trued as accurately as possible, the maximum permissible run-out both sideways and radially being plus or minus $\frac{1}{32}$ in.

Figs. 4A and 4B show the difference between the lacing when using Dunlop and Palmer rims. The key to correct lacing is the inside spokes to the large flange on the brake drum side which must slope in the direction shown in Fig. 4. With the Dunlop rim this spoke goes to the middle hole of one of the groups of three (see Subsection 12) and the rim must be built into the wheel so that these groups of three holes are on the right of the centre line when the brake drum is on the left, i.e. the inside spokes to the large flange cross from the left to the right of the centre line.

With the Palmer rim the spokes from the large flange on the brake drum side go to the more steeply angled holes in the rim which must be on the left of the centre line when the brake drum is on the left, i.e. none of the spokes crosses from left to right of the centre line.

15. Tyres

Standard tyres on the "250 Clipper" and "Model S" are Dunlop 3·00—19 in. Lightweight Reinforced and on the other models Dunlop 3·25—19 in. Ribbed.

When removing the tyre always start close to the valve and see that the edge of the cover at the other side of the wheel is pushed down into the well in the rim.

When replacing the tyre fit the part by the valve last, also with the edge of the cover at the other side of the wheel pushed down into the well.

If the correct method of fitting and removal of the tyre is adopted it will be found that the covers can be manipulated quite easily with the small levers supplied in the toolkit. The use of long levers and/or excessive force is liable to damage the walls of the tyre. After inflation make sure that the tyre is fitting evenly all the way round the rim. A line moulded on the wall of the tyre indicates whether or not the tyre is correctly fitted. If the tyre has a white mark, indicating a balance point, this should be fitted near the valve.

16. Tyre Pressures

The load which the tyre will carry at different inflation pressures is shown below:—

Tyre Section Inches	Inflation Pressure—lb. per sq. in.		
	18	20	24
	Load per tyre—lb.		
3·00	180	200	240
3·25	240	280	300

17. Lubrication

A greasing point is provided in the centre of the hub barrel. Unless the barrel is packed full with grease on assembly (which is apt to lead to trouble through grease finding its way past the felt seals on to the brake linings) this greasing point is of little value and the best way to grease the bearings is by packing them with grease after dismantling the hub as described above.

Note that the brake cam is drilled for a grease passage but the end of this is stopped up with a countersunk screw instead of being fitted with a grease nipple. This is done to prevent excessive greasing by over-enthusiastic owners. If the cam is smeared with grease on assembly it should require no further attention but in case of necessity it is possible to remove the screw, fit a grease nipple in its place and grease the cam by this means.

SECTION L1

Rear Wheel (Detachable Type)

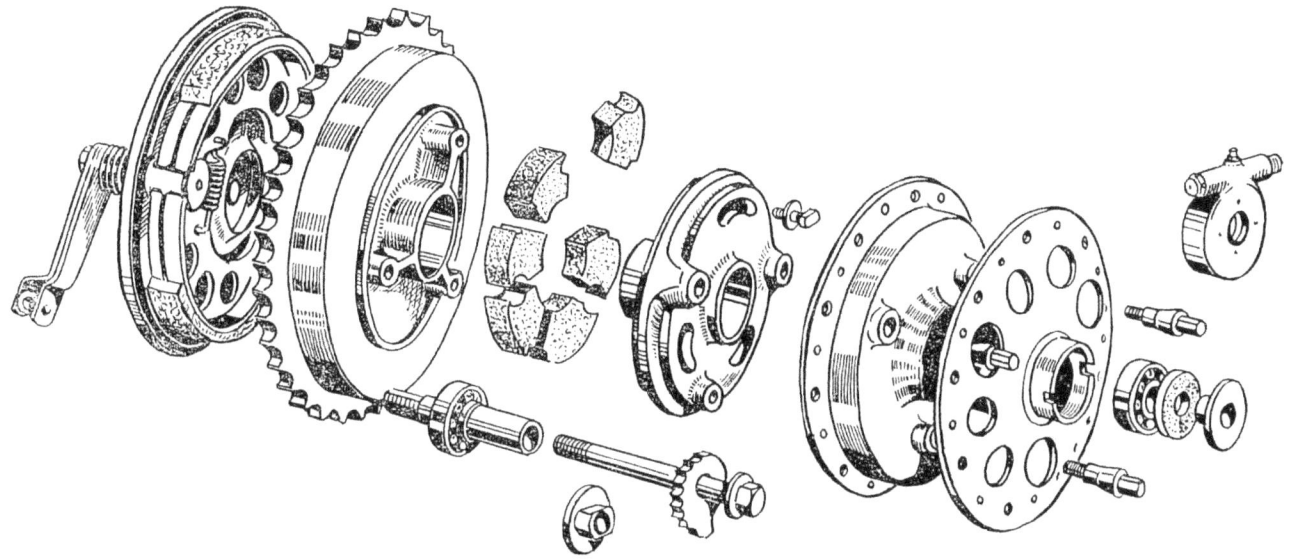

DETACHABLE REAR WHEEL
Fig. 1

1. Description

This wheel is of the "detachable" type which enables the main portion of the wheel to be removed from the machine without disturbing the chain or brake. The wheel incorporates the well known Enfield cush drive and also a 7 in. internal expanding brake.

2. Removal and Replacement of Main Portion of Wheel for Tyre Repairs, etc.

Place the machine on the centre stand, if necessary putting packing pieces beneath the legs of the stand to lift the wheel clear of the ground. Remove the dual seat (if fitted) and the detachable portion of the rear mudguard. Unscrew the three attachment bolts, 39316. Unscrew the loose section of the spindle, 39336, and withdraw this together with the chain adjuster cam, 36649, preferably marking this to ensure that it is replaced in the same position. Now slide the distance collar, 39323, out of the fork end and lift away the speedometer drive gearbox which can be left attached to the driving cable. The spacing collar, 39321, and the felt washer behind it may now be removed to prevent risk of them falling out when manipulating the tyre. If, however, these are too tight a fit in the hub to come out easily they may be left in place. The main body of the wheel can now be pulled across to the right hand side of the machine, thus disengaging it from the fixed section of the hub barrel and the cush drive shell and enabling the wheel to be lifted out of the machine.

When replacing the main portion of the wheel reverse the foregoing procedure, locating the wheel by the loose section of the spindle with the speedometer drive gearbox and distance collar in position before replacing the three attachment bolts, 39316. The cush drive shell can be prevented from rotating when turning the wheel to line up the holes for the attachment bolts if the machine is placed in gear or the rear brake is operated. When replacing the speedometer drive gearbox care must be taken to ensure that the driving dogs inside the gearbox engage with the slots in the end of the hub barrel. Before tightening the centre spindle make sure that the speedometer drive gearbox is correctly positioned so that there is no sharp bend in the driving cable.

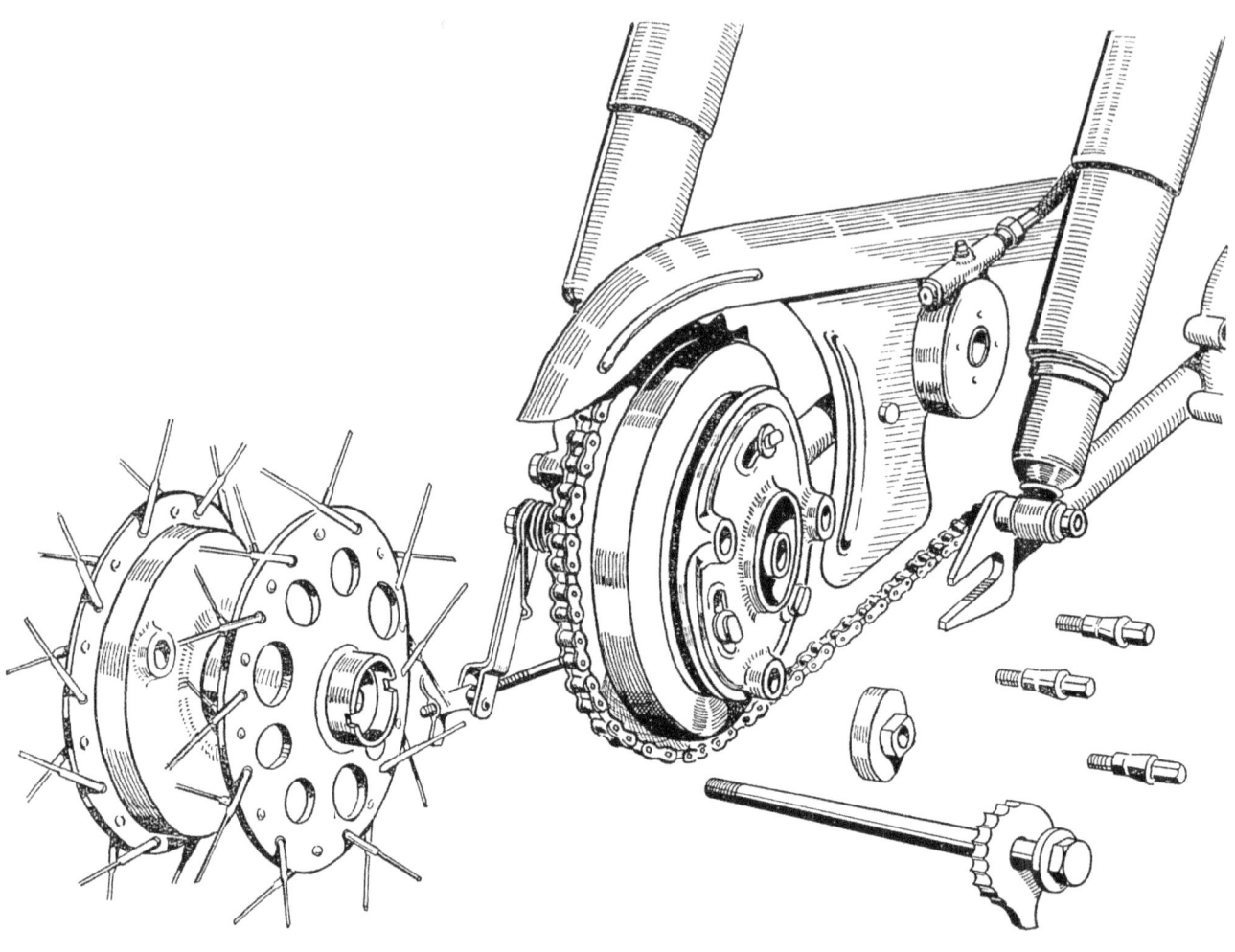

REMOVAL OF MAIN PORTION OF WHEEL
Fig. 2

3. Removal and Replacement of Complete Wheel for Access to Brake

Place the machine on the centre stand and remove the dual seat (if fitted) and detachable portion of the rear mudguard as if for removal of the main portion of the wheel only. Disconnect the rear driving chain at the spring link and remove the chain from the rear wheel sprocket leaving it in position on the gearbox countershaft sprocket. Unscrew the rear brake rod adjusting nut completely and depress the brake pedal so as to disengage the rod from the trunnion in the brake operating lever. Unscrew the brake cover plate anchor nut, 7598, and remove this together with the washer behind it. Unscrew the loose section of the spindle, 39336, two or three turns and the spindle nut, 36651, by a similar amount. Mark the chain adjuster cams to ensure replacing in the same position.* Disconnect the speedometer driving cable and slide the wheel out of the fork ends, tilting it so as to disengage the end of the brake shoe pivot pin from the slot in the fork end.

When replacing the wheel make sure that the dogs on the gear in the speedometer drive gearbox are engaged with the slots in the end of the hub barrel. Make sure also that the speedometer drive gearbox is correctly positioned so that there is no sudden bend in the driving cable. When

---

* Note that the wheel is not necessarily correctly lined up when the same notch position is used on both adjuster cams. Once the position of the cams which gives correct alignment has been found this alignment will, however, be maintained if both cams are moved the same number of notches.

replacing the connecting link in the driving chain make sure that the closed end of the spring link points in the direction of travel of the chain. Replace the chain adjuster cams in their original positions or, if necessary, turn each of them the same number of notches to tension the chain and maintain correct wheel alignment. Do not forget to refit the brake rod and adjust the brake so that the wheel turns freely when the brake is off, while at the same time only a small travel of the brake pedal is necessary to put the brake on.

4. Removal of Brake Shoes for Replacement, Fitting New Linings, etc.

Remove the complete wheel as described above, then remove the spindle nut, 36651, chain adjuster and the distance collar, 39315, thus permitting the complete brake cover plate with operating cam, pivot pin, shoes and return springs to be lifted off the hub spindle. The brake shoes can then be removed after detaching the return springs.

5. Replacing Brake Linings

Brake linings are supplied either in pairs ready drilled complete with rivets, 37787BX, or ready fitted to service replacement brake shoes, 38043. When riveting linings to shoes secure the two centre rivets first so as to ensure that the lining lies flat against the shoe. Standard linings are Ferodo MR41 which are drilled to receive cheese headed rivets.

6. Removal of Brake Operating Cam and Brake Shoe Pivot Pin

The pivot pin is threaded into the torque plate, from which it can be unscrewed after removing the locknut 39351. (Note the Part Number of the torque plate only is 36527 while the thin pressed steel cover plate is 36526. These two are riveted together and supplied as one unit Part Number 32525).

To remove the operating cam unscrew the nut, 10314, which secures the operating lever to the splines on the cam. A sharp tap on the end of the cam spindle will now free the lever after which the cam can be withdrawn from its housing.

7. Cush Drive

The sprocket/brake drum, 39301, is free to rotate on the hub barrel. Three radial vanes are formed on the back of the brake drum and three similar vanes are formed on the cush drive shell, 39302. Six rubber blocks are fitted between the vanes on the brake drum and those on the cush drive shell, thus permitting only a small amount of angular movement of the sprocket/brake drum relative to the hub barrel and transmitting both driving and braking torques and smoothing out harshness and irregularity in the former.

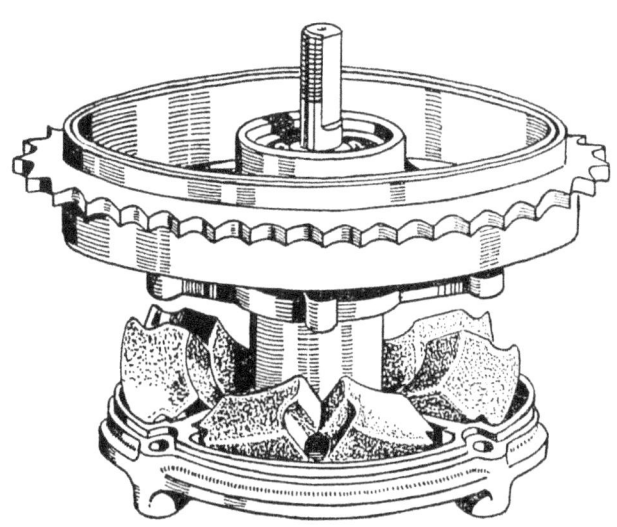

RE-ASSEMBLY OF CUSH DRIVE
Fig. 3

If the cush drive rubbers become worn so that the amount of free movement measured at the tyre exceeds $\frac{1}{2}$ in. to 1 in., the rubbers should be replaced. To obtain access to them remove the complete wheel as described above, then unscrew the loose section of the spindle, 39336, completely and also the three attachment bolts, 39316. The main portion of the wheel can then be lifted away from the assembly consisting of the fixed section of the hub barrel, fixed portion of the spindle, sprocket/brake drum complete with brake and the cush drive shell. Now remove the brake cover plate complete with brake shoes as described above, thus giving access to the three cush drive pin locking pins, 8718. Unscrew these and then unscrew the cush drive pins, 39310, thus enabling the sprocket/brake drum to be separated from the cush drive shell, after which the six cush drive rubbers can be lifted out.

When reassembling the cush drive the entry of the vanes between the rubbers will be facilitated if the latter are fitted into the driving shell first and then tilted. The rubbers should be liberally painted with soapsuds to facilitate entry of the vanes. The three cush drive pins, 39310, should be tightened as far as possible and then slackened back half to one turn to enable the locking pins, 8718, to be fitted.

When reassembling the cush drive, coat the inside of the bore of the sprocket/brake drum liberally with grease where it fits over the hub barrel. Put grease also behind the washers on the three cush drive pins, 39310.

8. Removal of Ball Bearings

To remove the ball bearings take the complete wheel out of the machine and separate the main portion of the wheel from the sprocket/brake drum, cush drive shell assembly as described above. To remove the bearing from the fixed section of the hub barrel first remove the brake cover plate complete with brake shoe assembly; then remove the felt washer, 9484, and distance collar, 11203. Now screw the loose section of the spindle into the fixed section and drive out the bearing by hitting the hexagon headed end of the loose section of the spindle.

To remove the bearing from the loose half of the hub barrel first lift away the distance collar, 39323, speedometer drive gearbox, the spacing collar, 39321, and the felt washer, 9484. Now enter the loose section of the spindle into the distance tube, 39312, from the driving sprocket end and drive out the distance tube with the two distance tube washers, 39313, and the bearing by means of a hammer and drift applied to the hexagon headed end of the loose section of the spindle.

9. Hub Bearings

These are deep groove single row journal ball bearings 5/8 in. i/d by 1 13/16 in. o/d by 5/8 in. wide. The Skefko Part Number is RMS5. Equivalent bearings of other makes are Hoffmann MS7, Ransome and Marles MJ 5/8 in., Fischer MS7.

10. Fitting Limits for Bearings

The fit of the bearings in the hub barrel is important. The bearings are locked on to the spindle by the various distance pieces. In order to prevent endways pre-loading of the bearings it is essential that, when everything is locked up, there is a small clearance between the inner edge of the outer race of the bearing and the back of the recess in each half of the hub barrel. To prevent any possibility of sideways movement of the hub barrel on the bearings it is, therefore, necessary for the bearings to be a tight fit in the barrel but this fit must not be so tight as to close down the outer race of the bearing and thus overload the balls. The following are the manufacturing tolerances which control the fit of the bearings. The figures for the bearings themselves are for SKF bearings but other manufacturers' tolerances are similar.

Bearing o/d	1·8122/1·8117 in.
Housing bore	1·8115/1·8110 in.
Bearing bore	·6252/·6247 in.
Shaft diameter (Loose side)	·624/·622 in.
Shaft diameter (Fixed side)	·6252/·6248 in.

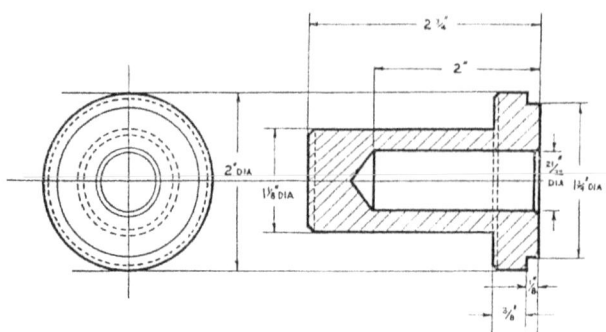

DRIFT FOR REFITTING BEARING (FIXED SECTION)
Fig. 4

11. Refitting Ball Bearings

In order to prevent the possibility of endways pre-loading of the bearings the following procedure should be followed carefully when fitting new bearings or refitting old ones—

(a) The bearing in the fixed section of the hub barrel should be fitted first together with the fixed section of the spindle using a special drift, as shown in Fig. 4, preferably under a press, if necessary using light hammer blows. This drift prevents the bearing being pushed right down to the bottom of its recess.

(b) The bearing in the loose half of the barrel is pressed in using either the drift part of E.4823,* or a suitable piece of tube 1 3/4 in. diameter with the end ground square so as to put pressure on the outer race of the bearing only. This bearing should be pressed or knocked only about half way into its recess at the present stage.

(c) The two parts of the wheel are put together and the three attachment bolts, 39316, are fitted and tightened.

(d) The bearing in the loose half of the barrel is now driven home by means of the same drift until further movement is prevented by the inner face of the inner race coming against the end of the distance tube, 39312.

As a check that the bearings are fitted correctly the loose section of the spindle and the spindle nut, 36651, can be fitted with suitable distance pieces beneath them so that, when the spindle and spindle nut are tightened, pressure is put on to the inner races of the bearings. When tightened solid the spindle should still be quite free to turn with the fingers. If the spindle is free before the nuts are tightened but not free afterwards, it is evident that there is end load on the bearings due to the bearing in the loose half of the hub not having been fitted deep enough in its recess. In this

---
* See Motor Cycle Service Tools Manual.

case the outer race should be tapped home with a tubular drift.

12. Reassembly of Brake Shoes, Pivot Pin and Operating Cam into Cover Plate

No difficulty should be experienced in carrying out these operations. Make sure that the pivot pin is really tight in the cover plate and put a smear of grease in the grooves of the pivot pin and on the operating face of the cam; also on to the cylindrical bearing surface of the operating cam if this has been removed. Fit the operating lever and trunnion, 23371, on its splines in a position to suit the extent of wear on the linings and secure with the nut. The range of adjustment can be extended by moving the lever on to a different spline.

13. Centering Cam Housing

Note that the bolt holes in the cam housing, 26347, are slotted, thus enabling the brake shoe assembly to be centered in the drum. It is not intended that on rear brakes the cam housing should be left free to float but the shoes should be centered by leaving the screws, 26309 and 35140, just short of dead tight. The brake cover plate assembly with the shoes should then be fitted over the spindle into the brake drum and the brake applied as hard as possible by means of the operating lever. This will centre the shoes in the drum. The screws should then be tightened dead tight and secured with the locknuts. If the shoes are not correctly centered the brake will be either ineffective or too fierce, depending on whether the trailing or leading shoe first makes contact with the drum. With the brake assembly correctly centered and the screws securing the cam housing correctly tightened wear on both linings should be approximately equal.

14. Final Reassembly of Hub before Replacing Wheel

Before replacing the felt washers which form the grease seals, pack both bearings with grease. Recommended greases are Castrolease (Heavy), Mobilgrease (No. 4), Esso Grease, Energrease C3 or Shell Retinax A. These are all medium heavy lime soap or aluminium soap greases. The use of H.M.P. greases which have a soda soap base is not recommended as these tend to be slightly corrosive if any damp finds its way into the hubs.

Make sure that the inside of the brake drum is quite free from oil or grease, damp, etc. Replace the felt washers, distance collars, the brake cover plate assembly, speedometer drive gearbox, distance collars, 39315 and 39323, chain adjuster cams, the loose section of the spindle and the spindle nut 36651. The wheel is then ready for reassembly into the machine.

15. Wheel Rim

The wheel rim is type WM2—19 in. plunged and pierced with forty holes for spoke nipples. The spoke holes are symmetrical, i.e. the rim can be assembled to the hub either way round. The rim diameter after building is 19·062 in., the tolerances on the circumference of the rim shoulders where the tyre fits being 59·930/59·870 in. The standard steel measuring tape for checking rims is $\frac{5}{16}$ in. wide, ·011 in. thick and its length is 59·964/59·904 in.

16. Spokes

The spokes are of the single butted type 8—10 gauge with 90° countersunk heads, angle of bend 95°—100°, length $6\frac{5}{8}$ in., thread diameter ·144 in., 40 threads per inch, thread form British Standard Cycle.

17. Wheel Building and Truing

The spokes are laced one over two and the wheel rim must be built central in relation to the outer faces of the distance collars 39315 and 39323. The rim should be trued as accurately as possible, the maximum permissible run-out both sideways and radially being plus or minus $\frac{1}{32}$ in.

18. Tyre

The standard tyre is Dunlop 3·50—19 in. Universal tread.

When removing the tyre always start close to the valve and see that the edge of the cover at the other side of the wheel is pushed down into the well in the rim.

When replacing the tyre fit the part by the valve last, also with the edge of the cover at the other side of the wheel pushed down into the well.

If the correct method of fitting and removal of the tyre is adopted it will be found that the covers can be manipulated quite easily with the small levers supplied in the toolkit. The use of long levers and/or excessive force is liable to damage the walls of the tyre. After inflation make sure that the tyre is fitting evenly all the way round the rim. A line moulded on the wall of the tyre indicates whether or not the tyre is correctly fitted. If the tyre has a white mark indicating a balance point, this should be fitted near the valve.

19. Tyre Pressures

The recommended pressures for the rear tyre are 16 lb. per square inch for wheel loads not exceeding 280 lb., 18 lb. per square inch for loads up to 320 lb., 20 lb. per square inch for loads up to 350 lb., 24 lb. per square inch for loads up to 400 lb., 28 lb. per square inch up to 450 lbs. and 32 lb. per square inch up to 500 lb.

20. Lubrication

A greasing point is provided in the centre of the hub barrel. Unless the barrel is packed full with grease on assembly (which is apt to lead to trouble through grease finding its way past the felt seals on to the brake linings) this greasing point is of little value and the best way to grease the bearings is by packing them with grease after dismantling the hub as described above.

Note that the brake cam is drilled for a grease passage but the end of this is stopped up with a countersunk screw instead of being fitted with a grease nipple. This is done to prevent excessive greasing by over-enthusiastic owners. If the cam is smeared with grease on assembly it should require no further attention but in case of necessity it is possible to remove the screw, fit a grease nipple in its place and grease the cam by this means.

SECTION L2

Rear Wheel (Non-Detachable Type)

Part No. 36788 for "500 Twin" and "350 Bullet"; Part No. 37278 for "Meteor 700" and "500 Bullet."

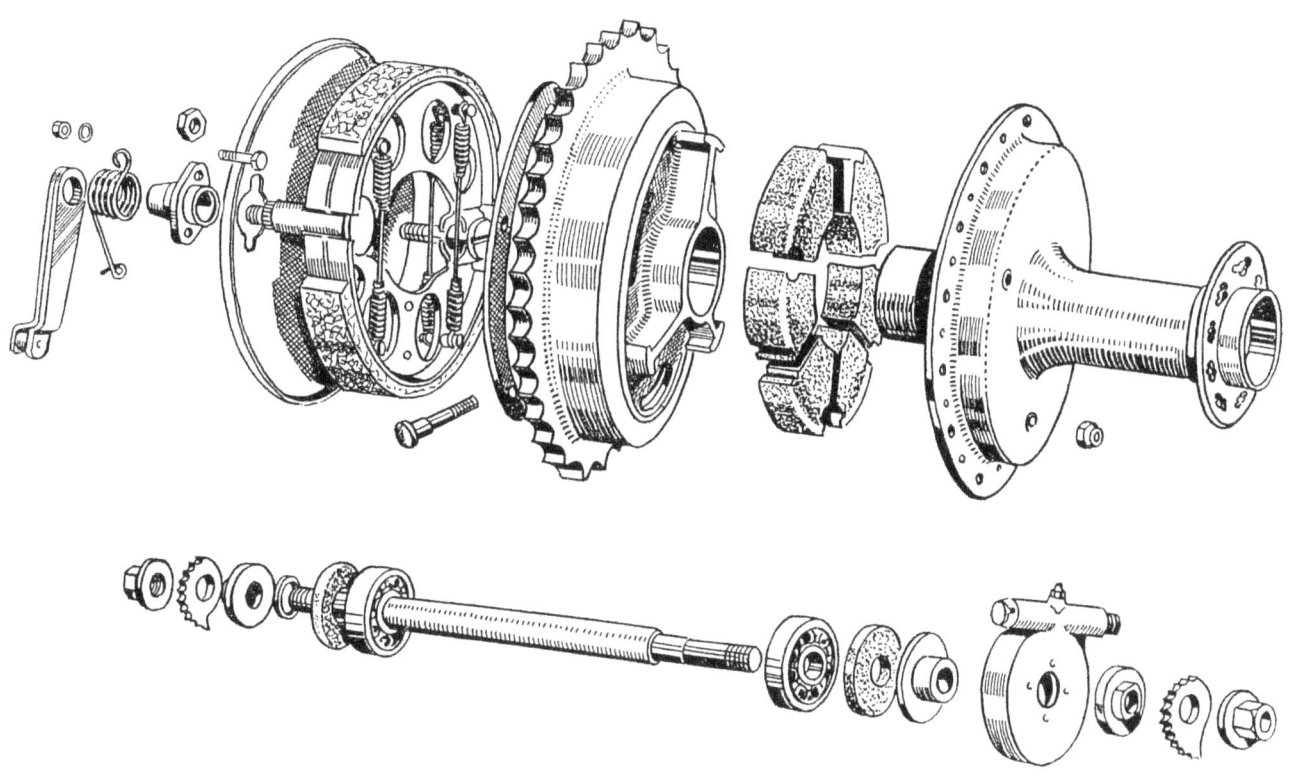

REAR HUB
Fig. 1

1. Description

These instructions cover the servicing of two different rear wheels, both of the non-detachable type incorporating a rubber cush drive and an internal expanding brake. Both types have a solid spindle and give a 3 in. chain line.

The heavier type used on the "Meteor 700" and "500 Bullet" has a 7 in. diameter brake drum while the lighter type used on the "500 Twin" and "350 Bullet" has a 6 in. diameter brake.

2. Removal and Replacement of Wheel

Place machine on the centre stand, if necessary putting packing pieces beneath the legs of the stand to lift the wheel clear of the ground. Remove the dual seat, if fitted, and the detachable portion of the rear mudguard. Disconnect the rear driving chain at the spring link and remove the chain from the rear wheel sprocket, leaving it in position on the gearbox countershaft sprocket. Unscrew the rear brake rod adjusting nut completely and depress the brake pedal so as to disengage the rod from the trunnion in the brake operating lever. Unscrew the brake cover plate anchor nut and remove this together with the washer behind it. Disconnect the speedometer driving cable, loosen the spindle nuts and mark the chain adjuster cams to ensure replacing in the same position. Slide the wheel out of the fork ends, tilting it so as to disengage the end of the brake shoe pivot pin from the slot in the fork end.

When replacing the wheel make sure that the dogs on the speedometer drive gearbox are engaged with the slots in the end of the hub barrel. Make sure also that the speedometer drive gearbox is correctly positioned so that there is no sudden bend in the driving cable. Make sure that the closed end of the spring link points in the direction of travel of the chain. Replace the chain adjuster cams in their original positions or, if necessary, turn each of them the same number of notches to tension the chain and maintain correct wheel alignment. Do not forget to refit the brake rod and adjust the brake so that the wheel turns freely while the brake is off, while at the same time only a small travel of the brake pedal is necessary to put the brake on.

3. Removal of Brake Shoes for Replacement, Fitting New Linings, etc.

Remove the complete wheel as described above, then remove the left hand spindle nut, chain adjuster and distance collar, thus permitting the complete brake cover plate with operating cam, pivot pin, shoes and return springs to be lifted off the hub spindle.

In the case of the 7 in. brake fitted to the "Meteor 700" and "500 Bullet" Models the brake shoes can then be removed, after detaching the return springs.

In the case of the 6 in. brake fitted to the "500 Twin" and "350 Bullet" Models, unscrew the pivot pin locknut and the operating lever nut, after which the assembly of the brake shoes, return springs, pivot pin and operating cam can be removed from the cover plate by unscrewing the pivot pin and applying light blows with a hammer and drift on the end of the operating cam. The return springs can then be unhooked from the spring posts in the brake shoes, thus allowing the whole assembly to fall apart.

4. Replacing Brake Linings

Brake linings are supplied either in pairs ready drilled complete with rivets, Part No. 37786BX (6 in. shoes) or 37787BX (7 in. shoes), or ready fitted to service replacement brake shoes, Part No. 38042 (6 in. shoes) or 38043 (7 in. shoes). When riveting linings to shoes secure the two centre rivets first so as to ensure that the lining lies flat against the shoe. Standard linings are Ferodo MR41 which are drilled to receive cheese headed rivets.

5. Removal of Hub Spindle and Bearings

To remove the hub spindle and bearings, having already removed the brake cover plate assembly and speedometer drive gearbox, lift out the felt washers and distance pieces then hit one end of the spindle with a copper hammer or mallet thus driving it out of the hub, bringing one bearing with it and leaving the other in position in the hub. Drive the bearing off the spindle and insert the latter once more in the hub at the end from which it was removed. Now drive the spindle through the hub in the opposite direction, when it will bring out the remaining bearing.

6. Hub Bearings

These are deep groove single row journal ball bearings. The lighter bearings used in the "350 Bullet" and "500 Twin" hubs are $\frac{5}{8}$ in. i/d by $1\frac{9}{16}$ in. o/d by $\frac{7}{16}$ in. wide. The Skefko Part No. is RLS5. Equivalent bearings of other makes are Hoffmann LS7, Ransome and Marles LJ $\frac{5}{8}$ in., Fischer LS7.

The heavier bearings used in the "Meteor 700" and "500 Bullet" Models are $\frac{5}{8}$ in. i/d by $1\frac{13}{16}$ in. o/d by $\frac{5}{8}$ in. wide. The Skefko Part No. is RMS5. Equivalent bearings of other makes are Hoffmann MS7, Ransome and Marles MJ $\frac{5}{8}$ in., Fischer MS7.

7. Fitting Limits for Bearings

The fit of the bearings in the hub barrel is important. The bearings are locked on the spindle between shoulders and the distance pieces, which in turn are held up by the cover plate nuts. In order to prevent endways pre-loading of the bearings it is essential that there is a small clearance between the inner edge of the outer race of the bearing and the back of the recess in either end of the hub barrel. To prevent any possibility of sideways movement of the hub barrel on the bearings it is, therefore, necessary for the bearings to be a tight fit in the barrel but this fit must not be so tight as to close down the outer race of the bearing and thus overload the balls. The following are the manufacturing tolerances which control the fit of the bearings. The figures for the bearings themselves are for SKF bearings but other manufacturers' tolerances are similar.

	"350 Bullet" and "500 Twin"	"Meteor 700" and "500 Bullet"
Bearing o/d	1·5622/1·5617 in.	1·8122/1·8117 in.
Housing bore	1·5620/1·5615 in.	1·8115/1·8110 in.
Bearing bore	·6252/·6247 in.	·6252/·6247 in.
Shaft diameter	·6252/·6248 in.	·6252/·6248 in.

8. Refitting Ball Bearings

To refit the bearings in the hub two hollow drifts are required, as shown in Figs. 2 and 3. One bearing is first fitted to one end of the spindle by means of the hollow drift; the spindle and bearing are then entered into one end of the hub barrel which is then supported on one of the hollow drifts. The other bearing is then threaded over the upper end of the spindle and driven home by means of the second hollow drift either under a press or by means of a hammer which will thus drive both bearings into position simultaneously.

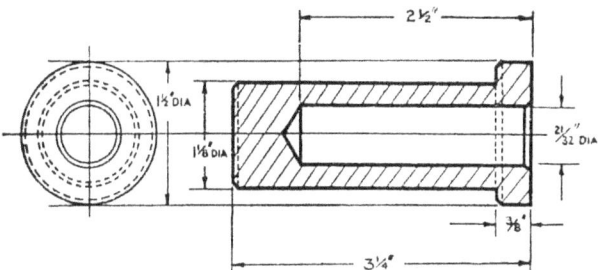

DRIFT FOR REFITTING BEARINGS
"350 Bullet"   "500 Twin"
Fig. 2

In order to make quite sure that there is clearance between the inner faces of the outer bearings and the bottom of the recesses fit the distance washers against the inner races of the bearings and either fit the assembly of brake cover plate, speedometer gearbox, etc., or make up this distance with tubular distance pieces. Fit and tighten the spindle nuts. Tightening the nuts

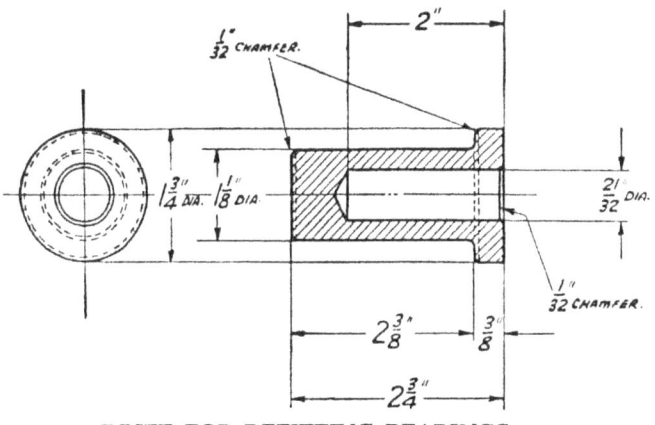

DRIFT FOR REFITTING BEARINGS
"Meteor 700"   "500 Bullet"
Fig. 3

should not have any effect on the ease with which the spindle can be turned. If tightening the nuts makes the spindle hard to turn this may be taken as proof that the bearings are bottoming in the recesses in the hub barrel before they are solid against the shoulders on the spindle. In this case the bearing should be removed and a thin packing shim fitted between the inner race and the shoulder on the spindle.

9. Removal of Brake Operating Cam and Brake Shoe Pivot Pin

The method of doing this has already been described in Paragraph 3 dealing with the 6 in. brake. The method is precisely the same for the 7 in. brake except that, owing to the different type of return springs used, it is, in this case, possible to remove the shoes from the pivot pin and operating cam before the latter are removed from the cover plate.

10. Cush Drive

The sprocket/brake drum is free to rotate on the hub barrel. Three radial vanes are formed on the back of the brake drum and three similar vanes are formed on the cush drive shell. Six rubber blocks are fitted between the vanes on the brake drum and those on the cush drive shell, thus permitting only a small amount of angular movement of the sprocket/brake drum relative to the hub barrel and transmitting both driving and braking torque and smoothing out harshness and irregularity in the former.

If the cush drive rubbers become worn so that the amount of free movement measured at the tyre exceeds $\frac{1}{2}$ in. to 1 in., the rubbers should be replaced. To obtain access to them remove the complete wheel as described above, remove the brake cover plate complete with the brake shoe assembly, unscrew the three Simmonds nuts at the back of the cush drive shell—if necessary holding the studs, 32431, by means of the flats on the heads inside the brake drum. Drive out the three studs into the brake drum after which the sprocket/brake drum can be separated from

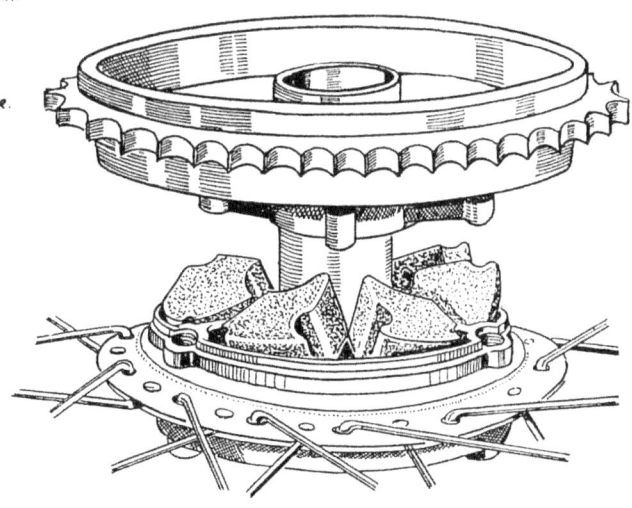

REASSEMBLY OF CUSH DRIVE
Fig. 4

the cush drive shell and the six cush drive rubbers can be lifted out.

When reassembling the cush drive the entry of the vanes between the rubbers will be facilitated if the latter are fitted into the driving shell first and then tilted. The rubbers should be liberally painted with soapsuds to facilitate entry of the vanes.

When reassembling the cush drive coat the inside of the bore of the sprocket/brake drum liberally with grease where it fits over the hub barrel and also put grease on the inner face of the lockring, 10097. The three Simmonds nuts should be tightened down solid as there is a shoulder on the stud which prevents tightening of the nuts from locking the operation of the cush drive.

11. Reassembly of Brake Shoes, Pivot Pin and Operating Cam into Cover Plate

No difficulty should be experienced in carrying out these operations. Make sure that the pivot pin is really tight in the cover plate and put a smear of grease in the grooves of the pivot pin and on the operating face of the cam; also on the cylindrical bearing surface of the operating cam if this has been removed. Fit the operating lever and trunnion on its splines in a position to suit the extent of wear on the linings and secure with the nut. The range of adjustment can be extended by moving the lever on to a different spline.

12. Centering Cam Housing

Note that the bolt holes in the cam housing are slotted, thus enabling the brake shoe assembly to be centered in the drum. It is not intended that on rear brakes the cam housing should be left free to float but the shoes should be centered by leaving the screws just short of dead tight. The brake cover plate assembly with the shoes should then be fitted over the spindle into the brake drum and the brake applied as hard as possible by means of the operating lever. This will centre the shoes in the drum. The screws should then be tightened dead tight and secured with the locknuts. If the shoes are not correctly centered the brake will be either ineffective or too fierce, depending on whether the trailing or leading shoe first makes contact with the drum. With the brake assembly correctly centered and the screws securing the cam housing correctly tightened wear on both linings should be approximately equal.

13. Final Reassembly of Hub before Replacing Wheel

Before replacing the felt washers which form the grease seals, pack both bearings with grease. Recommended greases are Castrolease (Heavy), Mobilgrease (No. 4), Esso Grease, Energrease C3 or Shell Retinax A. These are all medium heavy lime soap or aluminium soap greases. The use of H.M.P. greases which have a soda soap base is not recommended as these tend to be slightly corrosive if any damp finds its way into the hubs.

Make sure that the inside of the brake drum is quite free from oil or grease, damp, etc. Replace the felt washers, distance collars, the brake cover plate assembly, speedometer drive gearbox, distance collars, chain adjuster cams, the loose section of the spindle and the spindle nut. The wheel is then ready for reassembly into the machine.

14. Wheel Rims

The rim fitted to both types of wheel is WM2—19 in. pierced with 40 holes for spoke nipples. The internal width is 1·850 in. and the diameter after building 19·062 in., the tolerance on the circumference of the rim shoulders where the tyre fits being 59·930/59·870 in. The standard steel measuring tape for checking rims is $\frac{5}{16}$ in. wide, ·011 in. thick and its length is 59·964/59·904 in.

Note that two makes of rim are used—"Dunlop" and "Palmer Jointless." These differ in the positions of the pierced spoke holes. The Dunlop rims have a group of three holes on one side of the centre line, then a single hole on the other side, a further group of three and a single hole and so on. Palmer rims have the holes alternately spaced either side of the centre line. Both rims are interchangeable and both use the same length spokes but the method of lacing the wheel is different (see paragraph 16). Neither type of rim is symmetrical and care must be taken that they are built the right way round into the wheel.

15. Spokes

The spokes are of the single butted type 8—10 gauge with 90° countersunk heads, angle of bend 95°—100°, thread diameter ·144 in., 40 threads per inch, thread form British Standard Cycle. Spoke lengths are as follow:—
 "Meteor 700," and "500 Bullet,"
  Cush drive side, 7¾ in.
  Spoke flange side 8½ in.
 "500 Twin" and "350 Bullet,"
  Cush drive side, 7⅞ in.
  Spoke flange side 8⅝ in.

16. Wheel Building and Truing

The spokes are laced one over three and the wheel must be built central in relation to the outer faces of the distance collars which fit between the

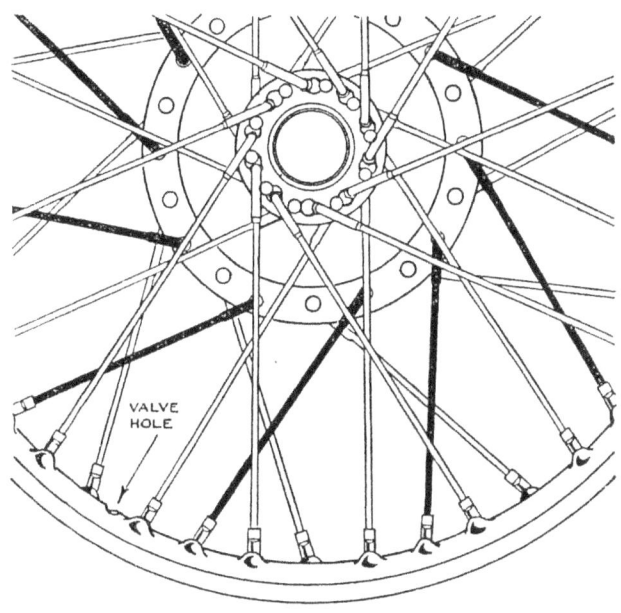

DUNLOP RIM
Fig. 5A

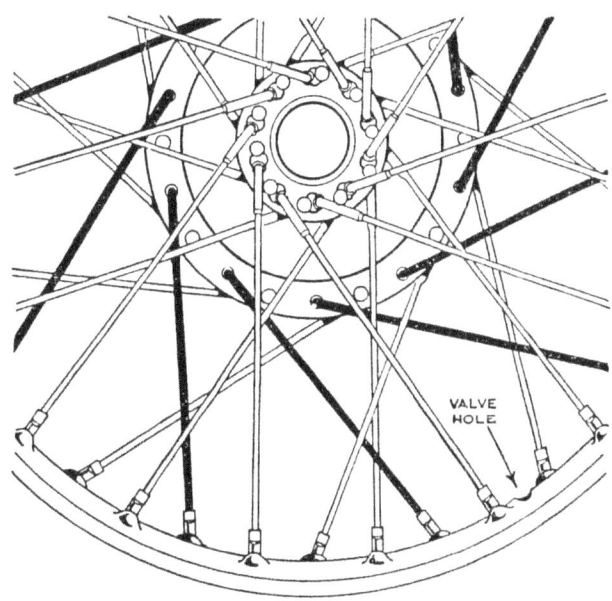

PALMER RIM
Fig. 5B

fork ends. The rim should be trued as accurately as possible, the maximum permissible run-out both sideways and radially being plus or minus $\frac{1}{32}$ in.

Fig. 5 shows the difference between the lacing when using Dunlop and Palmer rims. The key to correct lacing is the inside spokes to the large flange on the cush drive shell which must slope in the direction shown in Fig. 5. With the Dunlop rim this spoke goes to the middle hole of one of the groups of three (see paragraph 14) and the rim must be built into the wheel so that these groups of three holes are on the right of the centre line when the cush drive is on the left, i.e. the inside spokes to the large flange cross from the left to the right of the centre line.

With the Palmer rim the spokes from the large flange on the cush drive shell go to the more steeply angled holes in the rim which must be on the left of the centre line when the cush drive is on the left, i.e. none of the spokes crosses from left to right of the centre line.

17. Tyres

Standard tyres are Dunlop 3·50—19 in. Universal tread except on the "350 Bullet" where a 3·25—19 in. Universal tyre is used.

When removing the tyre always start close to the valve and see that the edge of the cover at the other side of the wheel is pushed down into the well in the rim.

When replacing the tyre fit the part by the valve last, also with the edge of the cover at the other side of the wheel pushed down into the well.

If the correct method of fitting and removal of the tyre is adopted it will be found that the covers can be manipulated quite easily with the small levers supplied in the toolkit. The use of long levers and/or excessive force is liable to damage the walls of the tyre. After inflation make sure that the tyre is fitting evenly all the way round the rim. A line moulded on the wall of the tyre indicates whether or not the tyre is correctly fitted. If the tyre has a white mark, indicating a balance point, this should be fitted near the valve.

18. Tyre Pressures

The load which the tyre will carry at different inflation pressures is shown below:—

Tyre Section Inches	Inflation Pressures—lb. per sq. in.					
	16	18	20	24	28	32
	Load per tyre—lb.					
3·25	200	240	280	350	400	440
3·50	280	320	350	400	450	500

19. Lubrication

A greasing point is provided in the centre of the hub barrel. Unless the barrel is packed full with grease on assembly (which is apt to lead to trouble through grease finding its way past the felt seals on to the brake linings) this greasing point is of little value and the best way to grease the bearings is by packing them with grease after dismantling the hub as described above.

Note that the brake cam is drilled for a grease passage but the end of this is stopped up with a countersunk screw instead of being fitted with a grease nipple. This is done to prevent excessive greasing by over-enthusiastic owners. If the cam is smeared with grease on assembly it should require no further attention but in case of necessity it is possible to remove the screw, fit a grease nipple in its place and grease the cam by this means.

SECTION M2

Special Tools

For "Bullet" Models

SECTION C2

Sub-Section	No.	Use	Page
4, 18	14835	Magdyno Pinion Extractor (Tool Kit)	2
7	TE.1124	Valve Spring Compressor	2
9	—	Valve Guide Mandrels	2
11	E.5477	Gudgeon Pin Extractor (Adaptor if necessary)	2
13	TE.1167	Valve Grinding Tool	3
16	E.5425	Pump Disc Lapping Tool	3
17	E.5451	Pump Worm Shaft Spanner	3
21	E.5410	Tappet Guide Extractor	3
23	E.5414	Clutch Centre Extractor	3

SECTION D2

3	E.5121	Crankshaft Extractor	5
4	E.4816	Roller Race Assembly, Timing Side	4
4	E.4817	Bearing Assembly, Driving Side	4
5	E.6462	Locating Plate for Assembly of Cam Spindles	5
6	E.2775	Crankshaft Pot or Jig ("350 Bullet")	5
6	E.2774	Crankshaft Pot or Jig ("500 Bullet")	5

SECTION H1

5	E.5431	Frame Expander	6

SECTION J1

3	E.4912	Gland Nut Grips	6
3	E.5418	Lockring Spanner	6

SECTION J3

3	E.4912	Gland Nut Hand Grips	6
3	E.5418	Lockring Spanner	6

SECTION J4

2	E.4912	Outer Tube Hand Grips	6
2	E.5417	Gland Nut Hand Grips	6
2	E.5418	Lockring Spanner	6

Special Tools for "Bullet" Engines

14835
MAGDYNO PINION EXTRACTOR

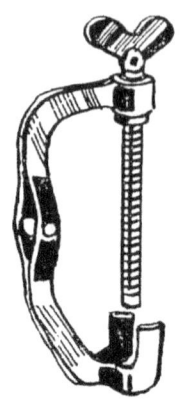

TE.1124
VALVE SPRING COMPRESSOR

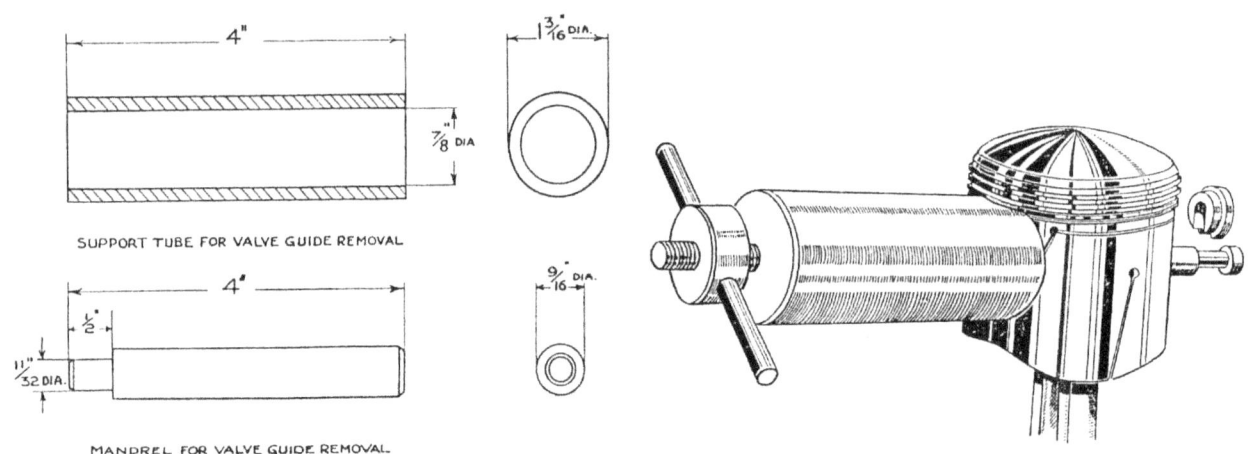

VALVE GUIDE MANDRELS

E.5477
GUDGEON PIN EXTRACTOR

Special Tools for "Bullet" Engines

TE.1167
VALVE GRINDING TOOL

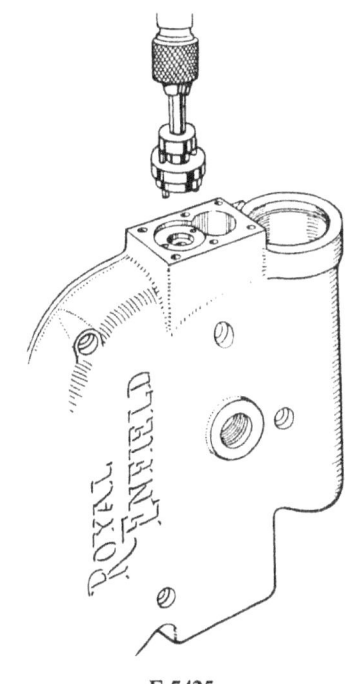

E.5425
PUMP DISC LAPPING TOOL

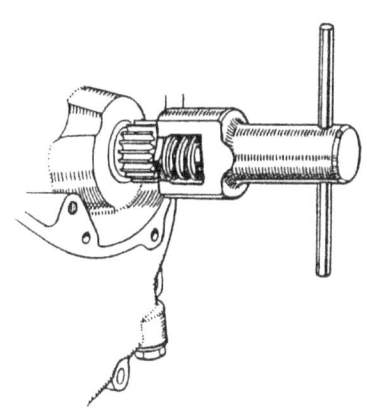

E.5451
PUMP WORM SHAFT SPANNER

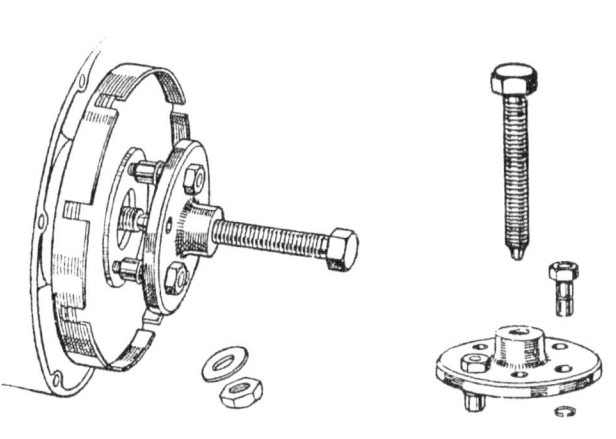

E.5414
CLUTCH CENTRE EXTRACTOR

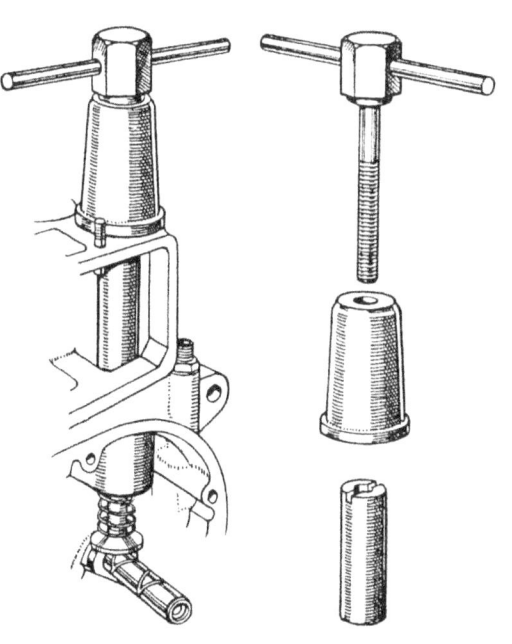

E.5410
TAPPET GUIDE EXTRACTOR

Special Tools for "Bullet" Engines

TOOLS FOR FITTING BUSHES

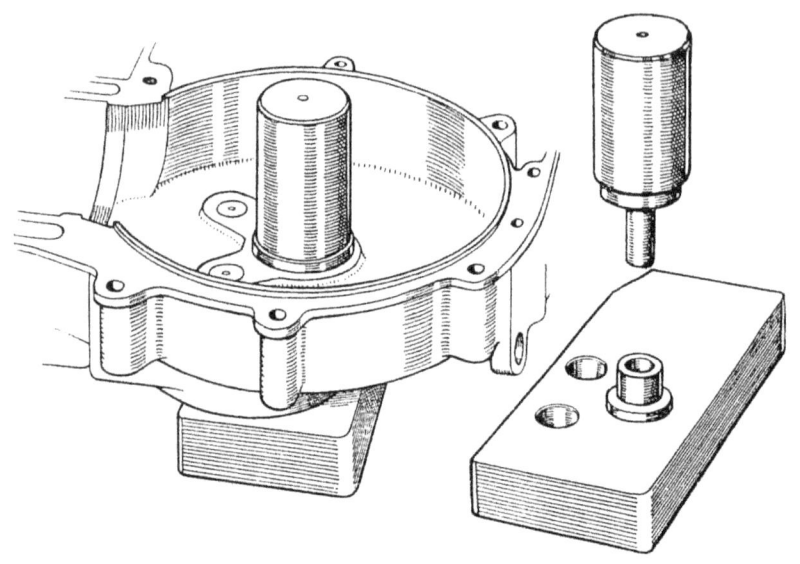

E.4816
ROLLER RACE ASSEMBLY, TIMING SIDE

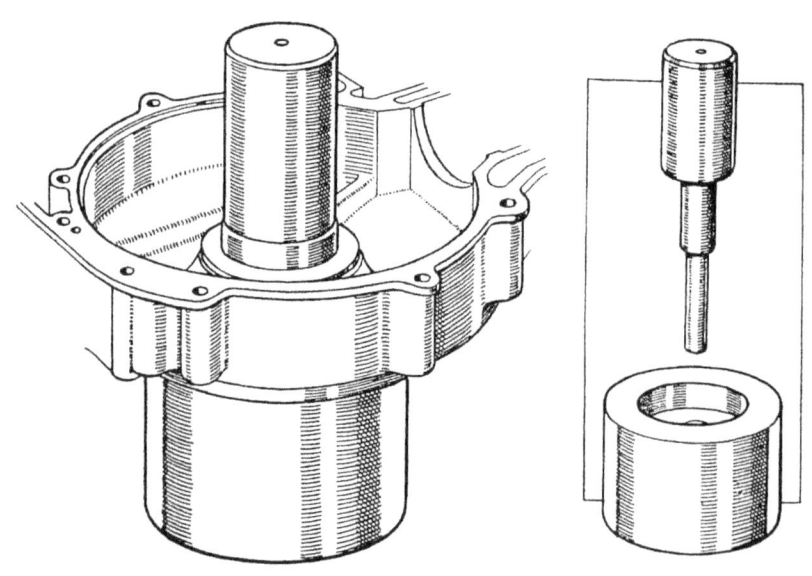

E.4817
BEARING ASSEMBLY, DRIVING SIDE

Special Tools for "Bullet" Engines

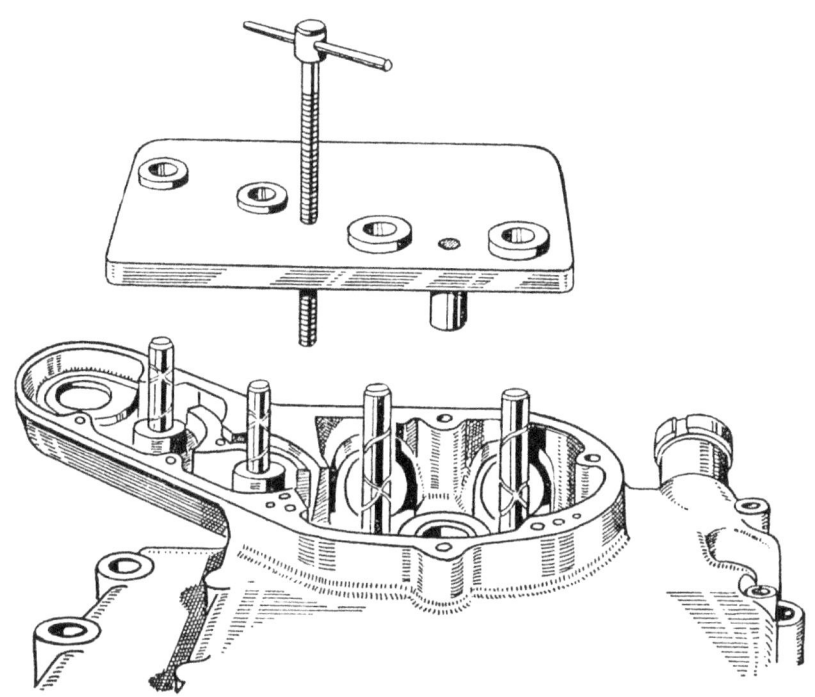

E.6462
LOCATING PLATE FOR ASSEMBLY OF CAM SPINDLES

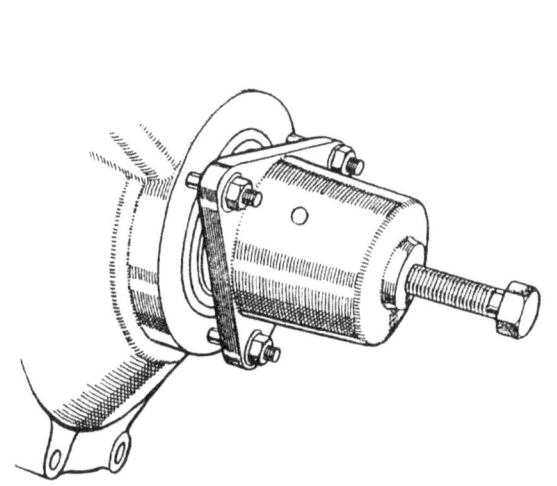

E.5121
CRANKSHAFT EXTRACTOR

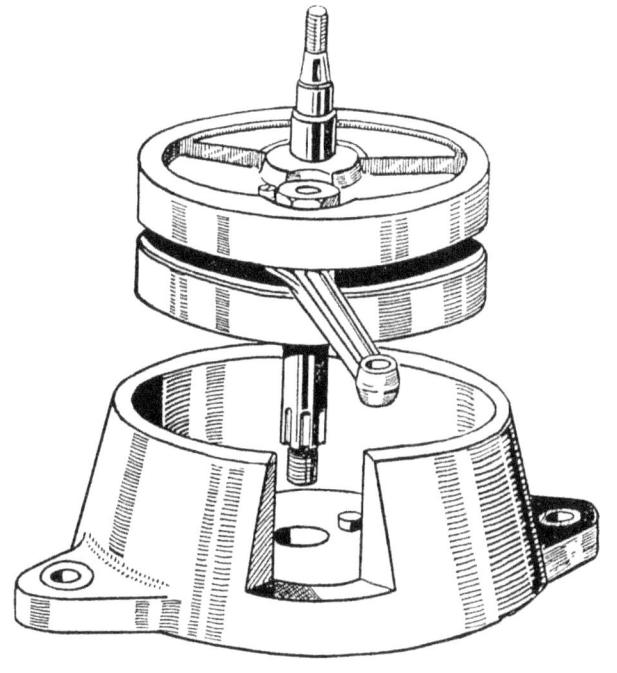

E.2774/E.2775
CRANKSHAFT POT OR JIG
for "350 Bullet" (E.2775) and "500 Bullet" (E.2774)

Special Tools for "Bullet" Frames and Forks

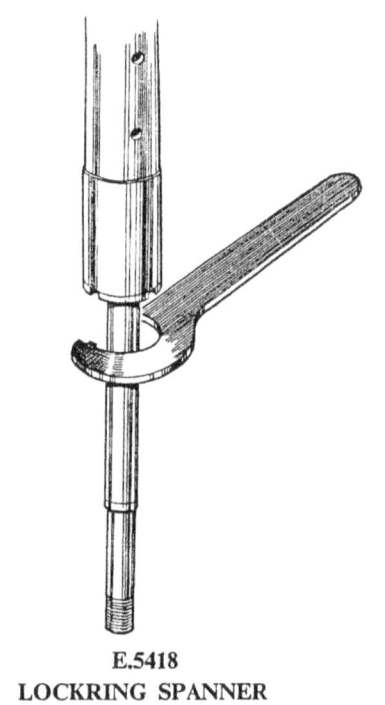

E.5418
LOCKRING SPANNER

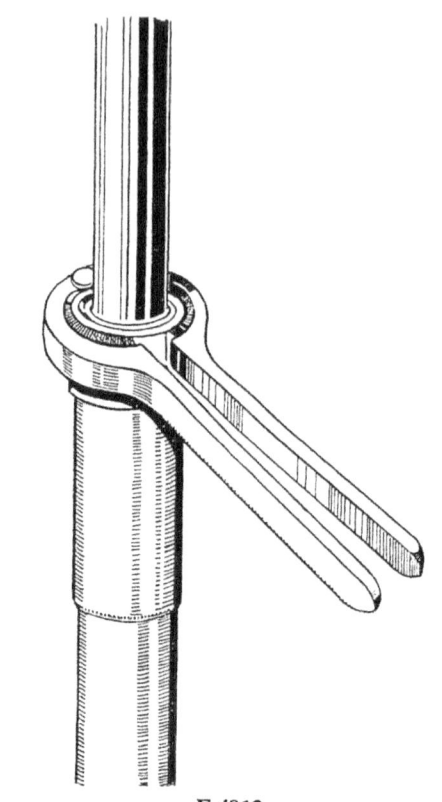

E.4912
GLAND NUT AND OUTER TUBE HAND GRIPS

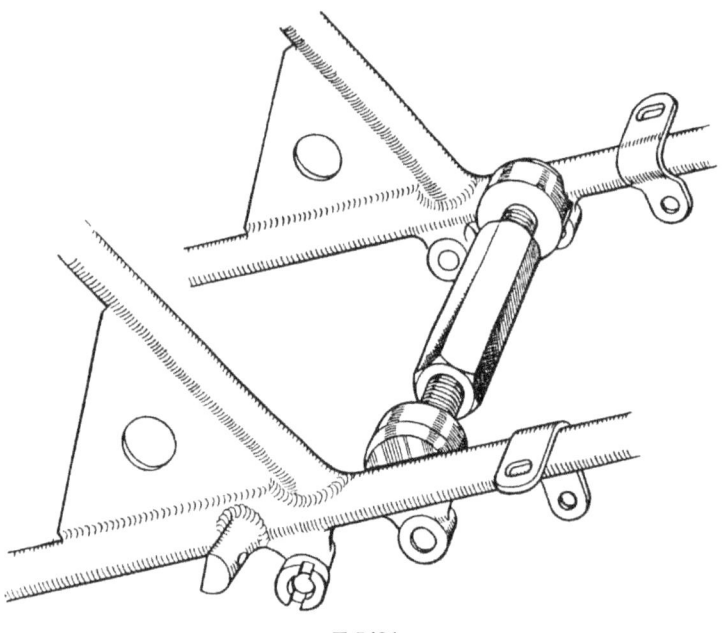

E.5431
FRAME EXPANDER

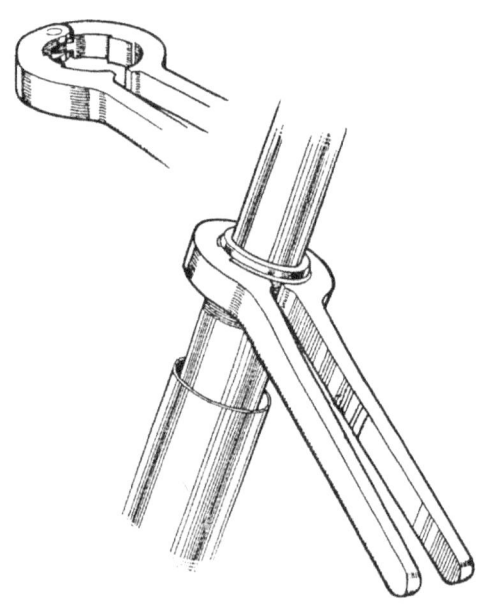

E.5417
GLAND NUT HAND GRIPS

WORKSHOP MAINTENANCE MANUAL

FOR THE

Royal Enfield
'Made like a Gun'

"350 BULLET" 1956-1962
"500 BULLET" 1956-1962
"350 CLIPPER" 1958-1962
"WORKS REPLICA" 1958-1962
MOTOR CYCLES
including "AIRFLOW" models

**A Floyd Clymer Publication
This edition published in 2024 by
www.VelocePress.com**

All rights reserved. This work may not be reproduced or transmitted in any form without the express written consent of the publisher.

IMPORTANT NOTE ON PAGE NUMBERING

The 1948 to 1955 manual starts on page 1 and ends on page 110. The 1956 to 1962 manual starts on page 111 and ends on page 206. The original manuals did not have page numbers and the contents were only identified by 'sections'. Consequently, the addition of page numbers can be useful as an 'identifier' in order to locate a particular 'section'.

INTRODUCTION

Welcome to the world of digital publishing ~ the book you now hold in your hand was printed using the latest state of the art digital technology. The advent of print-on-demand has forever changed the publishing process, never has information been so accessible and it is our hope that this book serves your informational needs for years to come. If this is your first exposure to digital publishing, we hope that you are pleased with the results. Many more titles of interest to the classic automobile and motorcycle enthusiast, collector and restorer are available via our website at www.VelocePress.com. We hope that you find this title as interesting as we do.

NOTE FROM THE PUBLISHER

The information presented is true and complete to the best of our knowledge. All recommendations are made without any guarantees on the part of the author or the publisher, who also disclaim all liability incurred with the use of this information.

TRADEMARKS

We recognize that some words, model names and designations, for example, mentioned herein are the property of the trademark holder. We use them for identification purposes only. This is not an official publication.

INFORMATION ON THE USE OF THIS PUBLICATION

This manual is an invaluable resource for those interested in performing their own maintenance. However, in today's information age we are constantly subject to changes in common practice, new technology, availability of improved materials and increased awareness of chemical toxicity. As such, it is advised that the user consult with an experienced professional prior to undertaking any procedure described herein. While every care has been taken to ensure correctness of information, it is obviously not possible to guarantee complete freedom from errors or omissions or to accept liability arising from such errors or omissions. Therefore, any individual that uses the information contained within, or elects to perform or participate in do-it-yourself repairs or modifications acknowledges that there is a risk factor involved and that the publisher or its associates cannot be held responsible for personal injury or property damage resulting from the use of the information or the outcome of such procedures.

WARNING!

One final word of advice, this publication is intended to be used as a reference guide, and when in doubt the reader should consult with a qualified technician.

ROYAL ENFIELD WORKSHOP MANUAL

Contents

1956-61 "350 Bullet" and "500 Bullet," 1958-61 "350 Clipper" (including "Airflow" models) and Trials "Works Replica" 1958 onwards

SECTION A14a	TECHNICAL DATA
SECTION A14b	TECHNICAL DATA
SECTION B14	ENGINE SPECIFICATION
SECTION C14	SERVICE OPERATIONS WITH ENGINE IN FRAME
SECTION D9	SERVICE OPERATIONS WITH ENGINE REMOVED
SECTION E9	GEARBOX AND CLUTCH
SECTION F4	CARBURETTOR
SECTION G1e	SRI MAGNETO
SECTION G2k	GENERATOR/RECTIFIER CHARGING SET
SECTION G4a	BATTERY
SECTION G5d	HEAD AND TAIL LAMPS
SECTION H5	FRAME
SECTION J1	FRONT FORK
SECTION J3	FRONT FORK
SECTION J6	FRONT FORK
SECTION J7	FRONT FORK
SECTION K3	FRONT WHEEL
SECTION K7	FRONT WHEEL
SECTION L12	REAR WHEEL (NON-DETACHABLE)
SECTION L13	REAR WHEEL (QUICKLY DETACHABLE)
SECTION M2 and M4	SPECIAL TOOLS
SECTION P1	"AIRFLOW" FAIRING

SECTION A14a
Technical Data

"350 Bullet" 1956 onwards, "350 Clipper" and Trials "Works Replica" 1958 onwards

Cubic Capacity ... ... 346 c.c.
Stroke ... ... 90 mm.
Bore ... ... Nominal ... 70 mm.
                  Actual   69·874 mm./2·751 in.
(Rebore to ·020 in. when wear exceeds ·0065 in. and again to ·040 in. after a further ·0065 in. wear.)
Compression Ratios—
    350 Bullet" to 1958, "350 Clipper"
    to 1959, and all "Works Replica"
    models ... ... 7·25 to 1
    "350 Bullet," 1959 onwards, and
    "350 Clipper," 1960 onwards ... 7·75 to 1
Piston Diameter—
    Bottom of Skirt— Fore and Aft   69·811/69·786 mm.
                    Top Lands ... 69·32/69·27 mm.
Piston Rings—
    Width—Plain Rings. (Two) ... ·0635/·0625 in.
             Scraper Ring. (One) ... ·156/·155 in.
    Radial Thickness ... ... 3·085/2·833 mm.
    Clearance in Grooves–Plain Rings ·003/·001 in.
                         Scraper Ring ·004/·002 in.
(Renew Piston Rings when gap exceeds $\tfrac{1}{16}$ in.)
Oversize Pistons and Rings available ... ·020 in. and ·040 in.
Piston Boss Internal Diameter ... ·7501/·7499 in.
Gudgeon Pin Diameter... ... ·7501/·7499 in.
Con. Rod Small End Diameter ... ·7507/·7505 in.
Con. Rod Big End Diameter ... 1·62625/1·62575 in.
Crank Pin Diameter ... ... 1·24900/1·24875 in.
Con. Rod Floating Bush—
    Outside Diameter ... ... 1·6235/1·6230 in.
    Inside Diameter ... ... 1·2502/1·2498 in.
    Width ... ... ·983/·980 in.
Driving Side Main Ball and Roller Bearings—
    Later type "350 Bullet" and "Works Replica," and "350 Clipper," 1960 onwards, use SKF.CRL.8 and SKF.RLS.8. Up to 1959 "350 Clipper" and earlier "Bullet" engines, use two SKF.RLS.8 bearings.
    Outside Diameter ... ... 2·25 in.
    Inside Diameter ... ... 1 in.
    Width ... ... ·625 in.
Timing Side Main Roller Bearing—
    Outside Diameter ... ... 1·876/1·875 in.
    Inside Diameter ... ... 1·5002/1·4998 in.
    Width ... ... ·750 in.
Size of Rollers—
    Nominal Size ... ... $\tfrac{1}{4}$ in. dia. × $\tfrac{21}{64}$ in. long
    Diameter ... ... ·2500/·2490 in.
    Length ... ... ·328/·327 in.
Graded rollers are available in steps of ·0001 from ·2490 to ·2500 in.
Rocker Bearing Inside Diameter ·626/·625 in.
Rocker Spindle Diameter ... ·6240/·6235 in.
Inlet Valve Stem Diameter ... ·3430/·3425 in.
Exhaust Valve Stem Diameter... ·3410/·3405 in.
Valve Guide Internal Diameter (All "Bullets" and "Trials;" "Clipper," 1960 onwards only) ... ... ·3447/·3437 in.
Valve Guide External Diameter (All "Bullets" and "Trials;" "Clipper," 1960 onwards only) ... ... ·6275/·6270 in.
Valve Guide Internal Dia. ("Clipper," up to 1959) ... ... ·3452/·3442 in.
Valve Guide External Dia. ("Clipper," up to 1959) ... ... ·625/·623 in.

Guide Hole in Cylinder Head (All "Bullets" and "Trials;" "Clipper," 1960 onwards only) ... ... ·622/·623 in.
Guide Hole in Cylinder Head ("Clipper" up to 1959) ... ... ·622/·623 in.
Tappet Stem Dia. (all models) ... ·375/·374 in.
Tappet Guide Internal Dia. (all models) ... ... ·3760/·3752 in.
Tappet Guide External Dia. (all models) ... ... ·7510/·7505 in.
Guide Hole in Crankcase (all models) ·750/·749 in.
Tappet Clearance with cold engine—
    Inlet ... ... Nil
    Exhaust ... ... Nil
Valve Spring Free Length—
    Inner ... ... 2·02 in.
    Outer ... ... 2·095 in.
(Renew when reduced by $\tfrac{3}{16}$ in.)
Valve Timing with ·012 in. clearance—
    Exhaust Opens ... ... 75° before B.D.C.
    Exhaust Closes ... ... 35° after T.D.C.
    Inlet Opens ... ... 30° before T.D.C.
    Inlet Closes ... ... 60° after B.D.C.
Cam Spindle External Diameter ... ·6240/·6235 in.
Cam Bush Internal Diameter ... ·6255/·6250 in.
Cam Lift ... ... ·3125 in.
Valve Lift (approximately) ... ·3125 in.
Contact Breaker (Coil Ignition)—
    Speed ... ... $\tfrac{1}{2}$ Engine Speed
    Points ... ... ·014/·016 in.
    Timing ... ... $\tfrac{1}{2}$–$\tfrac{7}{16}$ in. before T.D.C.
Magneto—
    Speed ... ... $\tfrac{1}{2}$ Engine Speed
    Points ... ... ·012/·015 in.
    Timing ... ... $\tfrac{1}{2}$–$\tfrac{7}{16}$ in. before T.D.C.
Engine Sprocket ("Bullet" and "Clipper") ... ... 25 Teeth
Engine Sprocket ("Trials") ... 20 Teeth
Clutch Sprocket (all models) ... 56 Teeth
Final Drive Sprocket ("Bullet") 20 Teeth
Final Drive Sprocket ("Trials") ... 17 Teeth
Final Drive Sprocket ("Clipper" up to 1959) ... ... 15 Teeth
Final Drive Sprocket ("Clipper," 1960 onwards) ... ... 20 Teeth
Primary Chain—
    Type... ... ... Duplex No. 114038 Endless
    Length ... ... 90 Pitches ("Trials" 88 Pitches)
    Width ... ... ·628 in.
    Pitch ... ... ·375 in.
Feed Oil Pump—
    Speed ... ... 1/12 Engine Speed
    Piston Diameter ... ... ·24975/·24950 in.
    Stroke ... ... ·5 in.
Return Oil Pump—
    Speed ... ... 1/12 Engine Speed
    Piston Diameter ... ... ·37475/·37450 in.
    Stroke ... ... ·5 in.
Sparking Plug—
    Type... ... Lodge H.14, KLG F.70, Champion L10S, ("Trials: Lodge HN)
    Diameter ... ... 14 mm.

SECTION A14b

Technical Data

"500 Bullet Engine" 1956 onwards

Cubic Capacity	499 c.c.
Stroke	90 mm.
Bore … Nominal	84 mm.
Actual	3·30725/3·30675 in.

(Rebore to ·020 in. when wear exceeds ·008 in. and again to ·040 in. after a further ·008 in. wear.)

Compression Ratio	6·5 to 1
Compression Ratio, 1959 onwards	7·25 to 1
Piston Diameter—	
Bottom of Skirt—Fore and Aft	3·3047/3·3042 in.
Top Lands	3·284/3·281 in.
Piston Rings—	
Width—Plain Rings (Two)	·063/·062 in.
Scraper Ring (One)	·156/·155 in.
Radial Thickness	·115/·108 in.
Clearance in Grooves—Plain Rings	·0035/·0015 in.
Scraper Ring	·0035/·0015 in.

(Renew Piston Rings when gap exceeds 1/16 in.)

Oversize Pistons and Rings available	·020 in. and ·040 in.
Piston Boss Internal Diameter	·7500/·7497 in.
Gudgeon Pin Diameter	·7500/·7497 in.
Con. Rod Small End Diameter	·7507/·7505 in.
Con. Rod Big End Diameter	1·62625/1·62575 in.
Crank Pin Diameter	1·24900/1·24875 in.
Con. Rod Floating Bush—	
Outside Diameter	1·6235/1·6230 in.
Inside Diameter	1·2502/1·2498 in.
Width	·983/·980 in.
Driving Side Main Ball and Roller Bearings SKF.CRL.8 and SKF.RLS.8.	
Outside Diameter	2·25 in.
Inside Diameter	1 in.
Width	·625 in.
Timing Side Main Roller Bearing—	
Outside Diameter	1·876/1·875 in.
Inside Diameter	1·5002/1·4998 in.
Width	·750 in.
Size of Rollers—	
Nominal Size	1/4 in. dia. × 21/64 in. long
Diameter	·2500/·2490 in.
Length	·328/·327 in.

Graded rollers are available in steps of ·0001 from ·2490 to ·2500 in.

Rocker Bearing Inside Diameter	·626/·625 in.
Rocker Spindle Diameter	·6240/·6235 in.
Rocker Spindle Dia., 1959 onwards	·5617/·5615 in.
Rocker Bush Diameter, 1959 onwards	·5627/·5622 in.
Inlet Valve Stem Diameter	·3430/·3425 in.
Exhaust Valve Stem Diameter	·3410/·3405 in.
Valve Guide Internal Diameter	·3447/·3437 in.
Valve Guide External Diameter	·6275/·6270 in.
Guide Hole in Cylinder Head	·626/·625 in.
Tappet Stem Diameter	·375/·374 in.
Tappet Guide Internal Diameter	·3760/·3752 in.
Tappet Guide External Diameter	·7510/·7505 in.
Guide Hole in Crankcase	·750/·749 in.
Tappet Clearance with cold engine—	
Inlet	Nil
Exhaust	Nil
Valve Spring Free Length—	
Inner (Earlier Type)	2·032 in.
Outer (Earlier Type)	2·095 in.
Inner (1959 onwards)	1·5 in.
Outer (1959 onwards)	1 11/16 in.

(Renew when reduced by 3/16 in.)

Valve Timing with ·012 in. clearance—	
Exhaust Opens	75° before B.D.C.
Exhaust Closes	35° after T.D.C.
Inlet Opens	40° before T.D.C.
Inlet Closes	70° after B.D.C.
Cam Spindle External Diameter	·6240/·6230 in.
Cam Bush Internal Diameter	·6255/·6250 in.
Cam Lift	·3125 in.
Valve Lift (approximately)	·3125 in.
Contact Breaker (Coil Ignition)—	
Speed	1/2 Engine Speed
Points	·014/·016 in.
Timing	7/16 in. before T.D.C.
Magneto—	
Speed	1/2 Engine Speed
Points	·012/·015 in.
Timing	5/16 in. before T.D.C.
Engine Sprocket	25 Teeth
Clutch Sprocket	56 Teeth
Final Drive Sprocket—	
Solo	21 Teeth
Sidecar	18 Teeth
Primary Chain—	
Type	Duplex No. 114038 Endless
Length	90 Pitches
Width	·628 in.
Pitch	·375 in.
Feed Oil Pump—	
Speed	1/12 Engine Speed
Piston Diameter	·24975/·24950 in.
Stroke	·5 in.
Return Oil Pump—	
Speed	1/12 Engine Speed
Piston Diameter	·37475/·37450 in.
Stroke	·5 in.
Sparking Plug—	
Type	Lodge HLN, KLG FE80, Champion NA8 (not 1959) Long Reach
Diameter	14 mm.

EXPLODED VIEW OF "BULLET" ENGINE Fig. 1

SECTION B14

Engine Specification

"350 and 500 Bullet" 1956 onwards, "350 Clipper" and Trials "Works Replica" 1958 onwards

1. Engine

The engine is a 346 or 499 c.c. vertical single-cylinder four-stroke with separate cylinder head and fully enclosed pressure-fed overhead valve gear. It has dry sump lubrication with the oil tank integral with the crankcase and a built-up steel crankshaft.

2. Cylinder Head

The cylinder head is die-cast from aluminium alloy with ample finning to ensure adequate cooling. The valve inserts are of austenitic iron and are shrunk in so that they are replaceable (except on early models).

The large bore induction port is streamlined and blended to the valve seating.

3. Cylinder

On all but the Trials "Works Replica" model, the cylinder barrel is of cast iron with internal tunnels enclosing the push rods.

On the Trials machine, an alloy barrel with a shrunk-in liner is used.

The bore of the 350 engine is nominally 70 mm. and the stroke 90 mm., giving a cubic capacity of 346 c.c.

The bore of the 500 engine is nominally 84 mm. and the stroke 90 mm., giving a cubic capacity of 499 c.c.

4. Piston

The piston is of low expansion aluminium alloy, heat treated, and form-turned oval. There are three piston rings, the top two of which are compression rings. The top ring is chromium plated and the bottom one taper ground. The third ring is for oil control and is slotted.

Different compression ratios are available as follows:

350 c.c. Engine   6, $6\frac{1}{2}$, $7\frac{1}{4}$, $7\frac{1}{2}$, $8\frac{1}{2}$ and $10\frac{1}{2}$ to 1.

500 c.c. Engine $6\frac{1}{4}$, 8 and $9\frac{1}{2}$ to 1.

5. Connecting Rod

The connecting rod is produced from a stamping of Hiduminium RR56 light alloy. There is no bush fitted to the little end, but in case of wear after long service the little end may be bored out and a bush fitted, although this is rarely necessary.

The big end has a hardened chrome steel bush pressed in and a floating bush made from mild steel and white-metalled.

6. Crankcase

The combined crankcase and oil tank are die-cast from light alloy in two halves, being split vertically.

7. Crankshaft and Flywheel

The crankshaft is built up from two steel flywheels bolted to the crank pin and bolted and keyed to the engine shafts, the whole being carefully balanced.

8. Main Bearings

On the driving side there are two bearings, all later models having one ball and one roller. The pre-1960 "Clipper" has two ball bearings, as does the early type "Bullet." Each bearing has an inner and outer race, while on the timing side there are a roller bearing, with the rollers running on the shaft, and a plain phosphor bronze bush for retaining oil in the timing chest.

9. Cams

The cams are integral with the cam pinions, being machined from carbon steel and case hardened. They have internal bronze bushes running on fixed spindles in the timing chest. The cam profiles are produced with silencing ramps to ensure quiet running.

10. Valves

The inlet valve is machined from a stamping of Silicon-chrome valve steel and the exhaust valve is of austenitic steel.

11. Valve Gear

The valves are operated from the cams by means of large flat-based guided tappets, high quality tubular steel push rods, with steel cups, and overhead rockers. Two compression springs are fitted to each valve.

12. Timing Drive

The cams are located in the timing chest and are driven at half engine speed from the crankshaft by a positive geared drive.

The magdyno, magneto or, on coil ignition models, the contact breaker, is driven from the inlet cam pinion through two idler pinions which also act as a gear pump to return the oil from the timing chest to the oil tank.

13. Ignition and Lighting System

The later "350" and "500 Bullet" and all "350 Clipper" models, are fitted with coil ignition as standard equipment, although some are fitted with a magneto to special order. This is the latest Lucas brushless type, with rotating magnet and stationary contact breaker. It runs at half engine speed and has a single cam.

Coil ignition models have the contact breaker unit driven from the same pinion that drives the magneto, and the coil is situated in the tool box.

An emergency starting system is incorporated.

The "Works Replica" is fitted with a waterproof magneto.

Lighting current is supplied by the battery, which is charged through a rectifier from an alternator consisting of a rotating magnet mounted on the crankshaft and running in a six-coil stator in the primary chaincase.

14. Carburettor (See Section F)

"350 Bullet," 1956-58, "350 Clipper," 1959 onwards, and all Trials Models. Amal type 376/29 Monobloc.

"350 Bullet," 1959 onwards—Amal 376/215.
"500 Bullet," 1959 onwards—Amal 389/34.
"500 Bullet," 1956-1958—Amal 389/9.

15. Air Filter

The air supply to the carburettor is cleaned by a Vokes Micro-Vee felt and gauze dry filter, housed in a box bolted to the frame behind the carburettor.

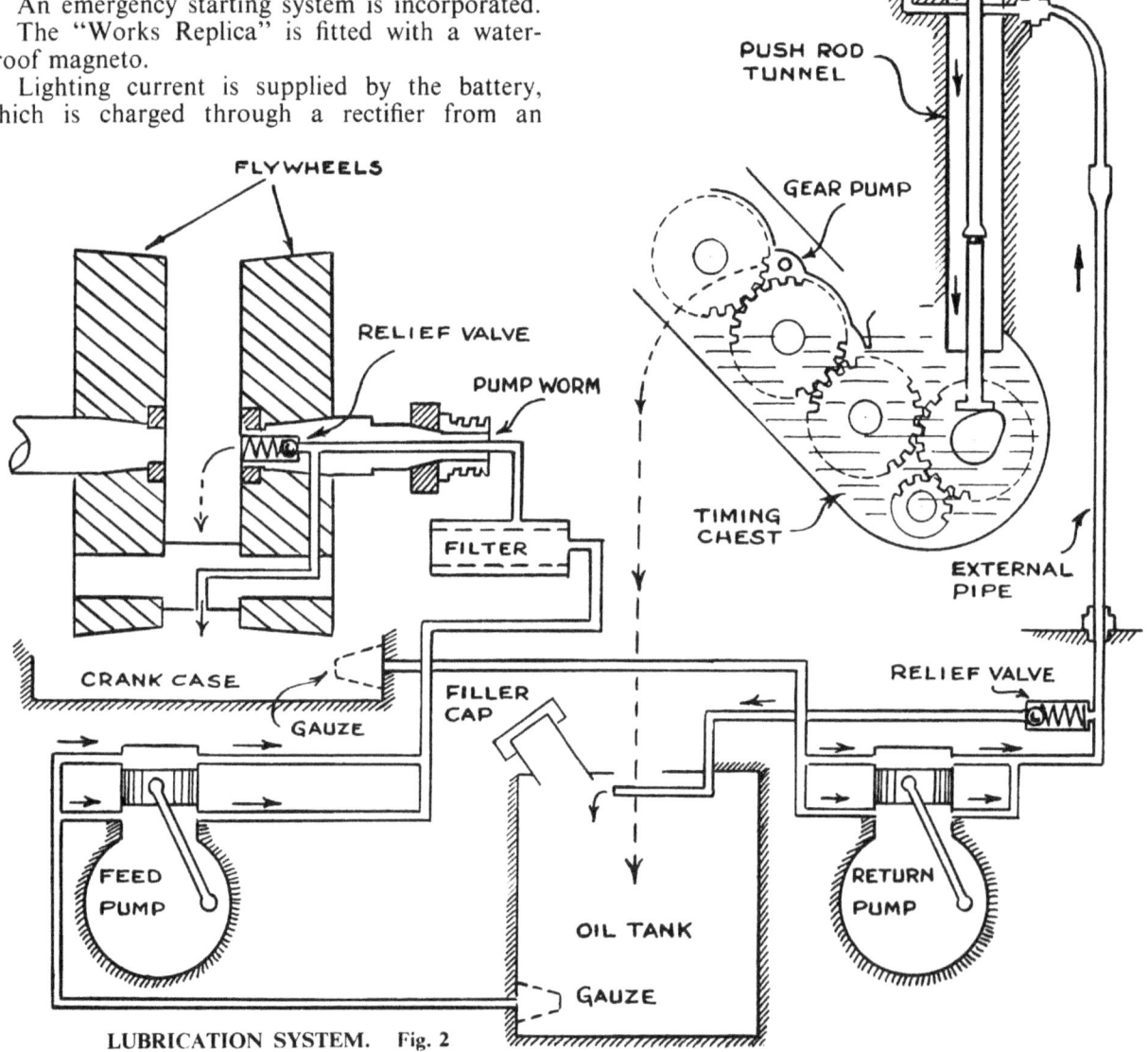

LUBRICATION SYSTEM.   Fig. 2

The "Trials" model has a Vokes Lightweight filter, oil wetted, which may be washed in petrol and refitted.

16. Lubrication System

Lubrication is by the Royal Enfield Dry-Sump which is entirely automatic and positive in action.

The oil tank is integral with the crankcase, ensuring the full rate of circulation immediately the engine is started and rapid heating of the oil in cold weather.

There are two piston type oil pumps running at $\frac{1}{1\frac{1}{2}}$ engine speed, positively driven from the timing side engine shaft through a worm gear.

The feed pump at the rear of the timing cover is for pumping oil from the tank to the big end bearing. This oil drains to the bottom of the crankcase and is pumped by the return pump back to the tank.

Some of the return oil is by-passed to the cylinder head for lubricating the rocker gear, whence it flows down the push-rod tunnels to the timing chest.

From here it is returned to the tank by the two idler pinions in the timing drive which act as a gear pump.

The return pump has a capacity of approximately double that of the feed pump, which ensures that oil does not accumulate in the crankcase.

Both pumps are double-acting, but the two sides of the feed pump are interconnected, thereby giving an augmented and more even supply to the big end. Both sides of the return pump are also interconnected for draining the crankcase.

Separate spring-loaded relief valves control the pressure to the big end and to the valve gear. The oil supply to the big end is through internally drilled passages and that to the valve gear is through an external pipe.

Gauze strainers are provided for the feed oil leaving the tank and for the return oil from the crankcase. In addition, the feed oil to the big end is pumped under pressure through a large capacity felt filter.

An important feature of the design of this filter is that the internal arrangement is such that, should it be neglected and become clogged, the oil pressure will lift the spring and cap off its seating thereby automatically by-passing the filter so that the big end will not be deprived of lubrication, even though the oil may be dirty.

17. Breather

The efficient operation of the breather is of paramount importance to the performance of the engine because it acts as a non-return valve between the crankcase and the outside atmosphere, causing a partial vacuum in the crankcase and rocker boxes which prevents the passage of oil into the cylinder and consequent smoking and oiling of the plug.

The breather on both the 500 c.c. and 350 c.c. models is located on the driving side of the crankcase. It consists of a small housing attached to the crankcase by three screws and having a short rubber tube with flattened end which acts as a non-return valve.

On some models the housing contains two small pen-steel discs, which form the valve, and this type has a metal breather pipe.

18. Gearbox

The gearbox is bolted on to the back of the crankcase and has four speeds, which are foot controlled, and a patented neutral finder. All gears are in constant mesh, changes being effected by robust dog clutches.

The standard gear ratios are as follows:

Solo

"350 Bullet"
  1956-7-8   5·72, 7·45, 10·35, 15·9
  1959 onwards   5·15, 7·03, 9·5, 14·32
"500 Bullet"
  1956-7-8   4·91, 6·4, 8·85, 13·65
  1959 onwards   4·91, 6·7, 9·05, 13·65
"350 Clipper"
  1958   5·67, 7·37, 10·2, 15·8
  1959 onwards   5·15, 7·03, 9·5, 14·32
Trials "Works Replica"
  1958 onwards   7·56, 10·58, 16·25, 22·68

Sidecar

"500 Bullet"
  1956-7-8   5·72, 7·45, 10·3, 15·9
  1959 onwards   5·72, 7·8, 10·5, 15·9

19. Clutch

On the "500 Bullet" the clutch has six pressure plates and five friction plates, including the sprocket which is lined on both sides with special friction material; the first two friction plates, in order of assembly, use inserts of this type of friction material. The outer two plates have four bonded-on segments on each side of a corky textured material, which give smooth operation and freedom from slipping in the presence of oil. The clutch centre is fitted with shock absorbers, consisting of rubber blocks.

The clutch on the "350 Bullet" and on all "350 Clippers" is similar to that described above, except that it has five pressure plates, and four friction plates; the first friction plate in order of assembly having inserts of the special friction material, and the outer two bonded-on segments of corky material. This clutch centre is solid.

"350 BULLET" AND "500 BULLET" OIL PUMP DIAGRAMS

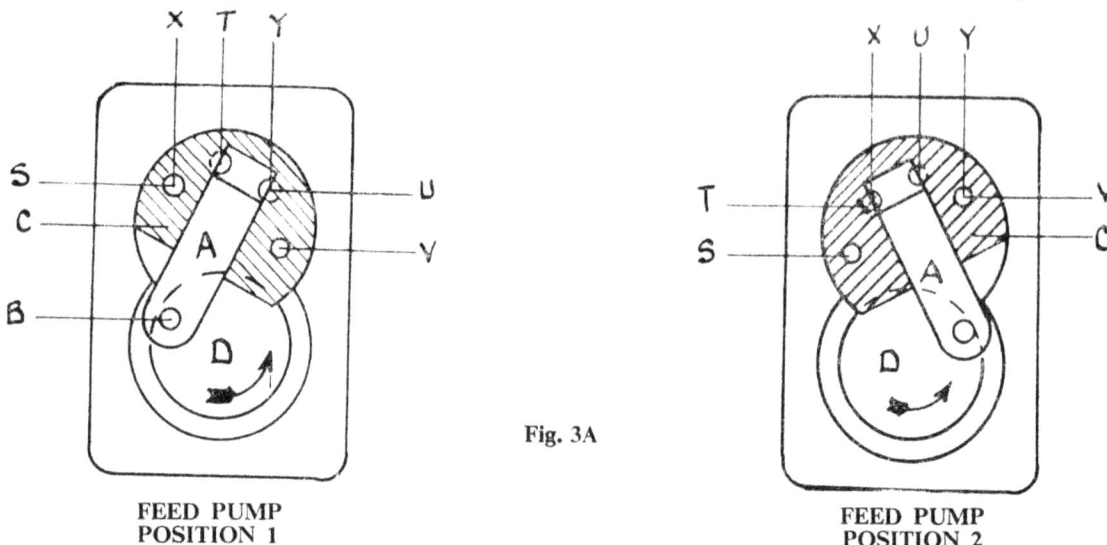

Fig. 3A

FEED PUMP POSITION 1

FEED PUMP POSITION 2

The ports are connected as follows:
X—in the housing is the delivery to the big end.
Y—in the housing is the suction from the oil tank.
S and V—are drilled through the disc.
T and U—are drilled from the underside of the disc into the cylinder hole.

Position 1. The plunger A is being drawn out of the cylinder hole in the disc C by the action of the peg B on the shaft D. The port U in the disc C registers with the suction port Y in the housing so that oil is drawn into the cylinder from the oil tank. At the same time the port S in the disc registers with the delivery port X in the housing so that oil below the disc in the housing is forced through S and X to the big end.

Position 2. The plunger A is being pushed into the cylinder hole in the disc C. The port T in the disc now registers with the delivery port X in the housing so that oil is forced out of the cylinder to the big end. At the same time the port V in the disc registers with the suction port Y in the housing and oil is drawn into the housing below the disc from the tank.

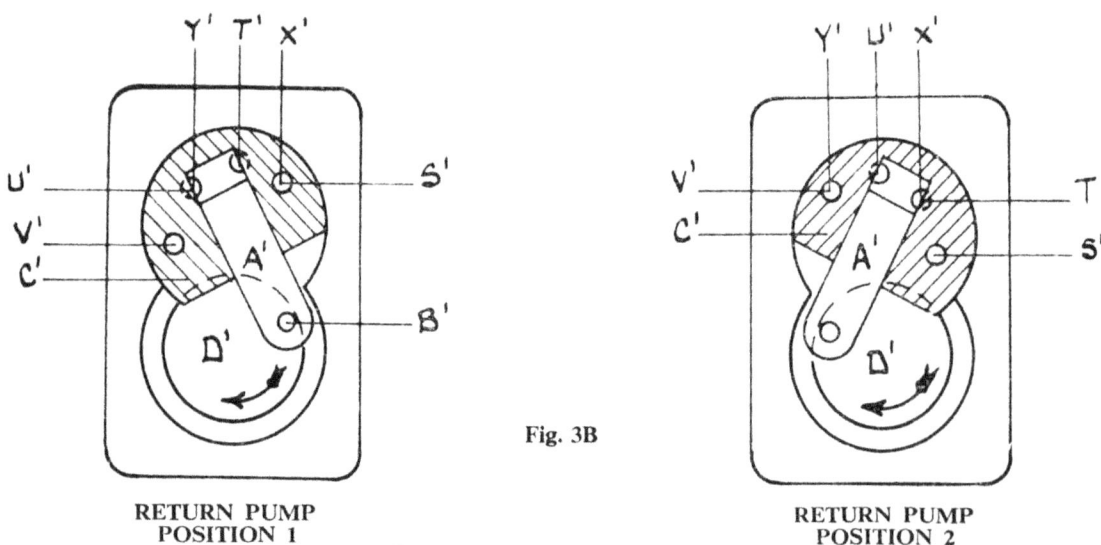

Fig. 3B

RETURN PUMP POSITION 1

RETURN PUMP POSITION 2

The ports are connected as follows:
X'—in the housing is the delivery to the rocker gear.
Y'—in the housing is the suction from the crankcase.
S' and V'—are drilled through the disc.
T' and U'—are drilled from the underside of the disc into the cylinder hole.

Position 1. The plunger A' is being drawn out of the cylinder hole in the disc C' by the action of the peg B' on the shaft D'. The port U' registers with the suction port Y' in the housing, so that oil is drawn into the cylinder from the crankcase sump. At the same time the port S' in the disc registers with the delivery port X' in the housing, so that oil below the disc in the housing is forced through S' and X' to the rocker gear.

Position 2. The plunger A' is being pushed into the cylinder hole in the disc C'. The port T' in the disc now registers with the delivery port X' in the housing, so that oil is forced out of the cylinder to the rocker gear. At the same time the port V' in the disc registers with the suction port Y' in the housing so that oil is drawn into the housing below the disc from the crankcase sump through V' and Y'.

SECTION C14

Service Operations with Engine in Frame

"350 and 500 Bullet," 1956 onwards, "350 Clipper" and
Trials "Works Replica" 1958 onwards

1. Removal of the Timing Cover

First place a tray under the engine to catch the oil which will escape when the cover is removed.

Remove the exhaust pipe and silencer.

Remove ten screws from the cover, taking care not to lose the sealing washers, one for each screw.

Draw off the timing cover, tapping it lightly if necessary.

In refitting the timing cover see that the joint washer is correctly located over the oil holes, using a little grease (not compound) to hold it in position.

See that the cork plug is in position in the hole in the pump worm. If the plug is damaged it should be renewed to ensure oil pressure to the big end bearing.

When refitting the timing cover it is important that the engine is turned gently forwards while the cover is being put in place. This will help the engagement of the pump worm with the pump spindle and prevent damage to the gears.

The filter chamber should be filled with clean oil before the timing cover is refitted.

To verify that the oil pumps are working after replacing the timing cover, start the engine up and remove the oil filler cap so that the oil return through the relief valve can be seen. It may take several minutes before there is sufficient oil in the engine for the return flow through the relief valve to commence.

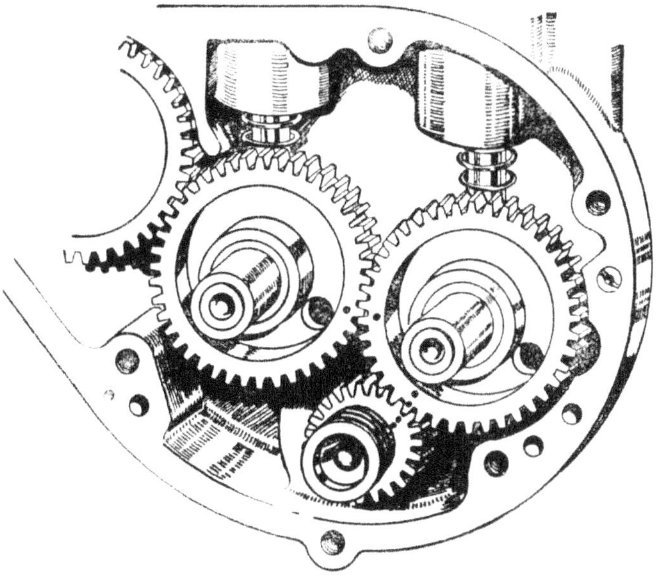

2. Valve Timing

The cams are integral with the cam pinions and the position for correct timing is marked on the pinions by small dots.

Rotate the engine to top dead centre and put the exhaust (or right-hand) cam pinion in position so that the pair of dots on it are opposite the pair of dots on the timing pinion on the crankshaft.

Put the inlet (or left-hand) cam pinion in position so that the single dot on it is opposite the single dot on the exhaust cam pinion.

The correct timing at ·012 in. tappet clearance is as follows:

"350 Bullet"
Exhaust opens 75° before bottom dead centre.
Exhaust closes 35° after top dead centre.
Inlet opens 30° before top dead centre.
Inlet closes 60° after bottom dead centre.

"500 Bullet"
Exhaust opens 75° before bottom dead centre.
Exhaust closes 35° after top dead centre.
Inlet opens 40° before top dead centre.
Inlet closes 70° after bottom dead centre.

3. Tappet Adjustment

The tappets are adjusted by the ball and socket joints which are located in a compartment at the side of the cylinder and access to which is obtained by removing the inspection cover.

Before checking the clearance or making any adjustment, rotate the engine until the piston is at the top of the firing stroke. This will ensure that both valves are closed and that the tappets are well clear of the silencing ramps on the cams. If the cylinder head has been dismantled, make sure that the end caps have been put back on the valve stems.

Later type "350 and 500 Bullet" valves have hardened ends and are not fitted with detachable end caps.

Because of the ball and socket joints at the bottom of the push rods, the tappet clearance cannot be measured there, but between the valve

VALVE TIMING MARKS
Fig. 1

stems and rockers, with the rocker box covers removed. To remove the rocker box covers the petrol tank must be taken off. (See Subsection 5.)

The correct clearance is nil or as little as possible with the engine **COLD**.

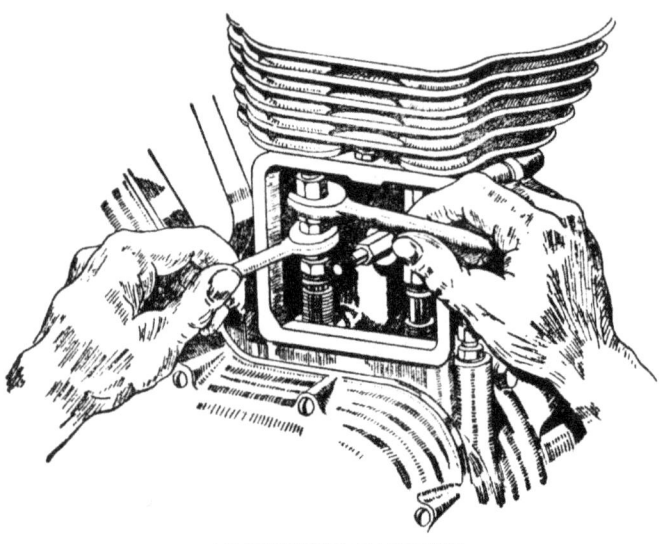

ADJUSTING TAPPETS
Fig. 2

To make the adjustment hold the push rod bottom end (top hexagon) and turn the locknut (middle hexagon) to the left. Screw the push rod cup (bottom hexagon) to the left to take up clearance or to the right to increase the clearance, at the same time holding the push rod bottom end (top hexagon). Lock the adjustment by tightening the locknut against the push rod end and then recheck the clearance.

Owing to the initial bedding down of the wearing surfaces, the tappets on new engines may require adjustment after the first few hundred miles.

4. Ignition Timing

The setting of the ignition depends upon the position of the magneto or contact breaker drive pinion relative to the shaft.

To obtain access to the pinion it is necessary to remove the timing cover (see Subsection 1).

On engines fitted with magneto and auto-advance mechanism, the latter is in unit with the driving pinion, and is held to the shaft on a smooth taper and secured by a nut having a right-hand thread.

There is some difference in all "350 Clipper" (see sub-section 18) and all "Trials" models, and in "350 and 500 Bullets" from 1960 onwards.

To remove the pinion and the auto-advance device, unscrew the nut and this will draw the pinion off.

Before setting the timing remove the magneto cover and adjust the contact breaker points to a clearance of ·015 in. when fully opened.

Because of the auto-advance mechanism, the timing is normally in the "retard" position when the engine is stationary. Rotate the two halves of the coupling relatively to each other against the springs, i.e. into the "advance" position, and hold it in this position by a piece of wire.

To set the timing, turn the engine until the piston is $\frac{1}{2}-\frac{7}{16}$ in. for the 350 c.c. Engine, or $\frac{3}{8}-\frac{5}{16}$ in. for the 500 c.c. Engine, before top dead centre on the compression stroke, i.e. with both valves closed.

Insert a thin piece of paper between the points of the contact breaker and turn the magneto forwards (or clockwise looking on the contact breaker) until the paper can just be pulled out.

Tighten the pinion and auto-advance device on to the shaft, taking care that it does not slip. Remove the piece of wire holding the auto-advance mechanism.

The timing can be checked by removing the cap from the magneto and holding the rotor in the advanced position by means of a screwdriver, without the necessity of taking off the timing cover.

On no account must the cam be altered from its original position on the rotor shaft or the efficiency of the magneto will be affected.

For all "350 Clippers," the auto-advance mechanism used is of a different type from that on the "350 Bullet" up to 1959, and the engine must be checked and set in the fully retarded position. This and the following remarks apply to "350 and 500 Bullets," 1960 onwards.

Gap setting should be ·015 in. to ·018 in. and the engine should be timed so that the contacts are on the point of opening when the piston is $\frac{1}{16}$ in. before top dead centre.

The best way to check the opening point is to switch on the ignition and rotate the engine slowly until the ammeter needle returns to its central position.

To adjust the timing, slacken the clamping bolt on the contact breaker housing and rotate the housing. If the timing cover has been dismantled, start with the contact breaker housing so that the name on the cover is roughly horizontal.

"Works Replica." The contact breaker should be set so that the points are just breaking when the piston is $\frac{7}{16}$ in. before top dead centre on the compression stroke, ignition fully advanced.

5. Removal of the Petrol Tank

Turn off the petrol tap.
Disconnect the petrol pipe.
Remove the bolt which holds the front of the tank to the frame, pull upwards to release the spring clip holding the tank at the rear.

6. Removal of the Cylinder Head

"350 Bullet," "350 Clipper," "Works Replica" and early "500 Bullet"

Remove the petrol tank (see Subsection 5).
Disconnect the engine steady.
Disconnect the plug lead and oil pipe.
Remove the exhaust pipe.
Push the carburettor back clear of the studs after removing the fixing nuts.
Remove the rocker box covers.
Remove the decompressor cable from the lever on the handlebar.
Turn the engine until both valves are closed.
Remove the rockers and bearings complete by undoing four $\frac{1}{4}$ in. nuts on each.
Lift out the push rods.
Remove six nuts, taking care not to lose the washers.
Remove the $\frac{1}{4}$ in. nut above the tappet chest to avoid possible damage to the crankcase.
Lift the cylinder head off the barrel, tapping it gently beneath the exhaust and inlet ports with a hide hammer to break the carbon seal. Do **not** tap the fins.

When fitting the head again, apply jointing compound to both sides of the gasket, replace the six nuts and tighten them progressively and diagonally from one side to the other to prevent distortion.

Replace the $\frac{1}{4}$ in. nut above the timing chest.
Replace the push rods with the adjustable parts downwards, remembering that the shorter rod is the inlet.
Replace the rockers and bearings, making sure that the oil feed holes are at the bottom and that the caps and bases are in line when tightened down. A sharp tap with a hammer on the end of

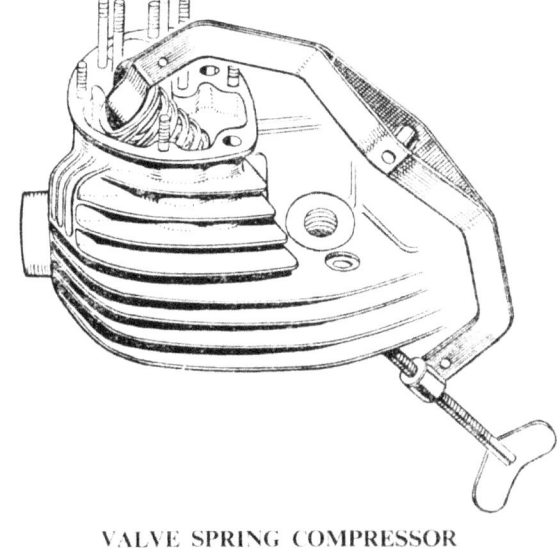

VALVE SPRING COMPRESSOR
Fig. 4

the rocker will help to ensure this. See that the valve stem caps are in place.

After the engine has been run long enough to get thoroughly hot, the tightness of the nuts should be rechecked.

It will be found convenient for this purpose to use a small auxiliary petrol tank while the engine is being warmed up on the stand, because all the cylinder head nuts are not accessible with the proper tank in position.

See that the rocker box gaskets are intact and replace the rocker box covers.

After tightening the cylinder head nuts with the engine hot, recheck the tappet clearance at some convenient time when the engine is cold.

"500 Bullet," 1959 onwards

Remove the cylinder head steady bar, exhaust pipe, carburettor, plug lead and the decompressor cable at the handlebar end. Disconnect the rocker oil feed pipes. Unscrew the five long nuts on the top of the head, the nut adjacent to the sparking plug and the sleeve nut by the decompressor. Withdraw the five studs from the crankcase—they have squared ends to take a spanner.

Remove the rocker covers, rockers and push rods. The rockers are removed by undoing the nuts at either end; one of these nuts is bored and tapped to take the oil union. Slide out the spindle, taking care that the spring washer at the push rod end and the plain washer at the other end do not fall down the push rod tunnel. Withdraw the push rods and lift the head.

For replacement reverse the order of the above instructions. Make the joint between cylinder

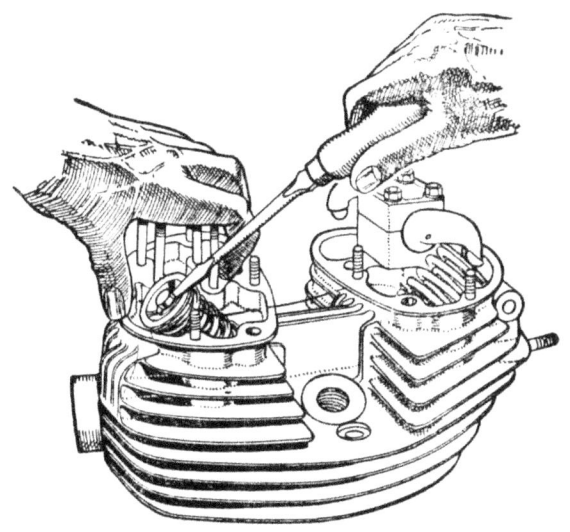

VALVE CAP REMOVAL
Fig. 3

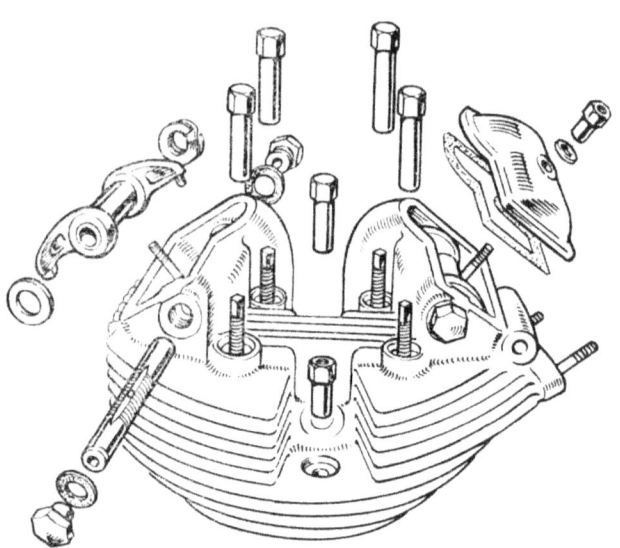

REMOVAL OF ROCKERS AND HEAD, "500 BULLET," 1959 ONWARDS
Fig. 5

head and barrel carefully as described in the foregoing paragraph. Replace the push rods and the five long studs in the crankcase, tightening these very carefully. Replace all the securing nuts, tightening them progressively to avoid distortion.

Replace the rocker spindles, inserting them through the box, through the spring washer held at the push rod end, through the rocker and the plain washer at the valve end and through the other side of the rocker box. Put on the nuts, test the rockers for freedom, replace the oil unions and the rocker box covers. Deal with the sparking plug, carburettor, exhaust pipe, decompressor cable and head steady and so complete the assembly.

7. Removal of the Valves

Remove the cylinder head and rockers (see Subsection 6).

Prise away the hardened steel thimble or end cap where fitted. If this has stuck it can be removed by means of a screwdriver.

Using a suitable compressing tool, compress the valve springs and remove the split conical collets from the end of the valve stem.

Slacken back the compressing tool and release the springs.

Withdraw the valve and place its springs, top spring collar (and bottom collar if it is loose), the end cap and split conical collets together in order that they may be reassembled with the valve from which they were removed.

Deal similarly with the other valve in the head.

If the valve will not slide easily through the valve guide, remove any slight burrs on the end of the valve stem with a carborundum stone. If the burrs are not removed and the valve is forced out, the guide may be damaged.

8. Removal of the Rockers

See Subsection 6.

9. Removal of the Valve Guides

To remove the valve guides from the head two special tools are required which can easily be made.

The first is a piece of tube with an internal bore of not less than $\frac{7}{8}$ in.

The second is a mandrel about 4 in. long made from $\frac{9}{16}$ in. diameter bar with the end turned down to $\frac{11}{32}$ in. diameter for $\frac{1}{2}$ in.

Support the cylinder head on the tube which fits over the collar of the valve guide. Using the mandrel, force the guide out of the head with a hand press or by using a hammer.

To fit a new guide, support the head at the correct angle and use a hand press and the same mandrel. If a hand press is not available and the guide is replaced by a hammer, use the mandrel to prevent damage to the guide.

It is necessary to recut the valve seat to the correct profile and grind in the valve after a guide has been replaced.

10. Removal of the Cylinder Barrel

Remove the Cylinder Head (see Subsection 6).
Put the piston at bottom dead centre.
Remove the $\frac{1}{4}$ in. nut above the tappet chest and lift the barrel off.

When replacing the cylinder barrel, clean off the joint faces and fit a new paper washer.

11. Removal of the Piston

Remove the cylinder head and cylinder barrel (see Subsections 6 and 10).

With the tang of a file remove the wire circlip retaining the gudgeon pin on the timing side.

Extract the gudgeon pin using Special Tool No. E.5477 (with adaptor if necessary), having first marked the pin so that it, and the piston, may be replaced the same way round, i.e. split skirt to the front.

During this operation put a piece of clean rag in the top of the crankcase to prevent foreign matter getting in. In particular, take care not to drop the circlip in the crankcase.

12. Decarbonising

Having removed the cylinder head as described in Subsection 6, scrape away all carbon, bearing in mind that you are dealing with aluminium which is easily damaged. Scrape gently to avoid scoring the combustion chamber or the valve

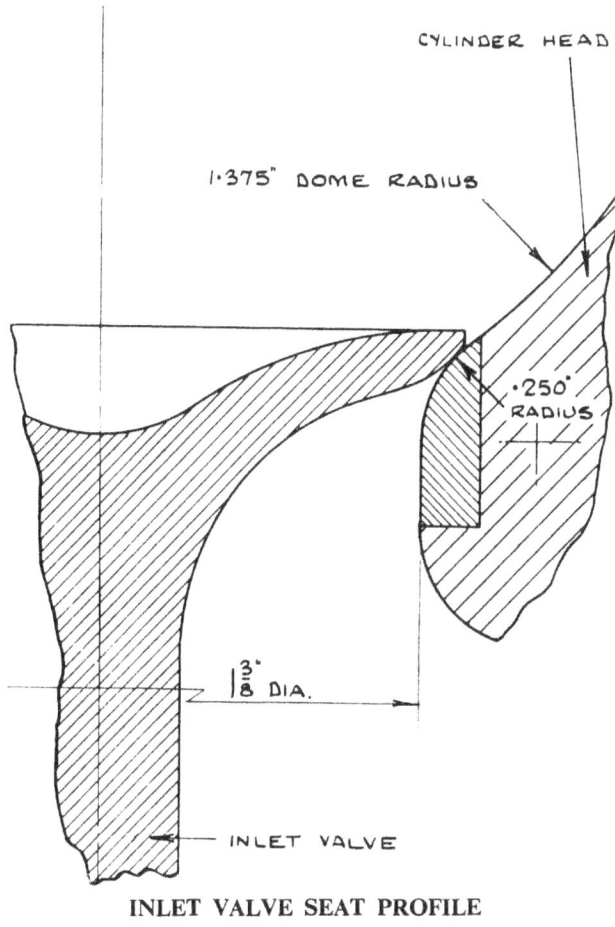

INLET VALVE SEAT PROFILE
Fig. 6

seats, which are of austenitic iron shrunk into the head. Be careful not to injure the joint face which beds down on to the head gasket.

Do not, in any circumstances, use caustic soda or potash for the removal of carbon from aluminium alloy.

Scrape away all carbon from the valve heads and beneath the heads, being careful not to cause any damage to the valve faces.

If the piston rings are removed, the grooves can be cleaned out and new ones fitted. For cleaning the grooves a suitable tool is a piece of broken ring thrust into a wooden handle and filed to a chisel point.

While the cylinder and piston are not in position, cover the crankcase with a clean cloth to prevent the ingress of dust and dirt of all kinds. Do not, of course, attempt to scrape the carbon from the piston when the mouth of the crankcase is open.

13. Grinding in the Valves

To grind a valve, smear the seating with a little grinding-in compound, place a light, short coil spring over the valve stem and beneath the head, insert the valve into its appropriate guide, press it on to the seat using a tool with a suction cup and with a backwards and forwards rotary motion, grind it on to its seat. Alternatively, a tool which pulls on the valve stem can be used. Frequently lift the valve and move it round so that an even and true seating is obtained. If no light spring is available, the lifting will have to be done by hand. Continue grinding until a bright ring is visible on both valve and seating.

The face and seat of the exhaust valve is cut at 45 degrees but the profile of the inlet valve is of a special streamlined design which eliminates pockets and sharp edges and allows a smooth flow of gas without eddies.

If the inlet valve or its seat is pitted and requires recutting, care must be taken to reproduce the correct profile as shown in Fig. 6.

The cylinder head should preferably be returned to the Works for the inlet valve seat to be recut, but if this is not possible a special tool consisting of an arbor and cutter is available. For the "350 Bullet" the arbor and cutter are No. T.2053 and T.1891; for the "500 Bullet," T.2053 and T.1892. Great care must be exercised in using this tool, as it is located off the valve guide and this may be damaged if suitable apparatus is not employed.

The inlet valve face and seat can be cut at 45 degrees in case of expediency but this may have a deleterious effect on the performance of the engine.

14. Reassembly after Decarbonising

Before building up the engine, see that all parts are scrupulously clean and place them conveniently to hand on a clean sheet of brown paper.

When reassembling the engine, it is advisable to fit a new paper washer between the cylinder barrel and the crankcase.

Smear clean oil over the piston and space the ring gaps, having replaced the rings if these have been removed. The taper ring is marked "TOP" on the upper face. Lower the piston over the connecting rod and insert the gudgeon pin. Fit the circlip securing the gudgeon pin.

If the piston ring gaps exceed $\frac{1}{16}$ in. when the rings are in position in the barrel, new rings should be fitted. The correct gap for new rings is ·011 in.–·015 in. The gap should be measured in the least worn part of the cylinder, which will be found to be the extreme top or bottom of the bore.

Oil the cylinder bore and lower the barrel over the piston and seat it gently on the paper washer. Tighten down the nut above the tappet chest and replace the cylinder head and rockers as described in Subsection 4.

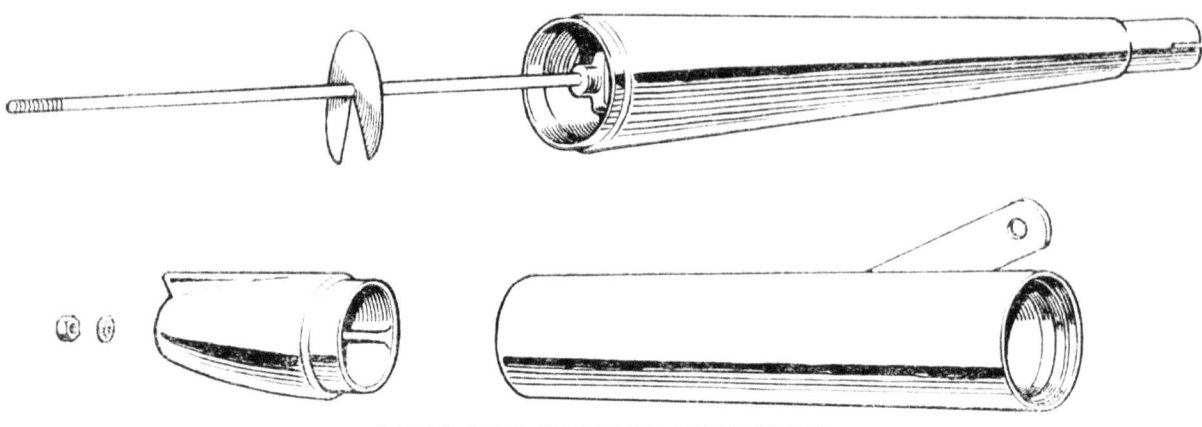

LATER TYPE SILENCER, DISMANTLED
Fig. 7

The silencer of the "350 and 500 Bullet" from 1961 onwards, may be dismantled for cleaning before refitting to the machine.

After removing the 3/16 in. nut and tab washer in the tail, the tail piece and central body may be drawn off the long central stud located in the front portion of the silencer.

15. Cleaning the Oil Filter

The oil filter is located in the timing cover immediately below the oil pumps. The felt element should be taken out and washed in petrol after the first 500 miles and every subsequent 2,000 miles. Fit a new element every 5,000 miles.

The filter element is removed by unscrewing the nut holding the end cap in position. When reassembling the filter after cleaning, take care that no grit or other foreign matter is sticking to it. After emptying the filter chamber it is essential to run the engine slowly for about five minutes to ensure that oil is reaching the big ends. If the timing cover has been removed, fill the filter chamber with clean oil before replacing the cover.

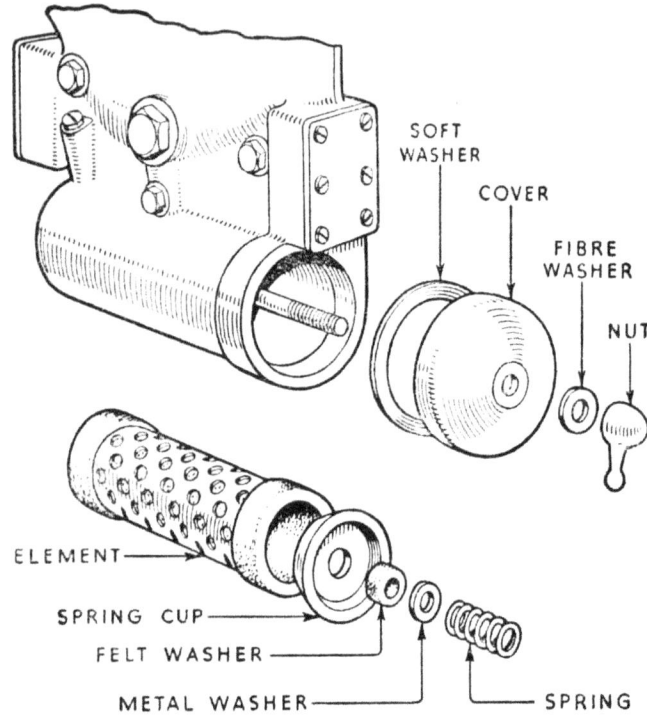

DETAIL OF FELT OIL CLEANER
Fig. 8

16. Overhaul of Oil Pumps

Remove the timing cover, as described in Sub-section 1.

Remove the end plates from both pumps.

Remove the pump discs and plungers.

Remove the pump spindle which can be pulled out from the front or return pump end.

Check the fit of the plungers in the pump discs which should have a minimum of clearance but should be able to be moved in and out by hand.

If, when fitting a new disc or plunger, the plunger is found to be too tight a fit, carefully lap with metal polish until it is just free. If the pump disc is not seating properly or if a new pump disc is being fitted, it should be lapped to the seating with Special Tool No. E.5425, using carborundum 360 fine paste or liquid metal polish until an even grey surface is obtained.

Replacement pump discs have a lip left on the flat, at the opposite side to the lapped face. The purpose of this is to hold the disc central in the housing during lapping-in. It should be filed off before the pump is finally assembled, care being taken not to damage the lapped face.

Wash all passages, etc., thoroughly with petrol after lapping to remove all traces of grinding paste.

Check the pump disc springs for fatigue by assembling in the timing cover and placing the pump covers in position. The latter should be held $\frac{1}{8}$ in. off the timing cover if the springs are correct.

In the case of the 500 c.c. engine see that the steel end pads are in position on the outer ends of the springs.

The pump spindle should be renewed if excessive wear has taken place on the teeth.

Reassemble the oil pumps, replacing the paper cover gaskets if necessary. Before fitting each cover fill the pump chamber with clean oil.

Having assembled the pumps, lay the timing cover flat and fill the oil ports by means of an oilcan. Turn the pump spindle with a screwdriver in a clockwise direction looking on the front and it can then be seen whether the pumps are operating correctly.

Before replacing the timing cover on the engine, fill the filter chamber with clean oil.

The oil feed to the big end can be checked by partially unscrewing the feed plug in the timing cover between the oil pumps while the engine is running and the oil return to the tank can be checked by removing the oil filler cap.

17. Removal of Pump Worm and Timing Pinion

Remove the timing cover as described in Subsection 1.

Unscrew the worm shaft by a hexagon head behind the worm, using Special Tool No. E.5451. This is a **left-hand thread.**

Withdraw the timing pinion by means of a flat chisel placed behind the pinion and tapped gently.

When refitting the timing cover see that the cork or rubber plug is in position in the hole in the pump worm and is undamaged.

18. Removal of the Magneto or Contact Breaker Pinion Unit

After first removing the timing cover of an engine having magneto ignition, the pinion of the type which incorporates an auto-advance unit is removed by unscrewing the centre nut. This will draw the pinion and auto-advance unit of the shaft.

Coil ignition models: The auto-advance mechanism in this case is in the contact breaker unit, and the pinion is drawn off by removing the securing nut and operating the extractor tool.

The "Works Replica," which employs magneto ignition, but no auto-advance mechanism, also follows this procedure.

19. Primary Chain Adjustment

Access to the primary chain adjuster is gained by removing the primary chain cover, which is

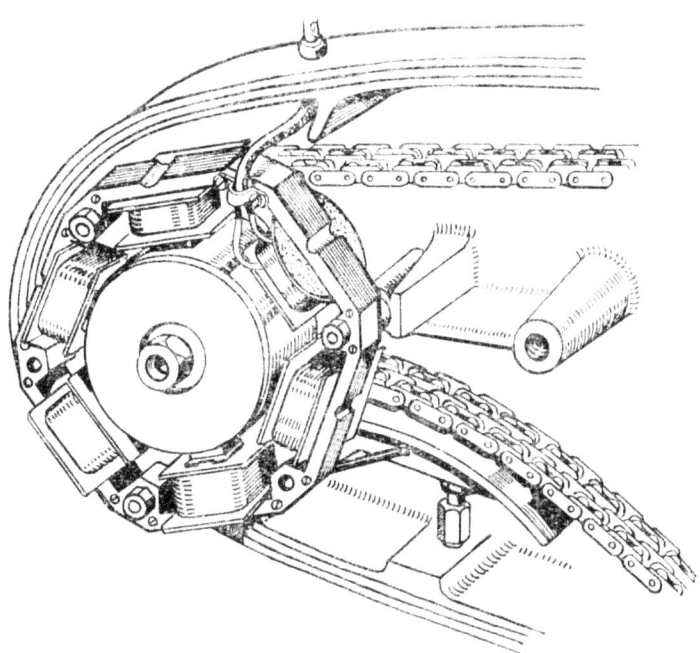

PRIMARY CHAIN ADJUSTMENT
Fig. 9

To take up slack in the primary chain, unscrew the locknut and turn the adjuster beneath the curved slipper until correct chain tension is obtained; retighten the locknut.

held in position by a single nut. Before removing the nut, place a tray under the engine to catch the oil from the chaincase.

Beneath the bottom run of the chain is a curved slipper on which the chain rests and which may be raised or lowered by turning the adjusting screw after having first slackened the locknut.

The chain should be adjusted so that there is $\frac{1}{4}$ in. up and down movement at the centre of the top run of the chain.

After replacing the chain cover, remember to replenish the chaincase with oil.

20. Removal of the Engine and Clutch Sprockets

The primary chain is endless so that it is necessary to remove both the engine and clutch sprockets simultaneously.

Remove the alternator stator by undoing three fixing screws.

Remove the central hexagon nut securing the alternator rotor, which can then be drawn off, taking care not to lose the key.

Unscrew the engine sprocket nut using Special Tool No. E.4877. The engine sprocket is mounted on splines and can then be removed with the clutch sprocket.

To remove the clutch sprocket unscrew the clutch spring pins then lift away the spring cap, springs and distance pieces, clutch front plate, centre retaining ring and the assembly of driving and driven clutch plates. The clutch sprocket can then be withdrawn from the centre after removal of the large circlip which secures it.

21. Removal of the Tappets and Guides

It is only necessary to remove the tappets and guides if they have become worn.

To remove the guides use Special Tool No. E.5410.

The guide should have an interference fit of ·0015 in. to ·0025 in. in the crankcase and can be driven in with a bronze drift, care being taken when the guide is nearly home to avoid damaging the collar. Excessive hammering may close up the bore of the guide which would necessitate removing the tappet and reaming again. In no circumstances should the guide be reamed in position on the 350 c.c. engine as swarf might get into the recess in the guide.

22. Dismantling the Breather

If the breather is not operating efficiently, it may cause pressure in the crankcase, instead of a partial vacuum, giving rise to smoking or over-oiling. If the breather is of the disc type, see that the discs and backplate are clean and undamaged and that the discs are seating properly.

When reassembling the breather, apply jointing compound very sparingly to the back of the steel plate taking great care to keep it away from the discs or their seatings.

If the breather is of rubber tube type, there are no moving parts and it is only necessary to see that the tube is not damaged or distorted.

If the breather body is detached from the driving side crankcase by removing the three screws, see that the faces are clean when refitting and apply jointing compound to ensure that the seal is airtight.

23. Removal of the Clutch

Remove the engine sprocket and clutch sprocket together as described in Subsection 20.

To remove the clutch centre, hold the clutch with Special Tool No. E.4871, and remove the centre retaining nut and washer with a box spanner.

The clutch centre can then be withdrawn from the shaft with Special Tool No. E.5414.

If the circlip is not removed the sprocket and clutch centre can be removed together.

24. Removal of the Final Drive Sprocket

Remove the clutch as described in Subsection 23.

Remove the primary chain tensioner.

Remove the rear half of the primary chaincase by taking out three socket screws.

Remove the grub screw locking the final drive sprocket nut.

Hold the sprocket and remove the nut (**right-hand thread**). The sprocket can then be withdrawn.

25. Pressure Relief Valves

There are two pressure relief valves in the oil feeds to the big end and to the rocker gear respectively. Their function is to prevent excessive pressure and their setting is not critical. The feed to the rocker gear comes from the return oil from the crankcase to the tank.

The pressure relief valves are set before leaving the Works and should not normally require to be disturbed. If, however, it is found necessary to dismantle either of them, they can be reset as follows:

Rocker Feed Relief Valve. This is located on the outside of the crankcase immediately below the lower end of the external oil pipe. It has a hexagon head and can be removed complete by unscrewing it out of the case.

The valve itself cannot be dismantled and, if found to be faulty, should be replaced by a new one.

Big End Relief Valve. This is located in the timing-side crankshaft and can only be adjusted when the crankshaft has been dismantled. It consists of a $\frac{5}{16}$ in. diameter steel ball and spring held in position by a screwed plug.

The valve is set to open when the oil pressure exceeds about 35 lb. per square inch and when set correctly there is a movement of about $\frac{3}{32}$ in. of the ball off the seat. This can be measured without dismantling the crankshaft by pushing a thin rod through the hole in the pump worm with the oil feed plug in the timing cover removed.

If the crankshaft is dismantled for any reason, it is always advisable to fit a new spring to the relief valve in case the original one has become weak.

If the valve is set to give too high a pressure, the pump disc will be forced off its seating.

26. Removal of the Magneto or Contact Breaker Unit

The magneto of all but "Works Replica" models, also the contact breaker unit fitted to "350 Clipper" and later "Bullets," is removed by taking off the timing cover (Sub-section 1) and the driving pinion (Sub-section 18), behind which are located three screws which secure the spigotted magneto or contact breaker unit.

The magneto on the "Works Replica" is held by a strap and when the nut securing this has been released, the magneto may be lifted from its locating dowels.

27. Fitting the Alternator

The alternator consists of two parts, the stator and the rotor. The stator of later models is mounted on to the three studs of the adaptor ring, which in turn is secured to the back half of the primary chaincase by three screws.

On earlier models the stator is of greater diameter and mounted on to the primary chaincase with three studs and distance pieces.

The rotor, which contains the permanent magnet, is mounted on the end of the crankshaft and is located by a key and secured by a special bolt and spring washer on 1960 models, and by a nut and tab washer on earlier models.

The radial air gap between the rotor and the poles of the stator should be ·020 in. in all positions and care must be taken when refitting to see that it is not less than ·010 in. at any point.

Fit the rotor first, making sure that it is located concentrically on the end of the crankshaft. Attention must be given to the seating of the key because a badly-fitting key may cause the rotor to run unevenly. Finally secure the rotor with the appropriate bolt or nut and washer.

Having fitted the rotor, secure the adaptor ring on later models with the three cheese-headed screws, and shake-proof washers, or, in the case of earlier models, place the three distance pieces over the three chaincase studs. The stator may then be fitted with the coil connections facing outwards, the leads on the inside at 12 o'clock.

Replace the nuts and shake-proof washers only finger-tight, and insert six strips (preferably of non-magnetic material) ·015 in. thick and about $\frac{1}{8}$ in. wide between the rotor and each pole piece.

Tighten the stator nuts and withdraw the strips.

Check the air gap with narrow feelers and, if less than ·010 in. at any point, remove the stator and file or grind the pole piece carefully until the correct gap is obtained.

An alternative, and more satisfactory method of assembling the alternator requires the use of Special Tool No. T2055. This is a gauge ·015 in. greater in radius than the rotor and fits over the adaptor on the end of the crankshaft in the rotor's place.

The stator is then put in position on the studs in the chaincase and the nuts tightened up.

Remove the gauge and fit the rotor, then check the air gap.

When refitting, note that the shaft may have a large or a small keyway. The small keyway is for the latest type of fitting and the large one for the old type. Do not fit a small key into the large keyway.

SECTION D9

Service Operations with Engine Removed

1956-60 "350 and 500 Bullet," 1958-60 "350 Clipper" and

1958-60 Trials "Works Replica"

1. Removal of the Engine from the Frame

Disconnect the battery leads and remove the battery.
Turn off the petrol and disconnect the petrol pipe.
Take the slides out of the carburettor.
Remove the air cleaner.
Remove the exhaust pipe.
Disconnect the electric horn leads.
Disconnect the control cable from the magdyno.
Disconnect the engine steady.
Remove the rear chain.
Remove the footrest bar.
Support the engine on a suitable box or wood block.
Remove the centre stand and the stand stop.
Remove the front engine plates.
Remove the bolt securing the rear engine plate to the frame.
Lift out the engine.

2. Removal of the Gearbox

Remove the primary chaincase, engine sprocket and clutch (see Section C, Subsection 24).

Remove four $\frac{3}{8}$ in. nuts and the gearbox can then be withdrawn from the engine.

3. Dismantling the Crankcase

Drain the oil tank by removing the drain plug.

Having removed the engine from the frame as described in Subsection 1, dismantle the cylinder head, barrel, piston, timing gear, magdyno, etc., as described in Section C.

Remove the nuts on the driving side of the engine from four fixed studs at the rear of the crankcase.

Remove six studs passing through the crankcase.

The two halves of the crankcase can then be separated.

The timing side double roller race and the bronze bush will remain in the timing side half of the crankcase.

The driving side outer races will remain in the driving side half of the crankcase.

The driving side inner races and the inner distance piece will remain on the engine shaft.

The flywheel assembly may be difficult to remove from the driving side of the crankcase owing to the shaft being a tight fit in the inner race of the ball bearings. This is particularly likely in the engines with two ball bearings. In this case push the shaft out of the bearings using crankshaft extractor E.5121.

4. Main Bearings

To remove the outer roller race(s) (or the inner ball race on earlier 350 Bullet engines or 350 Clipper) from the crankcase halves, heat to 100°C. or more and drop the half case sharply on a flat block of wood or bench, when the race(s) will drop out, together with the distance piece in the case of the driving side and the thrust washer in the case of the timing side.

Remove the circlip from the driving side crankcase and reheat to remove the second ball race.

To replace the bearings, heat the crankcase and press in the races in the following order:

Driving Side. Use Special Tool No. 4817.
Small steel washer.
Cork oil-retaining washer.
Large steel washer.
Ball bearing complete.
Circlip.
Outer distance piece ⎫ on
Outer roller race ⎭ 500 c.c. and later 350 c.c. engines;
or distance piece and inner ball race on 350 c.c. Bullet and Clipper engines.

Timing Side. Use Special Tool No. 4816.
Steel thrust washer.
Outer roller race(s).

Care must be taken to see that the lead on the outside of the outer roller race enters the case first to make sure that it is square with the housing.

5. Replacement of the Cam and Idler Spindles

To remove the cam spindles heat the crankcase and tap the spindles out from inside.

To remove the idler spindles heat the crankcase as before, hold the spindles in a vice and tap the crankcase lightly with a hide hammer.

To replace the spindles use Special Tool No. E.6462 which is a locating plate for all the spindles.

Start the spindles in the holes in the crankcase by tapping them lightly.

Offer the locating plate to the spindles, making sure that they are all upright. Tap the plate over the spindles until it touches the timing chest face, having first made sure that the latter is quite clean.

Drive the spindles home with a small hammer (not heavier than ½ lb.) and a drift.

Remove the locating plate.

6. Flywheel Assembly

The flywheel assembly consists of the crankshaft and the connecting rod.

To dismantle the crankshaft remove the set screws securing the crankpin nuts.

Holding the crankshaft in a special jig, No. E.2774 ("500 Bullet") or E.2775 ("350 Bullet" or "350 Clipper"), remove the crankpin nuts.

Using E.2774 or E.2775 with a pair of steel bars (about 1 in. × ⅜ in. × 9 in. long) placed across, press out the crankpin with a hand press.

The connecting rod can then be removed.

Turn the crankshaft over in the jig and repeat with the other side if necessary.

To remove the timing side mainshaft, take the set screw from the shaft nut and unscrew the nut. Drive the shaft out with a hammer and drift. To replace the timing side shaft, reverse the above process, making sure that the key is a good fit and that the nut is tightened securely by means of a box spanner with a 12 in. tommy bar.

The driving shaft has no nut but is secured by tightening the sprocket nut after the assembly of the engine. It should be pressed in and out with a hand press or a hammer and drift. If the latter is used care must be taken not to damage the centre.

To reassemble the crankshaft, press the crankpin into the timing side flywheel, making sure that the oil hole is in the correct position and that the thrust washer is facing the right way, i.e. with chamfer **away** from the flywheel.

Test the oil passages with an air line or oil gun to make sure that they are clear.

Put the floating bush over the crankpin.

Put the connecting rod over the floating bush.

Place the other thrust washer over the crankpin, **also with the chamfer away from the flywheel.**

Press the driving side flywheel on.

Put the flywheel in the assembly jig, to ensure that the flywheels and shafts are in line and replace the nuts, tighten securely and refit the set screws.

Test the oil passages again to ensure that they are clear.

If the same crankpin has been put back, it will be necessary to drill out the grub screw, in order to clean the oil passages after which a new grub screw must be fitted.

Mount the crankshaft between centres and true up to ·0005 in. on either side of the shafts.

If the readings for the two shafts are high on opposite sides, the error can be corrected by gently tapping either or both of the flywheels.

If the readings are high on the same side of the two shafts, it is probably due to dirt or foreign matter in the joints and the crankshaft should be dismantled again, carefully examined and cleaned and reassembled.

7. Reassembly of the Crankcase

Replace the bearings, etc., in the crankcase halves as described in Subsection 4.

Fit the inner distance piece and the rollers and cage, where fitted, in the driving side crankcase.

Lay the thrust washer on the bearing.

Assemble the flywheel into the bearing, if necessary using the sprocket nut with suitable packing piece to draw the driving shaft through the inner race(s) of the ball bearing(s).

Make sure that the crankcase face is clean and apply jointing compound to it.

Put the thrust washer on the timing side shaft and the rollers and cage.

Put the magdyno or magneto straps over the studs in the timing side crankcase and place the latter in position over the flywheel.

Bolt the two halves of the crankcase together, making sure that the joint matches correctly so that the cylinder base is flat.

SECTION E9

Gearbox and Clutch

"350 and 500 Bullet" 1956 onwards, "350 Clipper" and Trials "Works Replica" 1958 onwards

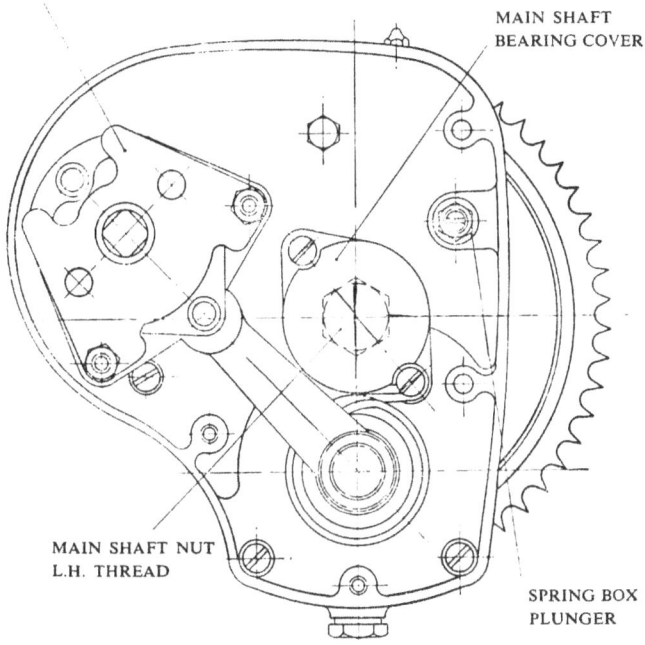

GEARBOX WITH OUTER COVER REMOVED
Fig. 1

1. Removal of Gearbox

This is described in Section D.

The gearbox can, however, be completely dismantled with the engine in the frame except for the removal of the inside operator and the bearings in the gearbox shell.

2. To Dismantle the Gearbox

First remove the kickstart crank, the change-gear lever and the neutral finder and pointer.

Remove the top small inspection cover and disconnect the clutch cable.

Remove four screws and the gearbox outer cover can then be detached.

Remove the change-gear mechanism by taking off the two nuts securing it.

Remove the main shaft bearing cover which is attached by two screws.

Remove four cheese-headed screws and one hexagon bolt.

Remove the spring box locating plunger nut and washer.

Remove the main shaft nut (**Left Hand Thread**).

The gearbox inner cover can then be removed.

The mainshaft can be drawn straight out if the clutch has been removed, which, however, should be done before taking off the gearbox inner cover. (See Section C.) The top gear pinion and dog will come away with the mainshaft.

The layshaft can then be removed and the 2nd and 3rd gears drawn off the final drive sleeve together with the operator fork.

To take out the final drive sleeve, the final drive

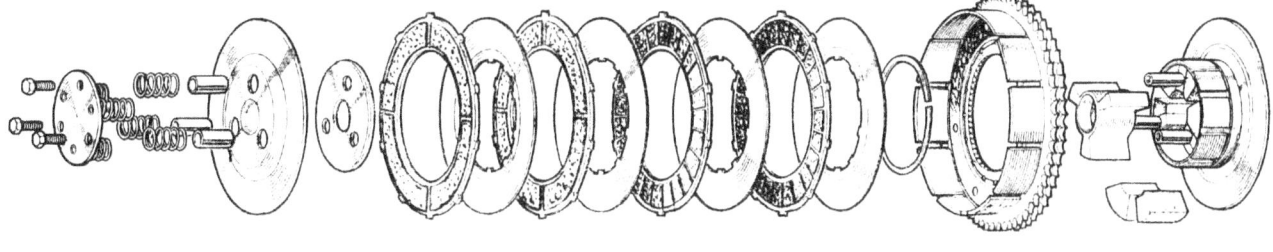

EXPLODED VIEW OF CLUTCH ("500 BULLET" AND TRIALS "WORKS REPLICA")
Fig. 2

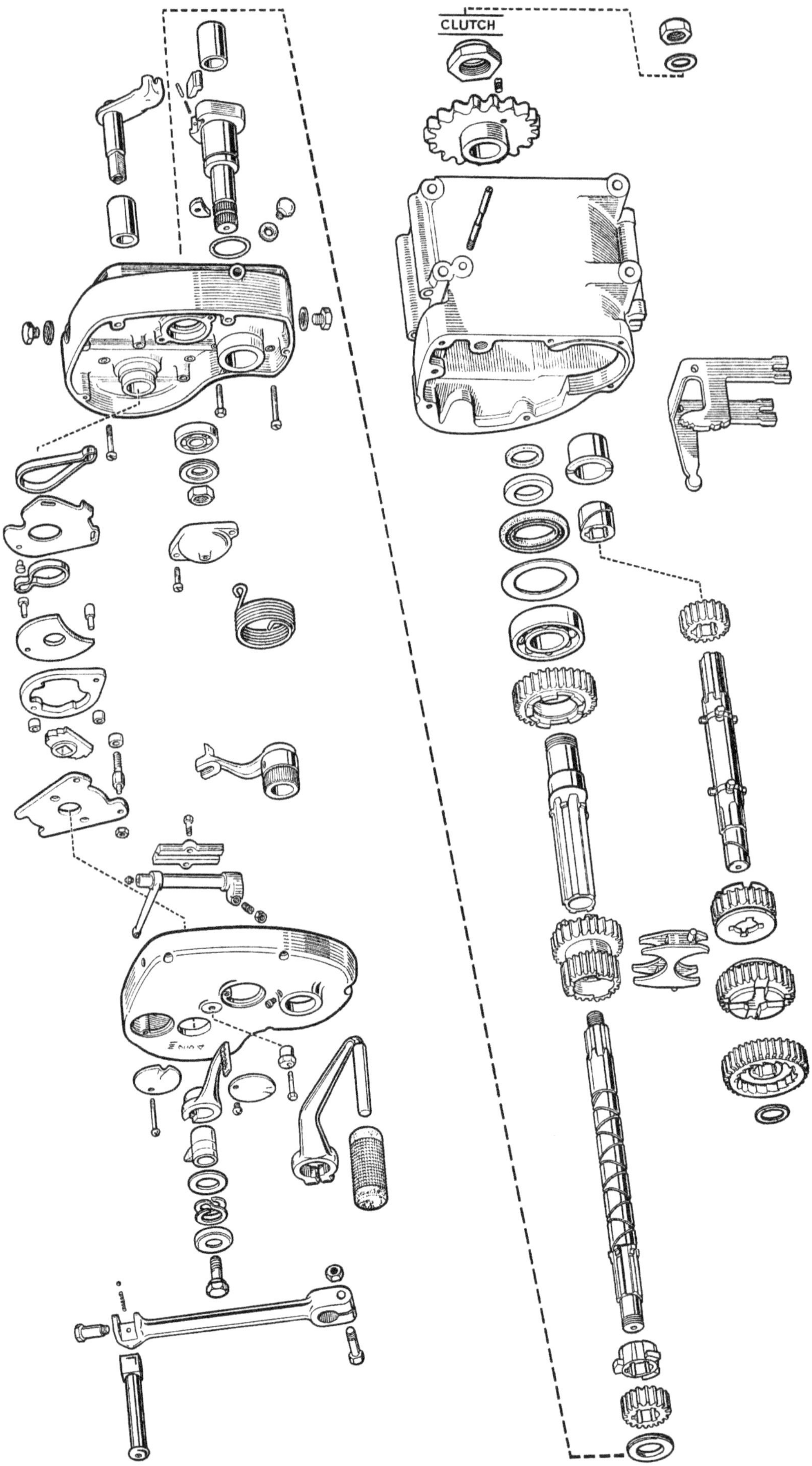

EXPLODED VIEW OF GEARBOX
Fig. 3

sprocket must be removed and this is preferably done before removing the inner cover. (See Section C.)

3. Removal of the Ball Races

The mainshaft ball bearings can be removed by using a stepped drift $1\frac{7}{16}$ in.—$1\frac{11}{64}$ in. diameter for the bearing in the box and $\frac{13}{16}$ in.—$\frac{39}{64}$ in. diameter for the bearing in the cover.

When refitting the bearings stepped drifts of $2\frac{5}{16}$ in.—$1\frac{11}{64}$ in. diameter and $1\frac{11}{16}$ in.—$\frac{39}{64}$ in. diameter must be used for the bearings in the box and cover respectively.

Note the felt washer in the recess behind the larger main shaft bearing and the dished pen-steel washer between the bearing and the felt washer. The second dished pen-steel washer, if fitted, has a smaller central hole and is on the other side of the main shaft bearing and is nipped between the inner face of the bearing and the shoulder on the final drive sleeve. See that both of the dished pen-steel washers have their raised portions facing towards the clutch and final drive sprocket.

4. Change-Gear Mechanism

If the two nuts securing the change-gear ratchet mechanism are slackened, the adjuster plate can be set in the correct position. In this position the movement of the gear lever necessary to engage the ratchet teeth will be approximately the same in each direction.

If the plate is incorrectly adjusted, it may be found that, after moving from top to third or from bottom to second gear, the outer ratchets do not engage the teeth on the inner ratchets correctly.

If, when fitting new parts, it is found that the gears do not engage properly, ascertain whether a little more movement is required or whether there is too much movement so that the gear slips right through second or third gear into neutral. If more movement is required, this can be obtained by filing the adjuster plate very slightly at the points of contact with the pegs on the ratchet ring.

If too much movement is already present, a new adjuster plate giving less movement must be fitted.

5. Re-assembling the Gearbox

The procedure is the reverse of that given in Subsection 2 but the following points should be noted:—

If the main shaft top gear pinion and dog have been removed, make sure that the dog is replaced the right way round or third and top gears can be engaged simultaneously.

Make sure that the trunnions on the operator fork engage with the slots in the inside operator.

See that the main shaft is pushed right home. (It may tighten in the felt washer inside the final drive shaft nut.)

The layshaft top gear and kickstarter pinion should be assembled on the layshaft and the kickstarter shaft and ratchet assembled on to it before fitting the end cover. Do not forget the washer on the layshaft between the kickstarter pinion and the kickstarter shaft.

The joint between the gearbox and the inner cover should be made with gold size, shellac or a similar jointing compound.

Make sure that all parts are clean before commencing assembly. In normal climates the recesses in the gearbox should be packed with soft grease and the box should be filled up to the correct level with engine oil. (See Subsection 9.) **On no account must heavy yellow grease be used.**

6. Dismantling and Re-assembly of the Clutch

The method of removing the clutch is described in Section C. When re-assembling, the following order must be observed:

"500 Bullet" and "Works Replica"
Plain dished plate (dish projecting outwards).
Friction plate (24 inserts).
Plain flat plate.
Friction plate (24 inserts).
Plain flat plate.
Friction plate (bonded $\frac{1}{4}$ segments).
Plain dished plate (dish projecting inwards).
Friction plate (bonded $\frac{1}{4}$ segments).

"350 Bullet" and "350 Clipper"
Order of assembly is as above, but with two friction plates (24 inserts) and one friction plate (bonded $\frac{1}{4}$ segments) only, and one plain plate less.

Do not forget to replace the cush rubber and retaining plate before fitting the pressure plate.

Make sure that the distance tubes inside three of the springs pass through the holes in the pressure plate. The other three springs are located by means of bosses on the clutch cap.

Tighten the spring pins as far as they will go.

If the clutch lifts unevenly it is probable that one of the springs has taken a set, in which case new springs should be fitted.

7. Adjustment of the Clutch Control

It is essential that there should be about $\frac{1}{16}$ in. free movement in the clutch cable, to ensure that all the spring pressure is exerted on the plates.

There are two points of adjustment for the clutch cable. The first is at the top of the gearbox just behind the oil filler plug and is provided for taking up any stretch in the cable. The adjustment is made by screwing the collar in or out of the gearbox shell. The connection between the end

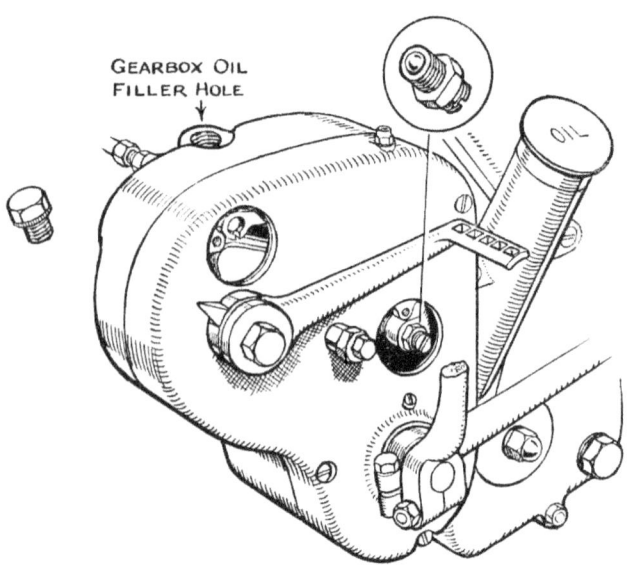

CLUTCH ADJUSTMENT ON CURRENT GEARBOXES
Fig. 4

of the cable and the horizontal lever can be seen if the top small inspection cover on the front of the gearbox is removed. Tighten the locknut on the screwed collar after adjustment has been made.

The other point of adjustment is behind the lower inspection cover on the front of the gearbox and is for compensating for wear on the clutch

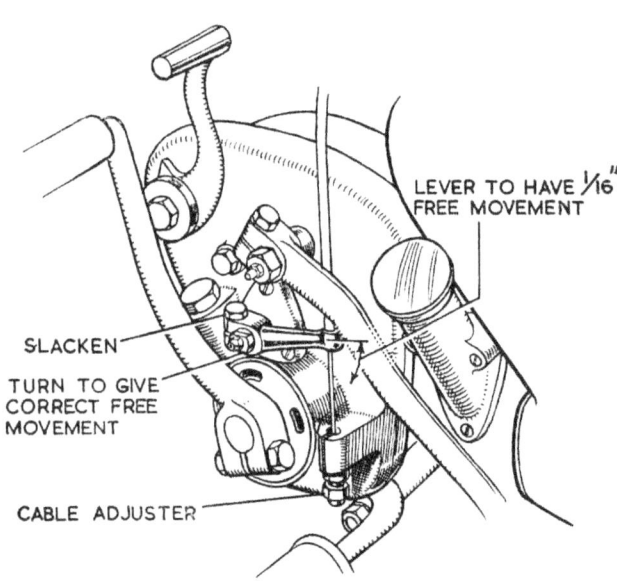

CLUTCH LEVER AND CABLE ADJUSTMENTS ON EARLY GEARBOXES
Fig. 5

plate inserts. To make the adjustment, remove the inspection cover, slacken the locknut and turn the central screw. Tighten the locknut after adjustment has been made.

The reason for the two points of adjustment is to enable the lever behind the cover to be kept in its proper position whether the need for adjustment is caused by plate wear or cable stretch.

Owing to initial bedding down of the clutch plate inserts, the clutch control may require adjustment after the first few hundred miles with a new machine. This point should therefore be examined soon after delivery and adjustment made if necessary.

On earlier models the clutch operating mechanism is exposed on the front of the gearbox, but the adjustments are, however, the same in principle as those described above.

The cable adjustment is at the bottom of the front of the gearbox just in front of the kickstart lever. The collar is screwed in or out of a lug on the gearbox cover and is secured by a locknut as before.

The other adjustment is made by slackening the clamping bolt in the horizontal lever and turning the lever on its spindle, which is the end of the operating worm in the gearbox cover.

When correctly adjusted, the lever should be approximately square with the cable when the clutch is fully lifted.

The position of the lever endwise on the worm spindle is important and it should be positioned so that it does not foul the kickstart lever.

8. Adjustment of the Neutral Finder

The neutral finder is adjusted by means of an eccentric stop secured to the front of the gearbox cover by a bolt which limits the travel of the operating pedal. Slacken the bolt and turn the eccentric until the correct movement of the pedal is obtained.

9. Gearbox Oil Level

The gearbox is replenished with oil by removing a plug in the top and the correct level can be checked by removing a second plug lower down on the right hand side looking at the cover.

On earlier models a dip-stick is attached to the filler plug for measuring the level of the oil or was provided loose in the tool kit.

On some models the filler plug is on the side of the gearbox and in such cases the oil should be level with the plug hole and no dip-stick is required. The oil will be found to run into the box more easily on these models if the engine is started up and allowed to tick over so that the gears and shafts rotate.

The oil capacity is $\frac{3}{4}$ pint.

SECTION F4

Amal Monobloc Carburetter

1. General Description

The Amal Monobloc Carburetter has been introduced as an improvement on the earlier standard needle type. In general it gives better petrol consumption, combined with improved starting and acceleration from low speeds and a small increase in maximum speed.

The float chamber is integral with the mixing chamber and contains a pivoted barrel-shaped float operating on a nylon fuel needle. There is a considerable leverage ratio between the float and the needle and, in consequence, flooding is rare unless there is dirt on the needle seating.

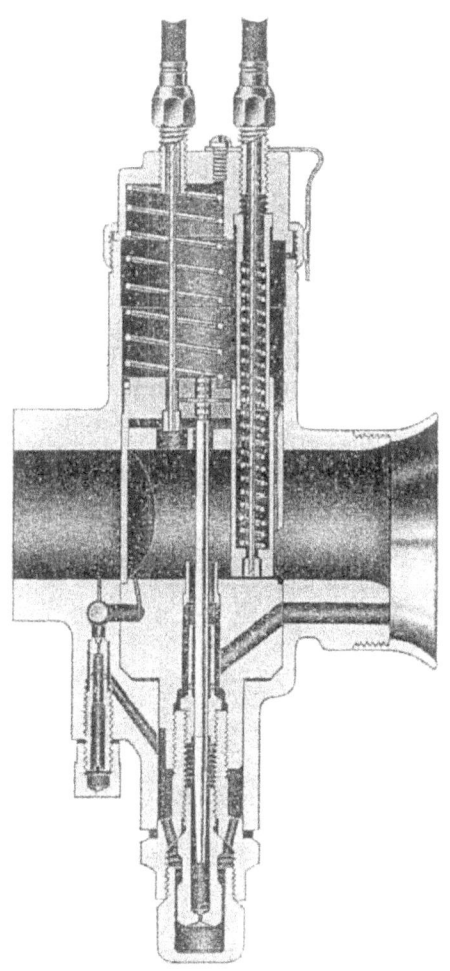

SECTION THROUGH MIXING CHAMBER, SHOWING AIR VALVE AND THROTTLE CLOSED

Fig. 1

The supply of air to the engine is controlled by a throttle slide which carries a taper needle operating in the needle jet. The needle is secured to the throttle slide by a spring clip fitting in one of five grooves and the mixture strength throughout a large proportion of the throttle range is controlled by the position of this needle in the slide and by the size of the jet in which it works. There is, however, a restricting or main jet at the bottom of the needle jet and the size of this controls the mixture strength at the largest throttle openings. At very small throttle openings petrol and air are fed to the engine through a separate pilot system, which has an outlet at the engine side of the throttle. The air supply to this pilot system is controlled by the pilot air screw and the slow running of the engine can be adjusted by means of this screw and a stop which holds the throttle open a very small amount. The throttle slide is cut away at the back and the shape of this cut-away controls the mixture at throttle openings slightly wider than that required for slow running. There is a compensating system to prevent undue enriching of the mixture with increasing engine speed, this system consisting of a primary choke surrounding the upper end of the needle jet through which air is drawn in increasing quantities as the depression in the main choke increases. This air supply and the supply to the pilot system are taken from two separate ducts in the main air intake to the carburetter so that all the air passing to the engine can be filtered by fitting an air cleaner to the main carburetter air intake.

Two small cross holes in the needle jet, at a level just below the static level in the float chamber, permit petrol to flow into the primary choke when the engine is not running or when it is running at very low speeds, thus forming a well of petrol which will be drawn into the engine on starting or accelerating from low speeds. At moderately high engine speeds the level of petrol in the float chamber falls slightly and in consequence no more fuel flows through the cross holes in the needle jet so that the petrol well remains empty until the engine slows down or stops.

A handlebar controlled air slide is provided to enrich the mixture temporarily when required.

2. Tuning the Carburetter(s)

The throttle opening at which each tuning point is most effective is shown in Fig. 2. It should be remembered, however, that a change of setting at any point will have some effect on the setting required at other points; for instance, a change of main jet will have some effect on the mixture strength at half throttle which, however, is mainly controlled by the needle position. Similarly an alteration to the throttle cut-away may affect both the needle position required and the adjustment of the pilot air screw. For this reason it is necessary to tune the carburetter in a definite sequence, which is as follows:

First—Main Jet. The size should be chosen which gives maximum speed at full throttle with the air control wide open. If two different sizes of jet give the same speed the larger should be chosen for safety as it is dangerous to run with too weak a mixture at full throttle.

Second—The pilot air screw should be set to give good idling. Note that the pilot jet is detachable and two sizes are available, 25 c.c. and 30 c.c. If the pilot air adjusting screw requires to be screwed out less than half a turn the larger size pilot jet should be used; if the air screw requires to be screwed out more than 2-3 turns fit the smaller size of pilot jet.

PHASES OF AMAL MONOBLOC CARBURETTER THROTTLE OPENINGS

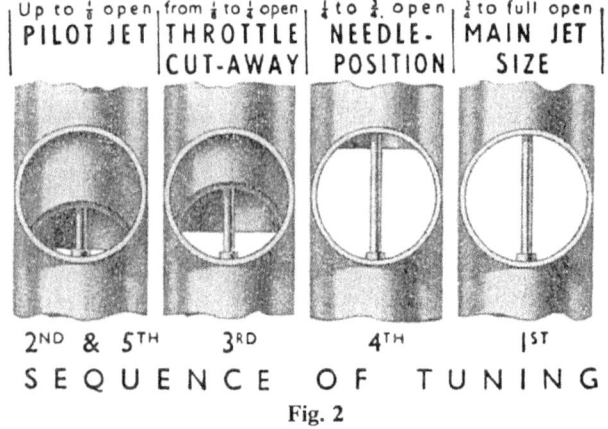

Fig. 2

Third—the throttle valve should be selected with the largest amount of cut-away which will prevent spitting or misfiring when opening the throttle slowly from the idling position.

Fourth—The lowest position of the taper needle should be found consistent with good acceleration with the air slide wide open.

Fifth—The pilot air screw should be checked to improve the idling if possible. When setting the adjustment of the pilot air screw this should be done in conjunction with the throttle stop. Note that the correct setting of the air screw is the one which gives the fastest idling speed for a given position of the throttle stop. If the idling speed is then undesirably fast it can be slowed down by unscrewing the throttle stop a fraction of a turn.

It will be noted that of the four points at which adjustments are normally made, i.e., pilot air screw, throttle cut-away, needle position and main jet size, the first and third do not require changing of any parts of the carburetter. Assuming that the carburetter has the standard setting to suit the particular type of engine any small adjustments occasioned by atmospheric conditions, changes in quality of fuel, etc., can usually be covered by adjustment of the pilot air screw and raising or lowering the taper needle one notch. If, however, the machine is used at very high altitudes or with a very restricted air cleaner a smaller main jet will be necessary. The following table gives the reduction in main jet size required at different altitudes:

Altitude, ft.	Reduction, %
3,000	5
6,000	9
9,000	13
12,000	17

In the case of carburetters for engine running on alcohol fuel considerably larger jets are needed. In most cases a No. 113 needle jet will be required and the main jet size will require to be increased by an amount varying from 50% to 150% according to the grade of fuel used.

If the engine is run on fuel containing a small proportion of alcohol added to the petrol, a rough and ready guide is that the main jet should be increased by 1% for every 1% of alcohol in the fuel. In most cases alcohol blends available from petrol pumps do not contain sufficient alcohol to require any alteration to the carburetter setting.

The range of adjustment of the taper needle and the pilot air screw are determined by the size of the needle jet and of the pilot outlet respectively. Standard needle jets have a bore at the smallest point of ·1065 in. and are marked 106. Alternative needle jets ·1055 in., ·1075 in., ·109 in. and ·113 in. bore are available and are marked 105, 107, 109 and 113 respectively.

The standard pilot outlet bore is ·025 in. but in some cases larger size pilot outlets are used. Since the pilot outlet is actually drilled in the body of the carburetter it is necessary to have a carburetter with the correct size pilot outlet if the best results are to be obtained.

The accompanying table shows the standard settings for Amal Monobloc Carburetters used on Royal Enfield motor cycles.

Both instruments used for the twin carburetter "Constellation" are identical in all respects but for the float chamber arrangement, which is as follows:

Carburetter type 376/242 supplies the left-hand cylinder and has an integral float chamber which

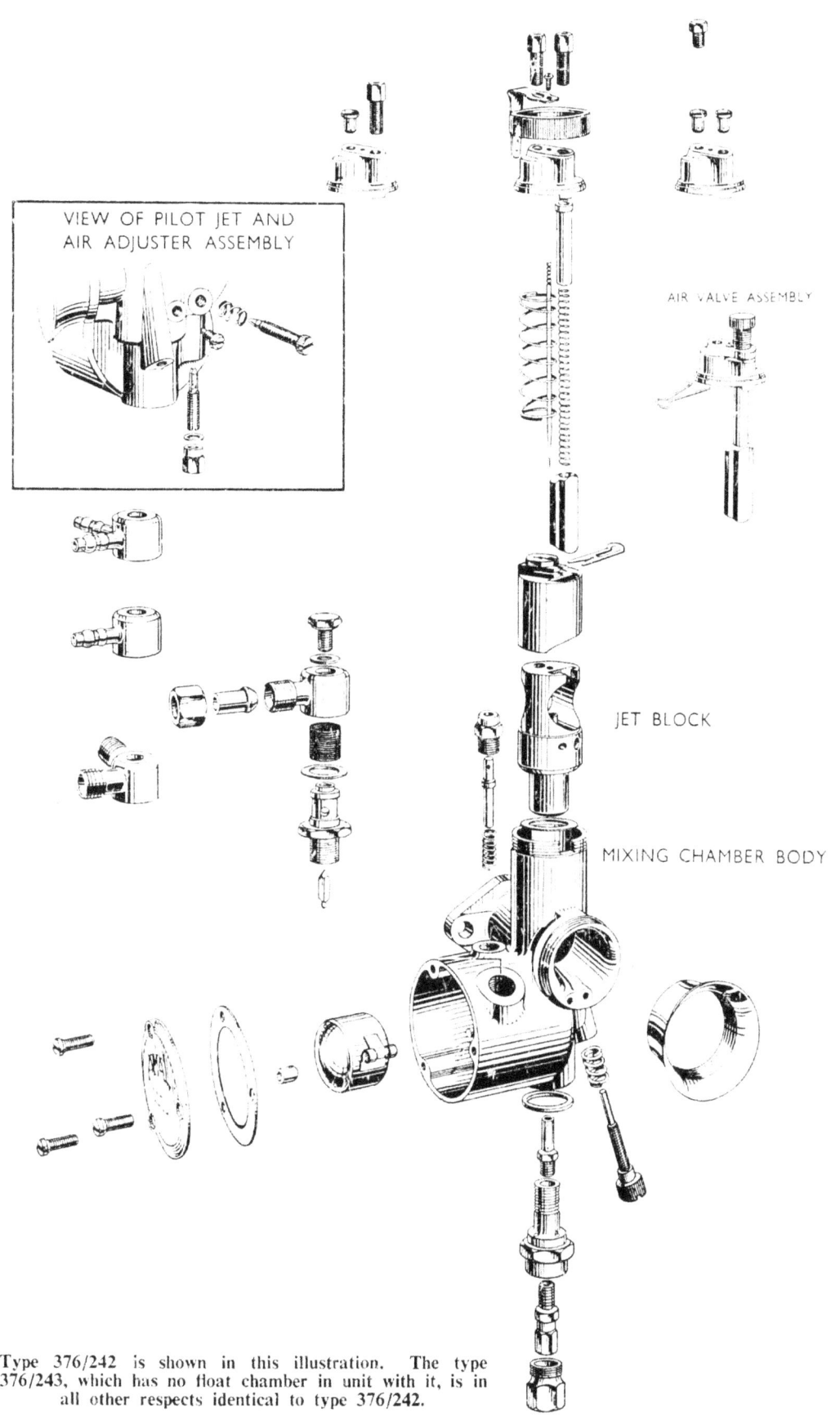

Type 376/242 is shown in this illustration. The type 376/243, which has no float chamber in unit with it, is in all other respects identical to type 376/242.

Fig. 3

also controls the fuel supply via a connecting pipe to the right-hand instrument type 376/243; this does not have a float chamber in unit with it.

It is important that the pilot air screws of both carburetters are in identical positions, relative to one another, the same applying to the throttle valves when seated on their stops. This is essential for an even smooth tickover and low-speed running. The speed of the tickover is regulated by these four adjuster screws. For an instant pick-up, both throttle valves must commence to rise from their stops simultaneously, when the twist grip is rotated. This is obtained by adjusting the twin control cables. Each main jet needle must be in the third groove.

Both air slides, operated from a single handlebar lever, must open and close identically, as failure to do this may result in one slide not opening fully, with a resultant loss of power.

It is most important that all of these adjustments are carried out in a thorough and careful manner if the maximum power and smoothness is to be obtained.

The "ears" to be found on the leading edges of the battery and toolbox lids are to shield the carburetter air intakes and so prevent misfiring at maximum revs.

3. Dismantling Carburetter

The construction of the carburetter is clearly shown in Fig. 3.

If the float chamber floods, first make sure that there is no dirt on the fuel needle seating. Owing to the use of a nylon needle and the leverage ratio between float and needle, flooding is very unlikely with this type of carburetter unless dirt is present or, of course, the float is punctured.

If it is necessary to remove the jet block note that this is withdrawn from the upper end of the mixing chamber after unscrewing the jet holder. Be careful not to damage the jet block when removing or refitting it. Note that the large diameter of the jet block pulls down on to a thin washer.

A single strand of an inner control cable is useful for clearing the small passages in the jet block and care must be taken not to enlarge these by forcing the wire through them. Compressed air from a pipe line or a tyre pump is preferable. A choked main jet should be cleared only by blowing through it.

4. Causes of High Petrol Consumption

If the petrol consumption is excessive first look for leaks either from the carburetter, petrol pipe, petrol tap(s) or tank. If coloured petrol is in use this will readily indicate the presence of any small leaks which otherwise might pass unnoticed. If the petrol system is free from leaks, carefully set the pilot adjusting screw as described in Subsection 2 to give the correct mixture when idling. Running with the pilot adjusting screw too far in is a common cause of excessive petrol consumption. If the consumption is still heavy try the effect of lowering the taper needle in the throttle slide by one notch. Do not fit a smaller main jet as this will not affect consumption except when driving on nearly full throttle and may make the mixture too weak at large throttle openings, thus causing overheating.

Settings for AMAL carburetters on ROYAL ENFIELD motor cycles

Machine	Carburetter Type No.	Choke Bore in.	Main Jet c.c.	Needle Jet	Needle Position	Throttle Valve	Pilot Jet c.c.
"250 Clipper" 1955 (late), 1956, 1957 and 1958 (early)	375/10	$\frac{25}{32}$	120	105	3	375/060/4	25
"Crusader 250" 1957 onwards "250 Clipper" 1958 (late) and 1959 onwards	375/16	$\frac{7}{8}$	120	105	3	375/060/3½	25
"Crusader Sports" 1959 onwards and "250 Trials" 1962 onwards	376/216	$\frac{15}{16}$	150	106	3	376/060/3½	25
"Crusader Super 5" 1962 onwards	376/283	1	170	106	3	376/3½	25
"350 Bullet" 1955 (late), 1956-7-8 and "350 Clipper" 1958 onwards	376/29	1	180	106	3	376/060/4	30
"350 Bullet" 1959 onwards	376/215	1 $\frac{1}{16}$	190	106	3	376/060/4	30
"Works Replica" 1958 onwards	376/29	1	180	106	3	376/060/4	30
"500 Bullet" 1956-58	389/9	1 $\frac{1}{8}$	200	106	2	389/060/3½	30
"500 Bullet" 1959 onwards	389/34	1 $\frac{3}{16}$	*220	106	3	389/060/3½	30
"Meteor Minor" 1958 onwards	376/92	1 $\frac{1}{16}$	250	106	2	376/060/3½	30
"Meteor Minor Sports" 1960 onwards	376/92	1 $\frac{1}{16}$	250	106	2	376/060/3½	30
"Super Meteor" 1956 onwards	376/41	1 $\frac{1}{16}$	240	106	3	376/060/3½	30
"Constellation" 1960 onwards	L/hand 376/242 R/hand 376/243	1 $\frac{1}{16}$	320	106	3	376/060/4	25

* With Air Cleaner. Main Jet 250 without Air Cleaner.

SECTION G1e

Lucas Rotating Magnet Magneto Model SR1

Used on "350 Bullet" 1956-59; "500 Bullet" 1956-59

1. General

The magneto rotor comprises a permanent magnet fitted with two laminated pole shoes. The stator consists of laminated pole pieces bridged by a laminated coil core. The coil has concentrically wound primary and secondary windings.

The rotor is driven by the engine through an automatic advance coupling and induces an alternating magnetic field in the laminated iron core of the coil. This field in turn induces alternating voltages in the primary and secondary windings of the coil. Magnetic flux due to current flowing in the primary winding tends to oppose any change in direction of the magnetic field in the laminated iron core. In this way, field reversals due to the rotating magnet are delayed until the contact breaker opens. This removes the restraining influence of the primary winding and the consequent rapid reversal of the magnetic flux linked with the coil causes a high voltage to be induced in the secondary winding.

The body of the magneto is formed of a single casting enclosed at the contact breaker end by a moulded cover. The cover is designed with the high tension cable outlet in a downward direction, thus preventing the retention of moisture at the terminal connection. The coil and capacitor are robustly constructed and specially treated to withstand very arduous conditions.

2. Routine Maintenance

(a) **Lubrication:**

TAKE GREAT CARE TO PREVENT OIL OR GREASE GETTING ON OR NEAR THE CONTACTS.

(i) After 1,000 running hours (say 30,000 miles) remove the moulded cover, slacken the nut securing the end of the contact breaker spring and lift off the moving-contact assembly. Smear the pivot pin with a small quantity of Mobilgrease No. 2 or its equivalent.

(ii) The magneto rotor is mounted on ball bearings. These bearings are packed with high melting point grease before leaving the factory and require no attention for a considerable time. About every two years, or when the engine is undergoing a general overhaul, the magneto should be dismantled by a Lucas Service Depot or Agent and the bearings repacked with high melting point grease.

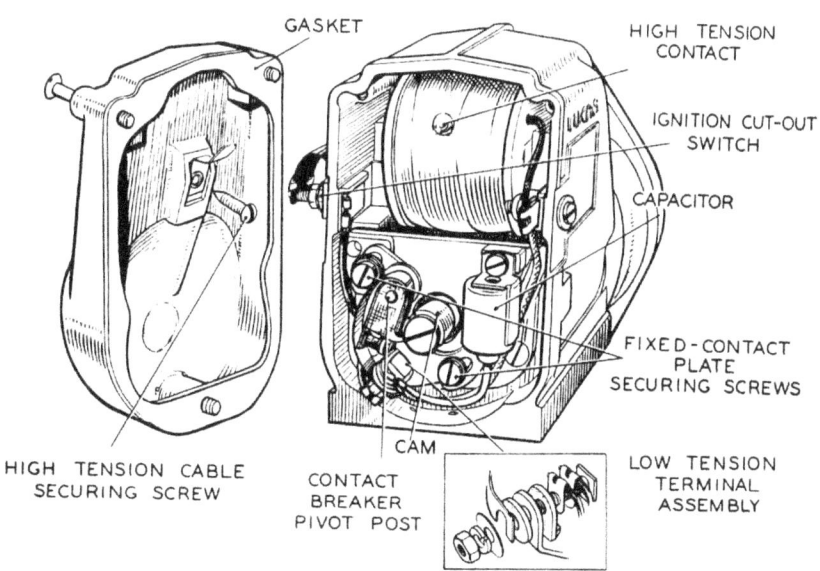

MAGNETO MODEL SR1 WITH COVER REMOVED
Fig. 1

(b) Cleanings

(i) Occasionally remove the moulded cover and wipe the inside of the cover with a soft dry cloth. Clean the outside of the cover before replacing it.

(ii) Examine the contact breaker. If the contacts are burnt or dirty clean them by polishing with a very fine carborundum stone or fine emery cloth. The contacts may be cleaned more easily if the moving contact assembly is removed, as Sub-section 2 (a) (i).

(c) Adjusting Contact Breaker

After cleaning check the gap between the contacts. Turn the engine until the contacts show the maximum opening which should measure 0·010 in. to 0·012 in. If the setting is incorrect slacken the two screws securing the fixed-contact plate and move the plate until the correct gap is obtained. Tighten the securing screws and measure the gap again.

(d) Replacement of High Tension Cable

Use 7 mm. neoprene-covered rubber ignition cable for the high tension lead. When connecting a new cable to the magneto do not bare the cable but cut it off flush to the required length. Remove the moulded cover, slacken the cable retaining screw and pull out the old cable. Push the new cable fully home and secure by tightening the screw. The pointed end of this will pierce the insulation, make contact with the cable core and lock the cable in place. After fitting a high tension cable a continuity test should be made between the cover electrode and plug end of the cable.

3. Servicing

To locate cause of misfiring or failure of ignition, check as follows :—

(i) Remove the sparking plug from the engine. Hold the end of the high tension cable about $\frac{1}{8}$ in. from the cylinder block and operate the kick-starter. If strong and regular sparking is produced the sparking plug should be cleaned and adjusted.

(ii) If no sparking is produced, examine the high tension cable and if necessary renew it as described in Sub-section 2 (d).

NOTE: In no circumstances must the contact breaker cam be removed from or turned on the spindle. The cam is correctly positioned when the magneto is built and the performance of the instrument depends on this position being maintained.

4. Automatic Advance Mechanism

This is automatically lubricated and requires no attention beyond making sure that it operates freely and the springs are securely fastened. For timing instructions see Section C5, Subsection 4.

SECTION G2k

Lucas A.C. Lighting-Ignition System

Used on "350 Bullet and 500 Bullet," "350 Clipper" and Trials "Works Replica" 1960 onwards

1. General

The Lucas A.C. Lighting-Ignition System comprises seven main components:

(1) Alternator with magnet rotor.
(2) Bridge-connected rectifier.
(3) Ignition coil.
(4) Contact breaker unit, and automatic timing control.
(5) Lighting switch.
(6) Ignition switch.
(7) 6-volt battery (see Section G4a).

Under normal running conditions, electrical energy in the form of rectified A.C. passes through the battery from the alternator, the rate of charge depending on the position of the lighting switch. When no lights are in use, the alternator output is sufficient only to trickle charge the battery. When the lighting switch is turned to the "Pilot" or "Head" positions the current increases proportionately.

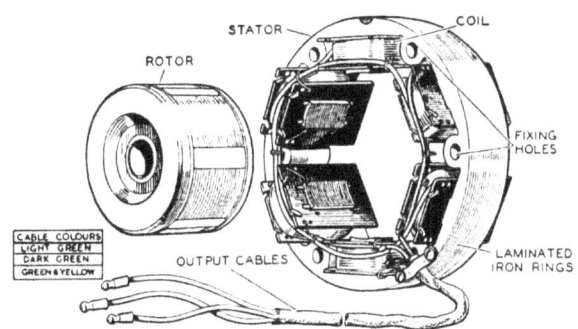

STATOR AND ROTOR OF ALTERNATOR RM15
Fig. 1

2. Alternator Models RM14 and RM15

Early models are fitted with type RM14 alternator, which has an outside diameter of $5\frac{7}{8}$ in. Later models are fitted with type RM15 (see Fig. 1) with an outside diameter of 5 in. They give a high output at low r.p.m. The alternator comprises two main components, a stator and a rotor. The stator is built up from iron laminations and carries three pairs of series-connected coils insulated from the laminations. The rotor has a hexagonal steel core, each face of which carries a permanent magnet keyed to a laminated pole tip. The pole tips are riveted circumferentially to brass side plates, the assembly being cast in aluminium and machined to give a smooth external finish. The stator and rotor can be separated without the need to fit magnetic keepers to the rotor poles.

As the rotor turns, rapid and repeated reversals of flux take place in the coil cores. These lines cut through the turns of the coil and induce alternating voltages in that coil. External connections are taken to these coils from a bridge-connected rectifier (see Fig. 2).

3. Circuit Detail

The alternator stator carries three pairs of series connected coils, one pair being permanently connected across the rectifier bridge network. The purpose of this latter pair is to provide some degree of charging current for the battery whenever the engine is running.

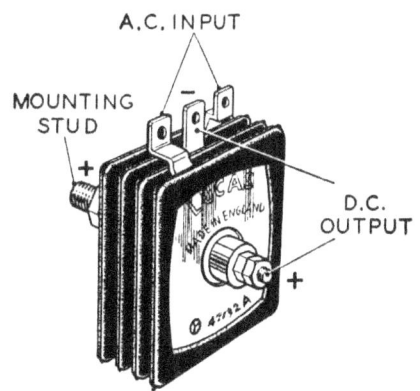

GENERAL VIEW OF RECTIFIER
Fig. 2

Connections to the remaining coils vary according to the position of the lighting and ignition switch controls, as shown schematically in Fig. 3.

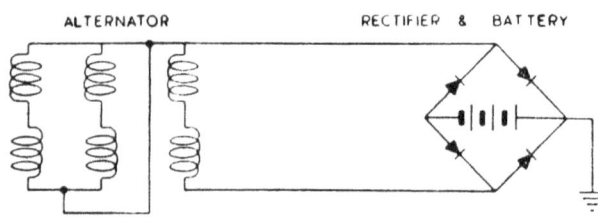

(a) LIGHTING SWITCH AT "OFF"

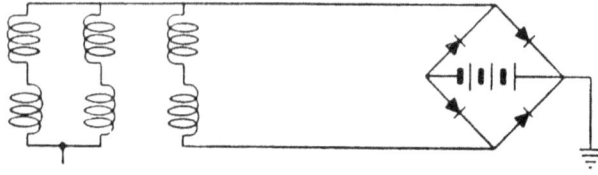

(b) LIGHTING SWITCH AT "PILOT"

(c) LIGHTING SWITCH AT "HEAD"
INTERNAL CONNECTIONS OF ALTERNATOR

CIRCUIT DIAGRAMS FOR POSITIONS OF LIGHTING SWITCH

Fig. 3

When no lights are in use the alternator output is regulated to its minimum value by interaction of the rotor flux and the flux set up by current flowing in the short-circuited coils.

In the "Pilot" position these coils are disconnected and the regulating fluxes are consequently reduced. The alternator output therefore increases and compensates for the additional parking light load.

In the "Head" position the alternator output is further increased by connecting all three pairs of coils in parallel.

4. Emergency Starting

An EMERGENCY starting position is provided on the ignition switch, for use if the battery has become discharged and a normal start cannot therefore be made. Under these conditions, the alternator is connected direct to the ignition coil, allowing the engine to be started independently of the battery. It should be noted that with the ignition switch at EMG and the engine running, the battery receives a charging current, so that its terminal voltage begins to rise. This rising voltage opposes the alternator voltage, and, on single-cylinder machines in the event of a rider omitting to return the ignition key to IGN after an emergency start has been made, misfiring may occur. This will cease on turning the ignition key to the normal running position, IGN.

This system, which on a single cylinder machine could cause trouble through unwanted sparks on the compression stroke of the engine, does not do so on the twin, owing to the fact that the distributor permits the passage of a spark only when the engine is near the firing position.

5. Direct Operation

Short journeys without the battery can be made with the switch in the "EMG" position. To do this, the cable normally connected to the battery negative terminal must be connected to an earthed point on the machine. If lights are required when the battery is disconnected, use only the headlights and keep the engine speed low to prevent excessive voltage rise.

6. Routine Maintenance

The alternator and rectifier require no maintenance apart from ensuring that all connections are clean and tight.

If the rotor, stator, engine crankshaft or rear half of the chaincase have been disturbed, the air gap between the rotor and stator should be checked. If a feeler gauge of at least ·008 in. thick cannot be passed between the rotor and each of the stator poles the alignment should be checked.

If removal of the rotor becomes necessary for any purpose, there is no necessity to fit keepers to the rotor poles. When the rotor is removed wipe off any metal swarf which may have been attracted to the pole tips. Place the rotor in a clean place.

The nuts which clamp together the rectifier plate assembly must not under any circumstances be slackened. They have been carefully set during manufacture to give correct rectifier performance. A separate nut is used to secure the rectifier to the frame of the motor cycle.

7. Ignition Coil Model Q6 or MA6

The ignition coil should be kept clean and the terminals kept tight.

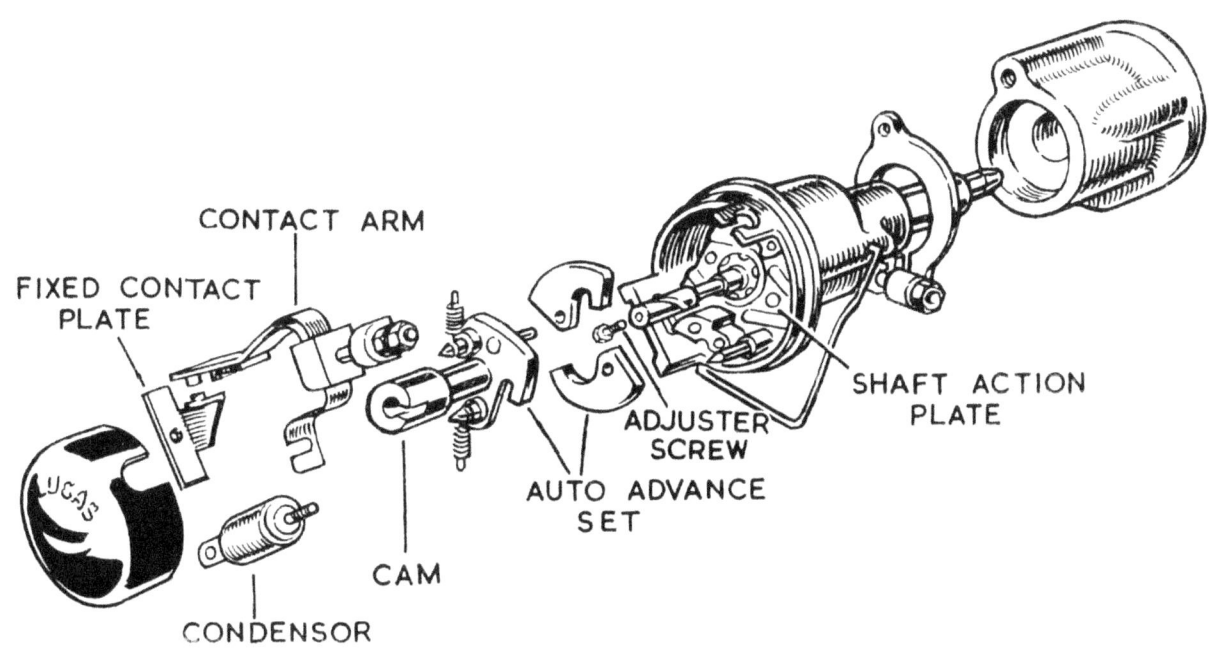

CONTACT BREAKER AND AUTOMATIC ADVANCE UNIT. MODEL 15D1

Fig. 4

8. Contact Breaker Unit

Early Models : Type CA1A

Later Models : Type 15D1

Lubrication every 3,000 miles. No grease or oil must be allowed to get on or near the contacts when carrying out the following procedure.

Smear the surface of the cam very lightly with Mobilgrease No. 2 non-creep oil or clean engine oil.

Place a spot of Ragosine oil or clean engine oil on the contact breaker pivot of type CA1A.

Contact Breaker Setting. The contact breaker setting should be checked after the first 500 miles running and subsequently every 6,000 miles. To check the gap, turn the engine over slowly until the contacts are seen to be fully open and insert a 0·014—0·016 in. feeler gauge between the contacts.

If the gap width is correct the gauge will be a sliding fit. To adjust the setting, set the engine in the position giving maximum contact opening. Slacken the two screws securing the fixed contact plate fitted to early models, and the single screw in the case of later models. Adjust the position of the plate until the gap is the thickness of the gauge, and tighten.

Automatic Timing Control

Early Models. Every 3,000 miles remove the central fixing bolt and inject a small amount of clean engine oil into the hole thus exposed. When the fixing bolt has been replaced and the engine run for a few minutes, the oil will be forced out over the automatic advance mechanism by centrifugal force.

To expose the automatic timing mechanism remove the two screws in the slotted holes of the C/B base plate.

Later Models. Remove the contact breaker cover and use clean engine oil to lubricate the automatic timing mechanism in the base of the unit. To obtain access, remove the contact breaker arm, contact plate, condenser and the screw in the end of the cam. The unit may then be lifted out.

Cleaning every 6,000 miles. Examine the contact breaker; the contacts must be free from grease or oil. If they are burnt or blackened, clean with fine carborundum stone or very fine emery cloth, afterwards wiping away any trace of dirt or metal dust with a clean petrol-moistened cloth. Cleaning of the contacts is made easier if the lever carrying the moving contact is removed.

9. Renewing High Tension Cables

If any of the high tension cables show signs of perishing or cracking they must be replaced, using 7 mm. neoprene-covered rubber ignition cable. To connect the cable to the distributor or to ignition coil model Q6, remove the metal washer and moulded terminal nut from the defective cable. Thread the new cable through the moulded terminal nut and cut back the insulation for about $\frac{1}{4}$ in. Pass the exposed strands through the metal washer and bend them back radially. Screw the terminal into the pick-up moulding.

To connect the cable to ignition coil model MA6, pass the cable through the rubber grommet, push the metal clip into the end of the cable (which should be cut off square), insert the cable and clip into the socket in the end of the coil, and slide the grommet into place to exclude water.

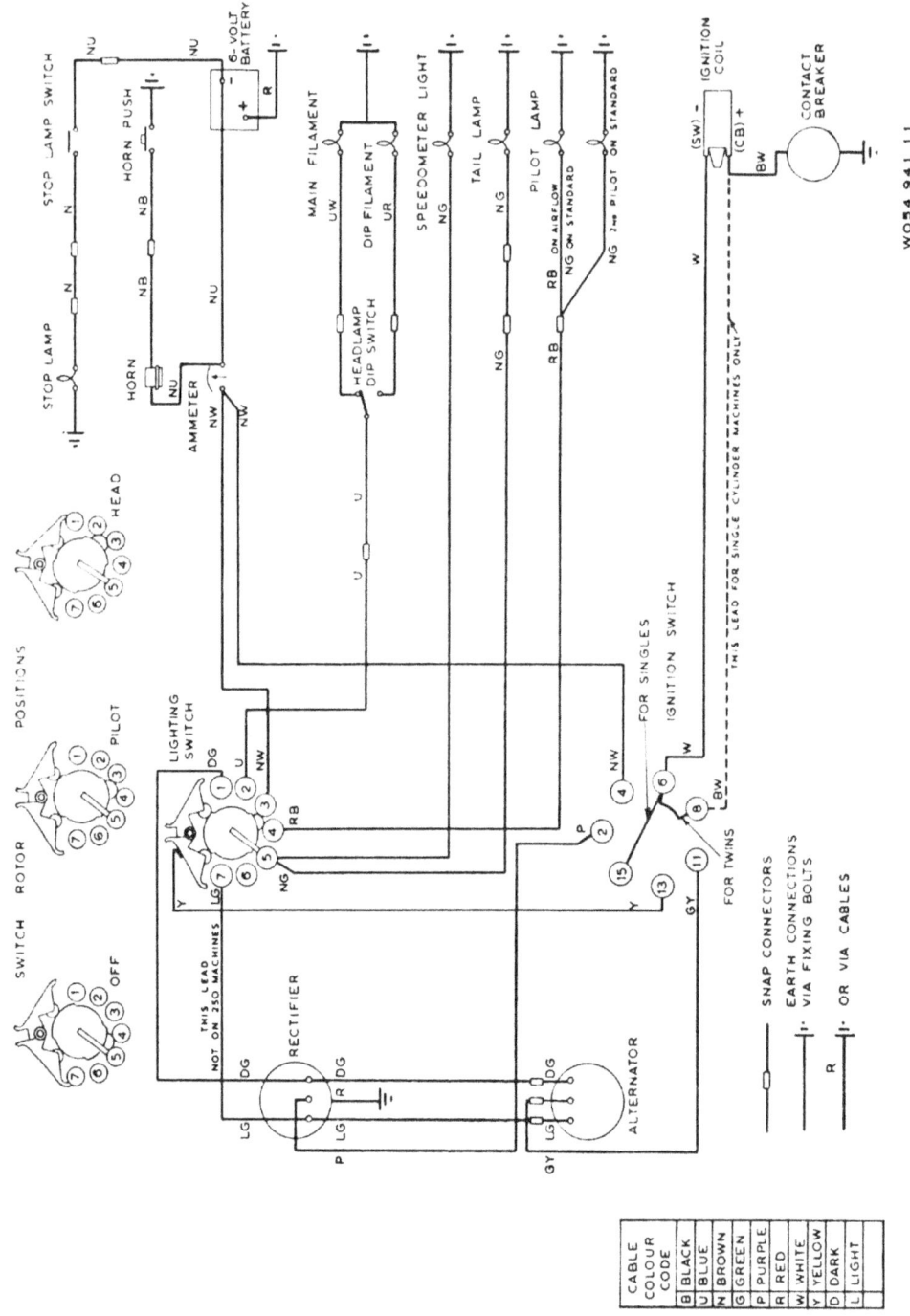

WIRING DIAGRAM

Fig. 5

SECTION G4a
Battery Model PUZ7E

1. General

The model PUZ7E (see Fig. 1) is a "dry-charged" battery and is supplied without electrolyte but with its plates in a charged condition. When the battery is required for service it is only necessary to fill each cell with sulphuric acid of the correct specific gravity. No initial charging is required, but the battery must be left to stand at least one hour after filling before putting the machine into service and then adjusting the acid level if necessary.

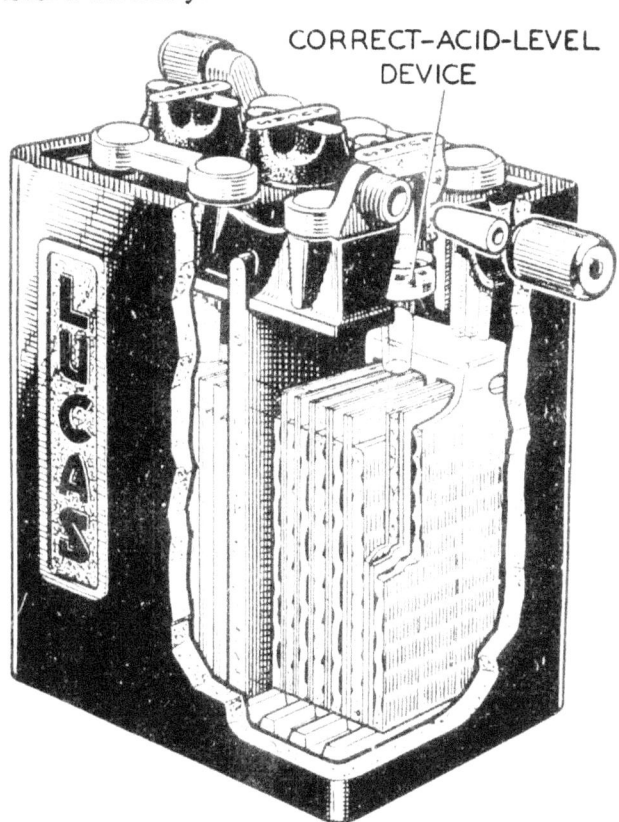

Fig. 1

2. Preparation for Service

The electrolyte is prepared by mixing together distilled water and concentrated sulphuric acid, using lead-lined tanks or suitable glass or earthenware vessels. Slowly add the acid to the water, stirring with a glass rod. Never add water to the acid, as this causes dangerous spurting of the concentrated acid. The specific gravity of the filling electrolyte depends on the climate in which the battery is to be used.

Specific gravity of electrolyte for filling "dry-charged" batteries:

Climates below 90°F. (32°C.)	Climates above 90°F. (32°C.)
Filling, 1·270	Filling, 1·210

The approximate proportions of acid and water to obtain these specific gravities:

To obtain specific gravity (corrected to 60°F.) of :	Add 1 vol. of 1·835 S.G. acid (corrected to 60°F.) to :
1·270	2·9 vols. of water.
1·210	4·0 vols. of water.

Heat is produced by the mixture of acid and water, the electrolyte should be allowed to cool before pouring it into the battery.

The specific gravity of the electrolyte varies with the temperature. For convenience in comparing specific gravities, they are always corrected to 60° F., which is adopted as a reference temperature.

The method of correction is as follows :—

For every 5°F. below 60°F., deduct ·002 from the observed reading to obtain the true specific gravity at 60°F. For every 5°F. above 60°F. add ·002 to the observed reading to obtain the true specific gravity at 60°F.

The temperature must be that indicated by a thermometer having its bulb actually immersed in the electrolyte and not the ambient temperature.

Fill the cells to the tops of the separators, *in one operation*. The battery filled in this way is 90% charged. When time permits, a short freshening charge for no more than four hours at the normal recharge rate of 1·5 amp. should be made.

3. Routine Maintenance

Fortnightly (or more frequently in hot climates) examine the level of electrolyte in the cells and if necessary add distilled water to bring the level up to the tops of the separators. The use of a Lucas Battery Filler will be found helpful, as it ensures that the correct electrolyte level is automatically maintained and also prevents distilled water from being spilled on the top of the battery (see Fig. 2).

Occasionally examine the terminals, clean and coat them with petroleum jelly. Wipe away all

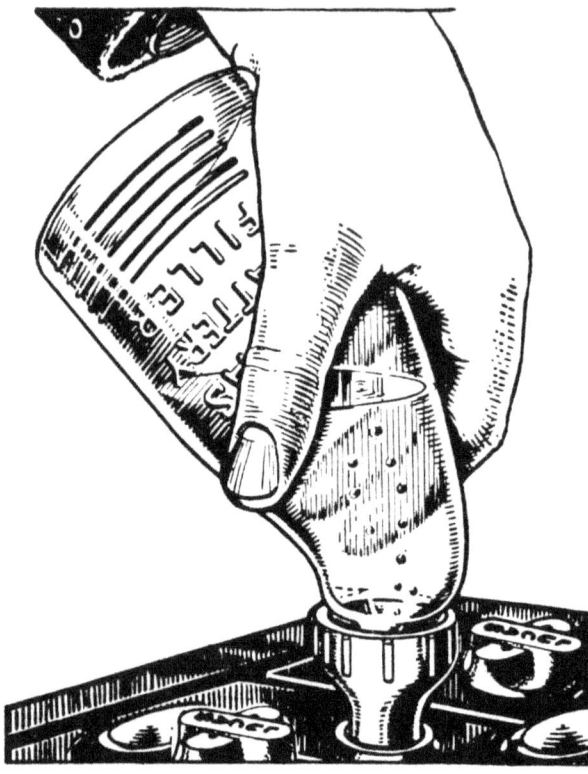

Fig. 2

The following table shows the state of charge at different values of specific gravities:

State of Charge	Temperature under 90°F.	Temperature over 90°F.
Battery fully charged	1·270—1·290	1·210—1·230
Battery about half charged	1·190—1·210	1·130—1·150
Battery fully discharged	1·110—1·130	1·050—1·070

If the battery is discharged, it must be recharged, either on the motor cycle by a period of daytime running or from an external D.C. supply at the normal recharge rate of 1·5 amp.

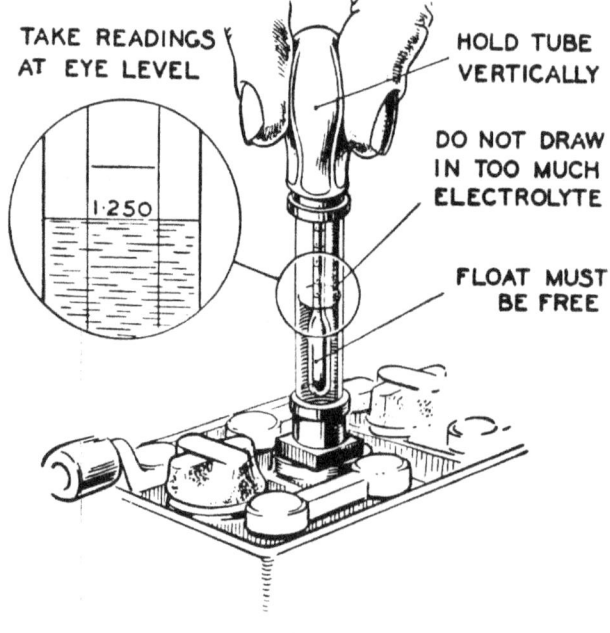

Fig. 3

dirt and moisture from the top of the battery and ensure that the connections are clean and tight.

4. Servicing

If the battery is subjected to long periods of night parking with the lights on, without suitable opportunities for recharging, a low state of charge is to be expected.

Measure the specific gravity of the acid of each cell in turn with a hydrometer (see Fig. 3).

SECTION G5d

Head and Tail Lamps

1. Headlamp

In all the above Models the headlamp incorporates the Lucas Light Unit MCF700. This is built into the Casquette fork head which contains twin parking lamps as well as the ammeter and switch.

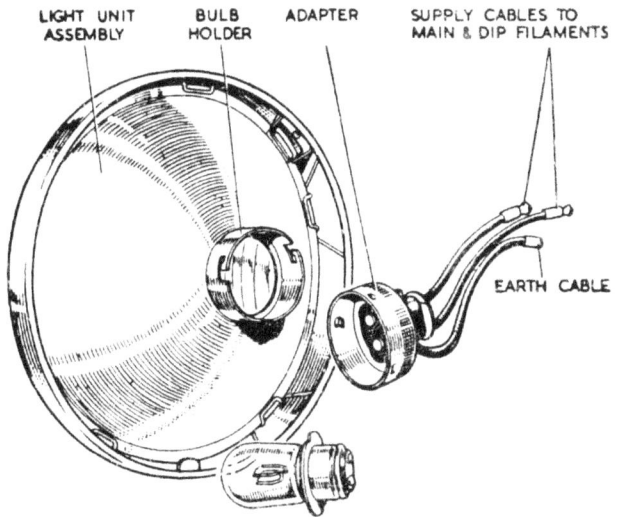

HEADLAMP MCF700
Fig. 1

2. Lucas Light Unit

The unit incorporates a combined reflector and front lens assembly (see Fig. 1). This construction ensures that the reflector and lenses are permanently protected, thus the unit keeps its high efficiency over a long period. A "prefocus" bulb is used, the filaments of which are accurately positioned with respect to the reflector, thus no focusing device is necessary.

The bulb has a large cap and a flange, which has been accurately positioned with relation to the bulb filaments during manufacture. A slot in the flange engages with a projection on the inside of the bulb holder positioned at the back of the reflector.

A bayonet-fitting adaptor with spring-loaded contacts secures the bulb firmly in position and carries the supply to the bulb contacts.

The outer surface of the lens is smooth to facilitate cleaning. The inner surface is formed of a series of lenses which determine the spread and pattern of the light beams.

In the event of damage to either the lens or reflector a replacement light unit must be fitted.

3. Replacing the Light Unit and Bulb

Slacken the securing screw at the top of the headlamp rim. Remove the front rim and Light Unit assembly.

Withdraw the adaptor from the Light Unit by twisting it in an anti-clockwise direction and pulling it off. Remove the bulb from its locating sleeve at the rear of the reflector.

Disengage the Light Unit securing springs from the rim and lift out the Light Unit.

Position the new unit in the rim so that the word "TOP" on the lens is correctly located when the assembly is mounted on the headlamp. Refit the securing springs ensuring that they are equally spaced around the rim.

Replace the bulb and adaptor. The bulb must be the Lucas "prefocus" type—6 v. 30/24 watt Lucas No. 312.

Locate the bottom of the Light Unit and front rim assembly in the headlamp shell or in the fixing rim attached to the Casquette fork head. Press the front on and tighten the securing screw at the top of the headlamp.

4. Parking Lights

Access to the parking bulbs is obtained by removing the parking lamp rim (see Fig. 2). This is forced over the edge of the rubber lamp body and is additionally secured by means of a small fixing

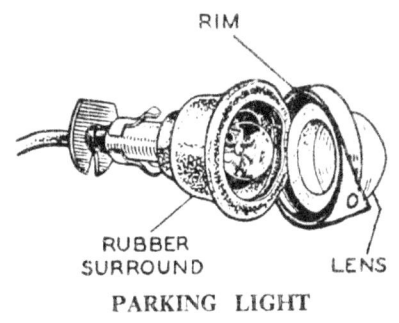

PARKING LIGHT
Fig. 2

screw. After removal of the lamp rim the parking lamp lens can be pulled out of the rubber body, after which the bulb will be accessible.

5. Tail Light

The Lucas lamp, Type 564 (Fig. 3) is a combined stop and tail light and also incorporates a reflector.

Access to the bulb is obtained by removing the two screws which secure the plastic cover.

The correct bulb is Lucas No. 384 6 volt 6/18 watt. The 6 watt filament provides the normal tail light, while the 18 watt filament is illuminated on movement of the brake pedal.

(**Note.**—6 watt bulbs are now required by law in Great Britain on machines of more than 250 c.c. capacity.)

Care must be taken that the leads to the stop tail lamp are correctly connected, as the use of the 18 watt filament on the normal tail light will not only discharge the battery but could cause trouble

STOP-TAIL LAMP L.564
Fig. 3

from excessive heat affecting the plastic cover. At the same time, the 6 watt filament, if used as a stop-tail light, will be ineffective in bright sunlight or at night when the tail light filament is illuminated.

SECTION H5

Frame

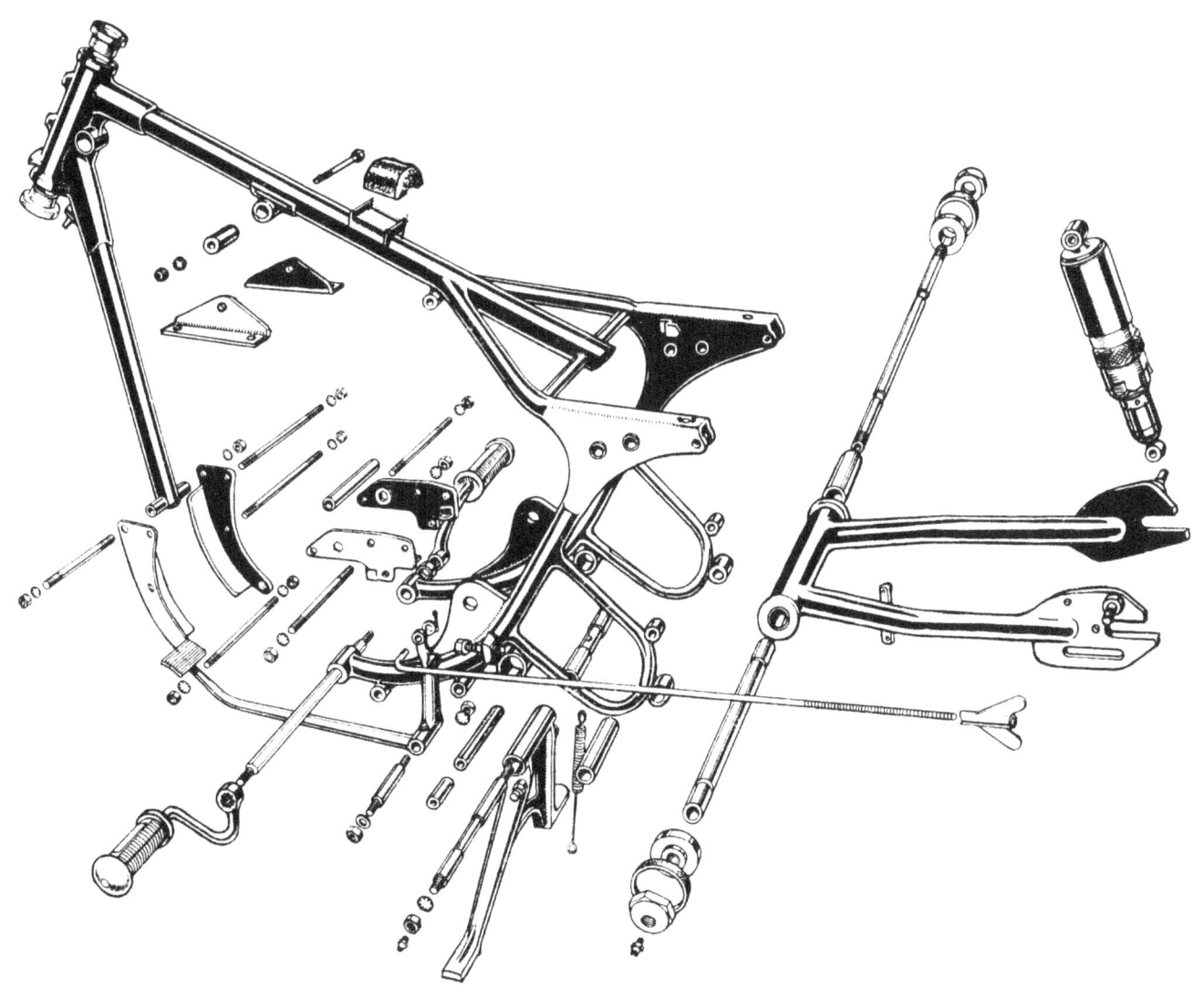

EXPLODED VIEW OF "CONSTELLATION" FRAME

Fig. 1

1. Description of Frame

The frame is built throughout of cold drawn weldless steel tubing with brazed or welded joints, liners being fitted where necessary for extra strength. All the main frame members are made of chrome-molybdenum alloy steel tubing which retains its strength and resistance to fatigue after brazing or welding.

The swinging arm unit which forms the chain stays is fitted with large diameter phosphor bronze bushes and pivots on a stout steel tube which is secured to the main frame by a long bolt passing through the pivot lugs. Hardened steel thrust washers are provided to deal with side thrust. The torsional rigidity of the swinging arm unit helps to maintain the rear wheel upright in the frame and thus relieves the wheel spindle of bending stresses to which it is subject with other types of rear suspension.

2. Steering Head Races

The steering head races, 34085, are the same at the top and bottom of the head lug and are the same for all models. They are easily removed by knocking them out with a hammer and drift and new races can be fitted either under a press or by means of a hammer and a wooden drift.

3. Removal of Rear Suspension Unit

On the "Constellation" and "Super Meteor" from 1961 onwards, the valances on either side of the frame must be removed to gain access to the top pivot pin. (See Section C, paragraph 8.)

The procedure for all models is then as follows. Remove the top pivot pin nut, drive out the pivot pin, then hinge the suspension unit back on the lower pivot pin. After removing the lower nut, the unit may be pushed off the pivot pin welded to the fork end.

4. Servicing Rear Suspension Units

The proprietary units fitted are sealed and servicing of the internal mechanism can be carried out only by the manufacturers.

The rubber bushes in the top and bottom eyes can easily be renewed and the spring can be removed by pushing down on the top spring cover so as to release the split collar above it. After removal of the split collar the top cover and spring can be lifted off. When reassembling, the spring should be greased to prevent rust and squeaking if it should come into contact with either of the covers.

The standard solo springs have a rate of 100—105 lb. per inch and it is not difficult to

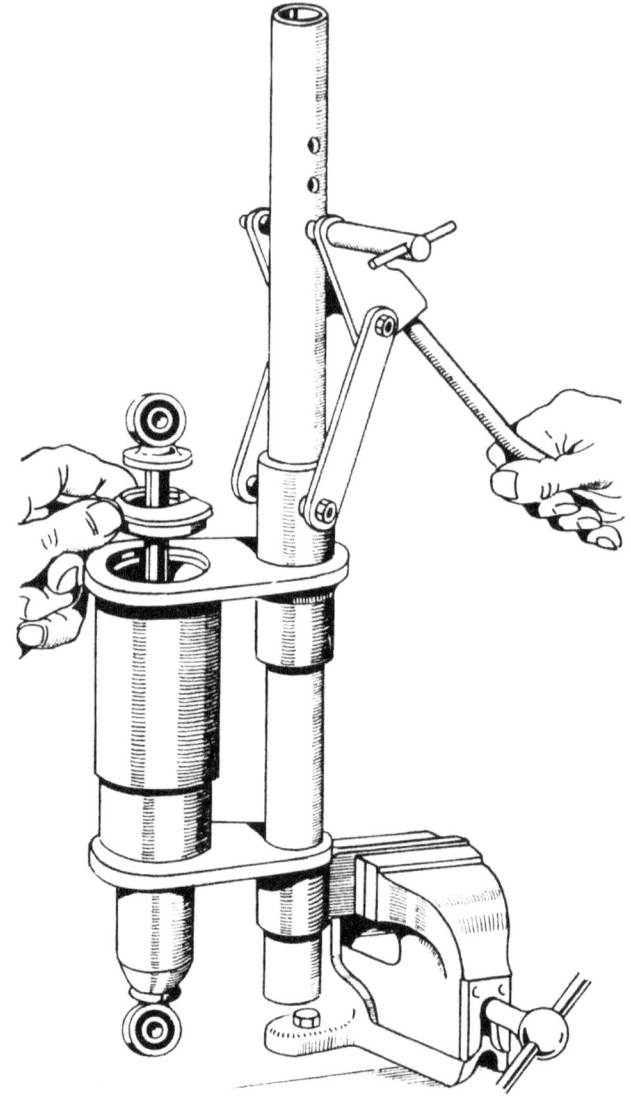

REAR SPRING COMPRESSOR
Fig. 2

compress these by hand. Heavier springs having a rate of 130 lb. per inch are available which may require the use of a spring compressor, as shown in Fig. 2.

5. Removal of Swinging Arm Chain Stays

First remove one of the pivot pin nuts and pull the pivot pin out from the other end. To release the pivot bearing it is necessary to spread the rear portion of the frame, using the frame expander E.5431, which will spread the frame sufficiently to enable the spigots on the thrust washers to clear the recesses in the pivot lugs forming part of the frame.

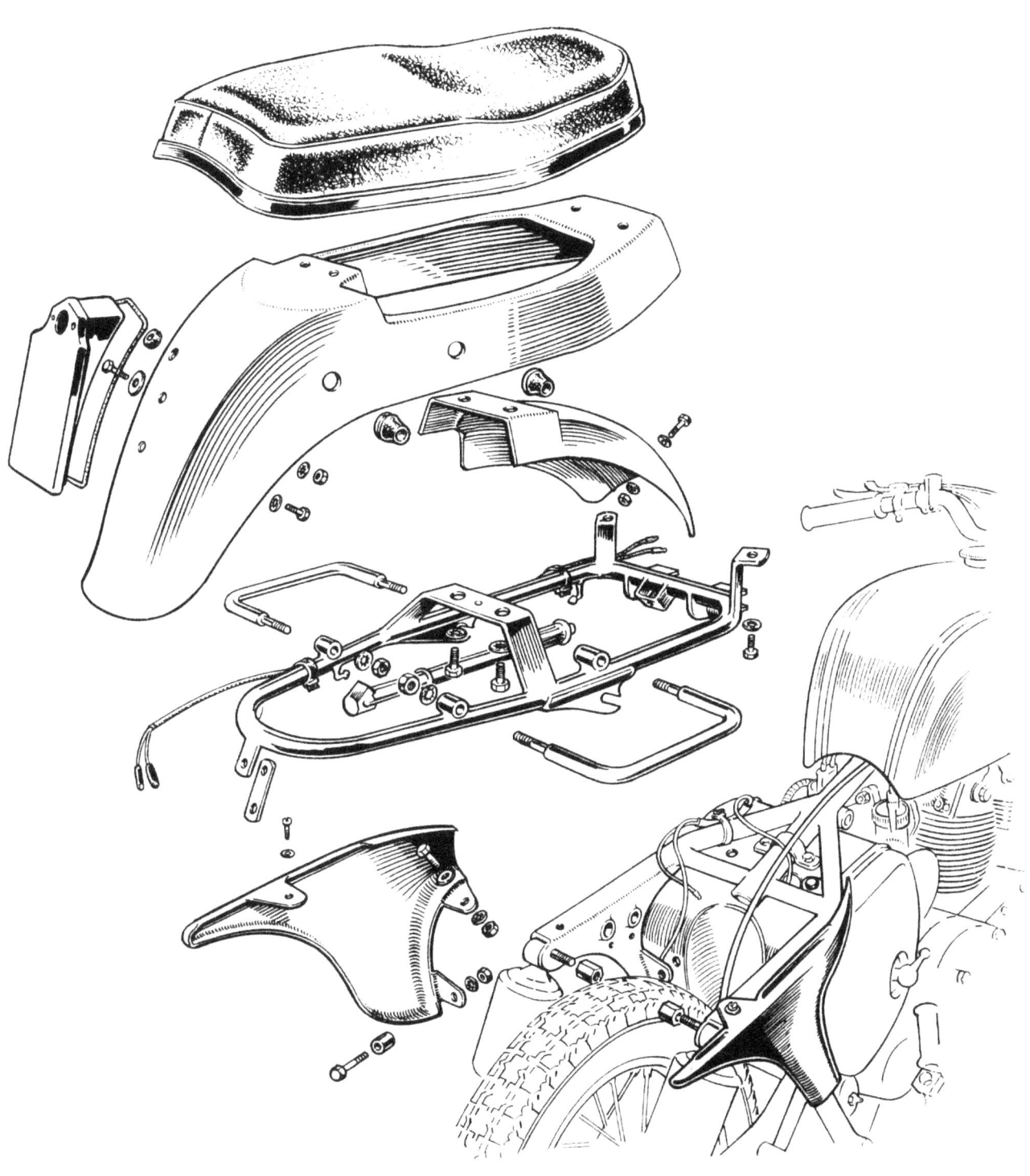

DUAL SEAT—MUDGUARD ASSEMBLY "CONSTELLATION" AND "SUPER METEOR," 1961 ONWARDS

Fig. 3

If it is necessary to remove the bronze bushes these can be driven out by means of a hammer and a suitable drift and new bushes can be fitted under a press without difficulty. After fitting the bushes they must be reamed to ·844/·843 in.

6. Centre Stand

To remove the centre stand unscrew the nut from one end of the stand spindle, knock out the latter and withdraw the stand complete with its bearing sleeve after disconnecting one end of the stand spring.

7. Wheel Alignment

Note that it is not possible to guarantee that the wheels are correctly aligned when the same notch position is used on both adjuster cams. It is therefore not sufficient to count the notches and use the same position on both sides of the machine. The only way to guarantee that the wheels are in line is to check the alignment from front wheel to back using either a straight edge or a piece of taut string. The alignment should be checked on both sides of the machine and if the front and rear tyres are of different section allowance must be made for this.

It is usual to check the alignment of the wheels at a point about six inches above the ground but, if the alignment is checked also towards the top of the wheels, it will be possible to ascertain whether or not the frame is twisted so as to cause one wheel to be leaning while the other is vertical. To do this it is always necessary to remove the mudguards and, unless a straight edge cut away in its centre portion is available, it will be necessary also to remove the cylinder, toolboxes, battery, etc., in order to allow an unbroken straight edge or a piece of taut string to contact the front and rear tyres.

8. Lubrication

The steering head races, swinging arm pivot bearing and stand pivot bearing should be well greased on assembly. The swinging arm pivot and stand pivot are provided with grease nipples but no nipples are provided for the steering head as experience has shown that the provision of nipples at this point causes trouble through chafing and cutting of control and lighting cables. If the steering head bearings are well packed they will last for several years or many thousands of miles.

Recommended greases are Castrolease (Heavy), Mobilgrease (No. 4), Esso Grease, Energrease C.3 or Shell Retinax A.

9. Dismantling the Rear Mudguard-dual Seat Assembly, 1961 onwards

Having removed the assembly from the frame, as described in Section C, paragraph 8, dismantling for repair or replacement is a simple matter.

First remove the single $\frac{3}{16}$ in. bolt securing the number plate, and disconnect the rear light wires at the junctions. The lifting handles are next pulled out, after undoing the two $\frac{5}{16}$ in. nuts on each handle. The grommets may be left in position in the mudguard.

Take out the two $\frac{3}{16}$ in. bolts in the nose of the mudguard. These screw into tapped holes in the dual seat. When replacing, the shakeproof washer must be next to the head of the bolt and the large plain washer must be against the underside of the mudguard.

Remove the single $\frac{3}{16}$ in. nut and bolt, attaching the rear of the mudguard to the carrier. Note the large plain washer, which must be under the bolt head, and bear against the top of the mudguard on assembly. Also the shakeproof washer and metal plate on the underside.

Lastly, the two $\frac{1}{4}$ in. bolts attaching the front of the carrier to the mudguard, and the two $\frac{5}{16}$ in. bolts in the carrier bridge piece, can be undone. They fit into tapped holes in the dual seat.

Note that shakeproof washers are fitted to all bolts and studs. Plain washers must be placed as described above and shown in Fig. 3.

On some early 1961 "Constellation" models, this mudguard is made from glass-fibre and in the event of damage small repair kits, consisting of a quantity of resin, catalyst and glass fibre, are available from our Service Department. Instructions for carrying out minor repairs are issued with this kit. All other models have the mudguard of pressed steel.

SECTION J1

Front Fork

With Casquette and Aluminium Alloy Bottom Tubes

1. Description

The telescopic fork consists of two legs each of which comprises a main tube of chrome molybdenum alloy steel tubing which is screwed into the Casquette fork head at the upper end and securely clamped to the fork crown. Fitted over the lower end of the main tube is the bottom tube made of high strength aluminium alloy with an integral lug which carries the wheel spindle. Fitted on the lower end of the main tube is a steel bush which is a close fit in the bore of the bottom tube. The upper end of the bottom tube carries a bronze bush which is a close fit over the outside diameter of the main tube. The bush is secured to the bottom tube by means of a threaded housing which contains an oil seal. A stud known as the "spring stud" is fitted in the lower end of the bottom tube and a valve port is secured to the lower end of the main tube. As the fork operates oil is forced between the spring stud and the bore of the valve port forming a hydraulic damping system. A compression spring is fitted inside the main tube between the upper end of the spring stud and the upper end of the main tube. The lower end of the main tube and upper end of the bottom tube are protected by a cover secured to the fork crown.

A special fork is available for sidecar machines. This has bottom tubes with extended wheel lugs giving less trail and is fitted with stronger springs and a steering damper.

2. Operation of the Fork

The fork provides a range of movement of 6 in. from the fully extended to the fully compressed position. The movement is controlled by the compression spring and by the hydraulic damping system. The hydraulic damping is light on the bump stroke and heavier on the rebound stroke, thus damping out any tendency to pitching or oscillation without interfering unduly with the free movement of the fork when the wheel encounters an obstacle.

The fork is filled with a light oil (S.A.E. 20) to a point above the lower end of the spring so that the damper chamber "B" is always kept

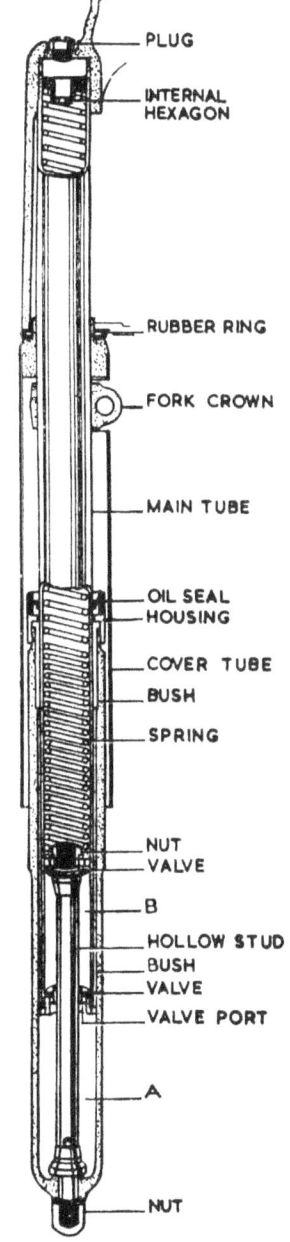

SECTION OF FORK LEG

Fig. 1

full of oil. Upward movement of the wheel spindle forces oil from the lower chamber "A" through the annular space between the spring stud (38067) and the bore of the main tube valve port (38138) into the damper chamber "B." During this stroke the pressure on the underside of the valve plate (38073) causes this to lift so that oil can also pass from "A" to "B" through the eight holes in the valve body. Since, however, the diameter of chamber "B" is less than that of chamber "A" there is not room in "B" to receive all the oil which must be displaced from "A" as the fork operates. The surplus oil passes through the cross hole in the spring stud and up the centre hole in the stud, spilling out through the nut (38076) which secures the upper end of the spring stud to the bronze guide at the lower end of the fork spring.

On the rebound stroke the oil in the damper chamber "B" is forced through the annular space between the spring stud and the bore of the main tube valve port. During this stroke pressure in chamber "B" closes the two disc valves at the upper and lower ends of the chamber so that the only path through which the oil can escape is the annular space between the spring stud and the port. Damping on the rebound stroke is therefore heavier than on the bump stroke. At the extreme end of either bump or rebound stroke a small taper portion on the spring stud enters the bore

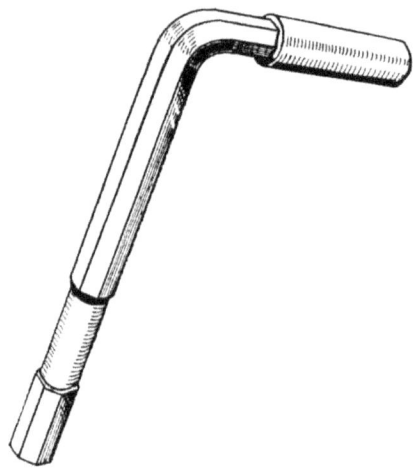

MAIN TUBE SPANNER

Fig. 2

of the valve port, thus restricting the annular space and increasing the amount of damping. At the extreme end of the bump stroke the larger diameter taper on the oil control collar (38075) enters the main counterbore of the valve port thus forming a hydraulic cushion to prevent metal to metal contact.

3. Dismantling the Fork to Replace Spring, Oil Seal or Bearing Bushes

Place the machine on the centre stand, disconnect the front brake control and remove the front wheel and mudguard complete with stays. Unscrew the bottom spring stud nut (38080) which will allow oil to run out of the fork down to

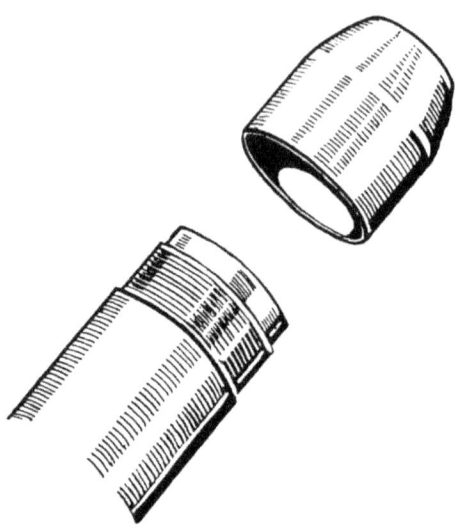

MAIN TUBE SEAL GUIDE

Fig. 3

the level of the cross hole in the spring stud. Now knock the spring stud upwards into the fork with a soft mallet, thus allowing the remainder of the oil to escape. Pull the fork bottom tube down as far as possible, thus exposing the oil seal housing (38157). Unscrew this housing either by means of a spanner on the flats with which it is provided or by using the gland nut hand grips (E.5417). The bottom tube can now be withdrawn completely from the main tube, leaving the bottom tube bush, oil seal housing and oil seal in position on the main tube.

Now unscrew the main tube valve port using "C" spanner (E5418). The spring stud and spring can now be withdrawn from the lower end of the main tube.

The steel main tube bush (38156) can now be tapped off the lower end of the tube, if necessary using the bottom tube bush for this purpose. Before doing this, however, it is advisable to mark the position of the bush with a pencil line so as to ensure reassembling it in the same position on the main tube. The reason for this is that these bushes are finish ground to size after fitting on to the tubes so as to ensure concentricity. After removal of the main tube bush the bottom tube bush, oil seal housing and oil seal can be removed.

In case of difficulty in removing the main tube bush it is possible to withdraw the oil seal housing after loosening the crown clip bolt 39038, removing the plug screw 38968 and unscrewing the main tube from the fork head by means of a hexagon bar ·500 in. across flats (Unbrako wrench W.11) or the special tool shown in Fig. 2.

4. Spring

Solo and Sidecar springs are available. The free length of each is 20½ ins. The spring should be replaced if it has closed by more than 1 inch.

5. Reassembly of Parts

When refitting the oil seal, or fitting a new one, great care must be exercised not to damage the synthetic rubber lip which forms the actual seal. If the seal has been removed from the upper end of the main tube and is refitted from this end a special nose piece (Fig. 3) must be fitted over the end of the tube to prevent the thread from damaging the oil seal.

The spring stud is a tight fit in the hole at the lower end of the bottom tube. Once the stud has been entered in the hole push the bottom tube up sharply against the spring until two or three threads on the stud project beneath the end of the bottom tube. Now fit the nut and washer and pull the stud into position by tightening the nut. If necessary fit the nut first without the washer until sufficient thread is projecting to enable the washer to be fitted.

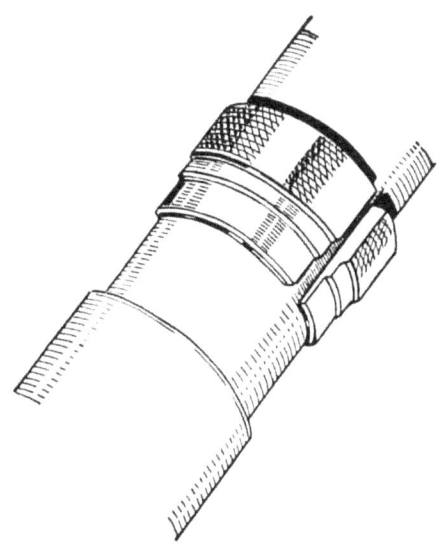

OUTER COVER CENTRALISING BUSHES

Fig. 5

6. Steering Head Races

The steering head bearing consists of two deep groove thrust races each containing nineteen ¼ in. diameter balls. The bearing is adjusted by tightening the steering stem locknut after loosening the ball head clip screw and both the fork crown clamp bolts. The head should be adjusted so that, when the front wheel is lifted clear of the ground, a light tap on the handlebars will cause the steering to swing to full lock in either direction, while at the same time there should be only the slightest trace of play in the bearings. When testing for freedom of movement the steering damper, if fitted, should be disconnected by unscrewing the anchor plate pin. Do not forget to tighten the ball head clip screw and fork crown clamp bolts. Before tightening the latter make sure that the cover tubes are located centrally round the main tubes so that the bottom tube does not rub inside the cover tube. A pair of split bushes (Fig. 5) is useful to ensure centralisation of the cover tubes.

7. Removal of Complete Fork

The fork complete with front wheel and mudguard can be removed from the machine if necessary by adopting the following procedure.

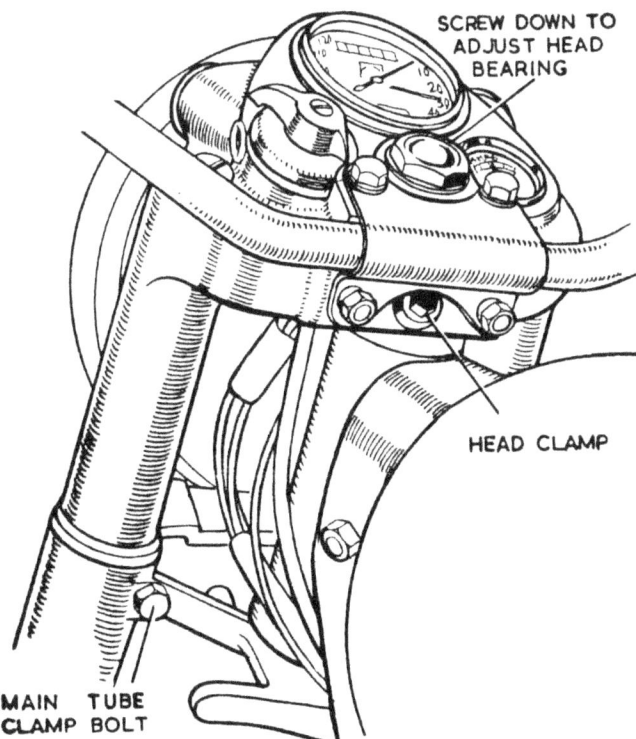

SHOWING THE POSITIONS OF THE CLAMP BOLTS SECURING THE STEERING STEM AND FORK TUBES

Fig. 4

The leads to the lighting switch and ammeter should be disconnected from the battery, regulator, tail lamp, etc. at their lower ends or by means of the plug and socket connectors when these are provided. The switch and ammeter are push fits into the rubber bushes in the fork head.

Disconnect the speedometer drive from the speedometer head and unscrew the steering damper knob and rod (on sidecar forks) after removal of the split pin through the lower end of the rod. Undo the steering damper anchor plate pin so as to disconnect the damper from the frame of the machine.

Remove the two plug screws (38968) and loosen the steering head clip bolt and the two fork crown clamp bolts.

Now unscrew the fork main tubes from the fork head and the steering stem locknut from the top of the steering stem, turning each tube and the nut a turn or two at a time. When the nut has been removed from the steering stem and the main tubes have been completely unscrewed from the fork head the complete fork and wheel with steering stem can be lifted out of the head lug of the frame.

8. Lubrication

The lubrication of the fork bearings is effected by the oil which forms the hydraulic damping medium. All that is necessary is to keep sufficient oil in the fork to ensure that the top end of the bottom spring stud is never uncovered even in the full rebound position. The level of oil in the fork can be gauged by removing the top plug screw and inserting a long rod about $\frac{3}{8}$ in. diameter. If slightly tilted this will ledge against the nut at the upper end of the bottom spring stud and indicate the level of oil above the stud. If the fork is empty to start with the quantity required is approximately $7\frac{1}{2}$ fluid ounces in each leg. Recommended grades of oil are Castrolite, Mobiloil Arctic, Essolube 20, B.P. Energol S.A.E. 20 and Shell X-100 20/20W.

9. Air Vents

The earlier forks of this type were provided with holes at the upper end of each main tube communicating with small vent holes in the Casquette head. Experience has shown that on rough roads oil may escape through these air vents which in consequence are now omitted. Escape of oil from the earlier forks can be largely eliminated by fitting specially long plug screws which are available. The Part Number is 40118. If these are fitted and the final vent hole is stopped up with a wooden plug leakage at this point is impossible. Fitting the special plug screws alone is sufficient in most instances.

SECTION J3

Front Fork

With Facia Panel and Aluminium Alloy Bottom Tubes

Used on "500 Bullet," 1953; "Meteor 700," 1953;
Trials "Works Replica" 1958 onwards

1. Description

(a) "500 Bullet" and "Meteor 700"

The telescopic fork consists of two legs each of which comprises a main tube of chrome molybdenum alloy steel tubing which is securely clamped to the Facia Panel Fork Head and to the fork crown. Fitted over the lower end of the main tube is the bottom tube made of high strength aluminium alloy with an integral lug which carries the wheel spindle. Fitted on the lower end of the main tube is a steel bush which is a close fit in the bore of the bottom tube. The upper end of the bottom tube carries a bronze bush which is a close fit over the outside diameter of the main tube. The bush is secured to the bottom tube by means of a threaded housing which contains an oil seal. A stud, known as the "spring stud," is fitted in the lower end of the bottom tube and a valve port is secured to the lower end of the main tube. As the fork operates oil is forced between the spring stud and the bore of the valve port forming a hydraulic damping system. A compression spring is fitted inside the main tube between the upper end of the spring stud and the upper end of the main tube. The main tube and upper end of the bottom tube are protected by a one-piece cover secured to the fork crown and carrying a pressed steel lamp bracket welded to it.

A special version of the fork is available for sidecar use. This has a modified fork head and fork crown setting the main tubes $1\frac{1}{2}$ in. further forward thus giving less trail and providing lighter steering when used with a sidecar. These sidecar forks also are fitted with a steering damper and have stronger springs.

(b) Trials "Works Replica"

There are minor internal differences in the fork for this model which are as follows. A distance piece is situated on top of the spring, and a long control collar is fitted to the hollow stud in place of the short control collar. The hollow stud itself has no external threads but is tapped internally to take the long cap stud which projects through the bottom of the leg and, with the short cap stud, secures the spindle cap.

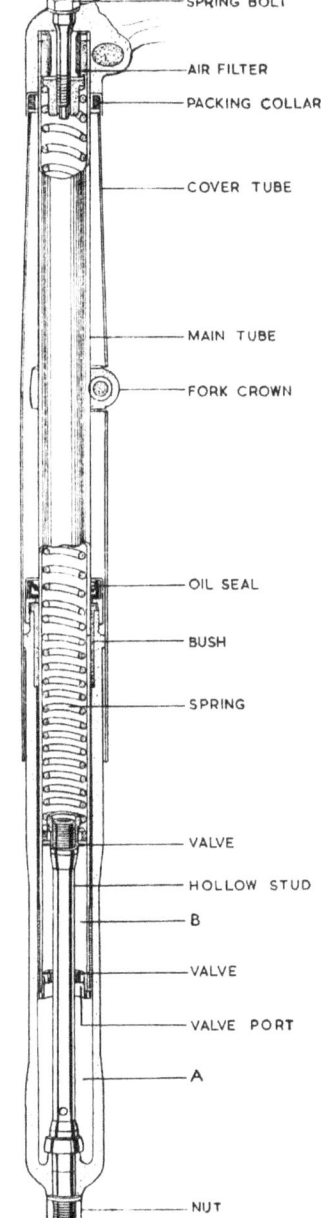

SECTION OF LEG

Fig. 1

2. Operation of Fork

The fork provides a range of movement of 6 in. from the fully extended to the fully compressed position. The movement is controlled by the compression spring and by the hydraulic damping system. The hydraulic damping is light on the bump stroke and heavier on the rebound stroke, thus damping out any tendency to pitching or oscillation without interfering unduly with the free movement of the fork when the wheel encounters an obstacle.

The fork is filled with a light oil (S.A.E. 20) to a point above the lower end of the spring so that the damper chamber "B" is always kept full of oil. Upward movement of the wheel spindle forces oil from the lower chamber "A" through the annular space between the spring stud (38067) and the bore of the main tube valve port (38138) into the damper chamber "B." During this stroke the pressure on the underside of the valve plate (38073) causes this to lift so that oil can also pass from "A" to "B" through the eight holes in the valve body. Since, however, the diameter of chamber "B" is less than that of chamber "A" there is not room in "B" to receive all the oil which must be displaced from "A" as the fork operates. The surplus oil passes through the cross hole in the spring stud and up the centre hole in the stud, spilling out through the nut (38076) which secures the upper end of the spring stud to the bronze guide at the lower end of the fork spring.

On the rebound stroke the oil in the damper chamber "B" is forced through the annular space between the spring stud and the bore of the main tube valve port. During this stroke pressure in chamber "B" closes the two disc valves at the upper and lower ends of the chamber so that the only path through which the oil can escape is the annular space between the spring stud and the port. Damping on the rebound stroke is therefore heavier than on the bump stroke. At the extreme end of either bump or rebound stroke a small taper portion on the spring stud enters the bore of the valve port thus restricting the annular space and increasing the amount of damping. At the extreme end of the bump stroke the larger diameter taper on the oil control collar (38075) enters the main counterbore of the valve port thus forming a hydraulic cushion to prevent metal to metal contact.

3. Dismantling the Fork to Replace Spring, Oil Seal or Bearing Bushes

Place the machine on the centre stand, disconnect the front brake control and remove the front wheel and mudguard complete with stays. Unscrew the bottom spring stud nut (38080) which will allow oil to run out of the fork down to the level of the cross hole in the spring stud. Now knock the spring stud upwards into the fork with a soft mallet, thus allowing the remainder of the oil to escape. Pull the fork bottom tube down as far as possible, thus exposing the oil seal housing (38157). Unscrew this housing either by means of a spanner on the flats with which it is provided or by using the gland nut hand grips (E5417). The bottom tube can now be withdrawn completely from the main tube, leaving the bottom tube bush, oil seal housing and oil seal in position on the main tube.

Now unscrew the main tube valve port using "C" spanner (E5418). The spring stud and spring can now be withdrawn from the lower end of the main tube.

The steel main tube bush (38156) can now be tapped off the lower end of the tube, if necessary using the bottom tube bush for this purpose. Before doing this, however, it is advisable to mark the position of the bush with a pencil line so as to ensure reassembling it in the same position on the main tube. The reason for this is that these bushes are finish ground to size after fitting on to the tubes so as to ensure concentricity. After removal of the main tube bush the bottom tube bush, oil seal housing and oil seal can be removed.

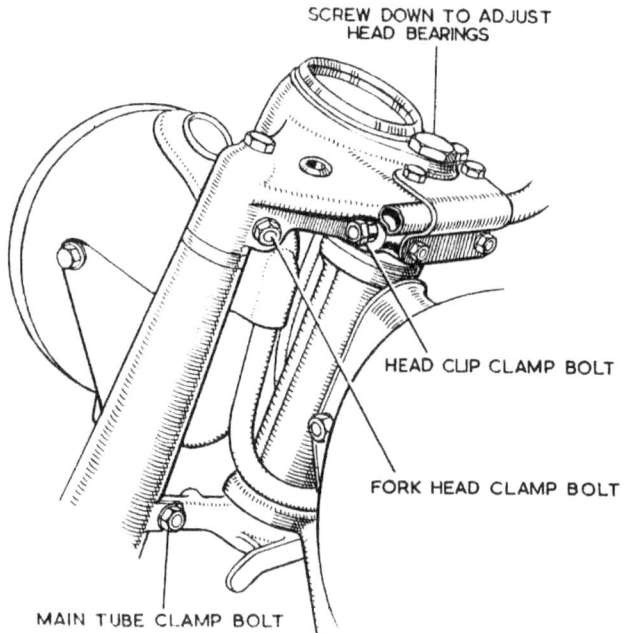

SHOWING THE POSITIONS OF THE CLAMP BOLTS SECURING THE STEERING STEM AND FORK TUBES

Fig. 2

In case of difficulty in removing the main tube bush it is possible to withdraw the oil seal housing from the upper end after removal of the main tube from the fork head and fork crown as described in paragraphs 6 and 7.

4. Spring

Solo and sidecar springs are available. The free length of each is $20\frac{1}{2}$ in. The spring should be replaced if it has closed by more than 1 inch.

5. Steering Head Races

The steering head bearing consists of two deep groove thrust races each containing nineteen $\frac{1}{4}$ in. diameter balls. The bearing is adjusted by tightening the steering stem locknut after loosening the nuts on the three pinch bolts which secure the fork head to the steering stem and to the two main tubes. The head should be adjusted so that when the front wheel is lifted clear of the ground a

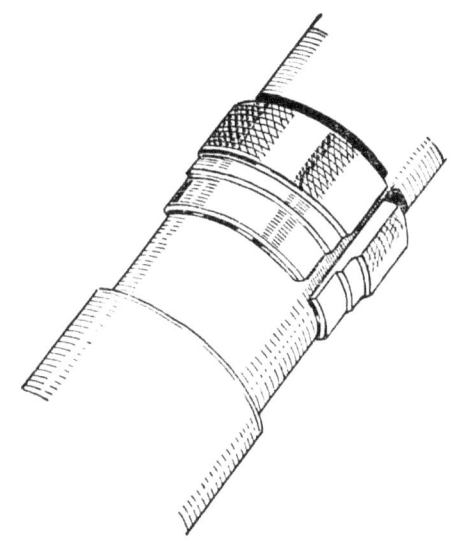

OUTER COVER CENTRALISING BUSHES

Fig. 3

light tap on the handlebars will cause the steering to swing to full lock in either direction, while at the same time there should be only the slightest trace of play in the bearings. When testing for freedom of movement the steering damper, if fitted, should be disconnected by unscrewing the anchor plate pin.

Adjustment of the steering head depends on the ability of the fork head to slide on the steering stem and on the fork main tubes. A rubber washer is interposed between the fork head and the top of the lamp bracket tube to permit the necessary movement. If this rubber washer is fully compressed while there is still some play in the steering head it will be necessary to remove the fork head (see paragraph 6) and shorten the lamp bracket tube by, say, $\frac{1}{32}$ in. Alternatively, if the lamp bracket tube is loose when the steering head is correctly adjusted, it can be tightened by fitting an additional steel washer (Part No. 35974) beneath the rubber washer.

It is also possible that the steering head cannot be adjusted because the main tube is bottoming in the recess in the fork head in which it fits. In this case the nuts on the fork crown clamp studs must be loosened and the sleeves separated (see paragraph 7) thus permitting the main tubes to slide through the fork crown. Do not forget to tighten the fork head pinch bolts and the nuts on the fork crown clamp studs after adjusting the steering head. Before tightening the latter make sure that the cover tubes are located centrally round the main tubes so that the bottom tube does not rub inside the lower end of the cover tube. A pair of split bushes (Fig. 3) is useful to ensure centralisation of the cover tubes.

6. Removal of Facia Panel Fork Head, Spring, etc.

To remove the Facia Panel Fork Head for access to the lamp bracket tubes (or to change the fork spring without disturbing the bearings) proceed as follows—disconnect all control cables at the handlebar end and remove the headlamp from the lamp brackets. The switch panel can conveniently be removed from the back of the lamp so that the body of the lamp can be removed completely.

Now remove the two Fork Spring Guide Bolts from the fork head, unscrew the nuts on the fork

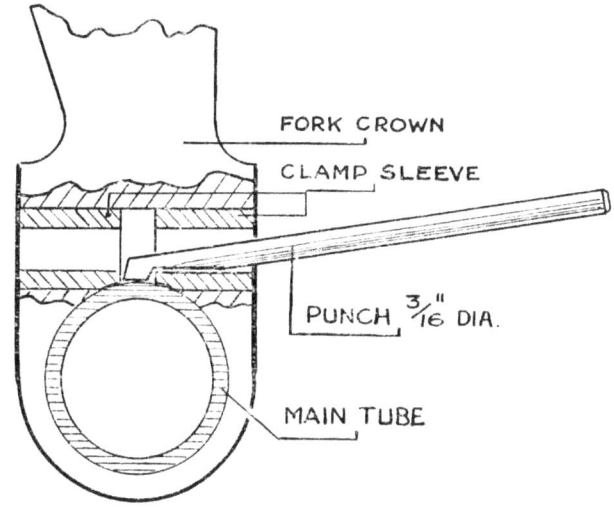

DRIFT FOR PARTING CLAMP SLEEVES

Fig. 4

head clip bolt and the two main tube clip bolts, remove the three clip bolt sleeves and knock out the three clip bolts. The facia panel fork head can now be tapped gently upwards with a hide mallet or a hammer and a wooden drift but care must be taken to hit only the more solid parts of the fork head, i.e. beneath the handlebar clip and at the back of the main tubes, avoiding the underside of the comparatively thin portion in front of the speedometer.

After removal of the fork head the lamp bracket tubes can be lifted straight off and the springs can be withdrawn from the upper end of the main tubes.

7. Removal of Main Tubes

To remove the main tubes first dismantle the fork as described in paragraph 3 then remove the facia panel fork head and lamp bracket tubes as described in paragraph 6. Now remove one nut from each of the fork crown clamp studs, remove the studs and separate the clamp sleeves with a drift of the form shown in Fig. 4. Now knock the main tubes out of the fork crown either upwards or downwards as may be most convenient. If the machine has been in an accident and the tube is badly bent both above and below the fork crown, it may be necessary to cut through the tube with a hacksaw before it can be withdrawn.

8. Reassembly of Parts

No difficulty should be experienced with this. When refitting the main tube use the lamp bracket tube as a guide to its correct position in the fork crown. The small shoulder some $1\frac{1}{2}$ in. from the upper end of the tube should be $\frac{1}{8}$ in. above the top of the lamp bracket tube when the latter is in position on the fork crown. With the main tube in this position tighten the fork crown clamp screws before fitting the facia panel fork head.

The cover tube must be fitted in position on the fork crown and the clamp sleeves placed in position before the main tube is fitted. To keep the clamp sleeves in position it is convenient to insert a short piece of tube or bar in the eye of the fork crown before putting the cover tube in position. The short piece of tube will be pushed out when inserting the main tube. Before tightening the nuts on the three fork head clip bolts make sure that the bolt heads and the sleeves are correctly positioned with the cut-away portion engaging the main tube or steering stem. Failure to do this may result in a cracked fork head.

When refitting the oil seal or fitting a new one great care must be exercised not to damage the synthetic rubber lip which forms the actual seal.

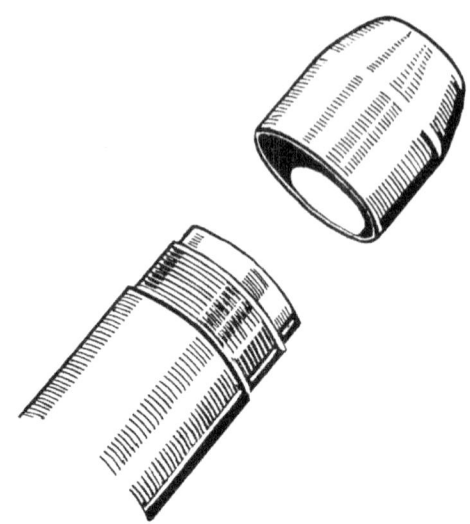

MAIN TUBE SEAL GUIDE

Fig. 5

If the seal has been removed from the upper end of the main tube and is refitted from this end a special nose piece (Fig. 5) must be fitted over the end of the tube to prevent the thread from damaging the oil seal.

The spring stud is a tight fit in the hole at the lower end of the bottom tube. Once the stud has been entered in the hole push the bottom tube up sharply against the spring until two or three threads on the stud project beneath the end of the bottom tube. Now fit the nut and washer and pull the stud into position by tightening the nut. If necessary fit the nut first without the washer until sufficient thread is projecting to enable the washer to be fitted.

9. Lubrication

The lubrication of the fork bearings is effected by the oil which forms the hydraulic damping medium. All that is necessary is to keep sufficient oil in the fork to ensure that the top end of the bottom spring stud is never uncovered even in the full rebound position. The level of oil in the fork can be gauged by removing the top plug screw and inserting a long rod about $\frac{3}{8}$ in. diameter. If slightly tilted this will ledge against the nut at the upper end of the bottom spring stud and indicate the level of oil above the stud. If the fork is empty to start with the quantity required is approximately $7\frac{1}{2}$ fluid ounces in each leg. Recommended grades of oil are Castrolite, Mobiloil Arctic, Essolube 20, B.P. Energol S.A.E. 20 and Shell X-100 20/20 w.

SECTION J6

Front Fork

With Casquette and Aluminium Alloy Bottom Tubes

1. Description

The telescopic fork consists of two legs each of which comprises a main tube of chrome molybdenum alloy steel tubing which is screwed into the Casquette fork head at the upper end and securely clamped to the fork crown. Fitted over the lower end of the main tube is the bottom tube made of high strength aluminium alloy with an integral lug which carries the wheel spindle. Fitted on the lower end of the main tube is a steel bush which is a close fit in the bore of the bottom tube. The upper end of the bottom tube carries a bronze bush which is a close fit over the outside diameter of the main tube. The bush is secured to the bottom tube by means of a threaded housing which contains an oil seal. A stud known as the "spring stud" is fitted in the lower end of the bottom tube and a valve port is secured to the lower end of the main tube. As the fork operates oil is forced between the spring stud and the bore of the valve port forming a hydraulic damping system. A compression spring is fitted inside the main tube between the upper end of the spring stud and the upper end of the main tube. The lower end of the main tube and upper end of the bottom tube are protected by a cover secured to the fork crown.

2. Operation of the Fork

The fork provides a range of movement of 6 in. from the fully extended to the fully compressed position. The movement is controlled by the compression spring and by the hydraulic damping system. The hydraulic damping is light on the bump stroke and heavier on the rebound stroke, thus damping out any tendency to pitching or oscillation without interfering unduly with the free movement of the fork when the wheel encounters an obstacle.

The fork is filled with a light oil (S.A.E. 20) to a point above the lower end of the spring so that the damper chamber "B" is always kept full of oil. Upward movement of the wheel spindle forces oil from the lower chamber "A" through the annular space between the spring stud (38067) and the bore of the main tube valve port (38138) into the damper chamber "B."

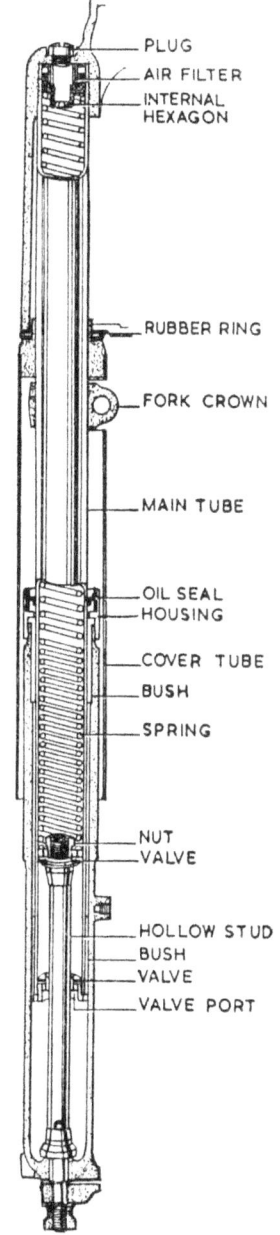

SECTION OF FORK LEG

Fig. 1

During this stroke the pressure on the underside of the valve plate (38073) causes this to lift so that oil can also pass from "A" to "B" through the eight holes in the valve body. Since, however, the diameter of chamber "B" is less than that of chamber "A" there is not room in "B" to receive all the oil which must be displaced from "A" as the fork operates. The surplus oil passes through the cross hole in the spring stud and up the centre hole in the stud, spilling out through the nut (38076) which secures the upper end of the spring stud to the bronze guide at the lower end of the fork spring.

On the rebound stroke the oil in the damper chamber "B" is forced through the annular space between the spring stud and the bore of the main tube valve port. During this stroke pressure in chamber "B" closes the two disc valves at the upper and lower ends of the chamber so that the only path through which the oil can escape is the annular space between the spring stud and the port. Damping on the rebound stroke is therefore heavier than on the bump stroke. At the extreme end of either bump or rebound stroke a small taper portion on the spring stud enters the bore of the valve port, thus restricting the annular space and increasing the amount of damping. At the extreme end of the bump stroke the larger diameter taper on the oil control collar (38075) enters the main counterbore of the valve port thus forming a hydraulic cushion to prevent metal to metal contact.

MAIN TUBE SPANNER
Fig. 2

3. Dismantling the Fork to Replace Spring, Oil Seal or Bearing Bushes

Place the machine on the centre stand, disconnect the front brake control and remove the front wheel and mudguard complete with stays. Knock the rearmost cap stud upwards into the fork with a soft mallet, which will allow oil to run out of the fork. Pull the fork bottom tube down as far as possible, thus exposing the oil seal housing (38157). Unscrew this housing either by means of a spanner on the flats with which it is provided or by using the gland nut hand grips (E.4912).

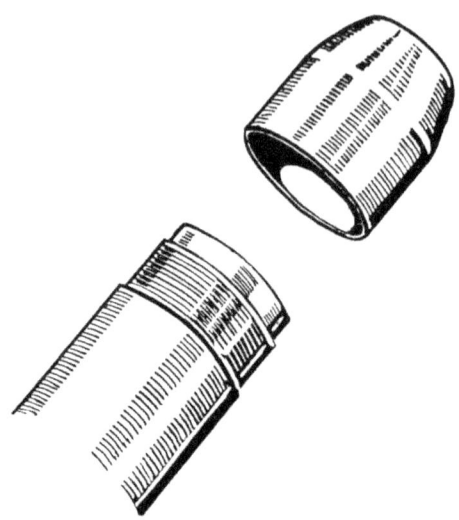

MAIN TUBE SEAL GUIDE
Fig. 3

The bottom tube can now be withdrawn completely from the main tube, leaving the bottom tube bush, oil seal housing and oil seal in position on the main tube.

Now unscrew the main tube valve port using "C" spanner (E.5418). The spring stud and spring can now be withdrawn from the lower end of the main tube.

The steel main tube bush (38156) can now be tapped off the lower end of the tube, if necessary using the bottom tube bush for this purpose. Before doing this, however, it is advisable to mark the position of the bush with a pencil line so as to ensure reassembling it in the same position on the main tube. The reason for this is that these bushes are finish ground to size after fitting on to the tubes so as to ensure concentricity. After removal of the main tube bush the bottom tube bush, oil seal housing and oil seal can be removed.

In case of difficulty in removing the main tube bush it is possible to withdraw the oil seal housing after loosening the crown clip bolt 39038, removing the plug screw 38968, and unscrewing the main tube from the fork head by means of a hexagon bar ·5 in. across flats (Unbrako wrench W.11) or the special tool shown in Fig. 2.

4. Spring

Solo and Sidecar springs are available. The free length of each is 20½ in. The spring should be replaced if it has closed by more than 1 in.

5. Reassembly of Parts

When refitting the oil seal, or fitting a new one, great care must be exercised not to damage the synthetic rubber lip which forms the actual seal. If the seal has been removed from the upper end of the main tube and is refitted from this end a special nose piece (Fig. 3) must be fitted over the end of the tube to prevent the thread from damaging the oil seal.

The spring stud is a tight fit in the hole at the lower end of the bottom tube. Once the stud has been entered in the hole push the bottom tube up sharply against the spring until two or three threads on the stud project beneath the end of the bottom tube. Now fit the nut and washer and pull the stud into position by tightening the nut. If necessary fit the nut first without the washer until sufficient thread is projecting to enable the washer to be fitted.

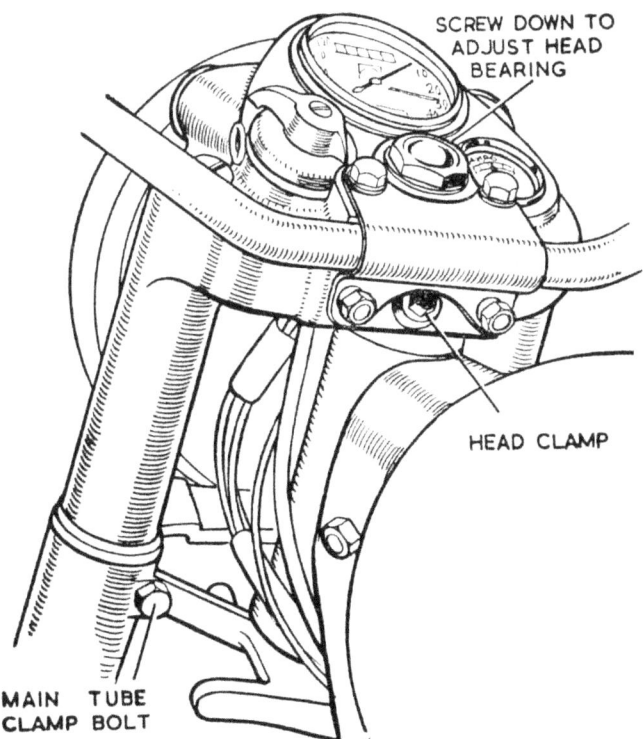

SHOWING THE POSITIONS OF THE CLAMP BOLTS SECURING THE STEERING STEM AND FORK TUBES

Fig. 4

6. Steering Head Races

The steering head bearing consists of two deep groove thrust races each containing nineteen ¼ in. diameter balls. The bearing is adjusted by tightening the steering stem locknut after loosening the ball head clip screw and both the fork crown clamp bolts. The head should be adjusted so

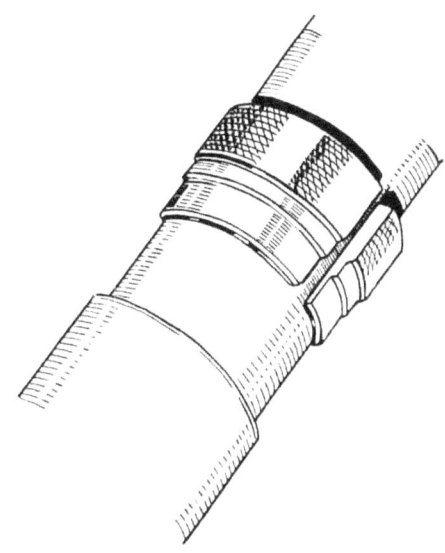

OUTER COVER CENTRALISING BUSHES

Fig. 5

that, when the front wheel is lifted clear of the ground, a light tap on the handlebars will cause the steering to swing to full lock in either direction, while at the same time there should be only the slightest trace of play in the bearings. When testing for freedom of movement the steering damper, if fitted, should be disconnected by unscrewing the anchor plate pin. Do not forget to tighten the ball head clip screw and fork crown clamp bolts. Before tightening the latter make sure that the cover tubes are located centrally round the main tubes so that the bottom tube does not rub inside the cover tube. A pair of split bushes (Fig. 5) is useful to ensure centralisation of the cover tubes.

7. Removal of Complete Fork

The fork complete with front wheel and mudguard can be removed from the machine if necessary by adopting the following procedure.

The leads to the lighting switch and ammeter should be disconnected from the battery, regulator, tail lamp, etc., at their lower ends or by means of the plug and socket connectors when these are provided. The switch and ammeter are push fits into the rubber bushes in the fork head.

Disconnect the speedometer drive from the speedometer head. Remove the two plug screws (38968) and loosen the steering head clip bolt and the two fork crown clamp bolts.

Now unscrew the fork main tubes from the fork head and the steering stem locknut from the top of the steering stem, turning each tube and the nut a turn or two at a time. When the nut has been removed from the steering stem and the main tubes have been completely unscrewed from the fork head the complete fork and wheel with steering stem can be lifted out of the head lug of the frame.

8. Lubrication

The lubrication of the fork bearings is effected by the oil which forms the hydraulic damping medium. All that is necessary is to keep sufficient oil in the fork to ensure that the top end of the bottom spring stud is never uncovered even in the full rebound position. The level of oil in the fork can be gauged by removing the top plug screw and inserting a long rod about $\frac{3}{8}$ in. diameter. If slightly tilted this will ledge against the nut at the upper end of the bottom spring stud and indicate the level of oil above the stud. If the fork is empty to start with the quantity required is approximately $7\frac{1}{2}$ fluid ounces in each leg. Recommended grades of oil are Castrolite, Mobiloil Arctic, Essolube 20, B.P. Energol S.A.E. 20 and Shell X-100 20/20W.

SECTION J7

Front Fork

With Casquette and Aluminium Alloy Bottom Tubes

"350 Clipper" and "Crusader Sports" 1959 onwards, "Crusader 250" 1957 onwards, "250 Clipper" late 1958 onwards and "250 Trials" 1962 onwards

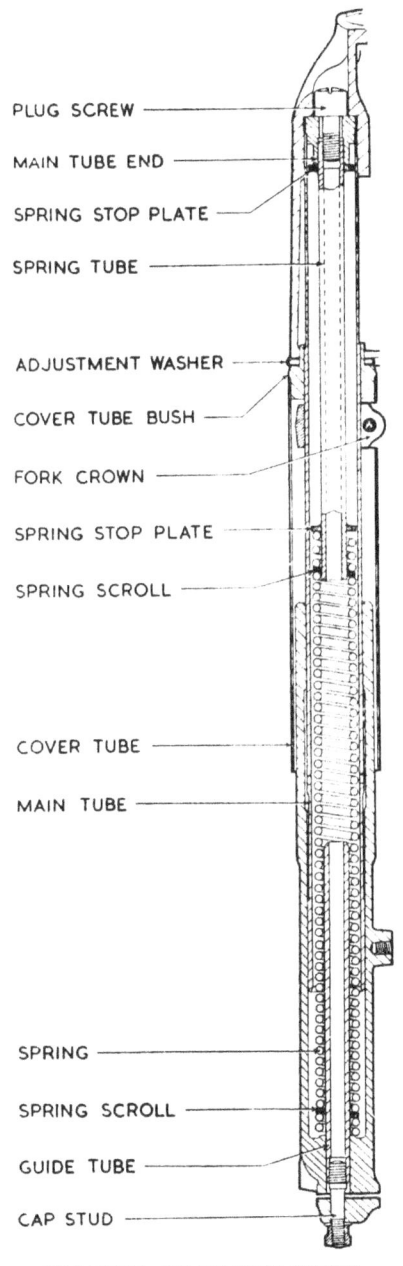

SECTION OF FRONT FORK
Fig. 1

1. Description

The telescopic fork consists of two legs, each of which comprises a main tube of chrome molybdenum alloy steel tubing which is screwed into the Casquette fork head at the upper end and securely clamped to the fork crown. Sliding over the lower end of the main tube is the cast aluminium alloy fork leg. Into the lower end of this is fitted a tube to which the bottom end of the compression spring is secured, the tube also acting as a guide for the spring. The top end of the spring is secured to a distance tube, which is held to the top of the main tube with a screw. The lower end of the main tube and upper end of the sliding fork leg are protected by a cover tube screwed to the fork crown.

The fork is filled with a light oil (S.A.E.20) to the level of a screw, for lubrication.

2. Dismantling Fork to Replace Spring

Place the machine on the centre stand, disconnect the front brake control and remove the front wheel and mudguard complete with stay. Unscrew the plug screws in the fork head, when the sliding fork legs, complete with springs and spring distance tubes can be withdrawn from the lower ends of the main tubes. The spring distance tube can now be unscrewed out of the spring and the spring, which is attached at the bottom end in a similar manner to that at the top, can be unscrewed from the sliding fork leg.

3. Spring

The original overall length of the spring is 16 in. A new spring should be fitted if the old one has set by more than 1 in.

4. Re-assembly of Parts

No difficulty should be experienced with this. Make sure that the spring is screwed right on to the scrolls at both ends. After assembling the sliding fork legs, springs and spring distance tubes,

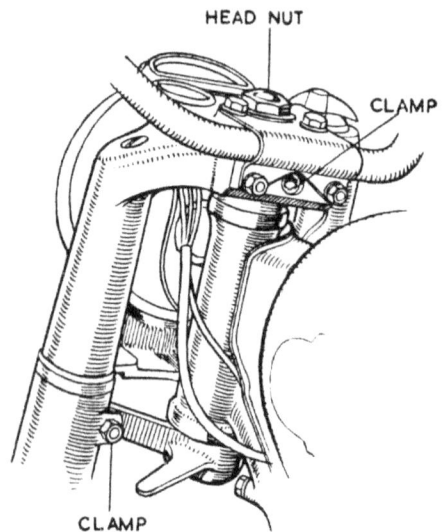

STEERING HEAD ADJUSTMENT
Fig. 2

line up the fork ends in the position in which they will be when the wheel is in position before tightening up the plug screws in the fork head.

5. Steering Head Races

The steering head bearing consists of two deep groove thrust races each containing nineteen ¼ in. diameter balls. The bearing is adjusted by tightening the steering stem locknut after loosening the ball head clip screw and both the fork crown clamp bolts. The head should be adjusted so that, when the front wheel is lifted clear of the ground, a light tap on the handlebars will cause the steering

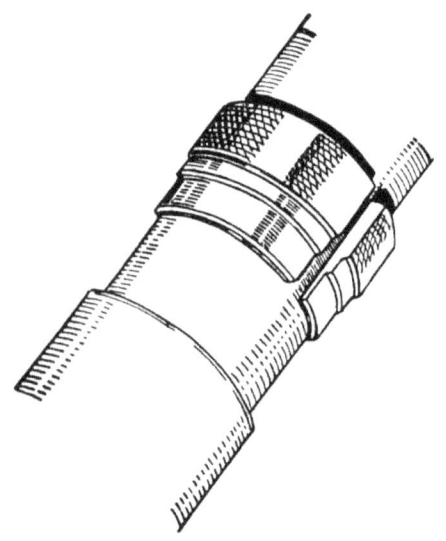

OUTER COVER CENTRALISING BUSHES
Fig. 3

to swing to full lock in either direction, while at the same time there should be only the slightest trace of play in the bearings. Do not forget to tighten the ball head clip screw and fork crown clamp bolts. Before tightening the latter, make sure that the cover tubes are located centrally round the main tubes so that the bottom tube does not rub inside the cover tube. A pair of split bushes (Fig. 3) is useful, to ensure centralisation of the cover tubes.

6. Removal of Complete Fork

The fork, complete with front wheel and mudguard, can be removed from the machine, if necessary, by adopting the following procedure.

The leads to the lighting switch and ammeter should be disconnected from the battery, rectifier, tail lamp, alternator and earth points at their lower ends, or at the plug and socket connectors when these are provided. If it is required to remove the lighting switch and ammeter, these are

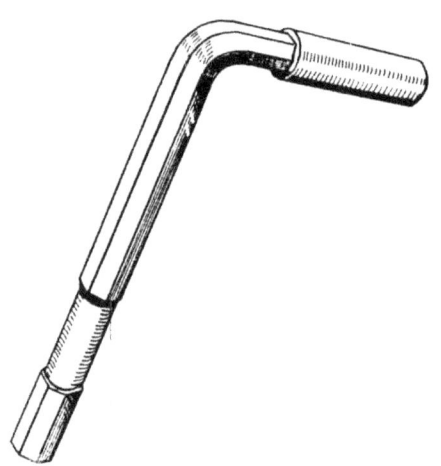

MAIN TUBE SPANNER
Fig. 4

push fits in the rubber bushes in the fork head. Disconnect the speedometer drive from the speedometer head and remove the two plug screws and loosen the steering head clip bolt and the two fork crown bolts.

Now unscrew the fork main tubes from the fork head by means of a hexagon bar ·500 in. across flats (Unbrako wrench W.11) or the special tool shown in Fig. 4. At the same time unscrew the steering stem locknut from the top of the steering stem, turning each tube and the nut a turn or two at a time. The main tubes have to be turned in a clockwise direction and the steering stem locknut anti-clockwise. When the nut has been removed from the steering stem and the main tubes have been completely unscrewed from the fork head, the complete fork and wheel with the steering stem can be lifted out of the head lug of the frame.

7. Lubrication

The oil level is determined by a small screw at the back of each sliding fork leg. First place the machine on the centre stand, thus allowing the forks to extend. To fill each fork leg to the correct level remove the plug screws from the fork head and the oil level screws at the back of the sliding fork leg. Pour oil in at the top until it runs out at the level holes. Wait until oil has stopped running and replace level plugs and plug screws.

Recommended grades of oil* are Castrolite, Mobiloil Arctic, Esso Extra 20W/30, B.P. Energol S.A.E. 20W, Shell X-100 20/20W or Havoline 20/20W.

8. "250 Trials"

A "Casquette" is not employed here, but the main fork tubes screw into the steering head and are secured to the fork crown by two clamp bolts as above. The forks differ in the following manner:

The bottom or sliding tube encases the lower part of the main tube and has, screwed to its upper end, an oil seal housing which, besides containing the oil seal, retains the top bush in the sliding tube. Screwed into the base of the main tube is a valve port which also secures the bottom bush.

In this fork a two-phase spring is used, and it abuts against spring guides at top and bottom.

Thrusting upwards from the base of the sliding tube is a hollow spring stud which passes through the bottom valve port and has the bottom spring guide attached to its upper end by a nut.

This spring guide has a ring of ports similar to those in the bottom valve port and each ring of ports is controlled by a valve plate or flap valve.

As the spring is compressed, both valve ports remain open, oil passes freely through them and no damping is achieved. Under very severe shocks, however, an oil control collar at the base of the sliding tube comes into play, trapping oil, and forming a cushion to check movement. On the rebound, both flap valves close and oil is forced to return through very restricted passages, thus damping the rebound movement of the fork.

*If temperature is above 90° F., use one of the following :—

| Castrol XL. | Mobiloil A. | Esso Extra 20W/30. |
| Energol S.A.E. 30. | Shell X-100 30. | Havoline 30. |

SECTION K3

Front Wheel

With Dual 6 in. Brake

Fitted to "Super Meteor,"
"500 Twin," "500 Bullet," "350 Bullet," 1956 onwards

1. Removal from Fork

To remove the front wheel from the fork place the machine on the centre stand and front stand, if fitted, or alternatively with sufficient packing (about 2 in.) beneath each side of the stand to lift the wheel clear of the ground when tilted back on to the rear wheel. Slacken brake cable adjustments and disconnect cables from handlebar lever and from operating cam levers on hub. Unscrew the four nuts securing the fork bottom tube lug caps (Part No. 38593) and allow the wheel to drop forwards out of the front fork. Make sure that the machine stands securely on the rear wheel and centre stand—if necessary place a weight on the saddle or a strut beneath the fork to ensure this.

2. Removal of Brake Cover Plate Assemblies

Lock the brake "on" by pressure on the operating lever, 38905 (R.H.) or 38906 (L.H.), and unscrew the cover plate nuts 31347. The right and left hand cover plate assemblies can then be withdrawn from the respective brake drums.

3. Removal of Brake Shoes and Springs

Unhook the springs from the shoes and lift away the latter. The pivot post and operating cam can then be withdrawn after removing the nuts which secure them.

4. Replacing Brake Linings

Brake linings are supplied either in pairs ready drilled complete with rivets (Part No. 42469BX)

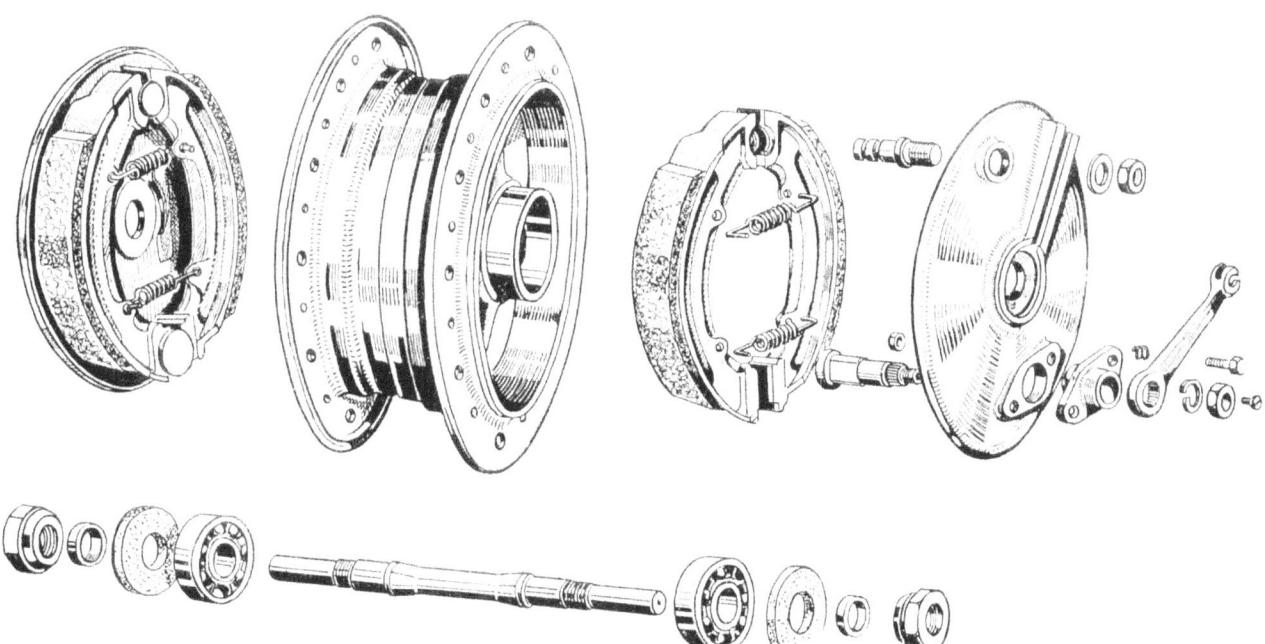

DUAL FRONT BRAKE
Fig. 1

or ready fitted to service replacement brake shoes (Part No. 41342SR). When riveting linings to shoes, secure the two centre rivets first so as to ensure that the lining lies flat against the shoe. Standard linings are Ferodo MS3, which are drilled to receive cheese-headed rivets.

Note : Some hubs were supplied fitted with bonded brake linings with no rivets. These can be serviced only by the use of the service replacement brake shoes (Part No. 41342SR).

5. Removal of Hub Spindle and Bearings

To remove the hub spindle and bearings having already removed the brake cover plate assemblies, lift out the felt washers, Part No. 21466, and distance washers, Part No. 30538. Now hit one end of the wheel spindle with a copper hammer or mallet, thus driving it out of the hub bringing one bearing with it and leaving the other in position in the hub. Drive the bearing off the spindle and insert the latter once more in the hub at the end from which it was removed. Now drive the spindle through the hub the other way, when it will bring out the remaining bearing.

6. Hub Bearings

These are deep groove single row journal ball bearings $\frac{5}{8}$ in. i/d by $1\frac{9}{16}$ in. o/d by $\frac{7}{16}$ in. wide. The Skefko Part No. is RLS5. Equivalent bearings of other makes are Hoffmann LS7, Ransome and Marles LJ$\frac{5}{8}$ in., Fischer LS7.

7. Fitting Limits for Bearings

The fit of the bearings in the hub barrel is important. The bearings are locked on the spindle between shoulders and the distance pieces, 30538, which in turn are held up by the cover plate nuts 31347. In order to prevent endways pre-loading of the bearings it is essential that there is a small clearance between the inner edge of the outer race of the bearing and the back of the recess in either end of the hub barrel. To prevent any possibility of sideways movement of the hub barrel on the bearings it is, therefore, necessary for the bearings to be a tight fit in the barrel but this fit must not be so tight as to close down the outer race of the bearing and thus overload the balls. The following are the manufacturing tolerances which control the fit of the bearings. The figures for the bearings themselves are for SKF bearings but other manufacturers' tolerances are similar.

Bearing o/d	1·5622/1·5617 in.
Housing bore	1·5620/1·5616 in.
Bearing bore	·6252/·6247 in.
Shaft diameter	·6252/·6248 in.

8. Refitting Ball Bearings

To refit the bearings in the hub two hollow drifts are required, as shown in Fig. 2. One bearing is first fitted to one end of the spindle by means of the hollow drift; the spindle and bearing are then entered into one end of the hub barrel which is then supported on one of the hollow drifts. The other bearing is then threaded over the upper

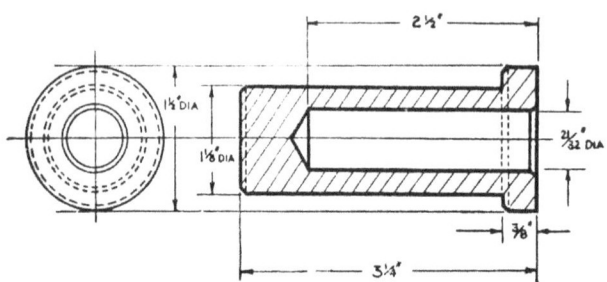

DRIFT FOR REFITTING BEARINGS
Fig. 2

end of the spindle and driven home by means of the second hollow drift either under a press or by means of a hammer which will thus drive both bearings into position simultaneously. In order to make quite sure that there is clearance between the inner faces of the outer bearing races and the bottom of the recesses, fit the distance washers, 30538, and the cover plate nuts, 31347, with either the cover plates themselves or additional packing washers behind the nuts. Tightening the nuts should not have any effect on the ease with which the spindle can be turned. If tightening the nuts makes the spindle hard to turn this may be taken as proof that the bearings are bottoming in the recesses in the hub barrel before they are solid against the shoulders on the spindle. In this case the bearing should be removed and a thin packing shim fitted between the inner race and the shoulder on the spindle.

9. Reassembly of Brake Shoes to Cover Plates

Assemble the pivot pin and operating cam into the cover plate, putting a little grease on the cylindrical portion of the cam. Smear a little grease on the pivot pin and on the flat portion of the cam. Assemble the shoes in position and hook the springs into them. The easiest way to do this is to hold the brake assembly in a vice by means of the locknut on the pivot pin and then pull the springs by means of a loop of fine strong string.

10. Floating Cam Housings

Note that the cam housings, Part No. 26836, are intended to be left free to float. The bolt holes in the cam housings are slotted and the securing pins, Part No. 252, are provided with double coil spring washers beneath their heads to enable them to be tightened sufficiently to prevent the cam housings moving under the influence of road shocks, while at the same time they can be, and should be, left free enough to be capable of being moved by hand in the direction of the slots. The pins, 252, are secured by locknuts, 7916, which are centre punched as an additional precaution.

The leading shoes (i.e. those towards the rear of the machine) have a servo action which render them more effective than the trailing shoes. This servo action causes the linings on the leading shoes to wear more quickly than those on the trailing shoes and at the same time tends to lift the leading shoes off the cams and press the trailing shoes harder on to the cams. With a fixed cam housing the result is that the majority of the cam pressure is applied to the less efficient trailing shoe. By leaving the housing free to float the cam can follow up the leading shoe thus maintaining equal pressure between the cam and the two shoes and so making full use of the more efficient leading shoe. Owing to the servo action the wear on the leading shoe with a floating cam housing is greater than that of the trailing shoe and in time the limit of float of the cam housing will be reached, after which the brake will continue to function as a fixed cam brake with some loss of efficiency. This can be restored by removing the shoes and fitting them in the opposite positions. Floating cam brakes are self-centering and there is no need to take any special precautions to see that the two linings are of equal thickness or that the brake shoe assembly is centered in the drum.

11. Refitting Brake Cover Plates

After assembling the brake shoe pivot pins and operating cams into the cover plates repack the hub bearings with grease. The recommended greases are Castrolease (Heavy), Mobilgrease (No. 4), Esso Grease, Energrease C3 or Shell Retinax A. These are all medium heavy lime soap or aluminium soap greases. The use of H.M.P. greases which have a soda soap base is not recommended as these tend to be slightly corrosive if any damp finds its way into the hubs.

Before fitting the distance washers and felt washers make sure that the inside of the brake drums are quite clean and free from oil or grease, damp, etc., and replace the brake cover plate assemblies. Securely tighten the cover plate nuts, 31347.

12. Wheel Rim

The rim is Type WM2—19 in. plunged and pierced with forty holes for spoke nipples. The spoke holes are symmetrical, i.e. the rim can be assembled to the hub either way round. Rim diameter after building is 19·062 in., tolerances on the circumference of the rim shoulders where the tyre fits being 59·930/59·870 in. The standard steel measuring tape for checking rims is $\frac{5}{16}$ in. wide, ·011 in. thick and its length is 59·964/59·904 in.

13. Spokes

The spokes are of the single butted type 8—10 gauge with 90° countersunk heads, angle of bend 95°—100°, length $6\frac{5}{8}$ in., thread diameter ·144 in., 40 threads per inch, thread form British Standard Cycle.

14. Wheel Building and Truing

The spokes are laced one over two and the wheel rim must be built central in relation to the nuts which secure the brake cover plates. The rim should be trued as accurately as possible, the maximum permissible run-out both sideways and radially being plus or minus $\frac{1}{32}$ in.

15. Tyre

The standard tyre is Dunlop 3·25—19 in. Ribbed tread.

When removing the tyre always start close to the valve and see that the edge of the cover at the other side of the wheel is pushed down into the well in the rim.

When replacing the tyre fit the part by the valve last, also with the edge of the cover at the other side of the wheel pushed down into the well.

If the correct method of fitting and removal of the tyre is adopted it will be found that the covers can be manipulated quite easily with the small levers supplied in the toolkit. The use of long levers and/or excessive force is liable to damage the walls of the tyre. After inflation make sure that the tyre is fitting evenly all the way round the rim. A line moulded on the wall of the tyre indicates whether or not the tyre is correctly fitted. If the tyre has a white mark, indicating a balance point, this should be fitted near the valve.

16. Tyre Pressure

The recommended pressure for the front tyre is 18 lb. per square inch for wheel loads up to 240 lb.

17. Lubrication

No grease nipple is provided on later hubs, due to the tendency to over-grease, resulting in grease finding its way past the felt seals on to the brake linings.

The correct method of lubrication is to pack the bearings with grease after dismantling the hub, as described above.

Note that the brake cams are drilled for grease passages but the ends of these are stopped up with countersunk screws instead of being fitted with grease nipples. This is done to prevent excessive greasing by over-enthusiastic owners. If the cams are smeared with grease on assembly they should require no further attention but in case of necessity it is possible to remove the screws, fit grease nipples in their place and grease the cams by this means.

SECTION K7

Front Wheel

With Single Brake

1959-60 " 350 Bullet," 7-inch Brake
1958-60 " 350 Clipper " and 1958-60 Trials " Works Replica," 6-inch Brake

1. Removal from Fork

To remove the front wheel from the fork place the machine on the centre stand with sufficient packing (about 2 in.) beneath each side of the stand to lift the wheel clear off the ground when tilted back on to the rear wheel. Slacken the brake cable adjustment and disconnect the cable from the handlebar lever and from the operating cam lever on the hub. Unscrew the four nuts securing the fork leg caps and allow the wheel to drop forward out of the front fork. Make sure that the machine stands securely on the rear wheel and centre stand—if necessary place a weight on the saddle or a strut beneath the fork to ensure this.

2. Removal of Brake Cover Plate Assembly

Lock the brake "on" by pressure on the operating lever and unscrew the cover plate nut. The cover plate assembly can then be withdrawn from the brake drum.

3. Removal of Brake Shoes for Replacement, etc.

The brake shoes can be removed after detaching the return springs. The brake linings are bonded to the shoes and if requiring to be renewed should be sent for servicing.

4. Removal of Brake Operating Cam

To remove the operating cam unscrew the nut, 10314, which secures the operating lever to the splines on the cam. A sharp tap on the end of the cam spindle will now free the lever, after which the cam can be withdrawn from its housing. **Do not try and remove the brake shoe pivot pin; it is cast into the brake cover plate and cannot be removed.**

5. Removal of Hub Spindle and Bearings

To remove the hub spindle and bearings having first removed the brake cover plate, unscrew the retaining nut and remove the dust excluder from the non-brake side of the hub. Now remove the felt washers and the distance washer from the brake side and hit one end of the spindle with a

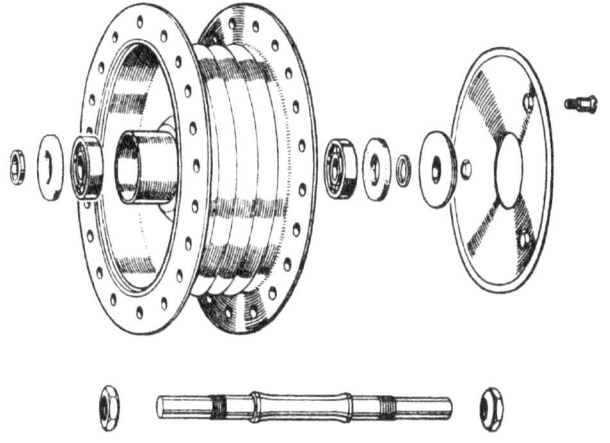

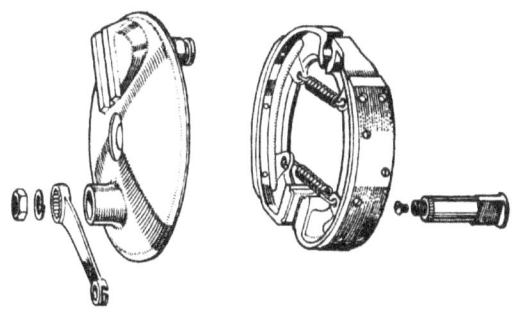

FRONT HUB AND BRAKE
Fig. 1

copper hammer or mallet, thus driving it out of the hub, bringing one bearing with it and leaving the other in position in the hub. Drive the bearing off the spindle and insert the latter once more in the hub at the end from which it was removed. Now drive the spindle through the hub the other way, when it will bring out the remaining bearing.

1959/1960 "350 Bullet" machines with 7 in. brakes have no loose, pressed cover on the non-brake side (see Fig. 1). Where this is fitted, the three screws holding it, and the cover plate, must be removed before attempting bearing removal.

6. Hub Bearings

These are deep-groove single-row journal ball bearings, $\frac{5}{8}$ in. i/d by $1\frac{9}{16}$ in. o/d by $\frac{7}{16}$ in. wide. The Skefko Part No. is RLS5. Equivalent bearings of other makes are Hoffmann LS7, Ransome and Marles LJ $\frac{5}{8}$ in., Fischer LS7.

7. Fitting Limits for Bearings

The fit of the bearings in the hub barrel is important. The bearings are locked on the spindle between shoulders and the distance pieces, 30538, which in turn are held up by the nuts on the spindle. In order to prevent endways pre-loading of the bearings it is essential that there is a small clearance between the inner edge of the outer race of the bearing and the back of the recess in either end of the barrel. To prevent any possibility of sideways movement of the hub barrel on the bearings it is, therefore, necessary for the bearings to be a tight fit in the barrel, but this fit must not be so tight as to close down the outer race of the bearing, and thus overload the balls. The following are the manufacturing tolerances which control the fit of the bearings. The figures for the bearings themselves are for SKF. Bearings, but other manufacturers' tolerances are similar.

Bearing o/d, 1·5622/1·5617 in.
Housing bore, 1·5620/1·5616 in.
Bearing bore, ·6252/·6247 in.
Shaft diameter, ·6252/·6248 in.

8. Refitting Ball Bearings

To refit the bearings in the hub, two hollow drifts are required, as shown in Fig. 2. One bearing is first fitted to one end of the spindle by means of the hollow drift; the spindle and bearing are then entered into one end of the hub barrel, which is then supported on one of the hollow drifts. The other bearing is then threaded over the upper end of the spindle and driven home by means of the second hollow drift either under a press, or by means of a hammer, which will thus drive both bearings into position simultaneously. In order to make quite sure that there is clearance between the inner faces of the outer bearing races and the bottom of the recesses, fit the distance washers, cover plate, dust excluder and the nuts on the spindle. Tightening the nuts should not have any effect on the ease with which the spindle can be turned. If tightening the nuts makes the spindle hard to turn this may be taken as proof that the bearings are bottoming in the recesses in the hub barrel before they are solid against the shoulders on the spindle. In this case, the bearing should be removed and a thin packing shim fitted between the inner race and the shoulder on the spindle.

9. Reassembly of Brake Shoes and Operating Cam into Cover Plate

No difficulty should be experienced in carrying out these operations. Put a smear of grease on the pivot pin and on the operating face of the cam; also on to the cylindrical bearing surface of the operating cam. Fit the operating lever, 38905, on its splines in a position to suit the extent of wear on the linings and secure with the nut and washer. Note that the position of the operating lever may have to be corrected when adjusting the brake after refitting the wheel. The range of adjustment can be extended by moving this lever on to a different spline. Limit of wear is reached when the cam is turned through nearly 90° with the brake hard on, so that there is a danger that the operating springs cannot return the brake to the off position.

10. Final Assembly of Hub before Replacing Wheel

Before replacing the felt washers which form the grease seals, pack all bearings with grease. Recommended greases are Castrolease (Heavy), Mobilgrease (No. 4), Esso Grease, Energrease C3 or Shell Retinax A. These are all medium heavy lime soap or aluminium soap greases. The use of H.M.P. greases which have a soda soap base is not recommended, as these tend to be slightly corrosive if any damp finds its way into the hubs.

Make sure that the inside of the brake drum is quite free from oil or grease, damp, etc. Replace the felt washers, distance collars, dust excluder and brake cover plate and securely tighten the spindle nuts.

11. Wheel Rim

1959 and 1960 "350 Bullet" and 1960 "Clipper": The wheel rim is WM2—17 in., plunged and pierced with forty holes for spoke nipples. The spoke holes are symmetrical, i.e. the rim can be assembled to the hub either way round. The rim diameter after building is 17·062 in., the tolerances

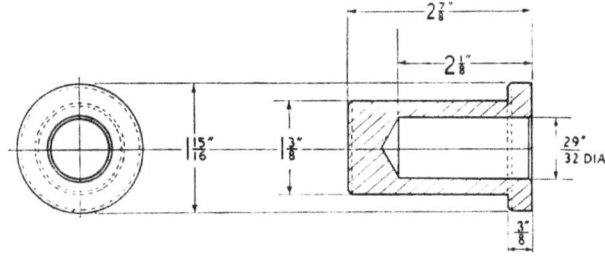

DRIFT FOR REFITTING BEARINGS
Fig. 2

on the circumference of the rim shoulders where the tyre fits being 53·642/53·582 in. The standard steel measuring tape for checking rims is $\frac{5}{16}$ in. wide, ·011 in. thick, and its length is 53·676/53·616 in.

Up to 1959 "Clipper," up to 1960 "500 Bullet," up to 1958 "350 Bullet": The wheel rim is WM2—19 in. plunged and pierced with forty holes for spoke nipples. The spokes are symmetrical, i.e. the rim can be assembled either way round. The rim diameter after building is 19·062 in., the tolerances on the circumference of the rim shoulders where the tyre fits being 59·930/59·870 in. The standard steel measuring tape for checking rims is $\frac{5}{16}$ in. wide, ·011 in. thick and its length is 59·964/59·904 in.

12. Spokes

"350 Clipper," 1960: The spokes are of the single-butted type, 8-10 gauge, with 90° countersunk heads, thread diameter ·144 in., 40 threads per inch, thread form British Standard Cycle. The inner spokes are $5\frac{5}{8}$ in. long with an angle of bend 100°, and the outer spokes $5\frac{3}{4}$ in. long with an angle of bend 80°.

The "Trials" model has a 6 in. brake, the front rim is WM1—21 in., there are forty spokes $7\frac{9}{16}$ in. long 10-8 gauge. On all "350 Bullets" up to 1958, "Clippers" up to 1959 and "500 Bullets" up to 1960, the inner and outer spokes are $6\frac{5}{8}$ in. long. "350 Bullets," 1959 and 1960 have spokes $6\frac{5}{16}$ in. long.

13. Wheel Building and Truing

The spokes are laced one over two, and the wheel rim must be built central in relation to the faces of the nuts on the spindle. The rim should be trued as accurately as possible, the maximum permissible run-out both sideways and radially being plus or minus $\frac{1}{32}$ in.

14. Tyre

The standard tyre is Dunlop 3·25-17 in. Ribbed. "350 Bullet" up to 1958, "350 Clipper" up to 1959, "500 Bullet" up to 1960: 3·25—19 in. When removing the tyre always start close to the valve and see that the edge of the cover at the other side of the wheel is pushed down into the well in the rim.

When replacing the tyre fit the part by the valve last, also with the edge of the cover at the other side of the wheel pushed down into the well.

If the correct method of fitting and removal of the tyre is adopted it will be found that the covers can be manipulated quite easily with the small levers supplied in the tool-kit. The use of long levers and/or excessive force is liable to damage the walls of the tyre. After inflation, make sure that the tyre is fitting evenly all the way round the rim. A line moulded on the wall of the tyre indicates whether or not the tyre is correctly fitted. If the tyre has a white mark indicating a balance point, this should be fitted near the valve.

15. Tyre Pressures

The recommended pressures for the front tyre are 16 lb. per square inch for wheel loads not exceeding 200 lb., 18 lb. per square inch for loads up to 240 lb., 20 lb. per square inch for loads up to 280 lb., and 24 lb. per square inch up to 350 lb.

16. Lubrication

Grease the bearings by packing them with grease after dismantling the hub as described above.

Note that the brake cam is drilled for a grease passage but the end of this is stopped up with a countersunk screw instead of being fitted with a grease nipple. This is done to prevent excessive greasing by over-enthusiastic owners. If the cam is smeared with grease on assembly it should require no further attention but in case of necessity, it is possible to remove the screw, fit a grease nipple in its place and grease the cam by this means.

SECTION L12

Rear Wheel (Non-Detachable Type)

1958-59 "350 Clipper"

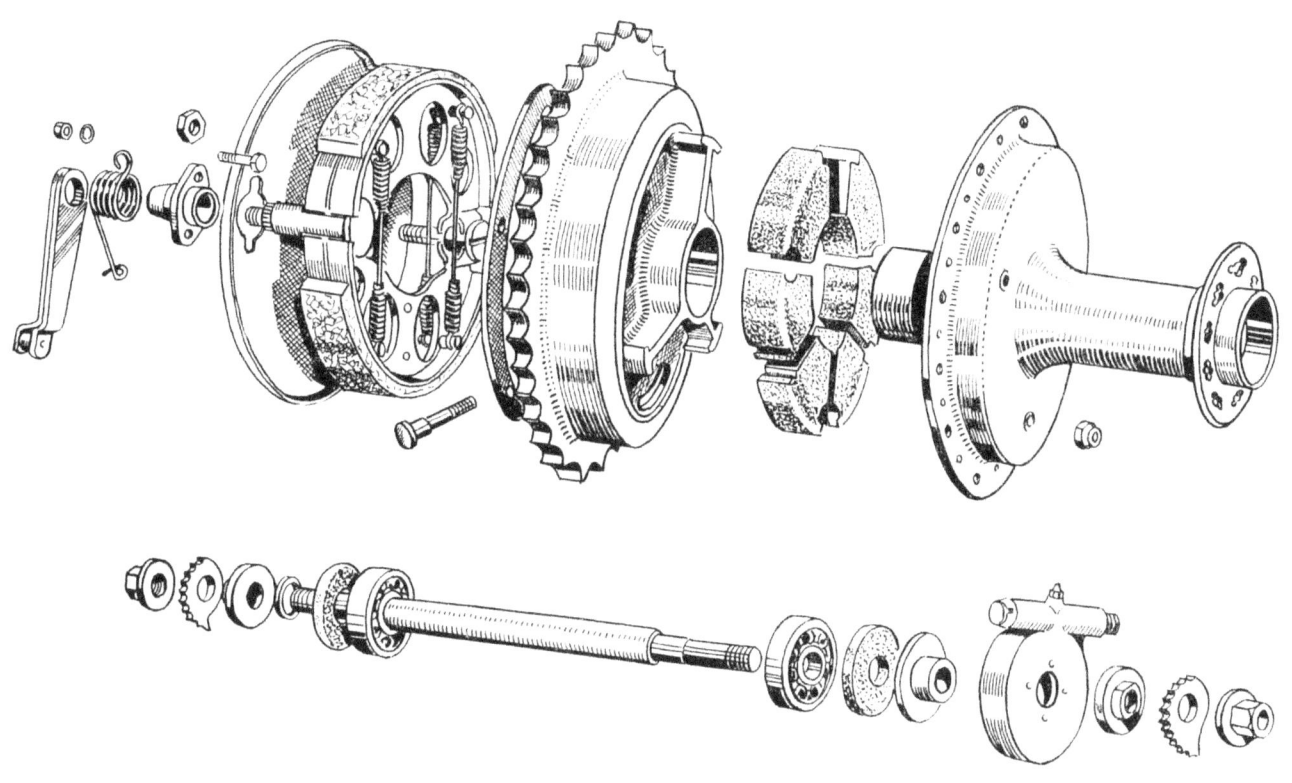

REAR HUB
Fig. 1

1. Description

These instructions cover the servicing of two different rear wheels, both of the non-detachable type incorporating a rubber cush drive and an internal expanding brake. Both types have a solid spindle and give a 3 in. chain line.

The heavier type used on the "Meteor 700" and "500 Bullet" has a 7 in. diameter brake drum while the lighter type used on the "500 Twin" and "350 Bullet" has a 6 in. diameter brake.

2. Removal and Replacement of Wheel

Place machine on the centre stand, if necessary putting packing pieces beneath the legs of the stand to lift the wheel clear of the ground. Remove the dual seat, if fitted, and the detachable portion of the rear mudguard. Disconnect the rear driving chain at the spring link and remove the chain from the rear wheel sprocket, leaving it in position on the gearbox countershaft sprocket. Unscrew the rear brake rod adjusting nut completely and depress the brake pedal so as to disengage the rod from the trunnion in the brake operating lever. Unscrew the brake cover plate anchor nut and remove this together with the washer behind it. Disconnect the speedometer driving cable, loosen the spindle nuts and mark the chain adjuster cams to ensure replacing in the same position. Slide the wheel out of the fork ends, tilting it so as to disengage the end of the brake shoe pivot pin from the slot in the fork end.

When replacing the wheel make sure that the dogs on the speedometer drive gearbox are engaged with the slots in the end of the hub barrel. Make sure also that the speedometer drive gearbox is correctly positioned so that there is no sudden bend in the driving cable. Make sure that the closed end of the spring link points in the direction of travel of the chain. Replace the chain adjuster cams in their original positions or, if necessary, turn each of them the same number of notches to tension the chain and maintain correct wheel alignment. Do not forget to refit the brake rod and adjust the brake so that the wheel turns freely while the brake is off, while at the same time only a small travel of the brake pedal is necessary to put the brake on.

3. Removal of Brake Shoes for Replacement, Fitting New Linings, etc.

Remove the complete wheel as described above, then remove the left hand spindle nut, chain adjuster and distance collar, thus permitting the complete brake cover plate with operating cam, pivot pin, shoes and return springs to be lifted off the hub spindle.

In the case of the 7 in. brake fitted to the "Meteor 700" and "500 Bullet" Models the brake shoes can then be removed, after detaching the return springs.

In the case of the 6 in. brake fitted to the "500 Twin" and "350 Bullet" Models, unscrew the pivot pin locknut and the operating lever nut, after which the assembly of the brake shoes, return springs, pivot pin and operating cam can be removed from the cover plate by unscrewing the pivot pin and applying light blows with a hammer and drift on the end of the operating cam. The return springs can then be unhooked from the spring posts in the brake shoes, thus allowing the whole assembly to fall apart.

4. Replacing Brake Linings

Brake linings are supplied either in pairs ready drilled complete with rivets, Part No. 37786BX (6 in. shoes) or 37787BX (7 in. shoes), or ready fitted to service replacement brake shoes, Part No. 38042 (6 in. shoes) or 38043 (7 in. shoes). When riveting linings to shoes secure the two centre rivets first so as to ensure that the lining lies flat against the shoe. Standard linings are Ferodo MR41 which are drilled to receive cheese headed rivets.

5. Removal of Hub Spindle and Bearings

To remove the hub spindle and bearings, having already removed the brake cover plate assembly and speedometer drive gearbox, lift out the felt washers and distance pieces then hit one end of the spindle with a copper hammer or mallet thus driving it out of the hub, bringing one bearing with it and leaving the other in position in the hub. Drive the bearing off the spindle and insert the latter once more in the hub at the end from which it was removed. Now drive the spindle through the hub in the opposite direction, when it will bring out the remaining bearing.

6. Hub Bearings

These are deep groove single row journal ball bearings. The lighter bearings used in the "350 Bullet" and "500 Twin" hubs are $\frac{5}{8}$ in. i/d by $1\frac{9}{16}$ in. o/d by $\frac{7}{16}$ in. wide. The Skefko Part No. is RLS5. Equivalent bearings of other makes are Hoffmann LS7, Ransome and Marles LJ $\frac{5}{8}$ in., Fischer LS7.

The heavier bearings used in the "Meteor 700" and "500 Bullet" Models are $\frac{5}{8}$ in. i/d by $1\frac{13}{16}$ in. o/d by $\frac{5}{8}$ in. wide. The Skefko Part No. is RMS5. Equivalent bearings of other makes are Hoffmann MS7, Ransome and Marles MJ $\frac{5}{8}$ in., Fischer MS7.

7. Fitting Limits for Bearings

The fit of the bearings in the hub barrel is important. The bearings are locked on the spindle between shoulders and the distance pieces, which in turn are held up by the cover plate nuts. In order to prevent endways pre-loading of the bearings it is essential that there is a small clearance between the inner edge of the outer race of the bearing and the back of the recess in either end of the hub barrel. To prevent any possibility of sideways movement of the hub barrel on the bearings it is, therefore, necessary for the bearings to be a tight fit in the barrel but this fit must not be so tight as to close down the outer race of the bearing and thus overload the balls. The following are the manufacturing tolerances which control the fit of the bearings. The figures for the bearings themselves are for SKF bearings but other manufacturers' tolerances are similar.

	"350 Bullet" and "500 Twin"	"Meteor 700" and "500 Bullet"
Bearing o/d	1·5622/1·5617 in.	1·8122/1·8117 in.
Housing bore	1·5620/1·5615 in.	1·8115/1·8110 in.
Bearing bore	·6252/·6247 in.	·6252/·6247 in.
Shaft diameter	·6252/·6248 in.	·6252/·6248 in.

8. Refitting Ball Bearings

Note that the two ends of the spindle are not identical. The end with the shorter plain portion between the thread and the shoulder must be fitted to the brake drum side of the wheel.

To refit the bearings in the hub two hollow drifts are required, as shown in Figs. 2 and 3. One bearing is first fitted to one end of the spindle by means of the hollow drift; the spindle and bearing are then entered into one end of the hub barrel which is then supported on one of the hollow drifts. The other bearing is then threaded over the upper end of the spindle and driven home by means of the second hollow drift either under a press or by means of a hammer which will thus drive both bearings into position simultaneously.

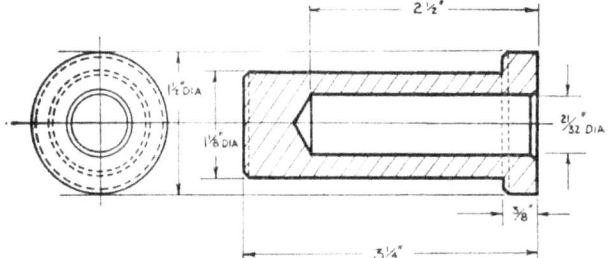

DRIFT FOR REFITTING BEARINGS
"350 Bullet"   "500 Twin"
Fig. 2

In order to make quite sure that there is clearance between the inner faces of the outer bearings and the bottom of the recesses fit the distance washers against the inner races of the bearings and either fit the assembly of brake cover plate, speedometer gearbox, etc., or make up this distance with tubular distance pieces. Fit and tighten the spindle nuts. Tightening the nuts

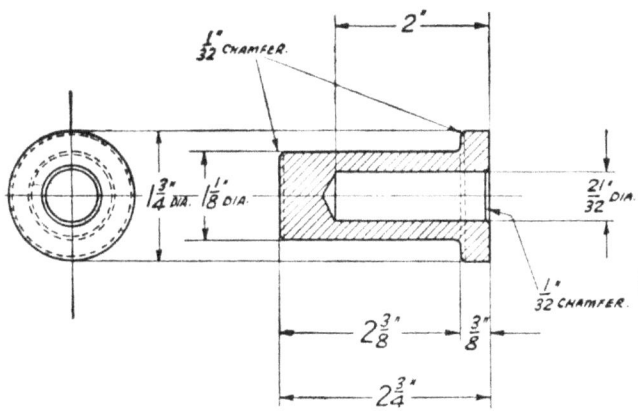

DRIFT FOR REFITTING BEARINGS
"Meteor 700"   "500 Bullet"
Fig. 3

should not have any effect on the ease with which the spindle can be turned. If tightening the nuts makes the spindle hard to turn this may be taken as proof that the bearings are bottoming in the recesses in the hub barrel before they are solid against the shoulders on the spindle. In this case the bearing should be removed and a thin packing shim fitted between the inner race and the shoulder on the spindle.

9. Removal of Brake Operating Cam and Brake Shoe Pivot Pin

The method of doing this has already been described in Paragraph 3 dealing with the 6 in. brake. The method is precisely the same for the 7 in. brake except that, owing to the different type of return springs used, it is, in this case, possible to remove the shoes from the pivot pin and operating cam before the latter are removed from the cover plate.

10. Cush Drive

The sprocket/brake drum is free to rotate on the hub barrel. Three radial vanes are formed on the back of the brake drum and three similar vanes are formed on the cush drive shell. Six rubber blocks are fitted between the vanes on the brake drum and those on the cush drive shell, thus permitting only a small amount of angular movement of the sprocket/brake drum relative to the hub barrel and transmitting both driving and braking torque and smoothing out harshness and irregularity in the former.

If the cush drive rubbers become worn so that the amount of free movement measured at the tyre exceeds $\frac{1}{2}$ in. to 1 in., the rubbers should be replaced. To obtain access to them remove the complete wheel as described above, remove the brake cover plate complete with the brake shoe assembly, unscrew the three Simmonds nuts at the back of the cush drive shell—if necessary holding the studs, 32431, by means of the flats on the heads inside the brake drum. Drive out the three studs into the brake drum after which the sprocket/brake drum can be separated from

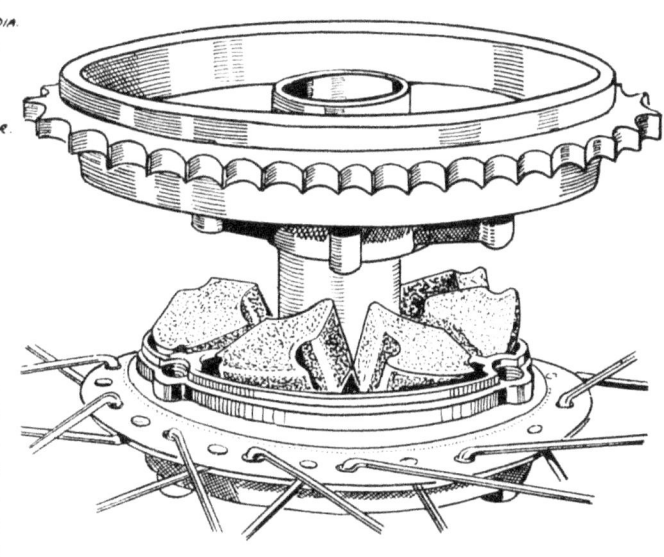

REASSEMBLY OF CUSH DRIVE
Fig. 4

the cush drive shell and the six cush drive rubbers can be lifted out.

When reassembling the cush drive the entry of the vanes between the rubbers will be facilitated if the latter are fitted into the driving shell first and then tilted. The rubbers should be liberally painted with soapsuds to facilitate entry of the vanes.

When reassembling the cush drive coat the inside of the bore of the sprocket/brake drum liberally with grease where it fits over the hub barrel and also put grease on the inner face of the lockring, 10097. The three Simmonds nuts should be tightened down solid as there is a shoulder on the stud which prevents tightening of the nuts from locking the operation of the cush drive.

11. Reassembly of Brake Shoes, Pivot Pin and Operating Cam into Cover Plate

No difficulty should be experienced in carrying out these operations. Make sure that the pivot pin is really tight in the cover plate and put a smear of grease in the grooves of the pivot pin and on the operating face of the cam; also on the cylindrical bearing surface of the operating cam if this has been removed. Fit the operating lever and trunnion on its splines in a position to suit the extent of wear on the linings and secure with the nut. The range of adjustment can be extended by moving the lever on to a different spline.

12. Centering Cam Housing

Note that the bolt holes in the cam housing are slotted, thus enabling the brake shoe assembly to be centered in the drum. It is not intended that on rear brakes the cam housing should be left free to float but the shoes should be centered by leaving the screws just short of dead tight. The brake cover plate assembly with the shoes should then be fitted over the spindle into the brake drum and the brake applied as hard as possible by means of the operating lever. This will centre the shoes in the drum. The screws should then be tightened dead tight and secured with the locknuts. If the shoes are not correctly centered the brake will be either ineffective or too fierce, depending on whether the trailing or leading shoe first makes contact with the drum. With the brake assembly correctly centered and the screws securing the cam housing correctly tightened wear on both linings should be approximately equal.

13. Final Reassembly of Hub before Replacing Wheel

Before replacing the felt washers which form the grease seals, pack both bearings with grease. Recommended greases are Castrolease (Heavy), Mobilgrease (No. 4), Esso Grease, Energrease C3 or Shell Retinax A. These are all medium heavy lime soap or aluminium soap greases. The use of H.M.P. greases which have a soda soap base is not recommended as these tend to be slightly corrosive if any damp finds its way into the hubs.

Make sure that the inside of the brake drum is quite free from oil or grease, damp, etc. Replace the felt washers, distance collars, the brake cover plate assembly, speedometer drive gearbox, distance collars, chain adjuster cams, the loose section of the spindle and the spindle nut. The wheel is then ready for reassembly into the machine.

14. Wheel Rims

The rim fitted to both types of wheel is WM2—19 in. pierced with 40 holes for spoke nipples. The internal width is 1·850 in. and the diameter after building 19·062 in., the tolerance on the circumference of the rim shoulders where the tyre fits being 59·930/59·870 in. The standard steel measuring tape for checking rims is $\frac{5}{16}$ in. wide, ·011 in. thick and its length is 59·964/59·904 in.

Note that two makes of rim are used— "Dunlop" and "Palmer Jointless." These differ in the positions of the pierced spoke holes. The Dunlop rims have a group of three holes on one side of the centre line, then a single hole on the other side, a further group of three and a single hole and so on. Palmer rims have the holes alternately spaced either side of the centre line. Both rims are interchangeable and both use the same length spokes but the method of lacing the wheel is different (see paragraph 16). Neither type of rim is symmetrical and care must be taken that they are built the right way round into the wheel.

15. Spokes

The spokes are of the single butted type 8—10 gauge with 90° countersunk heads, angle of bend 95°—100°, thread diameter ·144 in., 40 threads per inch, thread form British Standard Cycle. Spoke lengths are as follows:—

"350 Clipper" up to 1959, $8\frac{5}{8}$ in. and $7\frac{3}{4}$ in.

16. Wheel Building and Truing

The spokes are laced one over three and the wheel must be built central in relation to the outer faces of the distance collars which fit between the

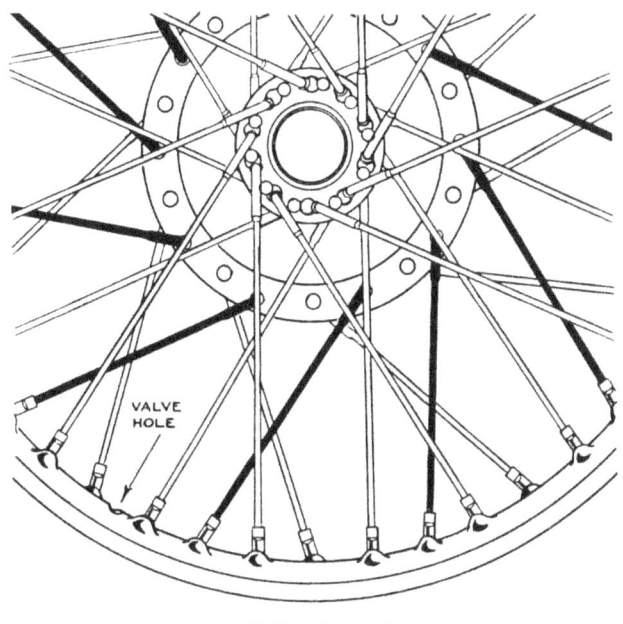

DUNLOP RIM
Fig. 5A

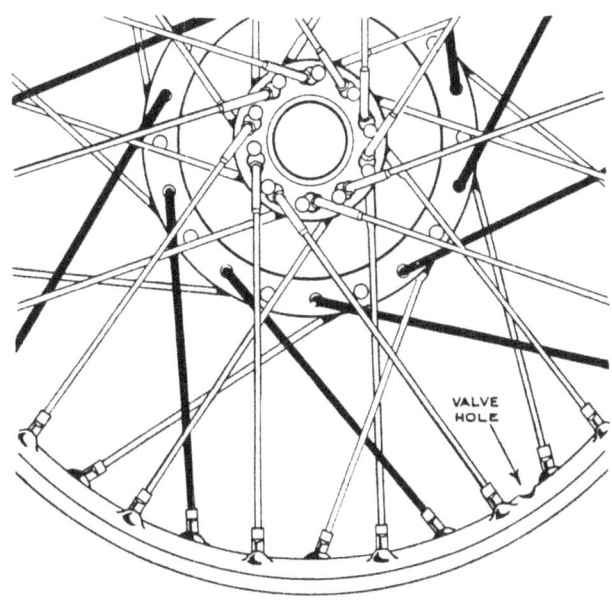

PALMER RIM
Fig. 5B

fork ends. The rim should be trued as accurately as possible, the maximum permissible run-out both sideways and radially being plus or minus $\tfrac{1}{32}$ in.

Fig. 5 shows the difference between the lacing when using Dunlop and Palmer rims. The key to correct lacing is the inside spokes to the large flange on the cush drive shell which must slope in the direction shown in Fig. 5. With the Dunlop rim this spoke goes to the middle hole of one of the groups of three (see paragraph 14) and the rim must be built into the wheel so that these groups of three holes are on the right of the centre line when the cush drive is on the left, i.e. the inside spokes to the large flange cross from the left to the right of the centre line.

With the Palmer rim the spokes from the large flange on the cush drive shell go to the more steeply angled holes in the rim which must be on the left of the centre line when the cush drive is on the left, i.e. none of the spokes crosses from left to right of the centre line.

17. Tyres

Standard tyres are Dunlop 3·50—19 in. Universal tread except on the "350 Bullet" where a 3·25—19 in. Universal tyre is used.

When removing the tyre always start close to the valve and see that the edge of the cover at the other side of the wheel is pushed down into the well in the rim.

When replacing the tyre fit the part by the valve last, also with the edge of the cover at the other side of the wheel pushed down into the well.

If the correct method of fitting and removal of the tyre is adopted it will be found that the covers can be manipulated quite easily with the small levers supplied in the toolkit. The use of long levers and/or excessive force is liable to damage the walls of the tyre. After inflation make sure that the tyre is fitting evenly all the way round the rim. A line moulded on the wall of the tyre indicates whether or not the tyre is correctly fitted. If the tyre has a white mark, indicating a balance point, this should be fitted near the valve.

18. Tyre Pressures

The load which the tyre will carry at different inflation pressures is shown below:—

Tyre Section Inches	Inflation Pressures—lb. per sq. in.					
	16	18	20	24	28	32
	Load per tyre—lb.					
3·25	200	240	280	350	400	440
3·50	280	320	350	400	450	500

19. Lubrication

A greasing point is provided in the centre of the hub barrel. Unless the barrel is packed full with grease on assembly (which is apt to lead to trouble through grease finding its way past the felt seals on to the brake linings) this greasing point is of little value and the best way to grease the bearings is by packing them with grease after dismantling the hub as described above.

Note that the brake cam is drilled for a grease passage but the end of this is stopped up with a countersunk screw instead of being fitted with a grease nipple. This is done to prevent excessive greasing by over-enthusiastic owners. If the cam is smeared with grease on assembly it should require no further attention but in case of necessity it is possible to remove the screw, fit a grease nipple in its place and **grease the cam** by this means.

SECTION L13

Rear Wheel

(Quickly Detachable Type with 7 in. diameter Brake and Full-Width Hub)

"350 and 500 Bullet," Trials "Works Replica" and "350 Clipper"—1960

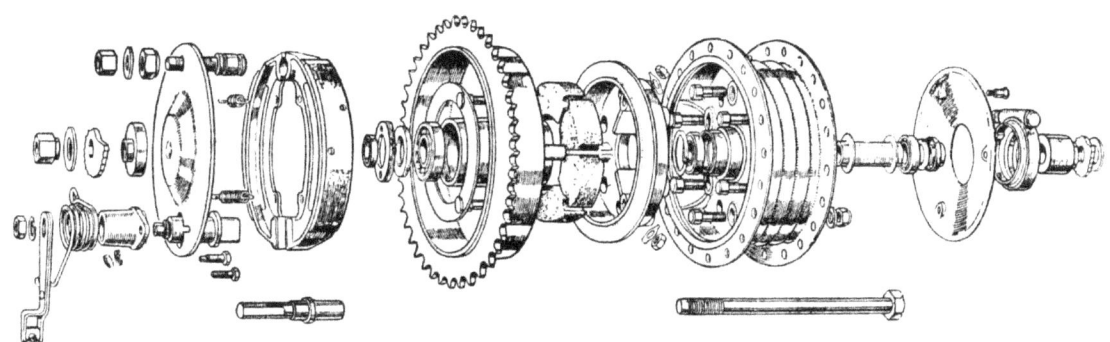

EXPLODED VIEW OF QUICKLY DETACHABLE REAR HUB
Fig. 1

1. Description

This wheel is of the "detachable" type, which enables the main portion of the wheel to be removed from the machine without disturbing the chain or brake. The wheel incorporates the well-known Enfield cush drive and also a 7-in. internal expanding brake.

2. Removal and Replacement of Main Portion of Wheel for Tyre Repairs, etc.

Place the machine on the centre stand, if necessary putting packing pieces beneath the legs of the stand to lift the wheel clear of the ground. Remove the dual seat (if fitted) and the detachable portion of the rear mudguard. Unscrew the loose section of the spindle, 41369, and withdraw this, together with the chain adjuster cam, 36649, preferably marking this to ensure that it is replaced in the same position. Now slide the distance collar, 41372, out of the fork end and lift away the speedometer drive gearbox, which can be left attached to the driving cable. The spacing collar, 40989, and the felt washer behind it may now be removed to prevent risk of them falling out when manipulating the tyre. If, however, these are too tight a fit in the hub to come out easily they may be left in place. The main body of the wheel can now be pulled across to the right-hand side of the machine, thus disengaging the six driving pins from the cush drive shell and enabling the wheel to be lifted out of the machine.

When replacing the main portion of the wheel, reverse the foregoing procedure. The cush drive shell can be prevented from rotating when turning the wheel to engage the six driving pins, if the machine is placed in gear or the rear brake is operated, taking care, when replacing the speedometer drive gearbox, that the driving dogs inside the gearbox engage with the slots in the end of the hub barrel. Before tightening the centre spindle make sure that the speedometer drive gearbox is correctly positioned so that there is no sharp bend in the driving cable.

3. Removal and Replacement of Complete Wheel for Access to Brake

Place the machine on the centre stand and remove the dual seat (if fitted) and detachable portion of the rear mudguard as if for removal of the main portion of the wheel only. Disconnect

REMOVAL OF WHEEL (OFFSIDE VIEW)
Fig. 2

the rear driving chain at the spring link and remove the chain from the rear wheel sprocket leaving it in position on the gearbox countershaft sprocket. Unscrew the rear brake rod adjusting nut completely and depress the brake pedal so as to disengage the rod from the trunnion in the brake-operating lever. Unscrew the brake cover plate anchor nut, 7598, and remove this together with the washer behind it. Unscrew the loose section of the spindle, 41369, two or three turns and the spindle nut, 28832, by a similar amount. Mark the chain adjuster cams to ensure replacing in the same position.* Disconnect the speedometer driving cable and slide the wheel out of the fork ends, tilting it so as to disengage the end of the brake shoe pivot pin from the slot in the fork end.

When replacing the wheel make sure that the dogs on the gear in the speedometer drive gearbox are engaged with the slots in the end of the hub barrel. Make sure also that the speedometer drive gearbox is correctly positioned so that there is no sudden bend in the driving cable. When replacing the connecting link in the driving chain make sure that the closed end of the spring link points in the direction of travel of the chain. Replace the chain adjuster cams in their original positions or, if necessary, turn each of them the same number of notches to tension the chain and maintain correct wheel alignment. Do not forget to refit the brake rod and adjust the brake so that the wheel turns freely when the brake is off, while at the same time only a **light pressure** on the brake pedal is necessary to put the brake on.

---

* Note that the wheel is not necessarily correctly lined up when the same notch position is used on both adjuster cams. Once the position of the cams which gives correct alignment has been found this alignment will, however, be maintained if both cams are moved the same number of notches.

4. Removal of Brake Shoes for Replacement, etc.

Remove the complete wheel as described above, then remove the spindle nut, 28832, chain adjuster and the distance collar, 41373, thus permitting the complete brake cover plate with operating cam, pivot pin, shoes and return springs to be lifted off the hub spindle. The brake shoes can then be removed after detaching the return springs. The brake linings are bonded to the shoes and if requiring to be renewed, should be sent for servicing.

5. Removal of Brake Operating Cam and Brake Shoe Pivot Pin

The pivot pin is threaded into the torque plate, 41109, from which it can be unscrewed after removing the locknut, 41375.

To remove the operating cam unscrew the nut, 10314, which secures the operating lever to the splines on the cam. A sharp tap on the end of the cam spindle will now free the lever, after which the cam can be withdrawn from its housing.

6. Cush Drive

The sprocket/brake drum, 41233, is free to rotate on the hub barrel. Three radial vanes are formed on the back of the brake drum and three similar vanes are formed on the cush drive shell, 40967. Six rubber blocks are fitted between the vanes on the brake drum and those on the cush drive shell, thus permitting only a small amount of angular movement of the sprocket/brake drum relative to the hub barrel and transmitting both driving and braking torques and smoothing out harshness and irregularity in the former.

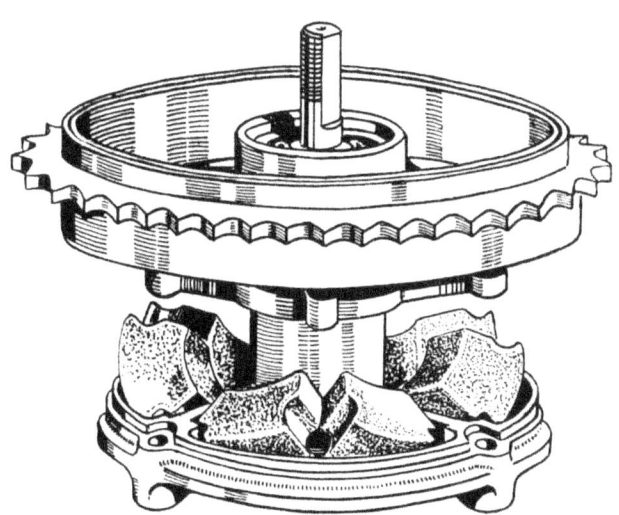

RE-ASSEMBLY OF CUSH DRIVE
Fig. 3

If the cush drive rubbers become worn so that the amount of free movement measured at the tyre exceeds $\tfrac{1}{2}$ in. to 1 in., the rubbers should be replaced. To obtain access to them remove the complete wheel as described above; then unscrew the loose section of the spindle, 41369, completely. The main portion of the wheel can then be lifted away from the assembly consisting of the fixed portion of the spindle, sprocket/brake drum complete with brake and the cush drive shell. Now remove the brake cover plate complete with brake shoes as described above, and unscrew the three nuts at the back of the cush drive shell after bending back the locking washers. The three studs, 41002, are brazed to the lockring, 10097, and should be driven out of the cush drive shell, each a little at a time to avoid distorting the lockring or bending the studs. The sprocket/brake drum can now be separated from the cush drive shell, and the six cush drive rubbers lifted out.

When reassembling the cush drive the entry of the vanes between the rubbers will be facilitated if the latter are fitted into the driving shell first and then tilted. The rubbers should be liberally smeared with soapsuds to facilitate entry of the vanes. Grease the inner face of the lockring, 10097, before assembling and tighten the three nuts down solid as there is a shoulder on the stud which prevents tightening of the nuts from locking the operation of the cush drive. Do not forget to bend up the tabs of the three locking washers.

When reassembling the cush drive, coat the inside of the bore of the sprocket/brake drum liberally with grease where it fits over the hub barrel.

7. Removal of Ball Bearings

To remove the ball bearings take the complete wheel out of the machine and separate the main portion of the wheel from the sprocket/brake drum, cush drive shell assembly, as described above. To remove the bearing from the sprocket/brake drum, first remove the brake cover plate complete with brake shoe assembly; then remove the distance collar, 41105, and unscrew the bearing retaining ring, 41108, with peg spanner. Now screw the loose section of the spindle into the fixed section and drive out the bearing by hitting the hexagon-headed end of the loose section of the spindle.

To remove the bearings from the loose half of the hub barrel, first lift away the distance collar, 41372, speedometer drive gearbox, the spacing collar, 40989, and the felt washer, 41006. Remove the bearing retaining circlip from the driving sprocket end of the barrel. Between the two bearings is a spacer, 40995, slotted at one end to enable a drift to be used on the bearing at that end.

Remove this bearing first, then enter the loose section of the spindle into the spacer and drive out the remaining bearing by means of a hammer and drift applied to the hexagon-headed end of the spindle.

8. Hub Bearings

These are deep-groove single-row journal ball bearings. The sprocket/brake drum bearing is a Skefko RLS7, $\frac{7}{8}$ in. i/d, by 2 in. o/d, by $\frac{9}{16}$ in. wide. Equivalent bearings of other makes are Hoffmann LS9, Ransome & Marles LJ. $\frac{7}{8}$ in., and Fischer LS9. The two bearings in the hub barrel are Skefko RLS5, $\frac{5}{8}$ in. i/d, by $1\frac{9}{16}$ in. o/d, by $\frac{7}{16}$ in. wide. Equivalent bearings of other makes are Hoffman LS7, Ransome & Marles LJ $\frac{5}{8}$ in., and Fischer LS7.

9. Removal of Hub Driving Pins

To remove the six driving pins from the aluminium full-width hub, first remove the hub cap after unscrewing the three screws attaching it to the hub. Unscrew the six Simmonds nuts and drive out the pins.

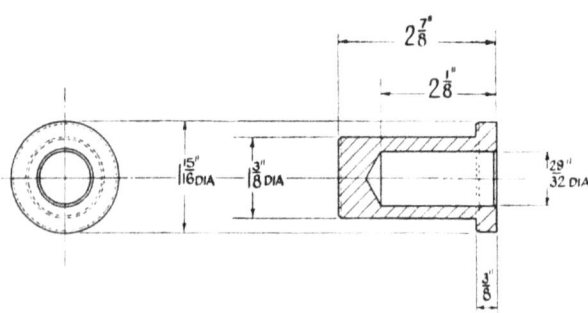

DRIFT FOR RE-FITTING BEARING

Fig. 4

10. Refitting Ball Bearings

To refit the sprocket/brake drum bearing, use a hollow drift as shown in Fig. 4. The bearing is first fitted to the fixed section of the spindle; the spindle and bearing are then entered into the sprocket/brake drum and driven home, preferably under a press or using light hammer blows.

The two bearings in the hub barrel are pressed in, using the drift part of E.4823. First assemble the bearing into the circlip grooved end of the barrel and fit the circlip. Replace the bearing spacer, the slot in the spacer can be at either end of the hubs, and assemble the second bearing, supporting the hub on the inner race of the other bearing. If the drift part of E.4823 is not available it is essential that the last bearing is assembled by applying pressure to both inner and outer races simultaneously to avoid pre-loading the two hub barrel bearings.

11. Reassembly of Brake Shoes, Pivot Pin and Operating Cam into Cover Plate

No difficulty should be experienced in carrying out these operations. Make sure that the pivot pin is really tight in the cover plate and put a smear of grease in the grooves of the pivot pin and on the operating face of the cam; also on to the cylindrical bearing surface of the operating cam if this has been removed. Fit the operating lever and trunnion, 23371, on its splines in a position to suit the extent of wear on the linings and secure with the nut. The range of adjustment can be extended by moving the lever on to a different spline.

12. Centering Cam Housing

Note that the bolt holes in the cam housing, 26347, are slotted, thus enabling the brake shoe assembly to be centred in the drum. It is not intended that on rear brakes the cam housing should be left free to float but the shoes should be centred by leaving the screws, 26309 and 35140, just short of dead tight. The brake cover plate assembly with the shoes should then be fitted over the spindle into the brake drum and the brake applied as hard as possible by means of the operating lever. This will centre the shoes in the drum. The screws should then be tightened dead tight and secured with the locknuts. If the shoes are not correctly centred the brake will be either ineffective or too fierce, depending on whether the trailing or leading shoe first makes contact with the drum. With the brake assembly correctly centred and the screws securing the cam housing correctly tightened wear on both linings should be approximately equal.

13. Final Reassembly of Hub Before Replacing Wheel

Before replacing the felt washers which form the grease seals, pack all bearings with grease. Recommended greases are Castrolease (Heavy), Mobilgrease (No. 4), Esso Grease, Energrease C3 or Shell Retinax A. These are all medium heavy lime soap or aluminium soap greases. The use of H.M.P. greases which have a soda soap base is not recommended as these tend to be slightly corrosive if any damp finds it way into the hubs.

Make sure that the inside of the brake drum is quite free from oil or grease, damp, etc. Replace the felt washers, distance collars, the brake cover plate assembly, speedometer drive gearbox, distance collars, 41373 and 41372, chain adjuster cams, the loose section of the spindle and the spindle nut, 28832. The wheel is then ready for reassembly into the machine.

14. Wheel Rim

The wheel rim is type WM2-19 in. plunged and pierced with forty holes for spoke nipples. The spoke holes are symmetrical, i.e., the rim can be assembled to the hub either way round. The rim diameter after building is 19·062 in., the tolerances on the circumference of the rim shoulders where the tyre fits being 59·930/59·870 in. The standard steel measuring tape for checking rims is $\frac{5}{16}$ in. wide, ·011 in. thick, and its length is 59·964/59·904 in.

The "350 Bullet" details are as given below:

The wheel rim is type WM2-17 in. plunged and pierced with forty holes for spoke nipples. The spoke holes are symmetrical, i.e. the rim can be assembled to the hub either way round. The rim diameter after building is 17·062 in., the tolerances on the circumference of the rim shoulders where the tyre fits being 53·642/53·582 in. The standard steel measuring tape for checking rims is $\frac{5}{16}$ in. wide, ·011 in. thick, and its length is 53·676/53·616 in.

The spokes are of the single-butted type, 8–10 gauge, with 90° countersunk heads, thread diameter ·144 in., 40 threads per inch, thread form British Standard Cycle. The inner spokes are $5\frac{5}{8}$ in. long with an angle of bend 100°, and the outer spokes $5\frac{3}{4}$ in. long with an angle of bend 80°.

15. Spokes.

The spokes are of the single butted type, 8-10 gauge, with 90° countersunk heads, thread diameter, ·144 in., 40 threads per inch, thread form British Standard Cycle. The inner spokes are $6\frac{5}{8}$ in. long with an angle of bend 100°, and the outer spokes $6\frac{3}{4}$ in. long with an angle of bend 80°.

"Trials" and "500 Bullets" up to 1960: inner and outer spokes $6\frac{5}{8}$ in.

"350 Bullet" up to 1958: $6\frac{5}{8}$ in. and $6\frac{3}{4}$ in.

"350 Bullet" 1959 and 1960, "350 Clipper" 1960: $5\frac{3}{4}$ in. and $5\frac{5}{8}$ in.

16. Wheel Building and Truing

The spokes are laced one over two and the wheel rim must be built central in relation to the outer faces of the distance collars 41373 and 41372. The rim should be trued as accurately as possible, the maximum permissible run-out both sideways and radially being plus or minus $\frac{1}{32}$ in.

17. Tyre

The standard tyre is Dunlop 3.50—19 in. Universal tread.

When removing the tyre always start close to the valve and see that the edge of the cover at the other side of the wheel is pushed down into the well in the rim.

When replacing the tyre fit the part by the valve last, also with the edge of the cover at the other side of the wheel pushed down into the well.

If the correct method of fitting and removal of the tyre is adopted it will be found that the covers can be manipulated quite easily with the small levers supplied in the toolkit. The use of long levers and/or excessive force is liable to damage the walls of the tyre. After inflation make sure that the tyre is fitting evenly all the way round the rim. A line moulded on the wall of the tyre indicates whether or not the tyre is correctly fitted. If the tyre has a white mark indicating a balance point, this should be fitted near the valve.

"350 Clipper" 1960: 3·25–17 in.

"350 Bullet" 1959 and 1960: 3·25–17 in.

18. Tyre Pressures

The recommended pressures for the rear tyre are 16 lb. per square inch for wheel loads not exceeding 280 lb., 18 lb. per square inch for loads up to 320 lb., 20 lb. per square inch for loads up to 350 lb., 24 lb. per square inch for loads up to 400 lb., 28 lb. per square inch up to 450 lb., and 32 lb. per square inch up to 500 lb.

19. Lubrication

Grease the bearings by packing them with grease after dismantling the hub as described above.

Note that the brake cam is drilled for a grease passage but the end of this is stopped up with a countersunk screw instead of being fitted with a grease nipple. This is done to prevent excessive greasing by over-enthusiastic owners. If the cam is smeared with grease on assembly it should require no further attention but in case of necessity it is possible to remove the screw, fit a grease nipple in its place and grease the cam by this means.

SECTION M2

Special Tools

For "Bullets", "350 Clipper" and Trials "Works Replica"

SECTION C

Sub-Section	No.	Use	Page
4, 18	14835	Magdyno Pinion Extractor (Tool Kit)	2
7	TE.1124	Valve Spring Compressor	2
9	—	Valve Guide Mandrels	2
11	E.5477	Gudgeon Pin Extractor (Adaptor if necessary)	2
13	TE.1167	Valve Grinding Tool	3
16	E.5425	Pump Disc Lapping Tool	3
17	E.5451	Pump Worm Shaft Spanner	3
21	E.5410	Tappet Guide Extractor	3
23	E.5414	Clutch Centre Extractor	3

SECTION D

Sub-Section	No.	Use	Page
3	E.5121	Crankshaft Extractor	5
4	E.4816	Roller Race Assembly, Timing Side	4
4	E.4817	Bearing Assembly, Driving Side	4
5	E.6462	Locating Plate for Assembly of Cam Spindles	5
6	E.2775	Crankshaft Pot or Jig ("350 Bullet" and "350 Clipper")	5
6	E.2774	Crankshaft Pot or Jig ("500 Bullet")	5

SECTION H

Sub-Section	No.	Use	Page
5	E.5431	Frame Expander	6

SECTION J1

Sub-Section	No.	Use	Page
3	E.5417	Gland Nut Grips	6
3	E.5418	Lockring Spanner	6

SECTION J6

Sub-Section	No.	Use	Page
2	E.4912	Outer Tube Hand Grips	6
2	E.5417	Gland Nut Hand Grips	6
2	E.5418	Lockring Spanner	6

Special Tools for "Bullets," "350 Clipper" and Trials "Works Replica"

14835
MAGDYNO PINION EXTRACTOR

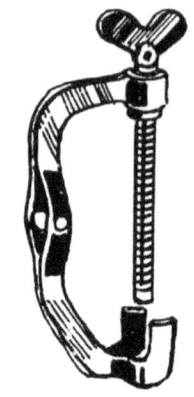

TE.1124
VALVE SPRING COMPRESSOR

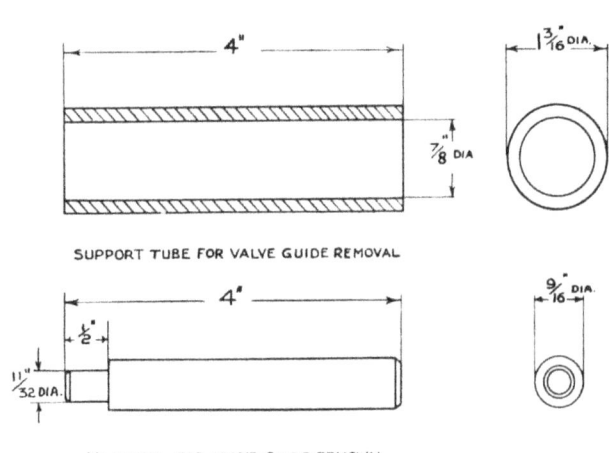

VALVE GUIDE MANDRELS

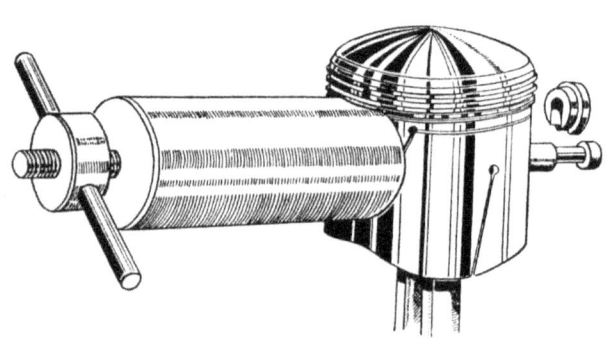

E.5477
GUDGEON PIN EXTRACTOR

Special Tools for "Bullets," "350 Clipper" and Trials "Works Replica"

TE.1167
VALVE GRINDING TOOL

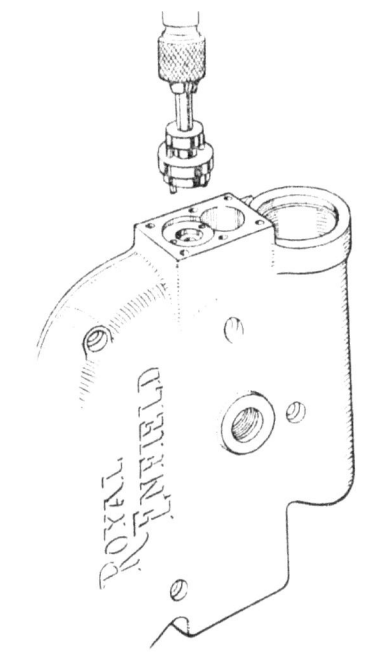

E.5425
PUMP DISC LAPPING TOOL

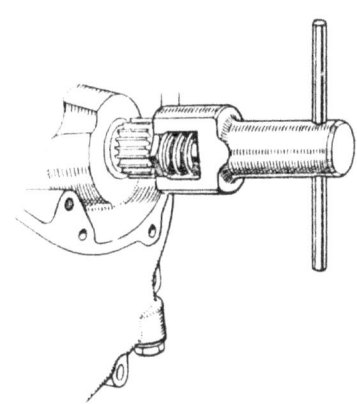

E.5451
PUMP WORM SHAFT SPANNER

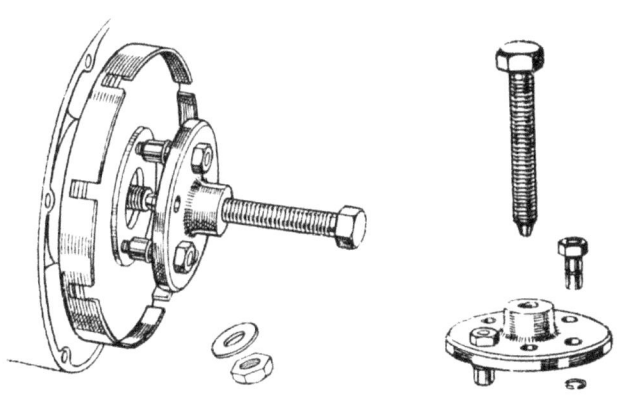

E.5414
CLUTCH CENTRE EXTRACTOR

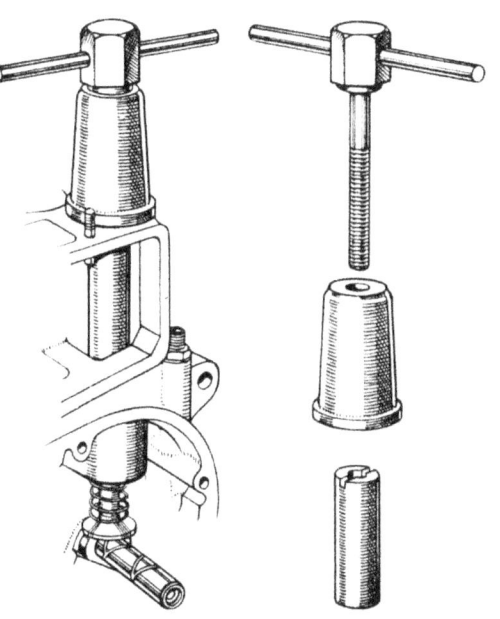

E.5410
TAPPET GUIDE EXTRACTOR

Special Tools for "Bullets," "350 Clipper" and Trials "Works Replica"

TOOLS FOR FITTING BUSHES

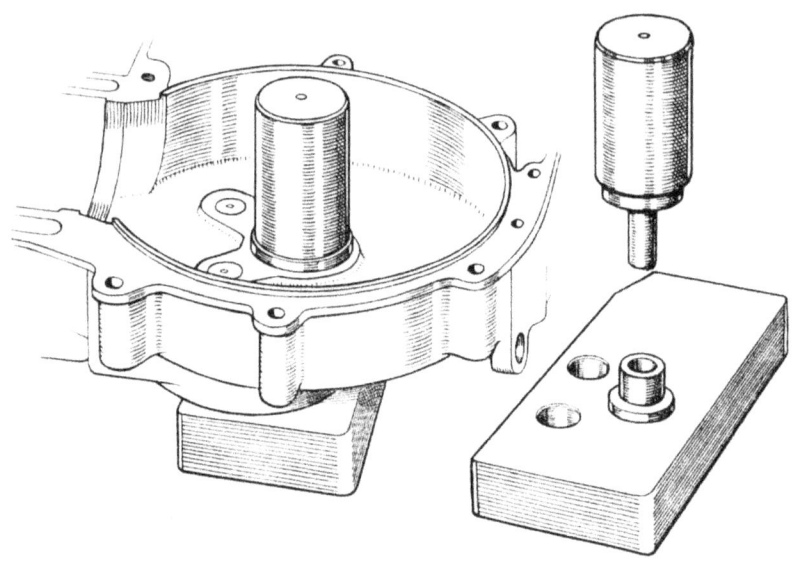

E.4816
ROLLER RACE ASSEMBLY, TIMING SIDE

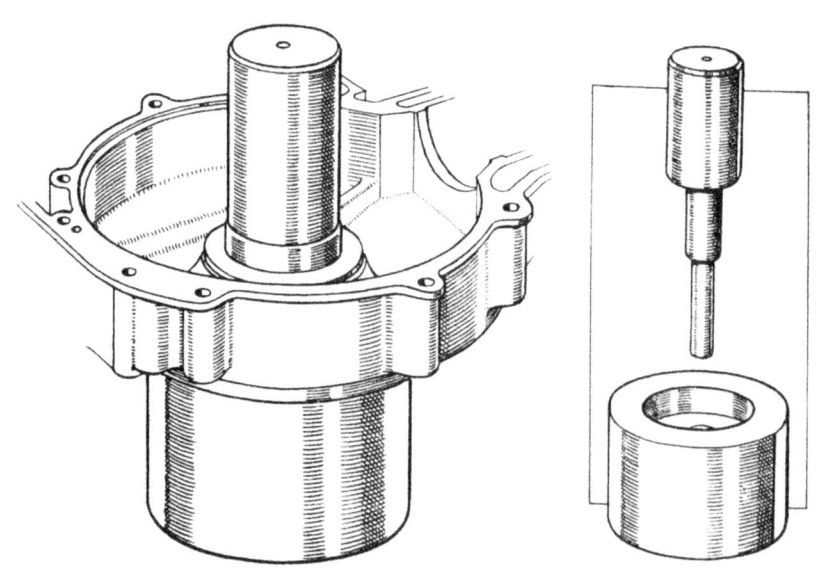

E.4817
BEARING ASSEMBLY, DRIVING SIDE

Special Tools for "Bullets," "350 Clipper" and Trials "Works Replica"

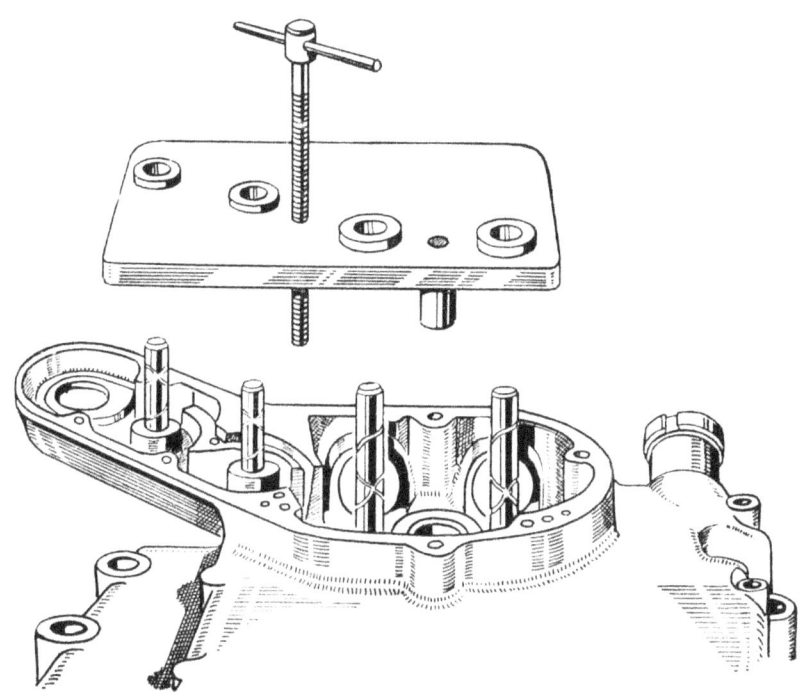

E.6462
LOCATING PLATE FOR ASSEMBLY OF CAM SPINDLES

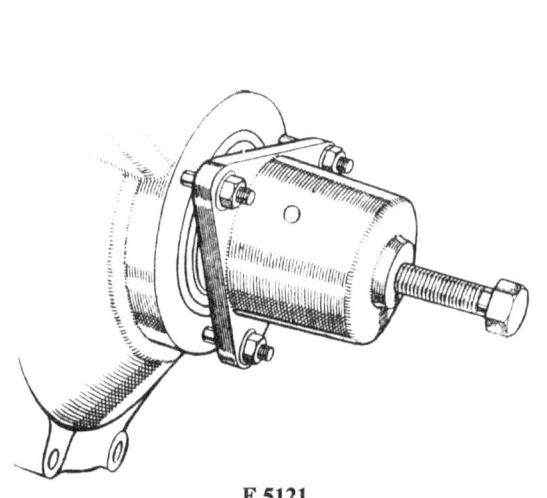

E.5121
CRANKSHAFT EXTRACTOR

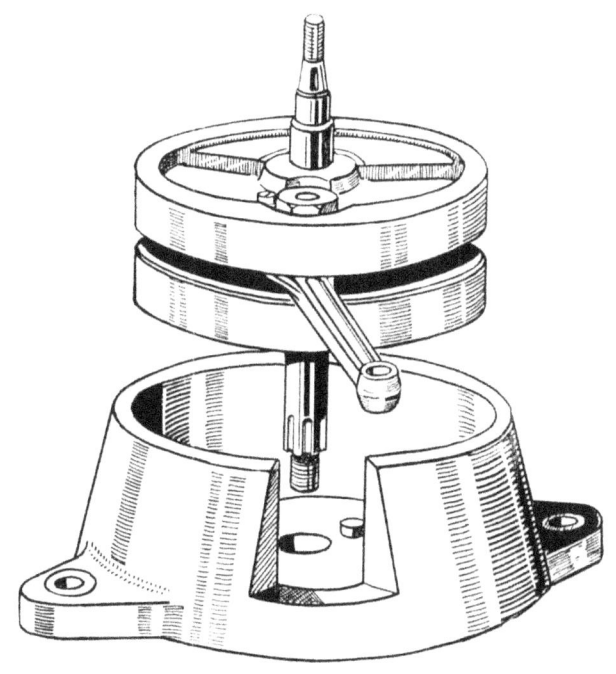

E.2774/E.2775
CRANKSHAFT POT OR JIG
for "350 Bullet" and "350 Clipper" (E.2775) and
"500 Bullet" (E.2774)

Special Tools for "Bullets," "350 Clipper" and Trial "Works Replica"

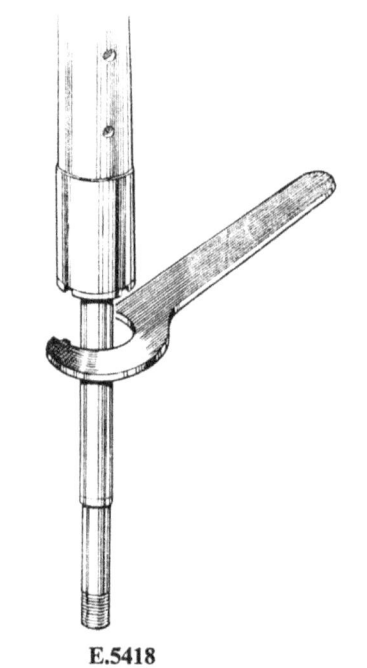

E.5418
LOCKRING SPANNER

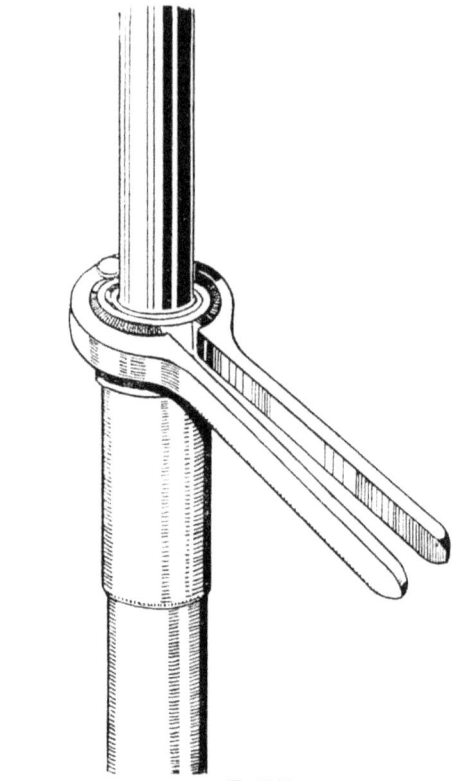

E.4912
GLAND NUT AND OUTER TUBE HAND GRIPS

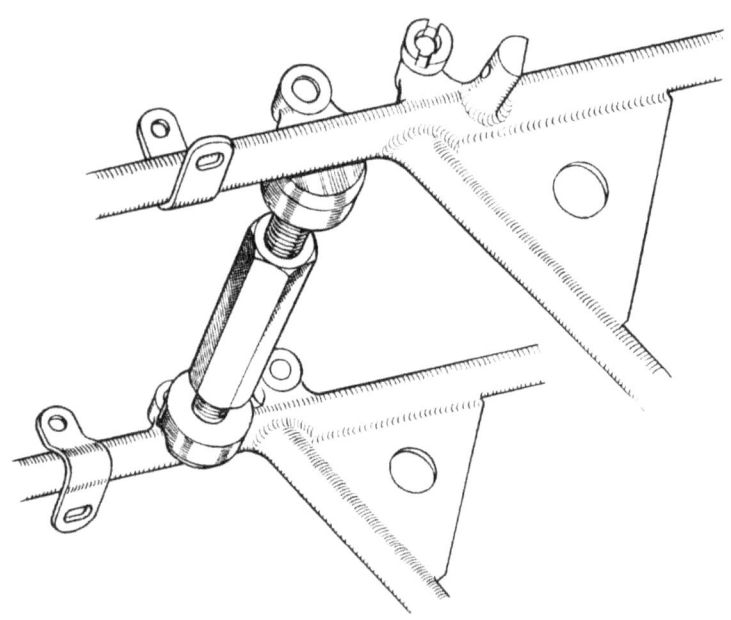

E.5431
FRAME EXPANDER

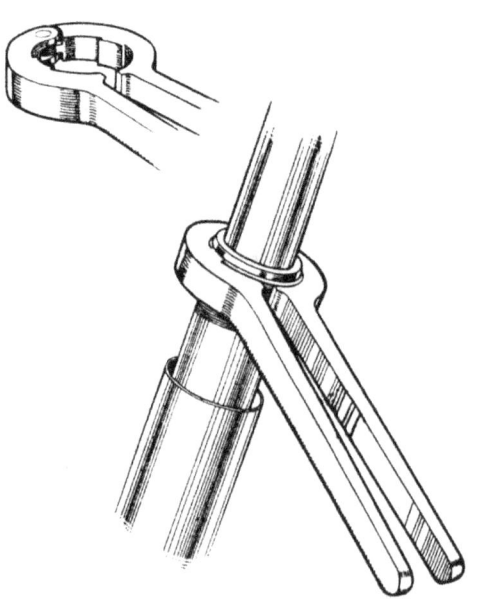

E.5417
GLAND NUT HAND GRIPS

SECTION M4

Special Tools

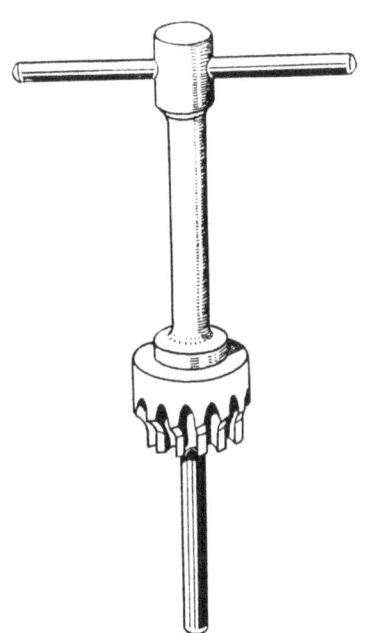

INLET VALVE SEAT ARBOR
T.2053 all models

INLET VALVE SEAT CUTTER
T.2054 Constellation, Super Meteor and Meteor Minor
T.2137 500 Twin
T.1892 500 Bullet
T.1891 350 Bullet

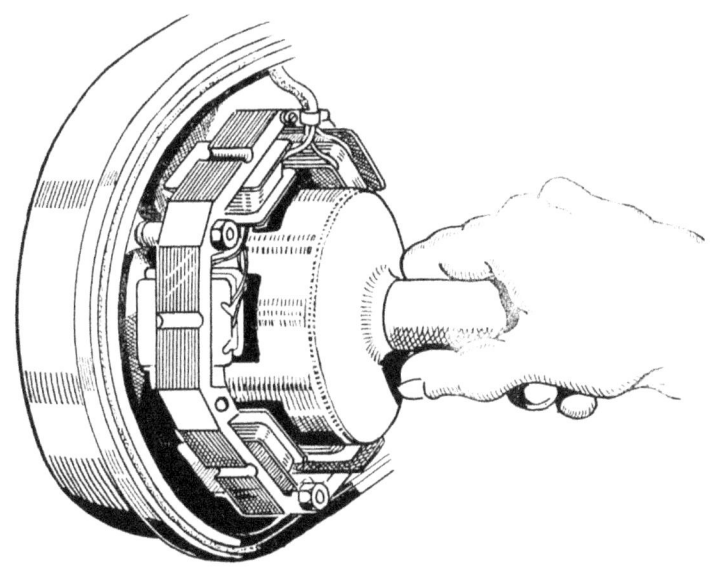

ASSEMBLY GAUGE IN USE TO CENTRALISE ROTOR

T.2055 Constellation, Super Meteor and Meteor Minor, also 350 Clipper, 350 Bullet and 500 Bullet

T.2138 1955-56 250 Clipper

SECTION P1

"Airflow" Fairing

1. Description of the Fairing

The "Airflow" fairing and front mudguard are fibre glass units and therefore very light, rigid and tough. The fairing, with the windscreen, provides full weather protection. It has two cubby holes and incorporates the headlamp, speedometer, ammeter and lighting switch.

On the rare occasions that it may be necessary to remove the mudguard and fairing from the machine, it will be found to present no difficulty if the following sequence is adopted:

2. Removal of the Windscreen

Remove the two screws which attach the number plate to the fairing. Removal of the number plate will expose a screw in the centre of the fairing which may now be taken out, together with the screws at each corner of the screen. The screen and metal back plate may now be lifted clear, taking care not to lose the five female screws with their plain steel and rubber washers.

3. Removal of the Headlamp

Take out the small screw from the underside of the headlamp rim. Raise the rim to clear its spigot plate from the slot in the lamp body shell and remove. Next take off the rubber ring from the light unit. By slackening the three light unit adjuster screws and rotating the light unit in an anti-clockwise direction, the unit may then be withdrawn sufficiently to disconnect the four leads.

Should it be necessary to remove the lamp body shell this may be done by unscrewing the four screws spaced round its flange. This also releases the rubber washer. Care should be taken not to lose the four screw locking plates inside the fairing.

4. Removal of the Headlamp Switch, Speedometer and Ammeter

Undo the switch knob screw and remove the knob. Unscrew the switch plate nut and remove the switch plate. The switch body may now be pulled out from beneath the fairing. Do not lose the plain washer situated beneath the switch knob.

Disconnect the speedometer drive, and, after removing two nuts, the spring washers and the bridge piece from the bottom of the speedometer, it may be removed.

To remove the ammeter it is only necessary to take off the rubber band from the body of the ammeter, after disconnecting the leads, and press down the small metal tabs which will be found turned outwards. The ammeter will then pull out from the top of the fairing.

5. Removal of the Front Wheel and Fork Legs

To remove the front wheel from the fork, place the machine on the centre stand with sufficient packing (about 2 in.) beneath each side of the stand to lift the wheel clear off the ground when tilted back on to the rear wheel. Slacken the brake cable adjustment and disconnect the cable from the handlebar lever and from the operating cam lever on the hub. Unscrew the four nuts securing the fork leg caps and allow the wheel to drop forward out of the front fork. Make sure that the machine stands securely on the rear wheel and centre stand—if necessary place a weight on the saddle or a strut beneath the fork to ensure this.

Unscrew the plug screws in the fork head, when the sliding fork legs, complete with springs and spring distance tubes, can be withdrawn from the lower ends of the main tubes.

6. Removal of the Front Mudguard

From the top of the fairing the two clamp bolts holding the mudguard to the fork crown can be reached. Unscrew the nuts and push out the bolts.

On Early Models it is necessary to remove the centre pin securing the guard to the bottom of the steering stem. The mudguard may now be withdrawn.

7. Removal of the Fairing

First take off the exhaust pipe. This is held to one of the front engine bearer bolts and to the pillion footrest stud at the rear.

Slacken the hose clips and remove the attachment caps from the ends of the attachment studs to which the lower part of the fairing is anchored.

Unscrew the nuts and push out the stud which secures the upper part of the fairing to the tube extending forward from the steering head.

If required the two bottom attachment studs may be removed.

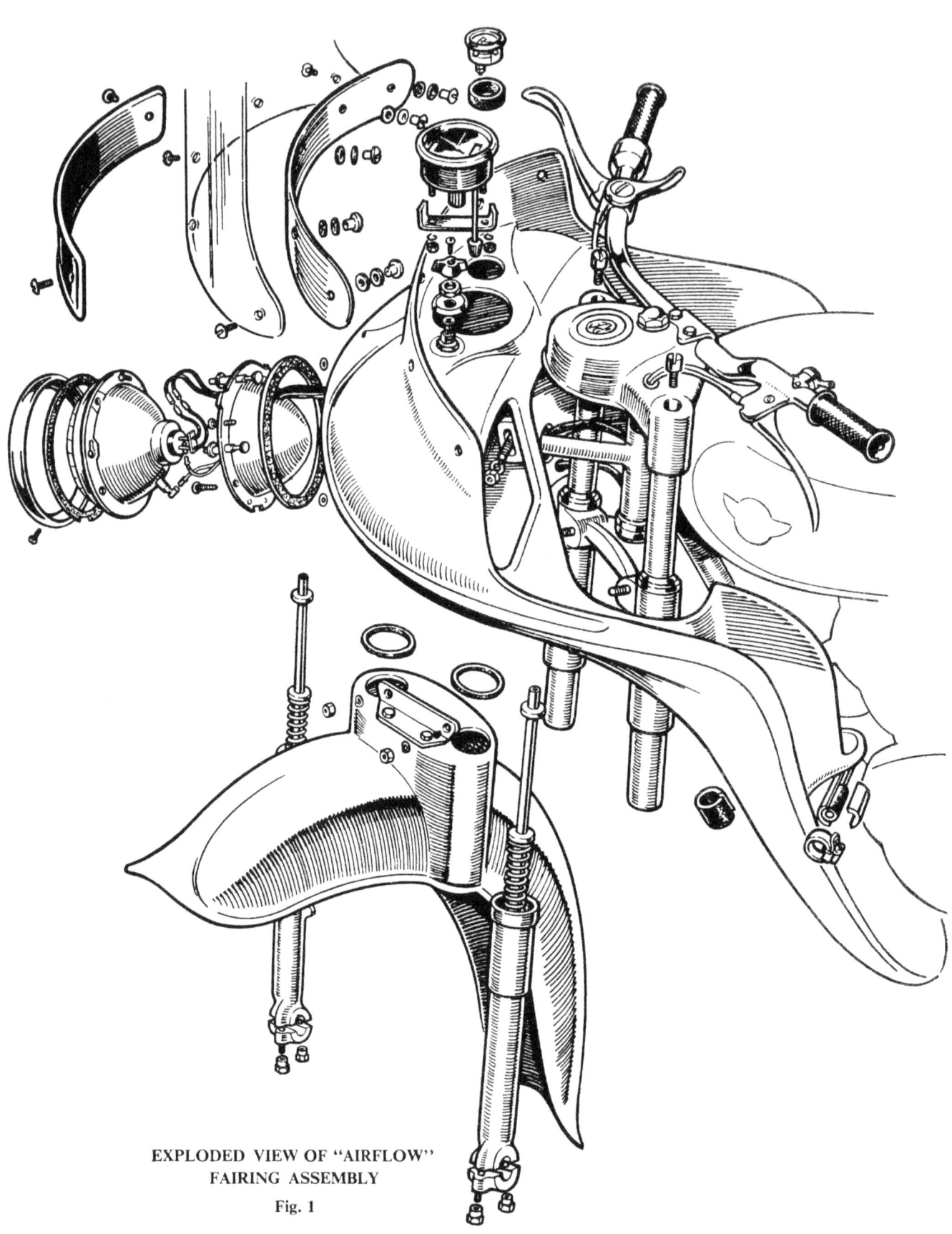

EXPLODED VIEW OF "AIRFLOW" FAIRING ASSEMBLY

Fig. 1

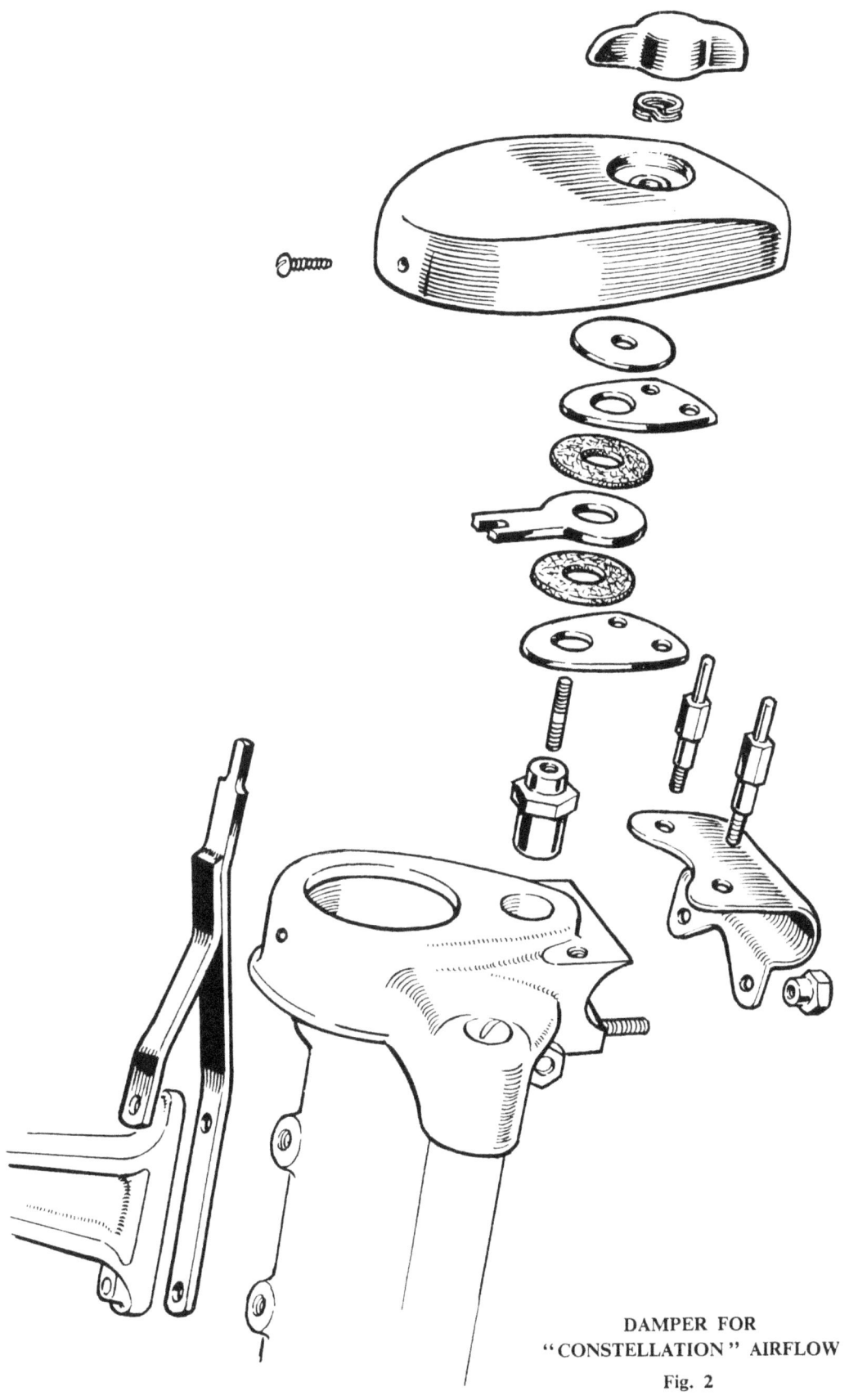

DAMPER FOR "CONSTELLATION" AIRFLOW

Fig. 2

8. Repairs

In the event of damage to the fairing, small repair kits consisting of a quantity of resin, catalyst and glass fibre are available from our Service Department. Instructions for carrying out minor repairs are issued with this kit.

9. Reassembly of the Fairing

If these have been removed replace the two bottom fairing attachment studs, also fit the rubber sleeve to the down tube. Next raise the fairing over the fork cover tubes, locating the bottom attachment plates on each leg shield over the attachment studs.

Incline the fairing outwards and thread the light and switch leads through the strut tube aperture, and the speedometer cable through the smaller hole below it. The fairing can then be pushed towards the forks until the strut tube, complete with buffer assembly, has entered the aperture and is positioned between the strut tube attachment plates. Fit the stud through the buffer assembly and attachment plates and secure washers and nuts to either end.

Complete the fairing assembly to the machine by fixing the attachment cap over the attachment stud rubber. Compress these parts together and secure with the attachment clip. The exhaust system may now be fitted.

10. Reassembly of Mudguard, Fork Legs and Wheel

Fit the two sealing washers to the fork cover tubes—not forgetting the small sealing washer for the fork crown extension tube on Early Models. Raise the mudguard, and thread the cover tubes (and the fork crown extension when fitted) through their respective holes. Line up the mudguard bracket holes with the fork crown clip bolt holes and fit the bolts, washers and nuts finger tight. (On Early Models fit the fork crown extension stud and washer.)

Slide the fork legs up into the fork head. Centralise the fork leg top with the cover tube, and push up to the full extent. Fit and tighten the plug screws in the fork head.

The fork crown clip bolts may now be tightened.

Replace the wheel and connect up the brake cable at both ends. **Do not forget to readjust the brake.**

11. Reassembly of Headlamp

Thread the red earth wire, the blue and red, and the blue and white main bulb wires from the dipper switch, and one green and brown pilot lamp wire, through the hole in the lamp body shell. Fit the body shell rubber washer between the fairing and the lamp body shell rim, and line up the holes in the shell rim, the washer and the fairing aperture rim. Secure with the four screws and locking plates, keeping the threaded plate at the bottom.

Connect the blue and red and the blue and white wires to the main bulb wires in the back of the light unit. Push the green and brown lead into the pilot lamp socket and the single red earth wire from the main harness into the socket on the main bulb fitting.

The light unit may now be pushed over the three adjusters, after first slackening them. Turn the light unit in a clockwise direction to secure. Afterwards tighten all the adjusters as far as possible.

Place the rubber ring over the light unit, with the face marked "BACK" facing the light unit rim. Locate the spigot plate, situated on the top underside of the rim, with the slot in the lamp body shell. Press the rim downwards and screw in the pin at the bottom of the rim.

Finally, adjust the aim of the light beam by turning the adjuster screws in a clockwise direction from the rear as necessary. Do not turn them further than required—not more than two screws will need adjusting.

12. Reassembly of Ammeter, Headlamp Switch and Speedometer

Insert the ammeter into the off-side hole in the fairing, turn up under the fairing the small tabs on the ammeter, and fit the rubber ring, pushing it up as far as possible. Connect up the two wires with the tab washer type connections to the ammeter terminals.

Push the switch up from the underside of the fairing, place in position the switch plate and secure with the nut. Finally, put on the small washer and the switch knob, and secure with the screw.

Push the speedometer into the fairing from above, and secure the bracket with the nuts and washers from below. Fit the speedometer drive and lamp.

13. Reassembly of Windscreen

Put the female screws, with their plain steel and rubber washers, into the back plate and windscreen, and line up with the holes in the fairing. Be sure to use the shortest male screw for the centre countersunk hole, and the two longest for attaching the number plate.

VELOCEPRESS MANUALS – MOTORCYCLE BY MAKE

AJS 1932-1948 SINGLES & TWINS 250cc THRU 1000cc (BOOK OF)
AJS 1945-1960 SINGLES 350cc & 500cc MODELS 16 & 18 (BOOK OF)
AJS 1955-1965 SINGLES 350cc & 500cc (BOOK OF)
AJS 1957-1966 FACTORY WSM - ALL SINGLES & TWINS
ARIEL UP TO 1932 (BOOK OF)
ARIEL 1932-1939 PREWAR MODELS (BOOK OF)
ARIEL 1933-1951 (WORKSHOP MANUAL)
ARIEL 1939-1960 4 STROKE SINGLES (BOOK OF)
ARIEL 1958-1964 LEADER & ARROW FACTORY WSM & PARTS LIST
ARIEL 1958-1964 LEADER & ARROW (BOOK OF)
BMW R26 R27 (1956-1967) FACTORY WORKSHOP MANUAL
BMW R50 R50S R60 R69S (1955-1969) FACTORY WORKSHOP MANUAL
BMW R50/5 R60/5 R75/5 (1969-1973) FACTORY WORKSHOP MANUAL
BRIDGESTONE 90 SERIES FACTORY WSM & PARTS CATALOGUE
BRIDGESTONE 175 SERIES FACTORY WSM & PARTS CATALOGUE
BRIDGESTONE 350 SERIES FACTORY WSM & PARTS CATALOGUES
BSA SERVICE SHEETS MASTER CATALOGUE ALL MODELS 1945-1967
BSA BANTAM D1 TO D7 1948-1966 FACTORY SERVICE SHEETS MANUAL
BSA BANTAM ALL MODELS FROM 1948 ONWARDS (BOOK OF)
BSA BANTAM D14 FACTORY SERVICE MANUAL
BSA DANDY FACTORY WORKSHOP MANUAL (COMPILATION)
BSA SINGLES & V-TWINS UP TO 1926 inc. 1927 SUPPLEMENT (BOOK OF)
BSA SINGLES & V-TWINS UP TO 1930 (BOOK OF)
BSA SINGLES & V-TWINS UP TO 1935 (BOOK OF)
BSA SINGLES & V-TWINS 1936-1939 (BOOK OF)
BSA C10, C11 & C12 1945-1958 FACTORY SERVICE SHEETS MANUAL
BSA OHV & SV SINGLES 250-600cc 1945-1959 (BOOK OF)
BSA C15 & B40 1958-1967 FACTORY SERVICE SHEETS MANUAL
BSA OHV & SV SINGLES 250cc (ONLY) 1954-1970 (BOOK OF)
BSA B31, B32, B33 & B34 1945-60 FACTORY SERVICE SHEETS MANUAL
BSA OHV SINGLES 350 & 500cc 1955-1967 (BOOK OF)
BSA M20, M21 & M33 1945-1963 FACTORY SERVICE SHEETS MANUAL
BSA TWINS A7 & A10 1948-1962 FACTORY SERVICE SHEETS MANUAL
BSA TWINS A7 & A10 1948-1962 (BOOK OF)
BSA TWINS A50 & A65 1962-1965 FACTORY WORKSHOP MANUAL
BSA TWINS A50 & A65 1962-1969 (SECOND BOOK OF)
DOUGLAS 1929-1939 PREWAR ALL MODELS (BOOK OF)
DOUGLAS 1948-1957 POSTWAR ALL MODELS FACTORY SHOP MANUAL
DUCATI 160cc, 250cc & 350cc OHC MODELS FACTORY SHOP MANUAL
HONDA 50cc ALL MODELS UP TO 1970 INC MONKEY & TRAIL (BOOK OF)
HONDA 90cc ALL MODELS UP TO 1966 (BOOK OF)
HONDA TWINS & SINGLES 50cc THRU 305cc 1960-1966 (BOOK OF)
HONDA TWINS ALL MODELS 125cc THRU 450cc UP TO 1968 (BOOK OF)
HONDA C100 50cc SUPER CUB O.H.C. 1959-1962 FACTORY WSM
HONDA C110 50cc SPORT CUB O.H.C. 1960-1962 FACTORY WSM
HONDA 50-65-70-90cc O.H.C. SINGLES 1959-1983 WSM
HONDA 100-125cc SINGLES CB/CD/CL/SL/TL 1970-1984 FACTORY WSM
HONDA 125-150cc TWINS C/CS/CB/CA 1959-1966 FACTORY WSM
HONDA 125-160-175-200cc TWINS 1965-1978 WORKSHOP MANUAL
HONDA 250-305cc TWINS C/CS/CB 1961-1968 FACTORY WSM
HOHDA 250-350cc TWINS CB/CL/SL 1968-1973 FACTORY WSM
HONDA 250-360cc TWINS CB/CL/CJ 1974-1977 FACTORY WSM
HONDA 350F & 400F 4-CYLINDER 1972-1977 FACTORY WSM
HONDA 450cc TWINS CB/CL 1965-1974 K0 to K7 WORKSHOP MANUAL
HONDA 500cc & 550cc 4-CYL 1971-1978 FACTORY WORKSHOP MANUAL
HONDA 750cc SHOC 4-CYL 1969-1978 K0~K8 WORKSHOP MANUAL
INDIAN PONYBIKE, BOY RACER & PAPOOSE ILL PARTS LIST & SALES LIT

J.A.P. ENGINES 1927-1952 & MOTORCYCLES 1934-1952 (BOOK OF)
MATCHLESS 1931-1939 ALL MODELS 250cc THRU 990cc (BOOK OF)
MATCHLESS 1945-1956 350 & 500cc SINGLES (BOOK OF)
MATCHLESS 1955-1966 350 & 500cc SINGLES (BOOK OF)
MATCHLESS 1957-1966 FACTORY WSM - ALL SINGLES & TWINS
NEW IMPERIAL ALL SV & OHV FROM 1935 ONWARDS (BOOK OF)
NORTON 1932-1939 PREWAR MODELS (BOOK OF)
NORTON 1932-1947 (BOOK OF)
NORTON 1938-1956 (BOOK OF)
NORTON 1945-1963 MODELS 16H, Big4, ES2, 19 & 50 WSM'S & PARTS
NORTON 1955-1963 MODELS 19, 50 & ES2 (BOOK OF)
NORTON 1948-1970 DOMINATOR TWINS FACTORY WSM'S & PARTS
NORTON 1955-1965 DOMINATOR TWINS (BOOK OF)
NORTON 1960-1970 TWIN CYLINDER FACTORY WORKSHOP MANUAL
NORTON 1970-1975 COMMANDO 850 & 750cc FACTORY WSM
NORTON 1975-1978 MK 3 COMMANDO 850 cc FACTORY WSM
PANTHER 1932-1958 LIGHTWEIGHT MODELS 250 & 350cc (BOOK OF)
PANTHER 1938-1966 HEAVYWEIGHT MODELS 600 & 650cc (BOOK OF)
PENTON-KTM-SACHS 1968-1975 100cc & 125cc WORKSHOP MANUAL
RALEIGH MOTORCYCLES 1919-1933 (BOOK OF)
ROYAL ENFIELD 1934-1946 SINGLES & V TWINS (BOOK OF)
ROYAL ENFIELD 1937-1953 SINGLES & V TWINS (BOOK OF)
ROYAL ENFIELD 1946-1962 SINGLES (BOOK OF)
ROYAL ENFIELD 1948-1962 350cc & 500cc PRE-UNIT BULLET WSM
ROYAL ENFIELD 1948-1963 500cc TWINS FACTORY WORKSHOP MANUAL
ROYAL ENFIELD 1952-1963 700cc TWINS FACTORY WORKSHOP MANUAL
ROYAL ENFIELD 1956-1966 250cc CRUSADER & 350cc NEW BULLET WSM
ROYAL ENFIELD 1958-1966 250cc & 350cc SINGLES (SECOND BOOK OF)
ROYAL ENFIELD 1962-1970 INTERCEPTOR WSM'S & PARTS (Compilation)
RUDGE 1933-1939 (BOOK OF)
SACHS 1968-1975 100cc & 125cc ENGINES WSM & M/CYCLE PARTS LIST
SUNBEAM 1928-1939 (BOOK OF)
SUNBEAM 1946-1957 S7 & S8 (BOOK OF)
SUZUKI 50cc & 80cc UP TO 1966 (BOOK OF)
SUZUKI T10 1963-1967 FACTORY WORKSHOP MANUAL
SUZUKI T20 & T200 1965-1969 FACTORY WORKSHOP MANUAL
SUZUKI TWINS 1962 ONWARDS 125-500cc WORKSHOP MANUAL
TRIUMPH 1935-1949 SINGLES & TWINS (BOOK OF)
TRIUMPH 1937-1961 SINGLES SV & OHV 250cc-600cc + TERRIER & CUB
TRIUMPH 1945-1955 PRE-UNIT 350cc, 500cc & 650cc TWINS WSM No.11
TRIUMPH 1945-1959 TWINS (BOOK OF)
TRIUMPH 1956-1969 TWINS (BOOK OF)
TRIUMPH 1956-1962 PRE-UNIT 500cc & 650cc TWINS WSM No.17
TRIUMPH 1957-1963 UNIT CONSTRUCTION 350-500cc WSM No.4
TRIUMPH 1963-1974 UNIT CONSTRUCTION 350-500cc FACTORY WSM
TRIUMPH 1963-1970 UNIT CONSTRUCTION 650cc FACTORY WSM
TRIUMPH 1968-1974 TRIDENT T150 & T150V FACTORY WSM
TRIUMPH 1971-1973 650cc OIL-IN-FRAME FACTORY WSM
TRIUMPH 1973-1978 750cc BONNEVILLE & TIGER FACTORY WSM
TRIUMPH 1979-1983 750cc T140, TR7 & TR65 FACTORY WSM
VELOCETTE 1925-1970 ALL SINGLES & TWINS (BOOK OF)
VELOCETTE 1933-1952 MOV-MAC-MSS RIGID FRAME FACTORY WSM
VELOCETTE 1954-1971 MSS-VENOM-THRUXTON-VIPER FACTORY WSM
VILLIERS ENGINE UP TO 1959 INC. 3 WHEELERS (BOOK OF)
VILLIERS ENGINE UP TO 1969 (BOOK OF)
VINCENT 1935-1955 (WORKSHOP MANUAL)
YAMAHA 1961-1967 YA5 & YA6 (WORKSHOP MANUAL & ILL PARTS LIST)
YAMAHA 1971-1972 JT1 & JT2 (WORKSHOP MANUAL & ILL PARTS LIST)

VELOCEPRESS MANUALS – SCOOTERS BY MAKE

BSA SUNBEAM SCOOTER WORKSHOP MANUAL 1959-1965
BSA SUNBEAM SCOOTER 1959-1965 (BOOK OF)
LAMBRETTA 1947-1957 ALL 125 & 150cc MODELS (BOOK OF)
LAMBRETTA 1957-1970 LI & TV MODELS (SECOND BOOK OF)
NSU PRIMA 1956-1964 ALL MODELS (BOOK OF)
TRIUMPH TIGRESS SCOOTER WORKSHOP MANUAL 1959-1965
TRIUMPH TIGRESS SCOOTER (BOOK OF)
VESPA 1951-1961 (BOOK OF)
VESPA 1955-1963 125 & 150cc & GS MODELS (SECOND BOOK OF)
VESPA 1955-1968 GS & SS (BOOK OF)
VESPA 1963-1972 90, 125 & 150cc (THIRD BOOK OF)

VELOCEPRESS MANUALS – MOPEDS & MOTORIZED BICYCLES

CYCLEMOTOR (BOOK OF)
NSU QUICKLY 1953-1963 ALL MODELS (BOOK OF)
PUCH MAXI N & S MAINTENANCE & REPAIR (3 MANUAL COMPILATION)
RALEIGH MOPEDS 1960-1969 (BOOK OF)

VELOCEPRESS MANUALS - THREE WHEELER'S

BOND MINICAR THREE WHEELER 1948-1967 (BOOK OF)
BMW ISETTA FACTORY WORKSHOP MANUAL
BSA THREE WHEELER (BOOK OF)
RELIANT REGAL THREE WHEELER 1952-1973 (BOOK OF)
VINTAGE MORGAN THREE WHEELER (BOOK OF)

VELOCEPRESS TECHNICAL BOOKS – MOTORCYCLE

1930'S BRITISH MOTORCYCLE CARBS & ELEC COMPONENTS (BOOK OF)
1930'S BRITISH MOTORCYCLE ENGINES (OVERHAUL & MAINTENANCE)
1930'S BRITISH MOTORCYCLE GEARBOXES & CLUTCHES (BOOK OF)
CATALOG OF BRITISH MOTORCYCLES (1951 MODELS)
LUCAS ELECTRONICS BRITISH M/CYCLES REPAIR & PARTS (1950-1977)
MOTORCYCLE ENGINEERING (P.E. Irving)
MOTORCYCLE ROAD TESTS 1949-1953 (Motor Cycle Magazine UK)
SPEED AND HOW TO OBTAIN IT (Motor Cycle Magazine UK)
TUNING FOR SPEED (P.E. Irving)
WIPAC (COMBO) MANUAL NUMBER 3 + M/CYCLE & SCOOTER MANUAL

VELOCEPRESS MANUALS – AUTOMOBILE BY MAKE

ALFA ROMEO GIULIA WORKSHOP MANUAL 1300 TO 2000cc 1962-1975
ALFA ROMEO GIULIA TECH MANUAL CARBURETED CARS FROM 1962
ALFA ROMEO GIULIA TECH MANUAL FUEL INJECTED CARS FROM 1969
ALFA ROMEO GIULIETTA & GIULIA 750 & 101 SERIES 1955-1965 WSM
AUSTIN-HEALEY SPRITE & MG MIDGET WORKSHOP MANUAL 1958-1971
BMW 600 LIMOUSINE FACTORY WORKSHOP MANUAL
BMW 600 LIMOUSINE OWNERS HAND BOOK & SERVICE MANUAL
BMW 2000 & 2002 1966-1976 WORKSHOP MANUAL
BMW 2500, 2800, 3.0 & BARVARIA WORKSHOP MANUAL
CORVAIR 1960-1969 WORKSHOP MANUAL
CORVETTE V8 1955-1962 WORKSHOP MANUAL
FERRARI HANDBOOK ROAD & RACE CARS (SERVICE/SPECS) 1948-1958
FERRARI 250GT SERVICE & MAINTENANCE by JIM RIFF 1956-1965
FERRARI 250GT & 250GTE FACTORY PARTS AND REPAIR MANUALS
FIAT 500 FACTORY WORKSHOP MANUAL 1957-1973
FIAT 600, 600D & MULTIPLA FACTORY WORKSHOP MANUAL 1955-1969
JAGUAR E-TYPE 3.8 & 4.2 SERIES 1 & 2 WORKSHOP MANUAL
JAGUAR MK 7, 8, 9 & XK120, 140, 150 WORKSHOP MANUAL 1948-1961
MERCEDES-BENZ 280 SERIES 1968-1972
METROPOLITAN FACTORY WORKSHOP MANUAL
MGA & MGB OWNERS HANDBOOK & WORKSHOP MANUAL
MG MIDGET TC, TD, TF & TF1500 WORKSHOP MANUAL
PORSCHE 356 1948-1965 WORKSHOP MANUAL
PORSCHE 911 2.0, 2.2, 2.4 LITRE 1964-1973 WORKSHOP MANUAL
PORSCHE 911 2.7, 3.0, 3.2 LITRE 1973-1989 WORKSHOP MANUAL
PORSCHE 912 WORKSHOP MANUAL
PORSCHE 914/4 & 914/6 1.7, 1.8, 2.0 LITRE 1970-1976 WSM
TRIUMPH TR2, TR3, TR4 1953-1965 WORKSHOP MANUAL
VOLKSWAGEN TRANSPORTER, TRUCKS & WAGONS 1950-1979 WSM
VOLVO 1944-1968 ALL MODELS WORKSHOP MANUAL

VELOCEPRESS TECHNICAL BOOKS - AUTOMOBILE

HOW TO BUILD A FIBERGLASS CAR
HOW TO BUILD A RACING CAR
HOW TO RESTORE THE MODEL 'A' FORD
MASERATI OWNER'S HANDBOOK
PERFORMANCE TUNING THE SUNBEAM TIGER
SOUPING THE VOLKSWAGEN
SOLEX CARBURETORS (EMPHASIS ON UK & EU AUTOMOBILES)
SU CARBURETORS (EMPHASIS ON UK AUTOMOBILES)
WEBER CARBURETORS (EMPHASIS ON ALFA & FIAT)

VELOCEPRESS BOOKS & GUIDES - AUTOMOBILE

COMPLETE CATALOG OF JAPANESE MOTOR VEHICLES
FERRARI 308 SERIES BUYER'S AND OWNER'S GUIDE
FERRARI BROCHURES AND SALES LITERATURE 1968-1989
FERRARI SERIAL NUMBERS PART I - ODD NUMBERS TO 21399
FERRARI SERIAL NUMBERS PART II - EVEN NUMBERS TO 1050
HENRY'S FABULOUS MODEL "A" FORD
MASERATI BROCHURES AND SALES LITERATURE

VELOCEPRESS BOOKS – AUTO RACING

CARRERA PANAMERICANA - MEXICAN ROAD RACE (BOOK OF)
DIALED IN - THE JAN OPPERMAN STORY
VEDA ORR'S NEW REVISED HOT ROD PICTORIAL

www.VelocePress.com

www.ingramcontent.com/pod-product-compliance
Lightning Source LLC
Chambersburg PA
CBHW080734300426
44114CB00019B/2588